Implementing

Baan™ IV

Implementing

Baan™ IV

Yves Perreault, Tom Vlasic, et al.

Implementing Baan

KPMG's involvment in this book was solely from the role of technical editor. As Technical Editor, KPMG reviewed and commented on the technical accuracy of the Baan sessions and the accompanying text. KPMG concurs with the author on the accuracy of this information.

KPMG however, does not follow or promote the methodology and procedures to implement Baan software that the author uses within this book. KPMG has their own proven methodology for the implementation of the Baan software which expands on the Baan Target Enterprise Methodology for implementation.

Screen reproductions in this book were created using Collage Plus from Inner Media, Inc., Hollis, NH and Capture from Mainstay, Camarillo, CA.

Contents at a Glance

Table of Contents

21 Understanding the Production Management Module   341

22 Understanding the Service Module   353

VI Appendixes

Credits

PUBLISHER
Joe Wikert

EXECUTIVE EDITOR
Bryan Gambrel

MANAGING EDITOR
Patrick Kanouse

ACQUISITIONS EDITOR
Tracy Dunkelberger

DEVELOPMENT EDITOR
Nancy D. Warner

SENIOR EDITOR
Elizabeth A. Bruns

COPY EDITORS
Tonya Maddox
Pat Kinyon
Kelli M. Brooks
Michael Brummitt
Keith Cline
Theresa Mathias

TEAM COORDINATOR
Michelle Newcomb

TECHNICAL CONSULTANTS
KPMG

BOOK DESIGNER
Ruth Harvey

COVER DESIGNER
Sandra Schroeder

PRODUCTION TEAM
Erin M. Danielson
Jennifer Earhart
Julie Geeting
Elizabeth San Miguel

INDEXER
Greg Pearson

Composed in Century and Franklin Gothic by Que Corporation. __ __ __ __ __ __ __ __ __ __

About the Authors

Yves Perreault is a consultant who has worked in the Baan environment for over six years. He was information technology manager for Wire Rope Industries, site of one of the first large Baan implementations in North America. He gained experience in the system implementation practice by working in more than 15 different projects. He is now working as a senior Baan project manager for SE Technologies Inc., in San Jose, California. He is also the Trustee of Communications for the Baan World User Group.

Tom Vlasic is the managing director of IT@Work, a consulting firm specializing in developing information technology strategic plans. Previously, he was the director of information technology for Husky Injection Molding Systems, Ltd., the site of one of North America's first multilogistic, multifinancial Baan implementations. While at Husky, Vlasic gained direct Baan experience as a project manager for a multisite Baan implementation.

Manoj Deshpande is a Baan implementer who specialized in the distribution and the manufacturing of packages. He has been implementing systems in India, Mexico, and California.

Bruno Dubreuil is a professional engineer with 14 years' experience. He has held many positions, such as project manager, project engineer, and university professor. For the the last two years, he has been implementing and promoting the Baan application.

Linda Gougeon was the finance key user during the implementation at Wire Rope Industries in 1992. She is now working for Cap Gemini and is using proven Baan software training techniques.

Jane Green is the manager of financial accounting at Gennum Corporation in Burlington, Ontario, Canada. Gennum was one of two North American beta sites for Baan's Triton 3.0 release. Jane was a member of the implementation team representing the finance area, and subsequently became the project manager for Baan's version IV upgrade. Jane is also a president of the Baan World User Group.

Peter Hingley is a senior business systems consultant with over 25 years experience in information technology and business process improvements. He has been involved in managing and directing many business systems' implementation initiatives throughout his career, including Wire Rope Industries' successful implementation of the Baan software. He has over six years' experience with Baan and is currently working for SE Technologies, Inc.

Ajay Jain, CPIM, is the vice president of operations for the western region of SE Technologies. Ajay has over 14 years of experience in the IT industry, primarily consulting in a variety of ERP/MRP systems. In addition to a degree in electronics engineering, he holds an M.B.A from San Jose State University.

Richard Joyce is the director of the National DEM Practice for SE Technologies. Richard has over 20 years of experience in the IT industry, primarily consulting in a variety of advanced manufacturing information systems. In addition to a degree in mathematics/computer science, he holds an M.S. in technology management.

Richard Lacombe has been working at Wire Rope Industries and Americ Disc for the last three years as a Baan developer and has been developing numerous customizations.

Mark Laliberte has been working with the Baan product since 1992, with experience ranging from version 2.0 to Baan IV. He was demand manager at Wire Rope Industries. Mark acquired 10 years' experience in distribution and manufacturing, which in turn created the opportunity for him to lead several project teams in optimizing business critical issues such as supply chain management reengineering, sales and operations planning structure, and forecasting accuracy. Mark is now a consultant with SE Technologies, and has been involved in various projects where customers are implementing Baan IV.

Serge LaPointe was on the selection team for the first Baan project in North America with Noranda in 1992. After 16 years of logistic management, Serge has decided to promote Baan as a business solution for high-tech and process industries. He has participated in many Baan implementations as a distribution and a manufacturing expert.

Sylvain Menard is a project manager for Process Technologies in Montreal, Canada. He is specializing in the Process module, but he is also very knowledgeable of the entire Baan environment.

Jörg Murawski is currently working as a consultant for Pico Soft Germany. He and his company are building a new office in the USA. His abilities contain a good overall view of the standard BAAN software and special skills of the Distribution module, the Manufacturing module, and the Tools module.

Mustapha Nakudha has been involved in the Baan environment since 1992. Although formerly involved with support operations, Mustapha is now a project manager for a large implementation in California.

Rajan Panchavarnam has accumulated a lot of experience on the Project module and the Enterprise Modeler through his involvement in various Baan implementations.

Paul J. Pretko is Director of Order Fulfillment Processes for the Sweetheart Cup Company. He is a graduate of Loyola College in Baltimore, and has over 10 years' experience in logistics/operations management system design and implementation.

Jaishankar Srinivasan is a Baan application specialist, specializing in the area of finance. He has over five years of industry experience in designing, developing, and implementing software systems—both PC- and network-based. Prior to working with SE, Jai worked for three and a half years with Rallis India Limited, the largest manufacturer of agricultural pesticides, fertilizers, and insecticides in Bombay, India. Jai was part of the team that successfully implemented Baan at Puma Technology, Inc., in a record time of two and a half months. Apart from being finance "guru," Jai has a good knowledge in distribution and tools and a fair amount of knowledge on the manufacturing aspect of Baan.

Cheryl Stanfield is the corporate accountant at Gennum Corporation. During the implementation of Triton 3.0, Cheryl was the key user responsible for the testing and training for accounts receivable, payable, and cash management. She continues to be the primary resource for those

Finance modules and is playing a significant role in Gennum's upgrade of Baan to version IV. Cheryl is frequently called upon by other member companies of the BWU to provide guidance in their operations.

In the last five years, **Sylvain Thauvette** has been implementing all packages of the Baan software. Also during this period, he designed many customizations and developed techniques to integrate third-party software with the Baan packages.

Subramanian Venkatesan is a tools developer for SE Technologies in San Jose, California.

Fred Vidican has over 30 years of business experience in business application and implementation, including six years of Baan-related involvement. Fred have been involved in various Baan implementations with the Noranda Group. He served as a founding member of the Baan World User (BWU) group, acting as secretary for two years and President for one. Fred is currently working for Deloitte Touche ICS in Toronto.

Fay Yen is a Baan implementation specialist with significant experience in the Distribution package, as well as the Dynamic Enterprise Modeler (DEM). She has worked with clients in the high technology and heavy equipment manufacturing industries focusing on order management, purchasing, distribution, and warehousing.

Acknowledgments

Yves Perreault   I would like to thanks all my colleagues at SE Technologies who helped me in this project, especially Sylvain Thauvette, Mark Laliberte, and Jaishankar Srinivasan. A special thanks also to Ajay Jain, who provided for the team to realize such a project.

I also need to mention all the hard work of colleagues from other Baan partners, like Sylvain Menard, Fred Vidican, and Serge Lapointe, who were very supportive.

Finally, I must thanks Jane Green, chairman of the Baan World User Group, and Cheryl Stanfield from Gennum Corporation, who did not hesitate to wake up early in the morning and put in all the necessary hours to create the financial chapters of this book. Those thanks are extended to all the other authors not mentioned here, but who have worked very hard; and to the staff at Que, particulary Tracy Dunkelberger and Nancy Warner, for their continuous support.

Tom Vlasic   To Wendy for supporting my time spent at the keyboard and to Karl for getting me in the loop.

We'd Like to Hear from You!

Que Corporation has a long-standing reputation for high-quality books and products. To ensure your continued satisfaction, we also understand the importance of customer service and support.

Tech Support

If you need assistance with the information in this book, please access Macmillan Computer Publishing's online Knowledge Base at **http://www.superlibrary.com/general/support**. If you do not find the answer to your questions on our Web site, you may contact Macmillan Technical Support by phone at **317/581-3833** or via e-mail at **support@mcp.com**.

Also be sure to visit Macmillan Computer publishing's Web resource centers for all the latest information, enhancements, errata, downloads, and more. It's located at **http://www.mcp.com/**.

Orders, Catalogs, and Customer Service

To order other Que or Macmillan Computer Publishing books, catalogs, or products, please contact our Customer Service Department at **800/428-5331** or fax us at **800/835-3202** (International Fax: **317/228-4400**). Visit our online bookstore at **http://www.mcp.com/**.

Comments and Suggestions

We want you to let us know what you like or dislike most about this book or other products. Your comments will help us continue publishing the best books available on computer topics in today's market.

Bryan Gambrel
Executive Editor
Macmillan Computer Publishing
201 West 103rd Street
Indianapolis, Indiana 46290 USA

Email: **bgambrel@mcp.com**

Fax: **317/581-4663**

Please be sure to include the book's title and author as well as your name and phone or fax number. We will carefully review your comments and share them with the author. Please note that due to the high volume of mail we receive, we may not be able to reply to every message.

Thank you for choosing Que!

Introduction

In this chapter

Who Should Use This Book

This book is written for anyone who works or is planning to work with Baan IV software.

If you are a new user, you find valuable tips to learning this Enterprise Resource Planning software quickly and efficiently. If you are an experienced user, you find valuable information that maximizes the use of Baan IV software. This book is also extremely valuable to you if you plan to start a career as a consultant, working for the Baan company, or working for one of the numerous third-party solutions partners and implementation partners.

This book teaches you how to use all the packages found in Baan IV software. You also learn the best techniques in various areas, from project management to problem solving.

How to Use This Book

This book is split into sections to help understanding the software's foundation, the different packages, and how to set the scene for a Baan implementation.

This book is designed to describe all of Baan's functions and to explain how to use the sessions. You also get help setting your parameters, which is a very crucial task when using a complete package like Baan IV.

How This Book Is Organized

The first section introduces the software and all its elements. The software's structure, as well as its navigation, are covered.

Part I: Corporate Readiness

Chapter 1, "The Baan Company," introduces the company behind the Baan IV software and details the history of this Enterprise Resource Planning software. Chapter 2, "Align the Order-to-Cash Business Process," describes a method that ensures that your organization's business processes are in shape for automation. This is referred to as *good-enough reengineering*. Chapter 3, "Focus the Information Technology Plan," introduces the elements to consider when refining your organization's information technology strategy to increase your return on your ERP investment. Chapter 4, "Follow a Proven Path," describes the best practice in implementing integrated business information system like Baan. It is a step-by-step, company-wide approach that helps you through the entire process and provides the structure and a roadmap while building the business case.

Part II: Implementation

Chapter 5, "Managing the Implementation," teaches you some aspects of project management to consider throughout the implementation process. Chapter 6, "The Baan Software," introduces the ERP package's elements. Each package is described, as well as other, external packages like Baan Synchronization and Hyperion. Chapter 7, "Using the DEM Tools," describes the powerful Enterprise Modeling tools. This chapter details all the elements of dynamic enterprise modeling and describes the best way to use the tools that accelerate the implementation rate. Chapter 8, "Getting to Know the Structure," introduces the key words and technical terms that every Baan user must know. Session code structures are explained. Chapter 9, "Navigating the Baan Software," explains how to use the various sessions found in the software. Each icon is described and explained. Chapter 10, "Corporate Readiness," highlights those issues that surround a Baan project that must be understood and well managed. Chapter 11, "Setting Up a Company," describes the steps to perform in order to create a company in Baan. Every file to be maintained is described in a checklist format. By following these steps, you can create a company to test Baan IV's software.

Part III: Modules

Chapter 12, " Understanding the Common Data Module," details the contents of the company data, employee master, customer master, and supplier master. Chapter 13, "Understanding the Financial Tables and the General Ledger," details all the steps required to set up the Financial package. See how the general ledger accounts are set up, as well as how you should create the dimensions to support the general ledger transactions. Chapter 14, "Understanding the Finance Subledgers," covers all the auxiliary functions of the Finance package, such as accounts payable, accounts receivables, and cash management functions. Using this information enables you to set up those modules, as well as process the payments to suppliers and apply cash receipts. Chapter 15, "Understanding the Item Control Module," shows you how to set up the item master file used throughout the software. Chapter 16, "Understanding the Distribution Module," introduces the Purchase Control module, the Distribution Requirement Planning module and the Replenishment Control module. Chapter 17, "Understanding the Inventory Module," details the functions found in the Inventory Control module, the Location Control, and the Lot Control module. This chapters reveals all the techniques to keeping inventory records in Baan and making the best use of the existing sessions. Chapter 18, "Understanding the Sales Control Module," explains the various methods used to manage pricing in Baan, as well as the use of the Sales Order Control module. Chapter 19, "Understanding the Transportation Module," describes this package, which allows management of the company fleet by tracking transportation orders and all the related information. Chapter 20, "Understanding the Manufacturing Module," introduces all the functions found to control the shop floor activities, the bill of material control, routing and hours accounting. Chapter 21, "Understanding the Production Management Module," details the functions that can be used to apply some controls over production, such as the recording of rejected quantities, the reporting of completed quantities, the monitoring of production costs, material usage, and utilities. This information is stored under production batches. Chapter 22, "Understanding the Service Module," introduces the function related to installation management and work to perform under warranties. Diagnostic and statistic functions are also covered in this chapter. Chapter 23, "Understanding the Project Module," explains the visibility of status and costs and early warnings about potential problems using the Project module. Chapter 24, " Understanding the Formula Management Module," explains that the product formula is the blueprint where information on ingredients, standard production quantities, and packaging configurations is stored as a guideline for production managed through the Process package. Chapter 25, "Understanding the Process Module," details how to manage process items, which are handled differently than regular manufactured items because of different features like containers. Chapter 26, "Understanding the Tools Package," describes all the elements of the development kit used to modify menus, forms, and reports. Version release control is also explained to ensure proper management of changes. Chapter 27, "Understanding the Integration Between the Modules," details how you convert transactions generated by the various packages into financial transactions. Find proposed integration setup for the most common type of transactions. Chapter 28, "Understanding the Utilities Module," explains how to import and export data from Baan IV software to an ASCII file.

Part IV: Migration

When you have a better understanding of all the Baan IV software packages, then you're in the position of setting your parameters in the most efficient way. In addition, you have to ensure that your Baan implementation is following the best techniques. Chapter 29, "Setting Your Parameters Properly," details how to set up all the parameters in the most efficient way. You find explanations of all the fields in every Parameters session. Chapter 30, "Managing Your Customizations," details what the process before deciding to modify part of the software is. The different approaches, as well as the available resources, are discussed in this chapter. Chapter 31, "Training and Simulating," describes all the elements to plan when preparing user training.

Part V: Going Live

Chapter 32, "Day 1 and Beyond," defines all the steps required to audit your implementation before going live and proposes some methods for evaluating the status of your implementation at a specific time. Chapter 33, "Finding Solutions to Users' Problems," shows useful tricks to quickly solving common users problems and details the procedure required to properly log any request for support.

Appendixes

Appendix A, "Samples of Customization," guides you in creating a table, generating a session to maintain it, and the required steps to building a report. Appendix B, "Understanding Baan BackOffice," introduces the newer version of Baan, which operates under the BackOffice environment. Appendix C, "Getting to Work in the Baan World," details the steps you should follow and the organization you should contact if you are interested in building a career working for Baan and its affiliates. Appendix D, "Networking Through the User Group," introduces the Baan World Users and describes this Group's activities. Instructions on how to use the BWU Internet Web site are included.

Corporate Readiness

The Baan Company

Understanding From Where Baan Came

The Baan Company is among the top software providers worldwide. They distribute Baan IV, which is a product highly ranked among the Enterprise Resource Planning (ERP) solutions available.

Founded in 1978 by Jan Baan in the Netherlands, this company is always innovating in the ERP world and has added functions to the base product developed over the last 10 years. Through Baan, along with his brother and the dedication of many employees, the technology that is driving the product named Baan IV was developed.

Requiring a Solid Structure

You need a solid information system structure to operate in an enterprise environment. Baan provides this structure, which is one of the reasons for its success. To complement their solid presence in the European market, Baan is expanding its presence worldwide. For example, Baan has United States offices in Menlo Park, California and Reston, Virginia. In addition, the Support Center for the Americas is located in Grand Rapids, Michigan.

Baan went public in 1995, and stocks for the company are traded on the NASDAQ Stock Exchange in New York and the Netherlands. Because of the strength of the product Baan develops, many people jumped on the stock, which is still doing very well as of this writing.

Understanding the Approach

Baan is using an approach in which customers and experts from different sectors of industry, as well as advisors from different universities, help develop the best practices in its software. That is what brought all the functionality in the current product and also ensures that the next releases contain the necessary elements to be one of the best products available.

Maintaining a Steady Growth

The Baan product has a very impressive track record. Here is the evolution of the open system software: Various technologies were developed prior to the launch of Baan IV. The tools used to maintain the products have been around for many years and have been improved over time. The same is true of the user interface.

Baan Release IV is the result of the hard work invested in developing the three major releases of Triton. The versions all had valuable improvements; Table 1.1 lists the previous releases and their major improvements.

Table 1.1   Release Improvements

Release	Characteristics
1.0	First release of the Triton ERP software
2.0a, b, c	Major enhancements in all modules
2.1	Major improvement of tools now to level 5
	Changes in file structure, all files now have a suffix
2.2	Addition of sales and marketing information
3.0, 3.1a, 3.1b	Revision of the Financial Package, Process Package, Transportation Package, and Orgware Package
4.0a	Graphical User Interface (GUI) Containerized items

Having difficulty securing rights for the name, Baan decided to stop using the name Triton for marketing reasons. Anyone who refers to Baan as Triton has likely been using the products for more than one release.

The following list contains some significant milestones for the Baan Company:

- 1978 Jan Baan founds the Baan Company and starts providing computerized solutions.
- 1982 Baan uses the UNIX platform.
- 1984 A Shell structure is created. This is the first step toward an Open System.
- 1985 A package is provided that includes Finance, Manufacturing, and Distribution for the construction business.
- 1986 Triton Tools are created.
- 1988 Database structure is modified to provide independence of data.
- 1989 First version of the ERP product, the Triton Software, is evolving toward MRP II concept.
- 1990 Client/server approach is taken.
- 1992 Joint venture with IBM and alliance with Origin.
- 1993 Creation of Orgware and development of the Process Module.
- 1994 Addition of Transportation, Project Control, and Executive Information System.
- 1995 Baan is a public company at both NASDAQ and the Amsterdam Stock Exchange.
- 1996 Baan IV is released.

The following table contains a few facts about the Baan Company:

Head Office	Ede, Netherlands
Main Offices	Menlo Park, California, USA
	Barneveld, Netherlands
	Singapore
Employees	More than 1,500
Support Centers	Grand Rapids, Michigan, USA
	Barneveld, Netherlands
	Mumbai, India
Installations	Nearly 2,000 at the end of 1996
Web Address	**www.baan.com**

Knowing Baan Customers

Any software manufacturer is always looking for major customers to build his or her credibility. Baan was very happy that many of the largest corporations implemented its software over the last five years. The list of installations is very impressive. At the end of 1996, the number of installations was nearly 2,000. Here is a list of the major corporations that have implemented modules of the Baan IV software:

- Acindar Industria Argentina
- Advanced Micro Devices
- Albert Richter GmbH & Company
- AP Parts
- Asea Brown Boveri Group (ABB)
- Autovaz, Incorporated
- Barlows Appliances
- Best Power Corporation
- Boeing Commercial Airplane Group
- Coemsa Ansaldo S.A.
- Colt Group
- Diebold
- Gennum Corporation
- Disques Amerique
- Europa Carton
- Flextronics International
- Ford Motor Company

- Friatec A.G.
- Fujitsu-ICL
- GEC Alsthom
- Grontmij
- HanJung
- Harris Heidelberg
- Hitachi
- Honda
- Hugues Aircraft
- Husky Injection Molding
- Industry Pininfarina
- Iskra Emeco
- Jeffrey Indescro
- John C. Nordt
- Kollmorgen Corporation
- KWO Kabel
- Mencey Quimica

- Mercedes Benz
- MG Industries
- MM Cable
- Noranda
- Nortel
- Novus
- Oki Electric Industry
- Philips
- Poliofelinas SA
- Puma Technology
- Rallis India
- Remploy
- Reuneuch Group

- Sensormatic
- Sierra Concepts
- Snap On Tools
- Solectron
- Stocko GmbH
- Sweetheart Cup Corporation
- Tait Electronics
- Tokyo Electron
- Trojan Technologies
- Van Geel Group
- Wyerhauser
- Zivi S.A. Cutelaria

 Take a look at Baan's Web site (**www.baan.com**) and Baan's World User Group Web site (**www.bwu.org**) if you are seeking employment for any of the sites using Baan and would like to get an updated list of customers.

Align the Order-to-Cash Business

Using Methodologies with the Dynamic Enterprise Modeler

The Orgware Dynamic Enterprise Modeler (DEM) is a very effective tool when combined with a thorough understanding of the three project models:

- Function
- Process
- Organization

As shown in Figure 2.1, the Organization model is similar to a traditional organization chart. The Process model is, in fact, a process flow chart, while the Function model describes the connection of the overall business process.

FIG. 2.1

An Orgware Project Model requires definition of a Function, Process, and Organization model.

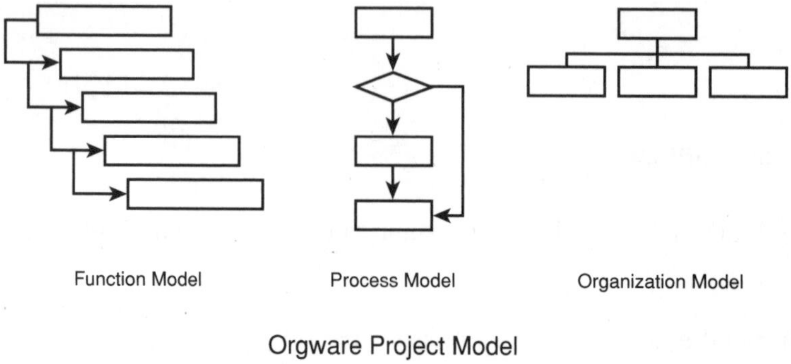

Function Model   Process Model   Organization Model

Orgware Project Model

The DEM used without a methodology has little value. This chapter discusses a methodology in which the DEM can be used to create an appropriate process and a function model. The methodology can be used independently of the DEM and still produce useful results, similarly to a continuous improvement program in which the focus is on the improvement of the process, not on the implementation of a technology solution. In that instance, there may be little to no requirement for information technology. However, a real benefit can be realized if the DEM is coupled with this methodology; that is, the generation of Baan system parameters and user desktops that correlate tightly with the business process.

Agreeing to Improve

The basis of any successful project is the belief that the project will succeed. The stronger the belief, the higher probability (in the minds of the participants) that the project will succeed. The more seniority a person has, enthusiasm captures, the more likely the project will receive support when needed most. Organizations tend to tire quickly and have less tolerance for long projects that produce soft benefits. Arguably, process improvement initiatives have historically been deemed as projects that return soft benefits. However, recent thinking points to the key role the business process plays in delivering value to the customer.

An organization must consider investment in the improvement of processes a priority. This is a change in thinking from the not-too-distant past when information technology seemed to dominate investment decisions. Now people look to the benefits from process improvement and understand that information technology is just the enabler. Thus, you must look to the return from the process improvement as the return from investment in information technology.

Information technology applied to processes that are not efficient simply help spread the negative effect of the process much more quickly. Process improvement initiatives can be independent of any decision to utilize information technology. However, the decision to leverage information technology should not be independent of a process improvement initiative. Some processes are best left to operate manually, while other processes' automation is simply cost prohibitive. This should not dampen the organization's interest in opportunities that further enhancing the process via information technology for. Information technology can increase the value of new processes, but to ensure its ability to bring value to the business, the process model must first be efficient. In other words, fix the process, then add technology— not the reverse. In this case, information technology can act as the enabler it is intended to be and disperse the positive effect of the process much more quickly.

Part
I
Ch
2

Fortunate is the organization that has strong leadership coupled with a clear business vision. The change initiative in these organizations comes from the top down. There is no time to rest; no lounging on laurels. Past accomplishments are merely watermarks for future goals. In these organizations the change initiative is a way of business life. Change is constant. The mandate for process improvement is clear and undisputed.

However, other organizations struggle with a clear mission toward process improvement. Process change initiatives may or may not come from the top down. If not, the challenge is to develop awareness at the senior level. In this case, a clear cost/benefit approach is the only real opportunity to get support and move ahead. It may not have to be hard-benefit; it may be strategic. A good example is the quality drive of the 1980s. Quality is no longer a competitive advantage, because there is no business without quality. You may have to deal with the perceptions of management; the "if it's not broken, don't fix it" attitude is one example. This rather conservative attitude is finding less acceptance in today's business climate, which has an ever-increasing rate of change. Few, if any, business leaders accept the status quo.

Who should manage the process? Business managers quickly assume ownership of the process. Who should manage process improvement? Business managers quickly assign information technology resources. Unfortunately, this must change. In progressive organizations, it's clearly the business groups that own the process and that are responsible for any process improvement initiatives. Historically, the information technology group has been labeled as the change agent within the organization. This is no longer the case. Business is the change agent. Information technology is perceived as the change agent, because it is providing technical enablers. Historically, IT found the process needing adjustment (positively, of course) in order to introduce a new system. More often than not, IT recognized the opportunity to improve processes. This is wrong. This breaks the rule of process improvement before technology application. Business understands business, and therefore must be charged with the responsibility to manage and continuously look for opportunities to improve the process.

A good indication that the organization's leaders support a process improvement initiative is the endorsement to create a dedicated process team, management steering team and part time working groups. Although these teams are reviewed in greater detail in Chapter 5, "Managing the Implementation," the structure is presented here to draw out those characteristics necessary to support successful process improvement initiatives.

The process team members need to be those who are closest to the process in each functional department (for example, Sales, Engineering, Purchasing, Manufacturing, and Finance). Avoid department managers. Further, leverage those closest to the processes under review.

Working groups are extensions of the process team members but are only required on a part-time basis. The working group members are chosen by the process team members to best represent the departments' processes. Rather than focus on other criteria (such as seniority or technology fluency), the process team wants the working group to have a broad coverage of all the processes under review. The organization chart in Figure 2.2 shows a typical team arrangement.

FIG. 2.2

Representation on the process team is directly related to the type of organization and processes under review.

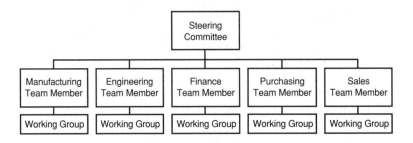

Process Alignment Teams
(Manufacturing Example)

NOTE The steering committee grants approval on all proposed process modifications. It should include department managers and the organizations leader. ■

Capturing the AS-IS Business Process

The primary reason to capture the AS-IS business process is to create process visibility. *Process visibility* is the ability to review the process steps as a third party and not as a participant. It provides the opportunity to see the process objectively, as a flowchart on a piece of paper, for example. Historically, having the AS-IS business process captured was considered mandatory. An organization wanted to know where it was before it took the next step. Until recently, organizations tended to be conservative in their approaches to altering the current business process. If the business was "making money," there appeared little reason to begin changing the way things were done. However, the exercise of capturing the AS-IS process can itself identify poorly defined processes.

TIP If the process is difficult to document, it's likely a good indicator that the process is difficult.

Organizations are typically divided along functional boundaries or vertical specialization, as shown in Figure 2.3 (for example, sales, engineering, purchasing, manufacturing, and finance). By virtue of this structure, members of these departments aren't typically exposed to processes occurring beyond their department wall.

Part

I

Ch

2

FIG. 2.3
Each department has vertical specialization.

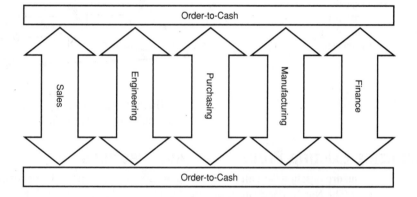

Vertical Specialization
(Manufacturing Example)

However, the customer does not see (or care about) any of these vertical micro-processes. The customer is only interested in the Order-to-Cash (horizontal) process. Take a look at Figure 2.4.

FIG. 2.4
The Order-to-Cash process flows horizontally across the organization.

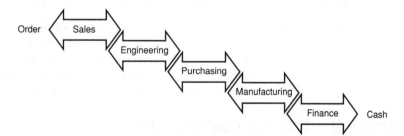

Horizontal Flow
(Manufacturing Example)

Unfortunately, the typical organization has very few (if any) individuals familiar with the Order-to-Cash process. The exercise to capture the Order-to-Cash process provides many employees a first look at how the organization really operates. Although each department may operate efficiently in its vertical process structure, it is the boundaries (or hand-off) between departments—vertical processes—in which the process ball gets dropped. The boundaries have no clearly defined ownership. The boundary does not necessarily fall into either bordering department. These orphan processes are to blame for many Order-to-Cash inconsistencies. It is easy to shift the blame when there is no ownership.

FIG. 2.5

The horizontal Order-to-Cash process includes Orphan processes that exist at the boundary between departments and are not well defined in any one department.

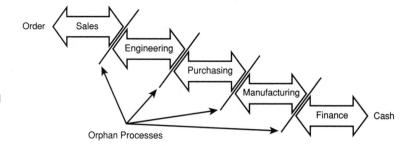

Boundary Conditions
(Manufacturing Example)

Utilizing Existing Procedures and Practices

Some organizations are unaware that they have already captured most of their business process. The North American automotive supply chain has the ISO/QS 9000 family of standards and is a good example. *ISO/QS 9000* is basically the definition of what and how an organization must document the processes it uses in its business. In other words, you document what you do and you do what you document. Unfortunately, ISO/QS 9000 is focused mainly on processes aligned closely with product or service quality. It does not guarantee that the process has been optimized (or aligned). Furthermore, this limits the completeness of the documents. It is impossible to consider this a complete AS-IS process description. However, it is an excellent starting point and likely captures the majority of the final AS-IS process.

If you need to be ISO/QS certified or need to meet a similar standard in your industry, consider this an opportunity for self-assessment. The self-assessment provides valuable material that can be reviewed by the standards auditors. In the case of ISO/QS 9000, consider the quality team leader the process team leader. The experience acquired with similar methods in the quality practice can be reused to model procedures and practices to create the AS-IS process.

Creating the Order-to-Cash Timeline

As a first step to capturing the AS-IS process in detail, consider developing a high level Order-to-Cash timeline. Similar to a typical project timeline, an Order-to-Cash timeline is steps that constitute the current business process. Another benefit to doing this exercise is that it educates the process team members on how the entire order-to-cash process operates.

An effective way to accomplish this is to use a recently completed production order or related concept in your industry. Use something that's recent enough that conditions in your organization are relatively the same. Choose a production order that did not involve significant changes, if any. Significant changes include customer changes with respect to terms and conditions, product configuration, or project deliverables. Engineering changes that were internally or externally introduced must be avoided. Manufacturing changes that resulted from part shortages or labor issues should be left out. Purchasing changes resulting from bill-of-material substitutions as well as manufacturing part shortages and finance cost accounting changes should all be set aside for this trial.

The benefit of a clean production order results in the Order-to-Cash timeline producing the best case order-to-cash cycle time. If the organization has existing targets or perceptions of the cycle time, this provides a good reality check. A clean production order helps the process team avoid getting bogged down with process issues that need not be addressed at this time. The objective is to produce a best case production order.

The Order-to-Cash timeline should include the following information:

- Department: Localize which functional group is responsible for the task.
- Task: The description of a particular vertical process in use in a particular department (for example, approval of inspected items).
- Role: The description of a particular set of skills required to complete the task (for example, shipper/receiver).
- Duration: The estimation of how long a particular task will take to complete by a person assuming a particular role.

Describing the Task   The task description should be small enough that one or two tasks are completed by an individual or role. If the task definition is too wide, the risk is that more than one role may be involved in the task. If the task definition is too narrow, then the risk is that the task detail adds complexity that overshadows the intention of the Order-to-Cash timeline.

Describing the Role   The roles need to be independent of any individual. When an organization creates roles and assigns these to tasks, the organization has the freedom to move individuals between roles. This provides an avenue for employee development and succession planning. Roles need to be thought out carefully with the help of the organization's Human Resources Department. This ensures that roles are developed and skills sets defined based on the need of the task and not based on the individual who happens to be currently completing the task.

Describing the Duration   Avoid conducting detailed time studies of task duration. It is best to obtain a solid estimate from the individuals currently completing the task in question.

N O T E   To avoid inflated/deflated estimates, obtain a duration estimate from more than one individual in the same role.

The process team is assigned the responsibility of gathering the necessary department, task, role, and duration information. The process team members are responsible for the department from which they were assigned. The process team members can collect this information in a relatively short time. It's not exact, and it's not overly detailed—the objective is to create an end-to-end description of the business in a short period of time. The process team leader is responsible for accumulating the data and creating the Order-to-Cash timeline. The timeline should include each task and role description. The duration is implied in the timeline itself. Figure 2.6 is an example of how the Order-to-Cash timeline would appear with all the information included.

FIG. 2.6

The Order-to-Cash timeline is a high-level, visual tool that estimates horizontal process characteristics.

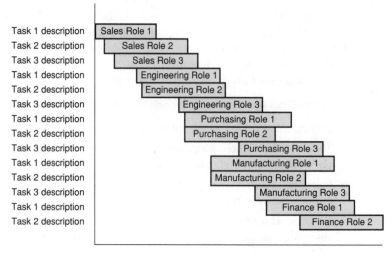

Task 1 description	Sales Role 1
Task 2 description	Sales Role 2
Task 3 description	Sales Role 3
Task 1 description	Engineering Role 1
Task 2 description	Engineering Role 2
Task 3 description	Engineering Role 3
Task 1 description	Purchasing Role 1
Task 2 description	Purchasing Role 2
Task 3 description	Purchasing Role 3
Task 1 description	Manufacturing Role 1
Task 2 description	Manufacturing Role 2
Task 3 description	Manufacturing Role 3
Task 1 description	Finance Role 1
Task 2 description	Finance Role 2

Production Time

Order-to-Cash Timeline
(Manufacturing Example)

The completed Order-to-Cash timeline is used by the process team to bring visibility to the organization's current business practices. Using the timeline as a guide, the process team can identify areas in which the potential for process risk is high. For example, engineering changes increase the time a design spends in engineering or preproduction before manufacturing is able to produce the product. Furthermore, the Order-to-Cash timeline can be used as a starting point for the Orgware DEM.

Performing a Reality Check

The reality check's purpose is for the process team to obtain clear direction from the steering committee on which processes it must include in the process alignment step. To accomplish this, the process team must complete the following:

- Collect relevant process statistics.
- Conduct a steering committee review meeting.

Collecting Process Statistics   Depending on your organization's particular industry and Order-to-Cash version, the statistics that are meaningful vary. Many interesting statistics exist in a manufacturing environment, such as the following:

- Number of engineering change notices (ECN) per production order
- Number of production orders that had ECNs
- Number of days the Materials Requirement Planning (MRP) changed
- Number of on-time deliveries
- Amount of work in progress
- Number of customer product configuration changes
- Number of days supplier deliveries were late

It may be an arduous task for the process team members, but the statistics need to be gathered to support any need for improvement. The process team must agree on which statistics are of importance to their particular process.

Conducting a Timeline Review Meeting   The purpose of the steering committee review meeting includes the following:

- Review the process timeline with senior management.
- Review the process statistics.
- Compare the statistics against expectations of senior management.
- Identify candidate processes to improve.

The process team leader is responsible for reviewing the Order-to-Cash timeline with the steering committee. If time and space permit, it is beneficial to have the entire process team attend the review meeting. Not only does that provide a solidarity in the findings, it allows detailed questions to be answered during the meeting and not deferred. A deferred decision requires another meeting and slows the process.

The purpose of reviewing the process statistics is to provide the steering committee with examples of reality to compare against (sometimes) different perceptions of management. Consider an organization that has a goal of delivering a product within a specific amount of time. The process statistics illustrated that the total duration was nearly equal to this time. However, when the total duration is calculated to include engineering change notices, the duration exceeds the delivery goal. Furthermore, it is shown that every production order exhibited at least one Engineering Change Notice (ECN). Hence, it is proven that the expectations of management with respect to delivery cycle time cannot be met. Although fictional, this simple type of reality setting is not uncommon.

The process team can now identify candidate processes for improvement. Consider, as candidates, processes that do the following:

- Slow the business
- Resist change
- Impede quality
- Create cost

The process team must be sure to prioritize the candidate processes for the steering committee. The steering committee is responsible for selecting which processes are to be aligned. This review meeting's result must be a clear agreement on which processes the process team will target for improvement.

Aligning the Order-to-Cash Business Process

Aligning a business process is less drastic than reengineering a business process. By alignment, it's assumed that the business is, to some degree, already on a path of continuous improvement. Reengineering a business is the tearing down of the process walls and a complete rebuilding from the ground up. The concept of process alignment is attractive to organizations that are already comfortable with the process of change.

N O T E Most organizations do not have the luxury of stopping what they are doing and rebuilding their business. In other words, the process alignment is referred to here as *good-enough reengineering.*

Processes that are aligned to what the organization most values produce results that benefit the organization. The objective of process alignment is to create processes that are well-defined, repeatable, and stable.

A *well-defined* process is one that can be easily explained by any participant in the process. These participants were previously defined as role players. Although each participant has a different role in the process, any single role player can define the entire process.

A *repeatable* process is one that, when initiated, follows the same set of steps to the conclusion. Given the same set of process inputs along the way, the process produces the same results. It's somewhat similar to a well-structured computer program.

A *stable* process is similar to a repeatable process, but is more resistant to process input variation. This input noise, although disturbing, can be dampened by the process enough to produce the expected result. The process noise may come into play when different participants (with varying skills) assume the same role. In all cases, the process inputs can be provided by several role players.

Some characteristics of Hammer & Champy's aligned processes are as follows:

- A role expands to consume additional process steps.
- Workers make decisions.
- Process steps are performed in natural order.
- Processes have multiple versions.
- Work is performed where it makes the most sense.
- Checks and controls are reduced.

For the process team to become comfortable with this definition it is best to develop some example processes in a pilot environment. The process team leader can facilitate an exercise in which each team member proposes an example of an aligned process and challenges the other team members to constructively criticize the process. With an understanding of an aligned process in place for the process team, its attention can be turned toward the task of aligning the candidate processes prioritized with the steering committee.

Creating the Process Blueprint

As described previously, the Orgware DEM is a tool that enables the creation of a business process model. Here, you review a methodology able to produce a valid business model independent of the DEM tool. The results obtained here can be used as a starting point for the DEM.

The members of the process team were originally chosen as representatives of specific functional areas. As such, the candidate processes need to be divided accordingly among the team. The division would occur naturally along functional department boundaries. Each team member has to adopt his or her share of any orphan processes found on the boundary between departments.

Reviewing Process Scenarios   Each process team member needs to generate a list of ideas or opportunities for the candidate processes or functional areas they have been assigned. This can range from improvement ideas to introducing new or replacement processes. They are referred to as *process scenarios*. This step can be done in preparation to entering the business function model into the DEM. The Process Scenario database should include the following:

- *Identification number.* An index to uniquely identify the process scenario.
- *Process scenario description.* A textual explanation of the scenario.
- *Process team originator.* A process team member not directly responsible for a functional area may contribute an applicable process scenario.
- *Date captured.* To provide the ability to age the process scenario list.

Reviewing Process Tasks   Each process team member is responsible for reviewing the available process scenarios and adopting (or dismissing) those that are relevant (or irrelevant) to their functional area. These are called *process tasks*. A process task is a high-level set of operations that must be complete in order to move the process on to the next stage. This step can be done in preparation to entering the business process model into the DEM.

Each adopted process scenario must be assigned to a particular role within a given functional department. This is the first point at which the process team members begin to order process tasks. Until this point, the process scenarios have been unordered. The Process Tasks database should include the following:

- *Functional area.* The department that this scenario currently belongs to (if it is an improvement) or the department that has to execute this process (if it is a new process).
- *Role.* The set of skills required to complete this process transaction. The role is filled by individuals within the department.
- *Task number.* An index that orders the process tasks for the role to complete.

Reviewing Process Steps   The process tasks must now be broken down into process steps. Process tasks occur based on business logic, whereas when a process task begins, the internal process steps run from start to finish. Each step is a finite action that is easily understood and actionable by the assigned role. Creating process steps aids development of the DEM business process model. For example, this could be the execution of a particular Baan session.

The Process Step database is sorted according to the process tasks. The Process Step database should include the following:

- A cross-reference to the parent process task, which then dictates the department and role
- A Process Step index to group the process steps according to the process tasks

Conducting Process Workshops

Process team members need to conduct several process workshops. Each process team member conducts a separate workshop that involves the working group from the respective functional area or department. The purpose of the process workshop is as follows:

- To introduce the working group to the new or proposed process alignments (changes)
- To provide an opportunity to get feedback from the working group regarding further improvements
- To provide an opportunity to review the decisions surrounding the process changes
- To get approval from the working group for each process task and process step

Each workshop should be held more than once. As the name implies, the intention is that this be a working group, to be provided with ideas in progress and to obtain feedback that can further improve the process improvement work.

This is the opportunity for any and all discussion of why a process decision has been made. The goal is to address all concerns during the workshops. This avoids any discussion of "Why?" during the training period and leaves adequate time for the real purpose of training.

N O T E   In the case of process steps being completed in Baan, the process team member can review the menu navigation with the working group.

The process team member should create and manage a Process Workshop journal. This journal should include each workshop's agenda. All issues raised and process approvals obtained are logged. Reasons and rationale for decisions reached are captured to support future review of the decision process. It is as important to capture the rationale leading to a decision as it is to capture the decision itself. The decision may be challenged in the future. If the rationale isn't clearly understood, the decision may be reversed; it would be hazardous to reverse the decision when the impact is unknown. In subsequent workshops, the participants have a chronological history of all the decisions reached. This avoids the process team member having to recap all decisions in all meetings.

Creating Step Action Result (STAR) Tables

The culmination of the new or aligned processes is their being put into production. Regardless of whether the processes are manual, automated, or a combination, a similar approach can be used to produce effective training and reference documentation. This detailed process step reference is called a *Step Action Result Table*, or *STAR table*.

Whether the documentation is paper-based or electronic, a consistent approach provides a method for easily introducing individuals into new roles. For example, when an employee transitions from Accounts Receivable to Accounts Payable. The process training can be accomplished largely by reviewing the STAR table document. The STAR table document includes the following:

Part

I

Ch

2

- *A description of the role responsible to execute the process steps.* This provides a new employee with an understanding of which departments are effected by this process and how the role itself is positioned within the department.

- *A description of the surrounding processes.* This particular process interacts with other processes up and down the process chain. It provides some insight into the impact this process has on other processes. When a larger order-to-cash process is not performing optimally, it makes it easier to determine which process tasks are involved. This eliminates starting at the beginning every time.

- *Terms and definitions that are common to this process.* Terminology changes throughout an organization's departments. The type and style of definitions depends upon where an individual works. This could include specific terms and definitions used with suppliers and customers to promote consistency and avoid misunderstanding. This becomes particularly helpful when roles are assumed by employees that may be transferred between other countries and languages.

- *The process steps are duplicated from the contents of the Process Task and Process Step database.* This could consist of a combination of manual and automated steps. In the case of Baan, this includes navigation within and between sessions. It is similar to the desktops generated by the DEM, but extended to include the manual steps.

- *Appendixes contain information that supports the process steps, such as Baan Company numbers.*

Installing the TO-BE Business Process

The installation of new or aligned processes does not require the same magnitude of effort as the migration to Baan. It is typically a subset of the Baan migration. Here, you review two issues important to the introduction of new or aligned processes.

Continuing Process Team Support

All too often, the process team is disbanded at the same time the new or aligned processes are implemented. This is the organization's most critical time, as a poorly implemented process can quickly cripple an operation. More often, the process is implemented properly, but there is no support for the individuals assuming the process roles. An otherwise simple issue with the process is unresolved and causes more severe problems. The process team members must be assigned directly to support the new or aligned processes. They can't yet be allowed to return to their previous roles. A journal of issues must be kept to ensure issues are resolved and as a reference when similar issues appear.

NOTE   A journal of issues is also used to meter the number of issues and is a gauge to determine when the process team members can (safely) return to their previous roles. ■

Depending on the length of the process team assignment, members may be asked to resume their original roles or remain with the process team for the next round of process improvement. Continuous improvement methods require that the process of looking for efficiency in the order-to-cash process is ongoing. There is never a point in time that the organization is considered to be at maximum efficiency.

Individuals assigned to the process team should be targeted as key employees—those who have a keen understanding of the current process within their department, but are also seeking to advance themselves across or up through the organization. Former team members are particularly well suited to become Baan project team members, because the method of process alignment is the basis for a successful Baan implementation.

Business Value for IT

The result of aligning business processes is not only an improved order-to-cash process, but also an opportunity for IT. The direct connection of IT initiatives to the business process is what determines *business value*, which is an estimation of the return from investment in IT.

Although many organizations undertake the Process Alignment methodology as part of a Baan implementation, it is also a methodology that can stand on its own. Clearly, a continuous improvement philosophy supports this practice. If a particular organization subscribes to continuous improvement, this methodology is already in place, albeit in a different form. It is unfortunate to think that every process improvement initiative had to involve technology. Not withstanding technology is the great enabler of our time. Beware, technology based on poor processes ends up processing poorly. ●

CHAPTER 3

Focusing the Information Technology Plan

Identifying Available Opportunities

The Information Technology (IT) plan must be more than a traditional description of technology evolution, more than an ingenious plan scripted to persuade the organization's financial decision makers to invest. The IT planning effort must move beyond the technical focus to include those issues of particular interest to the organization. A self-serving approach to the development of an IT plan based solely on technical content is unacceptable. Unfortunately, most reports remain unread, tucked away, out of view, in hope of not reminding the author of the questionable expense of the time resource expended. However, a properly structured approach to the research leading up to the creation of the report can be the real value. The end result is not necessarily the benefit, it is the journey, the uncomfortable questions that are asked, and the opportunities that are uncovered that produce the lasting benefit to the organization.

This chapter presents a two-part approach required to focus the IT plan. First, you will complete an information technology assessment and then, using the opportunities discovered, the process of developing an effective IT plan can occur. Figure 3.1 shows that in order to identify and estimate the opportunities available to an organization, an information technology assessment must be completed and the resulting information must then be used to shape the content of the IT plan.

FIG. 3.1
Opportunities occur when plans are compared to assessments.

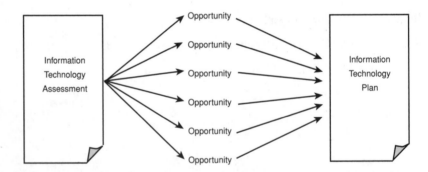

Performing an Information Technology Assessment

The information technology assessment methodology sets out to establish two things:

- To capture the state of deployment of information technology within the organization
- To rank the degree to which the organization utilizes the existing information technology it has already deployed

The first benefit in establishing these metrics is that you are able to determine the extent to which information technology is deployed throughout the organization. As you saw in the methodology of aligning the business process, there typically are few individuals in the organization who have a horizontal appreciation of the business, from the order point to the cash point. Unfortunately, there are probably fewer individuals who appreciate the breadth of application of information technology across the organization. Knowing how widely information technology is deployed throughout an organization can elicit a strong response from senior managers, who suddenly realize that without information technology, the organization would virtually come to a standstill.

This reality check for senior managers must be controlled and presented in the light of opportunity. You must leverage the fact that the organization is, to a degree, dependent on information technology. The dependence must be presented as an opportunity to further increase the positive return to the business. If the situation is not carefully presented, senior management can be left with a feeling of being held hostage by information technology. Rather than looking for opportunities to increase the use of information technology, the focus of senior management will quickly turn to options available to reduce the dependence on technology and ultimately get free of its grip.

As shown in Figure 3.2, the information technology assessment typically will cover the following areas:

Part

I

Ch

3

■ *Organizational Structure*. The IT Department will take on many forms depending on the organization's overall structure. Not only are there typical centralized and decentralized structures, there will be matrix structures inherited from the parent organization.

■ *Service Level*. Ultimately, the service level perception of the organization's information technology users is used to rank the effectiveness of the IT department. This must involve a service level survey, which can take many forms.

■ *Budget*. The organization likely is unaware of the true cost of supporting its information technology resources. The total cost of ownership (TCO) has been estimated by several industry analysts with some correlation. This study opens the door to opportunity in assigning costs directly to the appropriate business consumer of the technology.

■ *Project Mix*. Primarily the assessment is used to identify projects that do not need to be part of the information technology portfolio. These projects are shown to be business initiatives and not technology initiatives.

■ *Technology Portfolio*. This resembles a hardware and software inventory. Hopefully, one already exists that is relatively current.

FIG. 3.2

The common elements of an IT assessment or IT plan extend beyond the traditional technology components.

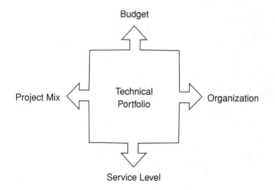

The fact that your organization will conduct an information technology assessment should be communicated to the entire business. The communication does not have to be elaborate or highly detailed. The purpose is to inform employees that the organization values its investment in information technology and that the result will be a report card used to highlight new opportunities to utilize technology even further. The communication can use any medium the organization currently utilizes (from bulletin boards to intranet postings). The information posting should include the following information:

- A definition of the assessment
- Who or which group is leading the assessment
- The expected duration
- Any activities in which the employees may be asked to participate
- The expected benefits
- A date when the next communication will be made available (this may be an interim status report if the duration is more than one month)
- A contact for further information or feedback

The assessment is, in fact, a preliminary measurement exercise. Employees become very interested in measurements because measurements can be used to rank employee performance. The old adage "what gets measured is what gets done" is both opportunity and risk for the organization. If the organization selects the right measurements, then the right things will get done. However, if the organization selects the wrong measurements, the wrong things will get done.

In the case of the information technology assessment, the measurements help produce the report card (discussed in the following section), but are more importantly used to identify opportunities in which you can leverage information technology to increase the return of business value. This opportunity model is addressed in the discussion on focusing the IT plan later in this section.

Creating the Information Technology Report Card

The second benefit of the information technology assessment is the ability to rank your organization against industry benchmarks. In large organizations there may be internal corporate benchmarks that can also be used. Table 3.1 provides a sample list of metrics that can be applied in each case.

Table 3.1   Metrics Available for the IT Assessment

Area	Metrics
Organization	Number of full-time personnel; number of external contractors and consultants; number of IT personnel as a percent of total employees; IT personnel cost as a percent of IT budget; IT personnel cost as a percent of revenue; IT spending per total number of employees; IT personnel and contractor/consultant turnover as a percent of total employee turnover; shift in IT personnel capabilities

Area	Metrics
Service Level	Number of information technology users per IT employees; support calls per employee and per IT employee; other support call metrics; satisfaction with applications
Budget	IT budget percent of sales; IT versus business unit investment; rate of IT budget change
	Training as a percent of total IT budget; IT spending per technology; total cost of ownership (TOC)
Project	Project completion; capital investment
	R&D investment; barriers to completion; legacy system replacement rate; BPR related project rate
Technology Portfolio	Platform distribution; rate of growth of client/server; package ERP systems

Measuring Organization Metrics   The following metrics can be used as a measure of compliance that your current organization exhibits with respect to industry standards. Once the assessment is completed, the gaps that exist between your organization and the industry can be used as opportunities for improvement.

- *Number of full-time IT personnel.* An absolute measure that is sometimes skewed with the (mis)definition of full-time employees, part-time employees, contract employees, and consultants.

- *Number of external contractors or consultants.* Using this measure along with the number of full-time IT personnel will provide a more precise comparison between organizations.

- *Number of IT personnel as a percent of total employees.* Typically used as a service metric, but in this context provides a normalized comparison between organizations of varying employee count.

- *IT personnel cost as a percent IT budget.* This will provide a normalized measure of the importance placed on human resources over technical resources.

- *IT personnel cost as a percent of revenue.* This provides a more consistent metric when comparing the human resource importance between organizations of varying revenue levels.

- *IT spending per total number of employees.* Used occasionally, but only within similar industries. Be cautious; the number of employees can vary dramatically between industries.

- *IT personnel and contractor/consultant turnover as a percent of total employee turnover.* Use this metric both alone and as compared to the rest of the organization. An improvement to this metric is to gather turnover by reason. The turnover reason can point out various root causes, some under the control of the IT department and some with the organization.

- *Shift in IT personnel capabilities.* Not an absolute measure, but a classification of the skills required to perform the required technical tasks. Over time it is important to develop adequate training programs to meet the emerging technical capability demands.

Part
I

Ch
3

Measuring Service Level Metrics The following service level metrics can be used as a measure of compliance that your current organization exhibits with respect to industry standards. Once the assessment is completed, the gaps that exist between your organization and the industry can be used as opportunities for improvement.

- *Number of information technology users per IT employee.* A common metric used throughout the industry for inter-company comparisons. This metric is best used to compare organizations in similar industries. Many users on a large, mainframe-based application can be supported by relatively few support personnel, while several distinct client/server applications and fewer end users require relatively more support personnel. Caution is required when using this metric because some organizations provide separate application and platform support. While the platform support is provided from within the IT department, the application support is provided by the business unit, thus skewing the metric to be low.

- *Support calls per employee and per IT employee.* This can be used as an inter-company comparison, but is primarily used as an internal measure of technical support loading.

- *Other support call metrics.* There are dozens of support call metrics that tend to provide better internal measurements than inter-company comparisons. However, these various support call metrics can be averaged to produce an estimation of customer satisfaction.

- *Satisfaction with applications.* This is different than customer satisfaction. Here you develop a measure of the usefulness of the tools provided to the information technology users. This is a useful metric, especially when considering upgrading legacy systems. It may be a surprise that the end users are quite satisfied with the benefits from the current system in place.

Measuring Budget Metrics The following financial metrics can be used as a measure of compliance that your current organization exhibits with respect to industry standards. Once the assessment is completed, the gaps that exist between your organization and the industry can be used as opportunities for improvement.

- *IT budget as a percent of sales.* Probably the most widely used metric when comparing IT departments between companies. Beware; it can be misleading. It's not clear what exactly is included in an IT budget. For example, some IT budgets used in this metric include only the operating expense, not capital projects.

- *IT versus business unit investment.* A recent trend shows that IT budgets are no longer tightly controlled within the IT Department, but rather each business unit is now being allocated an IT budget. Whether the IT budget is being distributed or the business units are simply allocating more of their existing budget to IT is not entirely clear. This certainly supports the notion that as an increasingly larger portion of technology dollars are controlled outside of the IT department, it follows that the decision making on the target of those budget dollars is being shared proportionally.

- *Rate of IT budget change.* Certainly an indicator of your organization's perception of the value that IT has brought to the business.

- *Training as a percent of total IT budget.* Particular to information technology is the increasing rate of change. Developing skills in every emerging technology is not feasible. However, the rate at which training dollars are invested can indicate the optimism an organization has towards information technology.

- *IT spending per technology.* A good comparison to ensure your shift in investment is correlating to the industry and its perception of emerging value-added technology.

Measuring Project Metrics   The following project metrics can be used as a measure of compliance that your current organization exhibits with respect to industry standards. Once the assessment is completed, the gaps that exist between your organization and the industry can be used as opportunities for improvement.

- *Project completion.* An indicator of whether the IT Department is profit or delivery focused. Primarily an internal benchmark.

- *Capital investment.* Also considered an IT budget metric. A relative internal comparison between the dollars invested in organization capital projects versus those in the IT department.

- *R&D investment.* Also considered an IT budget metric. A relative internal comparison between the dollars invested in product research and development and those invested in emerging technology opportunity development.

- *Barriers to completion.* A good cross-industry comparison. Determines whether a specific technology or method hampers completion of projects.

- *Legacy system replacement rate.* An indicator of the value your organization puts in new and emerging information technology. Can be combined with the project completion and the satisfaction with applications metrics to provide a realistic comparison.

- *BPR related project rate.* An indicator on the value your organization puts on the efficiency of the underlying business processes. Can be combined with the IT versus business unit investment metric.

Measuring Technology Portfolio Metrics   The following technology metrics can be used as a measure of compliance that your current organization exhibits with respect to industry standards. Once the assessment is completed the gaps that exist between your organization and the industry can be used as opportunities for improvement.

- *Platform distribution.* A ranking of the technologies used in your organization and the market leadership those technology vendors occupy.

- *Rate of growth of client/server.* Combined with the legacy system replacement rate, this metric is a good indicator of the risk level an organization is willing to accept.

- *Package (ERP) systems.* A good indicator of an organization's willingness to change its thinking from independent business units to a cross-functional model.

Part
I

Ch
3

Reviewing the Information Technology Report Card

The information technology assessment is not a trivial exercise for an organization to complete. Typically, the complexity of the information technology assessment is proportional to the organization's size. It follows that a large organization may have several facilities or sites to evaluate and may have to deal with a larger number of personnel. A large organization would also be challenged to uncover true financial statistics. However, the benefit of a large organization is that the metrics can be used internally as benchmarks between business units. The comparison will be much more realistic because the underlying definition and calculation of the metrics will be similar across the organization. A small organization will have to compare its metrics strictly to external organizations, where the metric definition can vary.

A completed information technology assessment allows the organization to produce a report card. The review of the report card should serve the entire organization. The IT report card does not have to be confined to the IT Department. This is an opportunity to alert senior management to any issues that have been identified. For example, a high personnel turnover rate in a specific technical area should prompt an investigation by the organization's human resource department to understand the reasoning. Better still, it is likely that several opportunities have appeared as a result of the IT assessment. In the next section, you will learn a method to structure and focus the IT plan on these opportunities.

Focusing the Information Technology Plan on Opportunity

The previous section discussed an approach to capturing the current state of an organization's utilization of information technology. It also reviewed some metrics used to help rank the efficiency of the information technology efforts. Given that an organization has completed the information technology assessment and report card, it is likely that several opportunities arose. Here you will look at a method to take advantage of these opportunities in preparing an IT plan.

IT plans are short lived. Unlike a typical business plan, IT plans do not have a life cycle of four or five years. As shown in Figure 3.3, the rate at which technology changes is about 12 to 18 months (that is, Moore's law). For example, a personal computer will double in processing capability in 12 months, but can be purchased at the same price as the current model.

With this in mind, the IT plan must be reviewed regularly. Typically, IT plans can span up to three years. Considering the previous performance model, the plan must accommodate changes in performance and capabilities of nearly 700 percent in three years' time. That's an enormous change to plan for in advance.

Recall that the objective is to focus the information technology plan on returning business value. The topic of aligning the organization's business processes was addressed earlier. With an aligned business process it is mandatory to ensure that every information technology initiative is directly connected to a business process. Given that the organization understands what value it places on a given business process, the organization can then estimate the return on the information technology used to support the process. Thus, it can begin to estimate what investment is reasonable.

FIG. 3.3
A typical cost/
performance curve of
computer processing
and cost over a 12
month period.

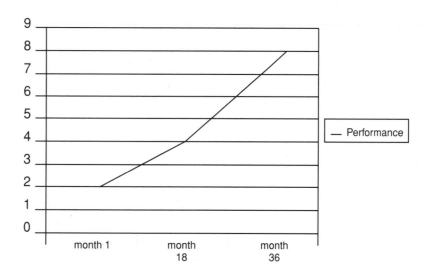

Reviewing the Information Technology Department Organization

Most organizations view the IT Department as a cost of doing business. That view is changing. As the need to carefully craft information technology solutions to support the business process becomes an absolute necessity to compete, the IT Department is being considered an equal partner in shaping the organization's direction. Although information technology solutions provide relief from mundane and labor intensive tasks, the new view has information technology being leveraged in areas that are strategic and providing organizations with competitive advantage.

This has created a new skill set for the IT leader in an organization. What was once a role strictly measured by technical fluency and competence has now changed. Today, IT leaders are expected to be business leaders first and technologists second. The IT leader must possess the necessary business acumen to participate in the organization's management process and business planning process. The IT leader must gain the credibility of his or her management peers in order to be trusted with the delivery of the information technology portfolio.

An addition to the change in the skill set of the IT leader, is the change required of the IT Department's organizational structure. The change in the IT leader's skill set has brought change in the measurement systems placed against the department from the rest of the organization. This prompts the IT Department to realign to best meet the new measurements systems.

IT Department reorganization is on the rise due to the new found sharing of information technology investment decisions. What was once a decision isolated within the IT Department is now seen as a cooperative decision made in consultation with the business units, possibly more heavily weighted on the business unit side.

Assessing the Organization   Several metrics could be gathered or calculated for the organization, such as the following:

- Number of full-time personnel
- Number of external contractors and consultants
- Number of IT personnel as a percent of total employees
- IT personnel cost as a percent IT budget
- IT personnel cost as a percent of revenue
- IT spending per total number of employees
- IT personnel and contractor/consultant turnover as a percent of total employee turnover
- Shift in IT personnel capabilities

It is important to remember that these are sample metrics. None, some, or all of these metrics could be applicable to a particular organization.

The organization's overall structure will have a great deal of influence over the demands placed upon the information technology organizational structure. In a large organization, the IT Department will tend to be less constrained for resources. This will allow the IT Department to focus some energy on more strategic initiatives. Whereas the small organization's IT department will likely be resource strained and will need to focus all its available energy on the tactical or operational task.

It follows that the assessment in a large organization will tend to show needs placed on the IT Department to be issues of standards and governance over technical delivery. Large organizations will experience technical services that spill beyond the IT Department boundaries and into the business units themselves. These larger business units are able to provide their own internal technical resources and are simply looking (or perhaps require approval) for overall guidance or direction. Thus, the IT Department will tend to be structured to have resources applied to these types of policy tasks. The small organization assessment will tend to show that demands on the IT Department are closely linked to delivery of technology. The small organization business units may not have the sufficient resources required to have their own technical capabilities.

Focusing the Organization   This section reviews available structural alternatives for an IT Department. Utilizing the results of the IT assessment and determining the type of organization being assessed will show the types of structures available. The intent is not to draw a completely new organizational chart, but to provide enough influence from the assessment that the current organizational chart has reason to bend to accommodate the findings.

Fundamentally, there are only two structures to apply to organize the IT Department. They are the following:

- *Centralized.* This structure provides tight control over all strategic, tactical, and operational technology issues. The advantage of the centralized organization is that it provides a clear source of direction. There is no doubt of this source. In a technical organization, a centralized structure will provide optimum definition and control of standards, policies, and procedures. This can lead to a better understanding (through visibility) and control of expense or total cost of ownership (TCO). Further, with a single set of standards, policies, and procedures, the organization provides itself with some flexibility to change as the need arises.

■ *Decentralized.* This structure provides loose control over all strategic, tactical, and operational technology issues. The advantage of the decentralized organization increases with overall company size. Although there may be more than one source of direction, having the input of more than a single source in a large company will provide more visibility to the needs of the organization. Responsiveness increases as local business units are able to react quickly to locally changing needs and requirements. Technical decisions can be averaged across the organization to provide a better overall result to the company.

Unfortunately, the optimum organizational structure will exist somewhere in between, typically referred to as a *hybrid*. Within the hybrid organizational structure, there are several degrees of freedom that must be understood and defined. These degrees of freedom can include the following:

■ Information technology steering committee

■ Competency centers

■ Application ownership

■ Hybrid model

In a large organization where some IT Department decentralization is expected, the overall information technology direction must be monitored and focused according to the business demands placed on it. A steering committee that includes technical members and key business unit members needs to be formed.

There is a distinct need to provide specialized services on a particular set of technology. This could be hardware, software, networking, or communications to name a few. An area of particular interest is the application support. In the case of implementing Baan, the organization will need to consider establishing a competency center for Baan. This would provide specialized Baan application support to users across the organization. It would be cost prohibitive to attempt having Baan application specialists in every business unit.

Closely tied with the competency center is the notion of distributing responsibility over the ownership of the application process and the underlying infrastructure. The trend in this area continues to be that business units are adopting the application and that the IT Department is retaining control of the infrastructure. This is not meant as a divide and run scenario; it is intended as a partnership. IT will leverage a common infrastructure to keep the business unit from having to have the resources available to provide this service. While the business unit will invest in the process it operates and the IT Department does not have to invest in resources to learn the specific of each business units processes. In the case of a Baan implementation, the business analysts or key users would be individuals located in the various business units. The technical support could come from the central IT Department.

N O T E An indirect consequence of the location of business analysts in the business units is that the quality and responsiveness of the IT Department service level must increase. Otherwise, IT risks loosing further service base to the business unit. ■

The data center is another functional area that can be organized centrally or be decentralized out to the business units. When the data center is decentralized out to the business units consider both the positive and negatives consequences. Technology consistency is more difficult to maintain. Each data center will tend to make decisions independently of the others, and technology fragmentation can occur. However, multiple data centers offer the opportunity to create redundant or backup data centers. However, there must be sufficient organization control to mandate data center standards. A slight variation on the decentralized model offers the benefits of both models. The campus model is similar to the decentralized model in that there are multiple centers supporting each business unit able to act as a backup. The campus model capitalizes on the centralized model value to provide consistency in standards. Unfortunately, the campus model is limited to organizations, who themselves are aligned along a campus model. If an organization locates business units independent of each other geographically, then the campus model reduces to the decentralized model.

Similarly, the technical help desk can be organized in either of the previous three models: centralized, decentralized, or campus. Each has advantages and disadvantages. However, it is best that the technical support help desk mirror the structure of the data center model. This will avoid duplication of resources.

The hybrid organization model shown in Figure 3.4 will vary in terms of its implementation in different organizations. This is primarily a result of how the decentralized technical members are viewed. Should they be IT Department members who live in the business unit or members of the business unit who act as technical representatives for the IT Department.

FIG. 3.4

The hybrid IT organization combines business unit participants with technologists.

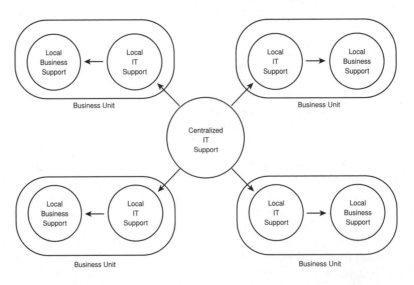

Some type of hybrid model will likely perform the best in your organization. This structure provides the benefits of central direction and standard setting while enjoying the participation of the business units in supporting applications.

Reviewing the IT Department Service Level

Of any of the functional areas reviewed in the assessment, the service level provided by the IT Department to the technology end users is probably the most interesting metric to review. The service level is usually estimated by considering the effectiveness of the organization's technical support help desk. Although this is a very important metric, you must understand that there are other considerations as well.

The technical support help desk is typically depicted as the phone that never gets answered. When the call for help does get answered, it is often to the callers disappointment. Most help desks will staff the front line with first-level support staff. This means the junior technicians taking the call are not what the caller anticipated. Callers expect the first line of support to be the person who can fix their problem. Unfortunately, the IT Department has neither the financial nor human resources to commit to this level of experience at the front line. The support mechanism is usually a tiered approach in which there is a many-to-one relationship between front line technicians and senior technical specialists.

The IT Department is interested to know how it is perceived from its customer base, the information technology end users. Do the end users view the IT Department as an operational or strategic partner? This dictates the importance the business units will place on the importance of the IT Department. Further, it is proportional to the investment the organization is willing to make in information technology in general and the IT Department specifically. This will also be concluded from the perception of how the IT Department is perceived to understand the underlying business needs and not just looking to deploy new technology.

The IT Department must take a proactive approach to the underlying business needs. It is very important to understand the business that is being supported. This provides the opportunity to determine whether the business is taking full advantage of the available technology.

As part of the IT assessment, try to include an end user survey. Properly structured, replies will provide a wealth of information in a number of areas. This information will help establish some of the metrics previously discussed as well as create awareness. Further, you need to get appreciation for the task at hand. End users need to understand that the IT Department is in a transition and that the final result will provide improved service level to the technology end users.

In addition to service level metrics, the survey can capture data that can support cost/benefit calculations leading to identification of new service opportunities. For example, an estimation from each end user as to the amount of data stored locally on the end users workstation can provide sufficient information to develop a business case for the need to protect important company assets: knowledge in the form of localized data.

Technology end users need more than help desks. Conducting a survey is one way to accumulate statistics and to produce a customer satisfaction benchmark. Using this benchmark, several opportunities may exist to provide increased support to the end user. For instance, the end users would surely appreciate the fact that the IT Department solicited their input to determine new service offerings.

Part

I

Ch

3

Assessing the Service Level   Several metrics have been presented that could be gathered or calculated for the service level, such as the following:

- Number of information technology users per IT employee
- Support calls per employee and per IT employee
- Other support call metrics
- Satisfaction with applications: several current packages could be included

This is not an exhaustive list of metrics. Your organization will likely develop metrics specific to its interest.

The IT assessment will attempt to capture information that can lead to conclusions on several issues related to the end user service level.

The first area to get focused feedback is those issues dealing with the end users first priority, that is, technology problem solving and support. This is usually an area where feedback is abundant. Unfortunately, it is usually negative feedback. However, it is the things done poorly that need to be improved. The intent is to categorize the feedback and look for patterns that may point to a particular application or infrastructure element or that may indicate additional training is needed on the part of the help desk technicians. This information could be coupled with the reorganization of the help desk discussed previously.

It is useful to gauge the interest level of the end users to contribute new ideas to the improvement of the information technology portfolio. The use of comment sections provides the opportunity for improvement suggestions. Still better is a comment section that has selections identified. This helps get feedback on specific proposed initiatives and prompts the end users to think of similar needs.

As end users become increasingly independent, there is a need to provide a "tool counter." End users need specific productivity tools. If there is a well-populated tool inventory ready for loan, then the end user is satisfied and the IT Department has the capability to keep track of frequently requested tools. This is preferred to the IT Department not being aware of the tools being deployed. Information archives must be made available or the data will inevitably be duplicated. The IT assessment can derive which sources of information are needed and at what frequency.

System availability is critical to most technology end users. The IT assessment can provide information about what expectations the end users have on system availability. Although system outages are always disruptive, it would be valuable to learn from the end users if preplanned outages would be acceptable and if so at what frequency, duration, and what times of the day or week.

Focusing the Service Level   This section uses the results from the IT assessment that highlight service level issues to suggest areas for consideration when developing the IT Department service level expectations.

A significant commitment to the end users would be to develop a mutually agreeable service level agreement, which is not unlike an agreement the organization would hold with an external supplier. Be very careful in this area. Committing to a service level agreement the IT Department is not prepared to meet will only destroy any credibility gained previously. Although there may be no legal recourse the end users can take, the lack of credibility will limit future success of any proposed initiatives.

The IT Department can organize itself sufficiently to develop and manage a service level agreement with the end users. There are likely to be several service level agreements in place. For example, the Baan application would have a separate service level agreement identifying such items as system availability, response time, data archival (backups), online history, MRP/PRP run frequency, master table update frequency, and so on.

Earlier you learned about the concept of a competency center. The competency center, as shown in Figure 3.5, could be used as a vehicle to package and deliver the services included in the end user application service level agreement. Various elements to consider are the following within this competency center:

- *A technical support help desk specifically trained in the supported application.* The service level agreement will identify the call resolution rate. That is, how many calls can be responded to in a given time period and what percentage will get resolved in a given time period. The help desk calls must be tracked and documented for several reasons. The two most important reasons are to enable repeat problem identification and to support a claim of meeting the service level agreement.

- *A facility to test application enhancements prior to production.* Regardless of whether the competency center delivers the enhancements, it should have the capability to test the enhancements in the organization's production environment.

- *The capability to make application changes or modifications.* The competency center is designed to serve the organization as a whole. It makes little sense to have end users responsible to outsource and project manage application enhancements.

- *A facility to test new releases of an application prior to production.* A new release of the application must be tested prior to release into production. The competency center provides an opportunity to utilize the organization's data and other unique attributes that the application vendor is unable to provide.

- *Training for both new and existing end users.* Training can be best organized within a competency center because the application expertise is already present. An external training organization will not be as familiar with day to day operation of the application, especially if the application has been customized to the organization.

- *The ability to market new application features and functions.* This is a proactive role for the competency center. The organization cannot afford to have all of its application end users responsible for monitoring new releases of the application for new feature function. The competency center can be responsible for targeting new feature function availability to the specific end users.

FIG. 3.5

The competency center provides shared central-ized resources to all business units.

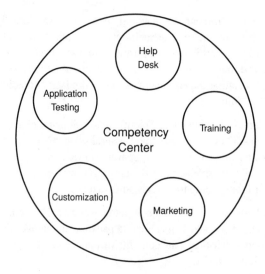

The IT Department should initiate the creation of a competency center focused on delivering specific application support, particularly in the case of major applications, such as Baan. The competency center is responsible for developing a service level agreement that is acceptable to the application end users.

Reviewing the IT Department Budget

Although the other areas in which you collect and analyze the IT assessment data are equally important, it is the IT Department's budget that receives the most attention from senior man-agement. This is probably due to the fact that the IT budget is void of technical content, on the surface at least. This is true in order to deal with the absolute expenditures, but to understand if there is value in the expenditure, there is little choice but to understand the information technology behind the expenditures.

Later you will review the topic of business value. This definition provides the organization an opportunity to increase the return on the investment in information technology. An organiza-tion must take two steps in its improvement in information technology investment.

First, the organization must analyze its current investment portfolio and refine the investment to ensure only those initiatives that are closely aligned with the business receive support. In other words, given the same investment an organization can increase its return on the invest-ment by simply realigning the current information technology initiatives. You will look more closely at this mix of strategic, tactical, and R&D projects in the next section.

Second, the organization can increase the investment in information technology initiatives. Given the first step to rationalize has been completed, the organization will now have a model of investment available to seek out new opportunities that return business value.

The metrics developed in the area of IT Department budget lead to the estimation of the total cost of ownership (TCO). A much touted metric in the information technology industry, the TCO metric first arose out of the personal desktop computer. The Gartner Group lead the way with TCO studies in the early 1990s. The TCO studies were the first real attempts to consolidate the total investment an organization must make to support the desktop environment.

The TCO metrics acumulate both operational expense and capital investment. The operational expense captures the cost of administration, support, and operations, while the capital investment includes the cost of capital in addition to the acquisition cost. To what extent direct end user costs are included tends to skew the comparison between TCO metrics between organizations.

In the focus of the IT plan, you will need to provide avenues of opportunity to reduce the TCO. During the review of the financial metrics, the goal is to identify those costs and categorize them into the operational or capital category. Within the operational expense category, the challenge is to identify the particular source of the expense, and hence the initiatives necessary to reduce the expense.

Assessing the Budget   Several metrics have been presented that should be gathered or calculated for the IT Department budget, such as the following:

- IT budget as a percent of sales
- IT versus business unit investment
- Rate of IT budget change
- Training as a percent of total IT budget
- IT spending per technology
- Total cost of ownership (TCO)

The intent of the IT assessment in this area is to gather sufficient financial information to formulate the TCO. The IT assessment should focus on the following areas:

- *Allocation of costs.* It is necessary to determine if a charge back policy exists. Do the end users of the technology have to pay from their departmental budgets or are the funds administered from the IT department budget? What decision cycle or methodology does the organization use to determine whether a particular information technology investment is appropriate? Is there a particular cost tracking mechanism in place to support the allocation of cost?

- *Administration costs.* This is a more difficult metric to quantify. However, it is important to understand the amount of time and expense that is invested in developing partnerships and alliances with information technology vendors. The degree to which partnerships are a success can be measured, in part, through the use of compatible technology.

- *Support costs.* Several areas of interest help develop an idea of support costs. Assess the use of standards, both technology standards (operating systems, network topologies and protocols, and so on) and product standards (brand names, models, and so on). Also determine the extent to which product suites are used.

Part

I

Ch

3

■ *Purchase costs*. Determine the level to which the organization takes advantage of volume purchasing agreements or has negotiated long-term purchasing agreements.

■ *Operational costs*. Determine the mix of purchase versus leasing of technology. How does older technology get allocated throughout the organization? Is it recycled, for example, by being trickled down to less demanding applications? How does the IT Department model its software licensing? Is it a concurrent user model or a named user model?

With these (and related) metrics, the TCO model will begin to take shape. In some cases it will be a revealing exercise. The TCO is traditionally a figure that greatly exceeds the purchase price. The purchase price typically is the only metric considered in most organizations.

Focusing the Budget   With the IT assessment results, the IT Department can begin to focus the IT plan with respect to financial planning.

The IT Department budget as a percent of revenue tends to pose a dichotomy to the reviewer. If the actual rate is lower than the industry rate, then it can be perceived that the organization is well positioned, because it is managing to spend less than its competitor on information technology. It can also be viewed that the organization is behind the industry and needs to invest more aggressively. If the actual rate is higher than the industry rate, it can be interpreted that the organization is spending too much on information technology and should consider a more conservative approach. It can also be interpreted that the organization is being aggressive with respect to its competitors.

Both cases can be highly influenced on whether senior management understands the return on investment from information technology or business value. The IT plan must focus on developing a mutually agreeable definition of business value. A value that can be used and understood when defending the IT budget position. Regardless, this is a metric that is probably the most widely used in the industry today.

The next most popular industry metric is the TCO, as shown in Figure 3.6. However, this metric is still relatively new in practice. As such, it may be the first time an organization will be exposed to the TCO. Be well prepared when using this measure in the IT budget. Although the resulting plan may be taking a very aggressive approach to controlling the newly found/allocated costs, the shock of tabling the TCO for the first time may present a barrier to overcome. In this section you will consider some of the ways in which the TCO parameters can be controlled.

To lower the purchase cost of technology, look into preconfigured units, which, in turn, drive the need for standards. If the organization can leverage many units at a standard configuration, the costs can be lowered. Look to vendors or resellers that can provide a preconfiguration service. The organization can provide the vendor with a standard profile or image to be installed in each unit. Typically, this is best leveraged in the workstation or desktop/laptop area.

To lower support costs, look at your organization's business model. If the organization is global, then it follows that the technology vendor must provide a global support model. Attempting to provide service and support across different time zones and different geography involving different languages and cultures can be an enormous challenge. Put simply, the vendor must be where your organization is located. Of course, product quality should obviate the need for extensive support and service. Ensure the vendor implements quality practices and procedures consistent with your organization's quality expectations.

To lower operating costs, the organization must consider the rate at which it wants to refresh technology. Historically, organizations used the trickle down method to reallocate older technology, especially in the computer desktop area. An emerging trend is to consider lease arrangements over capital purchases. Some programs offer the capability to hold the expense constant while replacing the technology as the performance increases.

Another key item to consider closely is the concept of volume license agreements. Historically, the volume required excluded the majority of organizations, however recent trends are clearly bringing the volume barrier to the point where most every company can participate. Be sure to clearly define the model as concurrent use and not per named user. Basically, the concurrent user model requires that you license only active users, while the named user model requires that you license every end user regardless of use. This should be applied to every support (email), productivity (word processor), or production application (Baan).

Allocation of costs is less a cost saving initiative than it is a visibility initiative. Historically, IT departments have been responsible for determining the benefit for all end users of technology. Recent trends now show the business units becoming more responsible for the benefit analysis. However, a clear definition of charge back is needed for those services provided by the IT Department. Historically, in the mainframe and mini-computer era, the CPU time that was consumed was used as a measure for cost allocation. However, with the recent trend to client server and desktop computing, it has become much more difficult to ascertain just how much (distributed) processing time is being consumed. In most organizations this tends to be allocated according to the number of end users located in each business unit.

FIG. 3.6
The TCO reveals the true cost of technology ownership.

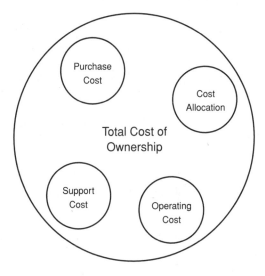

The TCO is an excellent opportunity for the IT Department to clearly identify costs to the organization. However, with the cost made visible, the pressure will increase to reduce these costs.

Reviewing the IT Department Project Mix

The IT Department has a portfolio of projects it must manage to completion. These projects are typically prioritized relative to the end user's persistence of getting the project delivered. However, the project list must reflect what the IT Department should be doing from an organization perspective and not an individual perspective. A common saying is that the IT Department must stop doing things right and start doing the right things.

Which initiatives are right depends on where the organization places itself on the spectrum of information technology use in its current business process. For example, the organization can utilize information technology to do the following (from simplest to most complex):

- Simply automate existing processes
- Bring together islands of information
- Align business processes
- Reengineer the business
- Completely redefine the scope of the business

The level of change the organization is promoting determines the number and type of projects the IT Department must manage.

There are three broad categories of projects.

- *Strategic*. These projects are focused on the initiatives in the organization's business plan that are categorized as capital investment initiatives. These projects will help support the organization in its new form planned for in the strategic plan.
- *Tactical*. These project are those initiatives that are currently in place supporting the business in its current or near term form. A tactical project evolves from a planned strategic project or it can be an operational project that may be dealing with infrastructure.
- *Development*. These projects typically support the strategic initiatives of evolving the technical infrastructure. These projects are coupled with training and development opportunities for the IT personnel. These projects will result in new infrastructure being deployed or new capabilities that can be offered to the organization.

There are two issues to learn more about. How aggressive is the organization in its process of change with respect to leveraging technology? Also, how does the current project mix support that degree of change?

Assessing the Project Mix   Several metrics have been presented that should be gathered or calculated for the IT Department project mix, such as the following:

- Project completion
- Capital investment
- R&D investment
- Barriers to completion
- Legacy system replacement rate
- BPR-related project rate

The IT assessment will attempt to draw out information that will lead to conclusions in the project mix. There are the three categories previously defined: strategic, tactical, and development. Furthermore, you must determine whether the IT Department is leading projects that it should otherwise not be leading. In fact there is a great opportunity to ensure that the business units are taking ownership of the projects that are directly related to their business processes.

The financial metrics related to capital and R&D investment are interesting to calculate and then compare with the organization's overall rate of investment in these categories.

End users should be questioned on their perception of whether various projects succeeded. Further, what is their definition of success? Historically, IT project leaders have been delivery focused rather than profit focused. Being delivery focused results from the project leader focusing on the due date as the overriding success factor. This then precludes other more important success factors from being achieved. The second issue is that the IT project leader likely is not aware or fluent in the success factors of the business unit requesting the project. In order for projects to be profit focused, the project leadership must emanate from the group that understands the business success factors.

Understanding the barriers to successful projects is valuable. More often than not the barrier will be an improperly assigned project leader. If the project is to support a strategic initiative of the organization the project leader needs to clearly understand that initiative. Just as an IT project leader will have difficulty managing a business unit project, it is equally difficult for a business unit project leader to manage what is really an information technology infrastructure project.

The rate at which legacy systems are being replaced for projects that utilize some sort of process reengineering can be indicators of success and should be drawn out in the IT assessment questions.

Focusing the Project Mix   The IT plan must be focused to clearly define the three types of projects, as shown in Figure 3.7, and the criteria to determine the type. Project ownership of each type of project must be clearly defined. The fact that all projects must be profit (or value) focused must replace the notion of delivery focused projects. This is not to say that project deadlines are not to be considered at all. Rather, timelines and milestones are evaluators of progress and really have little to do with success.

The strategic project should have a project leader assigned who resides in the business unit that owns the project. The appropriate business unit, through its understanding of the organization's strategic direction, will likely have initiated this type of project. If the business unit is not willing to manage the project, then the project objective needs to be re-examined. If an initiative is important to a department, that department will certainly provide leadership. It is in that business unit's best interest to take control in order to determine when the project success factor has been reached.

The tactical project is one that is currently in motion to support an existing business need. As with the strategic project, the probable leader for the tactical project is from the sponsoring business unit. This does not preclude the fact that the IT Department may have a major contribution to make to the project. Tactical projects need to complete and deliver the expected benefits in the organization's near term, typically between 2 and 12 months.

The development project is typically an internal IT Department project. It is tied to a strategic initiative, but is separate from the timeline of the strategic project. The strategic project may not begin for up to 12 months; however, the technology capabilities need to be understood and developed early and then maintained. As such, the project leader is usually from within the IT Department. The development projects should be organized to provide the majority of training that IT personnel will require. Training does not have to be a separate exercise.

In the section, "Focusing the Service Level," you learned about the concept of a competency center. This would be an area that could be assigned responsibility to organize and lead development projects. If the organization structure warrants, various IT personnel could be moved from the business unit into the competency center for the duration of the project. Hence, when the project is concluded, the IT personnel (support) would move back to the business unit for ongoing end user support. If the project were part of an enterprise-wide solution, the support should remain in the competency center.

FIG. 3.7

The organization's project mix will reflect the importance of business value.

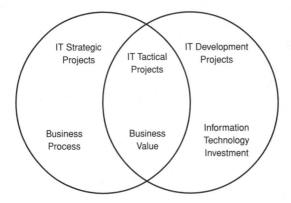

It is important to change the project success focus from delivery to value. This can be done by properly assigning project leadership to the three different project types.

Reviewing the IT Department Technology Portfolio

The fifth area to consider in the IT plan is the technology portfolio itself. Until this point, you have reviewed issues that surround and support the technology deployed in an organization. Here you will consider the types of information technology and tools typically used and you will define a way in which to group these into manageable families. It tends to look more like an organizational structuring, and in the end this may be the most efficient way to approach the technology classification.

The technology portfolio needs to capture several characteristics of the organization and the technology that is deployed.

From an organizational perspective, deployed application-level technology tends to follow the vertical functions within an organization. That is to say, certain applications will appear useful only in certain parts of the business (for example, a computer-aided design application is likely to appear in the Engineering Department and less likely to appear on a cost accountant's desktop). It follows from this that the hardware that supports the application will align along the same application and organizational lines (for example, a design workstation that supports the computer-aided design application will be less likely to show up on the cost accountant's desk).

As you look down into the layers of supporting technology and peer into the infrastructure, the alignment of the technology with the business is less clear. You see this trend continue: The further the technology is from the end user application, the more likely it is to be application independent. The infrastructure will begin to move from a vertical alignment to lay horizontally across the organization.

From the perspective of managing the technology, you can see that the technology alignment supports with your assumptions of the organizational alignment. Previously, you learned about the requirement of business unit leadership for strategic and tactical projects. It follows that the management or ownership of the technology should follow the same orientation. The business units should own and support the applications they use in their business. That is, as long as it is specific to that business unit. The challenge is then to locate technical resources within the business units, which is not difficult. What is more difficult is to decide if that technical resource is financially supported by the IT Department or is a member of the business unit. The latter is preferred, but is highly dependent on the overall organizational model.

As you move away from the end user application into the infrastructure, the alignment to the business is less and the technology begins to standardize across business units. The technical resource to support the infrastructure will likely be part of the IT Department. The goal is to leverage centralized support for a standard technical infrastructure.

Assessing the Technology Portfolio   Several metrics have been presented that should be gathered or calculated for the IT Department technology portfolio, such as the following:

- Platform distribution (inventory)
- Rate of growth of client/server
- Type of computing devices used
- Type of production systems used
- Type of productivity tools used
- Type of collaboration tools used

The IT assessment will draw primarily on technical personnel to gather data for the infrastructure area. In some cases this can be gathered from existing hardware and software inventories. The survey should include such items as database, collaboration, operating, and network systems, server hardware, and communications. Business unit personnel will have valuable input in the area of production applications, productivity tools, and collaboration needs.

The IT assessment, in addition to other questions, should include the following questions:

- *Uncover opportunity for new applications.* The end users can be queried on the time and recurrence of manual tasks. From this an estimation of labor costs can be calculated and form a base for cost/benefit analysis.
- *Form an opinion on computing effectiveness.* Are users satisfied with their computing environments? Are there hardware or software tools or applications that would improve their effectiveness?
- *Confirm inventory.* In large organizations it is difficult to capture every technology tool. This is an effective way to uncover isolated applications that could provide a benefit to the entire organization.

The IT assessment must be properly positioned to appeal to both the technical and business unit audience. Sufficient information must be gathered from both groups of individuals; otherwise, the results of only one group will skew the technology grouping to that particular group's alignment—vertically for production users and horizontally for technical support personnel.

Focusing the Technology Portfolio   There are many ways to organize the technology grouping within an organization. This section presents one that can be extended to cover most distributed organizations.

To address the business units needs, a vertical alignment is created. This application layer contains those production applications specific to each functional area (for example, engineering and business applications). Add a third functional area that will capture the productivity and collaboration tools called desktops. All production applications, production tools, and collaboration tools are captured in this layer. Any project initiated at this level requires business unit leadership. This is where the strategic and tactical projects occur.

To support the commonality or standardization across the organization, the horizontal layer is referred to as the *infrastructure*. This infrastructure layer can be further divided into a data layer, operating layer, hardware layer, and communications layer. This is where the development projects occur. Any project initiated here requires IT Department leadership. However, the development projects are undertaken only in response to a strategic or tactical initiative at the application level.

The infrastructure layer does not provide an organization with a competitive advantage; however, it is absolutely necessary and is referred to as the cost of doing business. The further down in the infrastructure you look, the more potential there exists for outsourcing. The reason is that at these lowest layers of infrastructure you have the most commonality and standardization. The golden rule is to outsource only what you understand. It is at these lowest layers that the IT Department will have the greatest experience in determining cost and service level.

The application layer (see Figure 3.8) is strategic and can provide an organization with distinct competitive advantage. These services should be the last if ever to be considered for outsourcing.

FIG. 3.8

The technical foundation for an organization is aligned with the business units at the application level, but assumes a more centralized model at the infrastructure level.

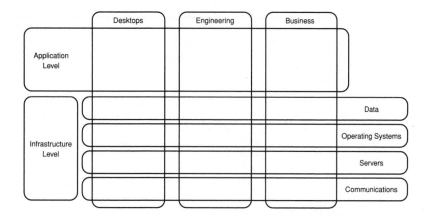

You've reviewed the opportunity for an organization to focus the IT plan using information recovered from an assessment of the current state. There are probably hundreds of metrics that could be calculated. The success lies with those who understand what they need from the assessment in order to develop a highly focused IT plan. ●

Follow a Proven Path

In this chapter

Using a Step-by-Step Approach

Following the proven path is the best practice when implementing an integrated business information system. It is a step-by-step, company-wide approach that helps you through the entire process, provides the structure and a roadmap while building the business case, and links it to your overall strategic company direction.

These proven path activities are designed to make sure a company makes an informed decision before proceeding to the next phase.

Project Initialization

The starting point is management's acceptance that the way you manage and control your business must change. This is where the company makes a formal commitment to proceed with the change. This phase is meant to help you gain an understanding of what is involved and the impact it will have on the business.

The project initialization phase consists of the following activities:

1. Scope of project—Identifies the areas of the business that will be affected by this implementation.
2. Objectives and deliverables—Identifies major business functions to be implemented and their time frames.
3. Project organization:
    - Appoint an executive torchbearer—Identifies the organization executive responsible for the successful implementation.
    - Establish a senior management steering committee—These are people within the organization accountable for the project and have the authority to approve funds, allocate resources, and resolving management level issues.
    - Establish a project team and a project manager—Select key business function experts within your organization and identify an internal project manager accountable for the project success.
    - Obtain outside assistance—Define their roles and responsibilities.
4. Work plan—What is to be done, by who, and on what dates.
5. Business assessment—Assess where your company is today and where it wants to go.
6. Education—Educate key managers.
7. Business case—Cost/benefit analysis.
8. Business performance goals.
9. Recommendation to steering committee—Work plan for next phase.
10. Authorization to proceed.

Requirements Definition

How you conduct business and all your business processes are examined, documented, and analyzed via requirements definition before they are reengineered to meet your future business and customer needs. These are design decisions regarding the way you plan to run your business in the future.

The requirements definition phase consists of the following activities:

1. Develop the current business model.
2. Document the current business processes.
3. Education—Educate employees working in specific functional areas.
4. Benchmark other companies with similar business processes.
5. Reengineer your business model and business processes—Functionality check list.
6. Establish performance indicators for your business processes.
7. Establish company policies.
8. Identify benefits of new business model.
9. Document technical specification:
   - Hardware
   - Operating system
   - Software
   - Network infrastructure
   - Vendors profile
   - Support requirements
10. Data management:
    - Identify key data elements.
    - Establish minimum data accuracy level.
11. People management:
    - Plan the people element.
    - Identify what has to change—Organizational structure, jobs, skills, behavior.
    - Management Sponsorship.
12. Update cost/benefit analysis.
13. Report to Steering Committee—Work plan for next phase.
14. Authorization to proceed.

Part
I

Ch
4

Selecting the Software

After your needs are defined, the next logical step is to look at what is available on the market that meets your requirements. The selection process is very demanding and must be prepared up front. There are a lot of details to consider and this exercise should be planned properly. The outcome of the search commits your organization for a long time—not to mention costing a lot of money and resources.

It is important to note at this stage that today the majority of companies do not develop their own software solution. It is far too costly and development and getting the solution into production take too much time.

Research and Selection Process

Match your business requirements with the vendor's profile and software functionality to find the best workable system solution for you. By evaluating the software's logic, a company can identify the customizations required.

This stage is generally referred to as the proof of concept stage, in which a company maps its processes to that of an ERP vendors' software. Regarding the following list: an RFI (Request for Information) is sent out to the 5 to 10 vendors that have been selected. A short list is made up of vendors who meet the selection criteria, and an RFP is then sent to these vendors.

The research and selection phase consists of the following activities:

1. Develop a request for proposal (RFP) package.
2. Establish a list of potential vendors.
   - Select 6&to 10 spltware vendors and issue your RFP to them.
   - Select 3 to 4 vendors that closely match your business needs.
   - Create a demonstration script and a method for evaluation.
   - Match your needs with the software functionality during vendor demonstrations.
   - Evaluate vendors' performance.
   - Determine missing functionality or improper logic.
   - Obtain alternatives, costs, and time constraints for missing requirements.
3. Modify your business model and business processes.
4. Complete vendors' profile analysis.
5. Visit customer sites.
6. Select software vendor.
7. Finalize hardware, operating system, network infrastructure requirements, and vendors.
8. Develop implementation plan.
9. Update the people management plan.
10. Finalize costs and prepare appropriation request (AR).

11. Update cost/benefit analysis.

12. Report to steering committee/work plan for next phase.

13. Authorization to proceed.

14. Sign vendor contracts.

In conclusion, it is very important to spend the appropriate amount of time choosing the right application, as well as ensuring that every element of the implementation is taken for account. Elements such as internal and external resource requirements must be accounted for at the time of planning.

Understanding the Importance of the References

It is important to base the software selection analysis on the comparison of your future use of the software with companies that are equivalent in size to yours and also, if possible, in the same line of business. Sometimes it is difficult to find the proper site with which to compare. Ask the vendor if you can see a customer and make it clear that you consider it very important it be someone to whom you can relate. This may mean that you have to travel to different parts of the globe to see an equivalent, but with the amount of money and resources you are about to invest, it is a point to consider.

When you have an agreement with a customer to go to their installation for a reference visit, prepare for this meeting by sending the host a profile of your company, a list of who will be visiting, and those employees' titles and functions. Also draft an agenda of the topics you would like to cover. Ask your host if you can spend some time with users of specific areas that interest you. Remember, at all times, that your host is doing you a favor; please have the courtesy of hosting prospects when you will be live. This process may seem to be a heavy burden on certain companies, but there is always something to learn on both sides from such a meeting. This also builds links between organizations that can help each other at a later point.

Prospective clients should also ask for reference letters or testimonials from current users of the software under consideration. If you can't visit the sites, you can always engage in a detailed interview with the user company.

Part
I
Ch
4

Outlining the Final Phase

You will not rest for long after selecting the software. After selecting, it is time to create your implementation plan. The following sections outline the points to consider in your final planning stage.

Implementation Approach

To ensure a safe and orderly transition from the old to new system, a three-phased approach is a must. Proving the new system works in-house, meets your business needs, and provides the benefits is more than just loading the software, testing it, and showing users how to push the buttons. The three-phase approach should include a computer room pilot, conference room pilot, and cutover go live:

■ Phase I—The computer room pilot is a technical testing of the hardware, database and software installation, and configuration.

■ Phase II—The conference room pilot is a functional piloting of your business processes using Baan (SIM I, SIM II, and SIM III).

■ Phase III—The cutover go live succeeds a successful SIM III process in which the organization agrees to go live. Keep in mind that you must establish cutover performance criteria. When you perform SIM III, you must identify the performance criteria (technical as well as business functions) that need to be met during SIM III in order to go live. You must also develop a cutover plan (a list of activities that need to be performed before going live).

In conclusion, it is most important that you follow the target methodology for a successful implementation.

Post Implementation Assessment

Following your new system's implementation is an appropriate time to reassess the company's situation, performance goals, problems, and opportunities. The outcome of this process should be a detailed plan (roadmap) of the company's continuous improvement journey.

The post-implementation assessment phase consists of the following activities:

1. Obtain feedback from users.
2. Assess business model and business processes performance indicators.
3. Review people management plan and assess impact.
4. Assess data accuracy performance.
5. Review business performance indicators.
6. Assess ongoing education and training plan.
7. Analyze issues of concern and determine cause and corrective action.
8. Report to steering committee/corrective action work plan.
9. Authorization to take action.

You may want to perform those tasks again during the implementation to ensure your project is going in the right direction. You must ensure that nobody deviated from the original plan, and if parameters have changed, that the impact has been measured and appropriate actions have been taken to correct the project plan.

Keys to Success

While the benefits to the business of implementing a new or improved system might be great, the risks of failure are also significant. The following are considered necessary for a successful implementation:

1. Top management support and participation
2. Project organization

3. Acceptable project management practices

4. Business justification

5. Business assessment

6. Education and training

7. Use of outside assistance

8. Data accuracy

9. Business performance indicators

10. People management

11. Pilot and cutover implementation approach

12. Post-business audit

These projects are high risk. They consist of three main elements: people, system and technology, and business processes. Most implementations focus on the technical and business processes aspects of the implementation and forget about the people element. Yet most failure (90 percent) of these implementations are caused by people issues. Your focus must be as much on the people element as it is on the technical and business process—if not more. ●

Part

I

Ch

4

Implementation

Managing the Implementation

Using a Conference Room Pilot

The conference room pilot is one of the most critically important phases of the Baan ERP implementation. This phase's objective is to identify and define all the business scenarios necessary to support the desired business model. The appropriate Baan functionality must be found to support the business process scenarios. In addition, the business process model, as it is implemented within Baan, must be approved for production rollout. The conference room pilot utilizes an iterative approach to arriving at the final business solution.

There are several elements required to ensure a successful conference room pilot. The conference room pilot can't be conducted in an organizational vacuum. You need the organization's help and thus, the organization must be well informed.

Don't expect your project leader to possess all the necessary experience to facilitate the conference room pilot. The reality is that you need help and will likely have to go outside your organization to find it. An average conference room pilot takes a few months. Try to make it as comfortable as possible for your team members, so that they remain focused and productive.

Whether you choose to use the Baan Orgware tools or some other productivity tools, you should select and implement a methodology that you are confident will produce the necessary results. You can look to your external facilitator or consultant for base methods, and then customize the method to fit your implementation.

Selecting the Pilot Team

The project team's structure will vary according to the size and type of the organization. Considering a typical Baan installation, the project would likely benefit from organizing the following three key groups:

- Project Leader—Not a group, but is a key individual for the project
- Key Users—A dedicated, full-time group with recruits from the various business units
- Working Groups—A part-time group with recruits from the various business units

Supporting groups can include the following:

- Steering Committee—To ensure best practices.
- Supplier Team—To ensure accountability between suppliers.
- Corporate Baan Team—If other business units have implemented Baan, the organization needs to consider standard implementations.

The conference room pilot results in a business process that may or may not resemble the organization's current process. The implementation introduces change to the organization, and change is always disruptive. The success of the project teams is measured by the degree to which they are able to manage the change and limit the disruption to the organization.

Recruiting a Project Leader

Unquestionably, the project leader is the most difficult position to recruit for a Baan implementation. A Baan implementation is a complex project to manage—the project leader must exhibit traditional qualities inherent in successful project managers: good organization, business savvy, good people skills, leadership, and the like.

The project leader should not be from the Information Technology Department. It is strongly recommended that the project leader be more experienced in the business than with technical matters. He or she must clearly understand the difference between the delivery focus and the profit focus project delivery metric. The project leader needs to clearly understand the factors leading to a successful project based on the profit focus metric.

A Baan implementation must be more of a business project than an information technology project. The opportunities the organization is looking to exploit should be business-driven. If the sole reason for implementing Baan is to acquire new information technology, the project will likely fail. At the very best, it will provide a poor return on investment. In this case, the organization will not reap Baan's benefits.

The Baan project team leader must understand that his or her performance—and ultimately, success or failure—is judged by the success of his or her key user and working group teams. Clearly, the project leader can't succeed on his or her own. The project leader needs to view the role located at the tip of an inverted pyramid. The project leader is to provide the necessary resources to the project teams in order to keep them moving in the right direction. The project teams are responsible for doing things correctly, while the project leader is responsible for choosing the correct things. The project leader spends a great deal of time resolving issues on the behalf of the project team members. In addition, the project leader is responsible for the following:

- Making decisions that move the project forward
- Clearly identifying the roles and responsibilities of each team member
- Moving obstacles out of the way

N O T E Ultimately, it is the project leader that must represent the entire project team to the steering committee. The project leader is held accountable for all the decisions made by the project team, but does not make all the decisions.

Recruiting Key Users

The key user team is responsible for identifying, testing, and configuring the automated business processes within Baan. It's also responsible for training the end users of the Baan system. The key user team members become both business process and Baan application specialists.

To support this requirement, the key user team should always consist of personnel from the business units throughout the organization. They must be dedicated full-time to the project.

Key users should be the best and brightest from the business units. The business units, on the other hand, will loudly object to the best and brightest being siphoned off to work on the Baan project—unless, of course, the project has been positioned properly within the business units.

N O T E If the business units are driving the project, and hence, understand the critical importance to the organization's well being, they will not hesitate to sponsor their best and brightest for the project team. ▪

Historically, when a key user joined a project team, he or she was considered information technology personnel for life (or for their career, at least). This is no longer the case. The role as a key user must be positioned with the employee as an assignment that provides them with a significant advantage within the organization. The combination of both business process and Baan application expertise serves the key user very well in terms of value to the organization. Key users should be identified as key employees whose value to the business is more than simply connected to the Baan implementation. The key user also gains valuable business process and Baan application exposure and knowledge in other business functions. Information at the heart of the Baan application is an extremely valuable asset to an organization. These people are involved in the migration of legacy data to the Baan application, and during the process make decisions on the configuration and definition of the data within Baan.

After the completion of the business process implementation within Baan, the key user's primary role is to train and mentor the end users. The key user's success is measured by the success of the end users they have trained.

Using Working Groups

The working groups are responsible for approving the business scenarios and their manifestation within Baan. There are several working groups, typically one from each major department or functional area. Examples include:

- ▪ Sales
- ▪ Engineering
- ▪ Purchasing
- ▪ Manufacturing/Assembly
- ▪ Finance

The key user from each functional area is responsible for organizing sessions with the working group to review the business scenarios and the resulting implementation within Baan. Rather than strict approval sessions, the key user is looking for the working group to highlight business scenarios that were overlooked or to ensure the business scenarios reflect reality on the business.

N O T E The working groups are required only part-time. Their contribution is on a periodic basis over the life of the conference room pilot. ▪

The working groups are end users, but not all end users are part of working groups. Depending upon the organization, it might make sense to rotate new end users through the working groups to provide an opportunity for as many end users as possible to have input regarding the implementation.

Planning to Communicate

Every project benefits when its objectives and progress are well communicated throughout the organization. Good ideas are not restricted to the key users or to the working groups. Good ideas can come from anywhere in the organization. Key users should encourage and openly consider business process scenarios from any part of the organization.

Secret projects do not breed good company support. Because the application effects most parts of the organization, it is best to discuss it early in the project lifecycle—especially during the pilot phase. This is an opportunity to encourage drop-in sessions for the curious. The organization as a whole may not get excited about the implementation, but you want everyone to be aware of the impending change.

Using an Implementation Blueprint

The implementation blueprint can be considered the project's diary. Creating the blueprint during an organization's first implementation is extremely beneficial. Subsequent implementations or upgrade efforts can utilize the lessons learned from the first implementation. The blueprint should be revised during each new installation or upgrade. A typical table of contents includes the following:

■ Introduction—An overview of the project that provides the background leading to the decision to implement Baan. Include the objectives and the risks. Include your particular methodology as it pertains to Baan Orgware, indicating which phases will be included. Any assumptions with respect to the business model must be made up front. Document how the project teams will communicate with the rest of the organization and list the members of the various teams.

■ Organization Background—An overview of the entire organization and which business units have been selected to implement Baan under this project (if more than one exists). Describe the business topology in terms of legal, logistical, and financial entities. For example, is the organization composed of business units that make a supply chain or do they produce independent products? Include a description of the various technical and non-technical systems in place to support this topology.

■ The As-Is Order-to-Cash Business Process—Capture the current business process that has been selected for Baan implementation. If the project is using a compact implementation model, then the as-is process will also be the to-be process.

■ The To-Be Order-to-Cash Business Process—If the project is using a comprehensive implementation model, then the to-be business process will be the newly aligned or reengineered business process defined by the key user team and approved by the steering committee.

Part

II

Ch

5

■ Order-to-Cash Business Process Gaps—If the comprehensive implementation model is used, there will be differences between the as-is and the to-be business process models. This section identifies and proposes solutions for the process gaps that must be closed in order to migrate from the as-is process to the to-be process.

■ Mapping the To-Be Order-to-Cash Business Process to Baan—This section captures the majority of the work completed during the conference room pilot. The key user team identifies the appropriate functionality within Baan to support the to-be business process.

■ System Configuration—Captures more than the hardware and software platform configuration. The documentation for items such as business scenario definition, logical tables, parameters, and menu structures is as important.

■ Migration Plan—The migration issue can be complex. The migration from one technology platform to another is one issue. However, the migration of legacy data consumes most of the migration issue agenda. The mapping of legacy data is both an obstacle and an opportunity. The obstacle is that the data dictionary or data definition will likely be different between your legacy system and Baan. Your team has to define a custom mapping. The opportunity is that the legacy data can be reviewed, redefined, deleted, cleansed, and so on before being migrated into the Baan system. The migration plan should also detail how the transition from the legacy system to the Baan system will occur. In other words, how long will the two systems run parallel and how will you transition from legacy to Baan?

■ Support Plan—A service-level agreement must exist between the Information Technology Department and the business units. System management procedures, backups, system availability, archive frequency, and so on must be documented. This could also include disaster recovery or business continuation plans.

■ Optimization Plan—This section details plans to review the business process if the project uses a compact implementation methodology. There are many possibilities for optimization, even in a comprehensive implementation project. Integration with other systems is an example.

■ Appendixes—Captures the detailed information referred to in the body of the blueprint.

The blueprint is more than just a document to capture the conference room pilot—it is a project lifecycle document. Although not useful as a proactive communication tool, it is very valuable as a historical reference. It forces the project leader to cover all areas of the project, particularly with respect to reasons for certain decisions.

NOTE An implementation blueprint can be very useful to the next project leader responsible for a new implementation or upgrading the current installation. ■

Communicating with the Steering Committee

The steering committee ideally consists of the organization's senior management team. Its primary role is to ensure that the implementation's business objectives are being met. To this end, the steering committee must ensure that the best practices are utilized and that the business process to be implemented is clearly understood.

The steering committee has final approval over the to-be business process in a comprehensive implementation. In the compact implementation, the steering committee ensures that the organization understands that the process, albeit not optimized, will be implemented in Baan. Any business process improvement is slated for the optimization phase.

The steering committee should be briefed monthly. This provides sufficient time for key users to map additional processes. The steering committee meeting also consists of reviews of the major milestones in the target methodology.

The steering committee meetings must be well organized and to-the-point. The agenda could be similar to the following:

- Interim Project Update—Review the highlights (of interest to the steering committee) that occurred since the last meeting.
- Previous Meeting Minutes Review—Review the status of action items raised from the last meeting.
- New Process Issues—Major business process issues that require a management decision to proceed.
- Updated Process Issues—Major business process issues that were deferred from the previous meeting pending additional detail. Present the detail and move for closure.
- Closed Process Issues—A reminder of major business process issues that were resolved at the previous steering committee meeting.

Each steering committee member should be provided a briefing handbook. The handbook captures the meeting activities. Thus, the project leader does not have to review the project history at each steering committee meeting. The project leader should distribute a process issues background document prior to each steering committee meeting. It provides each team member the opportunity to review the issues and related background information prior to the meeting. The background documents must be short and to-the-point.

TIP The project leader should briefly visit each steering committee member prior to the meeting to ensure that the background information is understood and whether any additional information is required.

N O T E The concept of using paper documents is for illustration. Use the medium that best suits your organization. That could be collaboration tools, browser tools, email, and so on. ■

Communicating with Key Users

The connection between the project leader and the key users should include as much face-to-face interaction as possible. This clearly depends on the size of project. Most decision making occurs in short, issue resolution meetings scheduled by either the project leader or a key user.

The results of the process and data mapping work by the key users must be detailed in the blueprint document appendexes. The key users must understand the sections in the blueprint that they are responsible for maintaining.

Project team meetings should be held between the steering committee meetings. They should be held as frequently as required, but limited to avoid wasting time. Action items must be recorded and assigned accordingly.

N O T E   The key user team is clearly aware of the project timeline and must understand the deliverable required at each of their individual milestones. ■

Communicating with the Rest of the Organization

Communicating pilot status to the rest of the organization is typically overlooked. The project leader and the key user team solicit the help of others throughout the conference room pilot, and it certainly helps others if they have an understanding of the project's background and, specifically, the conference room pilot. Consider organizing an open house to allow employees to get a firsthand look at the Baan application, and the process the key user team is conducting in the conference room pilot.

N O T E   Although you can never overcommunicate, a broadcast frequency of no more than the steering committee meetings is recommended. ■

Facilitating the Pilot

The project budget must have sufficient funding for external support. Although your project leader and key user team are carrying out the majority of the work, you benefit from the experience of others in specific areas of the project. The project relies on several types of external support from consultants and partners. Exposure to Baan installations should be the common theme. For example, the following might be helpful:

- ■ Hardware Suppliers—Those able to configure the necessary hardware platform to support your specific implementation. This also includes those responsible for the communications infrastructure.

- ■ Software Suppliers—Those able to configure operating systems and database applications specific to your implementation.

- ■ Implementation Experts—Those who have successfully managed Baan implementation projects in other organizations. You are investing in the experience of these implementation experts. They bring with them a wealth of experience with various configurations of Baan in other organizations. For example, the variation in logistical and financial company structures: one:one, many:one, one:many, many:many.

- ■ Module Experts—Those who are familiar with the internal feature and functions of the Baan application. You will likely have several module experts, because there are very few individuals available that understand (or need) the entire application. The module experts will likely contribute most of their time to specific key users who, in turn, are responsible for a particular piece of Baan functionality. Although the absolute number of module experts will be high, the number on-site with the key users team will be minimal. Module experts come in and out of the project timeline.

- Methodology Experts—Those who have managed change projects in your organization or other organizations. This is particularly important in the comprehensive implementation, when business processes are reviewed and optimized. This expert contributes experience outside the pure Baan implementation. They have organized and project-managed business process reengineering projects at other organizations (or even within your organization). They help merge the process alignment timeline with the Baan implementation timeline.

It was previously proposed that several project teams be formed to support the pilot effort, one of which was termed a supplier/consultant team. This team provides the opportunity for each of the suppliers and consultants to meet in a non-adversarial environment. This team also provides an opportunity for solutions to be proposed proactively, before issues arise. The team reduces the time demand on the project leader, who has to follow up with each supplier/consultant individually, and reduces the finger-pointing from one supplier to the next for unresolved issues.

Understanding the Pilot Environment

The environment within which the key user team conducts the conference room pilot is an important consideration. The pilot's objective is to configure, test, and confirm the operation of Baan to support the organization's business process. To do this in small, physically separated groups does not allow the interaction necessary to resolve the many border issues between functional areas.

Using a Conference Room

Your organization's resources limit the flexibility in establishing a dedicated area for the conference room pilot. The key users spend a great deal of time together. It is in their best interest to make the conference room as convenient, and hence, as productive as possible.

Given the key user team has been dedicated full-time to the pilot, some will likely find that the conference room is their new home. Ensure that sufficient storage space for the key users belongings exists in the conference room. This reduces the key users having to go to their previous location to retrieve materials or information.

Consider environmental issues such as proper lighting, including sunlight (if possible), acceptable airflow, and temperature control. Consider the location of washroom facilities, cafeteria, or beverage locations. Consider having a small supply of beverages and similar items located within the conference room. This feature is valuable during times the facility cafeteria is not open.

The conference room should include all the necessary administration tools and supplies: pens, pencils, paper, binders, and so on. There should be a conference room phone.

Seating arrangements, although informal, should reflect the amount of interaction between key users. For example, there will likely be more interaction between the purchasing and assembly key users then there will be between the sales and assembly key users. Try to avoid cubicles;

large conference tables that allow the key users to spread out a great deal of documentation is required. There is usually small group discussions to review common material. The tables allow this. Furthermore, paper wall hangers are beneficial. They provide a method for wall mounting an abundant amount of common information. Having to duplicate each piece, reduce revision control, and facilitate group discussion can be avoided by wall mounting.

Using a Test System

The conference room pilot should have a test system dedicated to its use. The system is initially used for training key users, and then during the pilot, it is used to configure the Baan system. When the team completes the pilot and moves into migration, the team switches to the production system to complete data migration and test sizing of the application. Because it may require that the database or parameters be reset to a known state (several times), flexibility is important during the pilot. Thus, keeping the database to a working minimum is recommended. For example, include a few complete bills of materials rather than hundreds of similar bills of materials, which would occur during sizing.

Key users must be free to experiment with Baan functionality. Undoubtedly, there will be error conditions that cause the system to corrupt data, application parameters, the database, and even the operating system itself. If the pilot team is expected to share a system with other production applications, there is a risk of production interruption on the other systems.

 TIP The pilot system can be used after the pilot is complete in order to support review of Baan application upgrades, or customizations and personalization.

The key users should use PC-based clients that support the additional tools that may be required as part of the project methodology. Although you may decide to use the Orgware tools, the key users will probably require word processors, spread sheets, presentation graphics, access to company email, and Internet access (for Baan World Users discussion groups and Baan itself). Consider providing your key users with remote access to the test system. This encourages key users to be active at times that may be more convenient (and productive).

Understanding Pilot Methodology

This section presents a method for facilitating the conference room pilot. The method can be adapted to most any set of tools used by the pilot team. The progression is straightforward. The methodology is primarily for a project that is considering some level of business process change. If the business processes are stable and will be implemented as is, then this method can be used with the existing processes. The conference room pilot workflow is captured in Figure 5.1.

The method begins at the scenario level. Business process scenarios are added to this level. Each business process scenario is then broken into specific transactions. Each transaction is reduced to individual tasks and finally, the tasks are broken into discrete steps (the keyboard strokes necessary to complete the task).

FIG. 5.1

The conference room pilot team needs to have a workflow to guide its efforts.

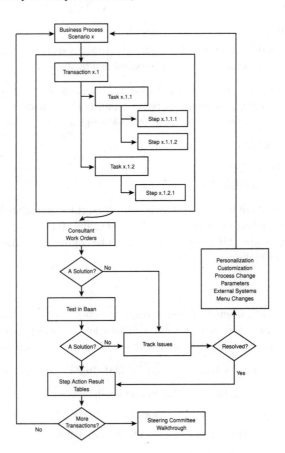

Using a Concept List of Scenarios

A business process scenario is a high-level description of a process that has a fairly wide scope. It's sometimes referred to as a business object. For example, Figure 5.1 illustrates a business process scenario as bill of material (BOM) administration. There are many variations and types of responsibilities that need to be defined in order to actually complete this process scenario. The business process scenarios are the foundation upon which the order-to-cash process resides. In other words, the business process scenarios are what define the organization's order-to-cash workflow.

An organizational role is closely linked with the process scenario. The person who occupies this particular role is responsible for completing the necessary transactions defined by the process scenario. The transactions are ordered and must normally be completed in the prescribed order.

Using Transactions

One or more transactions are needed to complete a process scenario. The transactions for a specific process scenario may or may not be completed by the same role (most often they are).

The transactions are not ordered steps, but appear as branches or options in the process scenario. There are several transactions required to complete the scenario in your BOM administration process scenario example. For example, the following steps might have to be completed:

- Create template BOM.
- Attach standard items.
- Copy E-BOMs to P-BOMs.

These transactions do not have to be ordered with respect to each other. There is no strict workflow relationship between transactions. These example transactions, along with other transaction defined under this process scenario, can be combined in different ways to produce different workflow variations.

Using Tasks

Tasks are functions that, when combined in a specific workflow order, produce the expected results for a transaction. This is the level at which the key users begin to investigate Baan functionality in support of each task. Each task should roughly correspond to a Baan session.

You could have several tasks from your copy E-BOMs to P-BOMs transaction example.

- Create a copy of an E-BOM for the production database.
- Create the copy data for an E-BOM for transfer to the production database.
- Finalize the E-BOM copy data into the production database.

Key users are required to identify Baan sessions that provide the functionality of each task.

Using Steps

The steps fall out fairly easily after a task is mapped to a specific Baan session. The steps are basically the necessary keystrokes required to complete the task. The data required for input, or expected as output, may not be defined at this point. The complete definition is documented when the transaction testing in Baan is complete. At this point, the steps have been defined, but not necessarily tested with real production data.

Using Work Orders for Consultants

As discussed previously, external consultants are needed as part of the conference room pilot. Specifically, the need is greatest for Baan module consultants. The module experts provide key users with help in discovering the appropriate Baan functionality to support the defined tasks.

In addition to leading the project team, the leader also has to monitor the consultants' progress and contributions. It is important to see what demand has been placed on the consultants for capacity planning purposes. Be sure the specific consultants are providing value to your key user team.

Consider creating a consultant work order process. This provides a formal mechanism by which key users can request specific tasks be completed by the consultants. It provides the project leader with the necessary background to ensure progress is being made by the consultants. The work order provides a source of information if a decision is ever questioned.

The consultants can use the work order as a means to prioritize and manage their workload. The consultants, along with the project leader, can agree to a suitable delivery schedule.

N O T E If the consultants can't find suitable Baan functionality, the work order will contain the necessary information to support any request for customization and personalization.

Using Transaction Testing in Baan

When suitable Baan functionality is defined for each transaction, key users must test the functionality to ensure the expected results occur. This requires that some company-specific data exist in the database. The Baan demo companies do not provide much value in the transaction-testing phase.

The key users are also configuring the system with parameters that can be altered to change the Baan application's behavior. As these transactions are proven within Baan, the key users need to review the functionality with the working groups. The working groups highlight any missing functionality or issues that may have been missed during the transaction definition step.

There needs to be a list of transactions from this activity, including tasks and steps, and those that have been approved and those that await approval.

Part
II

Ch
5

Using Step Action Result Tables

The creation of step action result tables is culmination of the key user team's efforts. These *tables* are essentially the handbooks (or whatever medium makes sense) that each person who assumes a role within the Baan application uses. It starts as their training manual and turns into their reference manual. When a new employee begins working at the organization, the step action result table document can be used as the introduction and training manual.

The document should include the following:

- Document revision information
- Table of contents
- A description of the role
- A description of the process scenario
- Terms and definition specific to the role
- The steps defined to complete the transaction
- Appendixes that include supporting information, such as company numbers

The content and format should be defined early in the conference room pilot. The key users must clearly understand that this is their deliverable.

Using an Issue List

There may be transactions that do not have a clear equivalent function in Baan during the conference room pilot. In this case, there are several options on proceeding. Some examples include:

- Customizations—This typically requires a change to the Baan source code. A customization should only be considered in extreme cases where the business process cannot be changed to accommodate the available Baan functionality.
- Personalization—This is a less drastic change to the application. It is typically a superficial modification, such as changing the text description of data fields on a report.
- Menu changes—This is a more common modification. Menus are sometimes created to reflect more of a workflow than the standard Baan sessions provide.
- Data conversions—The redefining of data may be required to support a particular type of transaction.
- External system interfaces—Data may be required from an external system in order to complete a transaction.
- Parameter settings—The functionality of the Baan system can be greatly effected by changing the parameters. Changes in the parameters must be well documented to allow rollback to a known state. The consultants can provide experience with the interaction between parameters. This area of Baan requires a great deal of experience.

Obtaining Steering Committee Approval

The conference room pilot's objective is to demonstrate the to-be business process implemented within the Baan application to the steering committee. The goal is to receive approval from the steering committee to proceed with the migration phase.

The approval stage cannot be completed in a single meeting. Several days have to be designated for the steering committee's attendance. Key users have to process typical company transactions from the order point to the cash point. The key user team verifies transaction results and corresponding data at strategic points throughout the process.

The pilot phase is complete with the approval of the steering committee team. The key user team then focuses on the task of migrating from the conference room pilot system to the production system. The migration phase defines those tasks necessary to bring the Baan system into production. ●

The Baan Software

Understanding the Baan Software

Originally know as Triton, the Baan Software has come a long way since Jan Baan wrote a Customer Application on a Commodore 64 in the 70s. Major corporations worldwide now use this package, which ranks second among the enterprise resource planning packages available.

Using an Integrated Solution

The Baan Software is a group of integrated enterprise resource planning tools that take advantage of all the actual technologies and business principles in the market world. The strong basic applications—such as the distribution and manufacturing functions—are supported by unique tools—such as the Business Organizer—to ensure a rapid implementation of the product and as well as a proper fit to the customer's process.

Baan, which benefits from the open system architecture and the client/server approach, is one of the most technologically advanced packages available. The team approach, leaders in technology, and business analysts raised this product to a very interesting level. Having seen the evolution of Baan products, it can be predicted that the next release of products will contain even more functionality that ensures the best return on investment for the user.

Choosing Your Solution

The Baan software can run on many different platforms. It can be run on any servers of the Hewlett Packard 9000, the IBM AIX servers, and on equipment produced by Bull, Sun, Sequant, and Digital. Baan IV's software is also introducing a Windows NT version that takes advantage of Microsoft BackOffice.

The software can use various databases. You can use one provided by the software manufacturer or use third-party databases like Oracle and Ingres.

Understanding the Main Modules

The Baan main modules are designed to allow corporations to manage the flow of information necessary to manage their businesses. Any other module can be run independently or can be linked to another package—that is the concept of the open computer systems.

This chapter defines the different modules and highlights their major components. There are 10 main modules in Baan. Each of these modules contains business objects to help users manage their businesses. All business objects are classified under their main modules, so you can have an appreciation of all the functions of the software and will know where to look to for an application

Understanding the Common Data Module

This is the nervous system of the software. All the files that are used in more than one module are stored and managed in this area. You find maintenance for the employee file, the supplier file, and all the logistics tables. Detailed information about this module can be found in Chapter 12, "Understanding the Common Data Module."

Each module has a module designator. TC is the designator for the Baan Common module. The Baan Common module contains the following tables:

- Logistic Tables
- Financial Tables
- Employee Master
- Customer Master
- Supplier Master

▶ **See** "The Main Modules," **p. 105**

Understanding the Finance Module

The financial package contains all the functions you find in any regular package. The normal day-to-day operations are simplified by a very flexible integration package that allows users to extract financial transactions from the sales and manufacturing areas and post them to the general ledger without having to key any transactions. The Financial module also comes with a Budget System, an Activity Base module, and a Fixed Assets module. Chapter 13, "Understanding the Financial Tables and the General Ledger," and Chapter 14, "Understanding the Finance Sub-Ledgers," contain more information about this module.

TF is the package designator for finance. This module contains the following modules:

- General Ledger
- Accounts Payable
- Accounts Receivable
- Cash Management
- Fixed Assets
- Financial Statement
- Financial Budget
- Cost Allocation

Understanding the Distribution Module

The Distribution module manages all the finish goods, raw materials, and services. It is here you find all the programs to create and manage the sales orders. This is also where you find all the inventory-related functions like Inventory Control, Location Control, Distribution Requirement Planning, and Replenishment Control. A detailed description of this module can be found in Chapter 16, "Understanding the Distribution Module."

TD is the module designator for the Distribution module. This module contains the following business objects:

- Item Control
- Cost Accounting

Part
II
Ch
6

- Purchase Control
- Sales Control
- Sales and Marketing Info
- Electronic Data Interchange
- Replenishment Order Control
- Inventory Control
- Lot Control
- Location Control
- Distribution Requirement Planning
- Tables
- Common Data
- Distribution Parameters

Understanding the Manufacturing Module

The Manufacturing module is designed to control all the operations related to products' fabrication, labor management, and capacity required. Planning functions such as Master Production Schedule, Material Requirement Planning, and Capacity Planning complement this module. More information on the Manufacturing module can be found in Chapter 20, "Understanding the Manufacturing Module."

TI is the module designator for the Manufacturing module. This module contains the following business objects:

- Engineering Data Management
- Item Control
- Bill of Material
- Routing
- Master Production Schedule
- Material Requirement Planning
- Capacity Requirement Planning
- Repetitive Manufacturing
- Shop Floor Control
- Hours Accounting
- Project Budget
- Product Configuration
- Product Classification
- Project Control
- Quality Management System

Understanding the Service Module

The Service module allows corporations that support installations in the field to manage all the repair and warranty information. Different functions help those corporations analyze similar failures and better diagnose the cause of problems. A detailed definition of each of this module's functions can be found in Chapter 22, "Understanding the Service Module."

TS is the module designator for the Service module. This module contains the following business objects:

- Installation Control
- Contract Control
- Service Order Control
- Service Analysis Control

Understanding the Transportation Module

The Transportation module was introduced in Baan's third release to help companies that specialize in the transportation of goods or have their own fleet to move those goods between the different points of inventory. Various programs are available to manage transportation orders and to maximize equipment use. Chapter 19, "Understanding the Transportation Module," contains detailed information on each of the functions for this module.

TR is the module designator for the Transportation module. This module contains the following business objects:

- Employee Control
- Address Control
- Transport Fleet Management
- Transport Fuel Control
- Hours and Expense Control
- Central Data Entry
- Transport Control
- Packing Control
- Warehouse Control

Part
II

Ch

Understanding the Process Module

Baan introduced the Process module with its third release. This is a unique solution designed for a different market segment than traditional Baan users. The Process module helps companies that produce identical product in different containers or have to keep track of the various batches processed. Baan's Process module is able to account for the potency, the acidity, and the grade of items. You can find detailed definitions of each of this module's functions in Chapter 24, "Understanding the Formula Management Module," and Chapter 25, "Understanding the Process Module."

The Baan Process module is designed to help manage the entire supply chain of any company operating in a process environment, such as the chemical industry.

PS is the module designator for the Process module. This module contains the following business objects:

- Formula Management
- Routing
- Master Production Scheduling
- Material Requirement Planning
- Quality Management System

Understanding the Project Module

Tailored for the project-oriented business, the Project module offers all the tools necessary for control over project accounting and planning. The Planning requirement process unique to Baan is also offered with functions to accurately track costs for the project-related industries.

This module links with all the software's other functions to provide the information necessary to successfully manage within an enterprise environment. Chapter 23, "Understanding the Project Module," contains more information about this module's functions.

PS is the module designator for the Project module. This module contains the following business objects:

- Project Estimating
- Project Definition
- Project Budget
- Project Planning
- Project Requirements
- Project Progress
- Project Monitoring
- Project Invoicing

Understanding the Tools Module

The Tools module regrouped all the programs designed to maintain and customize the application. The Form Manager, Report Writer, and Sessions Manager are the options used by developers to tailor Baan to users' needs. In addition to those programming tools, you find programs to manage the database, devices, and user profiles. Each of the functions for this module is discussed further in Chapter 26, "Understanding the Tools Module."

TT is the module designator for the Tools module. This module contains the following business objects:

- Software Installation
- Application Configuration
- User Management
- Device Management
- Job Management
- Database Management
- Audit Management
- Text Management
- Menu Management
- SQL Queries
- Business Objects
- Application Customization
- Application Development
- Terms and Definitions
- Translation
- Documentation
- Conversion
- Software Distribution
- Desktop Management

Understanding the Utilities Module

The existing utilities allow users to easily import or export information between Baan and any other system. The concept is simple: An ASCII-file format of a table is created and this can be uploaded or downloaded to Baan software either from or to the operating environment. This module eases the implementation of the software, facilitating the creation of master files imported from other software. This module's exchange functions are discussed further in Chapter 28, "Understanding the Utilities Module."

TX is the module designator for the Utilities module. This module contains the following business objects:

- Import Module
- Export Module
- Generate Exchange Scheme

Part
II

Ch
6

Understanding Other Baan Packages

To complete the basic modules of its package, Baan developed new applications. Those packages' main functions are outlined in the remaining sections of this chapter.

With all the Baan Company's recent acquisitions, as well as with the growing number of companies that want to interface their software with Baan, the number of packages is growing exponentially. The following sections cover some of the packages already on the market.

Understanding Enterprise Modeling

Enterprise Modeling, formerly known as Orgware, is a process in which the customers can map all the processes used, and then develop an accurate and complete implementation plan. After this plan is generated and the project started, Orgware becomes a tool used to follow the project's evolution and helps identify where processes can be improved.

This tool is certainly one of the most advantageous in Baan's suite of products. Using the DEM process can cut several months from the implementation process by ensuring the accuracy of the plan followed. Chapter 7, "Using the DEM Tools," defines the use of the DEM tools.

Understanding Enterprise Performance Manager

The Enterprise Information System's (EIS) tools are designed to give various levels of management access to the data in the Baan tables. Baan achieved this by adding functions found in most of the EIS systems found on the market to the regular product.

The data of the Distribution, Finance, and Manufacturing modules are available in this module and they can be displayed using various formats. Those formats include an Ishikawa fishbone diagram or direct interface with another database system.

Understanding Baan Synchronization

Developed by Berclain, a Montreal-based software manufacturer, Moopi is a planning tool that complements Baan's planning functions very well. Future Baan releases will be using functions of this very complete planning software.

 Using the Baan synchronization software, you can complement all of Baan software's capacity planning functions and work at a more detailed level of planning. Now Baan Synchronization can be used as an integral component of the Baan software. You can get additional information on the Baan Synchronization software at **www.berclain.com**.

Understanding Supply Chain Automotive

The flexibility of the Baan package was a big factor in developing an automotive version of the package. Baan ensured the participation of world leaders in the automotive industry and came up with a package that is used by such companies as Mercedes Benz and Honda.

The major functions required in this industry, such as the Just in Time Delivery Process (JIT) and the Electronic Data Interchange (EDI), are part of the functionality of the Baan software.

Other automotive industry concepts, such as retroactive billing and Kanban delivery, have been included to meet the needs of this important segment of the industry.

The functionality of the main Baan modules have been adapted to this automotive environment and users will find the familiar make-to-stock, make-to-order, and assemble-to-order concepts in the regular Baan modules.

Understanding Hyperion

Hyperion is a financial reporting software that can be used in conjunction with the Baan finance package. Users find tools to create reports and drill down facilities to manipulate all the general ledger information.

Creation of budgets, as well as consolidation of information among various financial companies, is easy when using Hyperion software. Hyperion also offers Analytical Accounting functions as well as Web Access functions.

Additional information on the Hyperion Software can be found at **www.hyperion.com**.

Understanding Safari

Safari is a report writer package that can be used to complement Baan software. This software allows you to create reports using the information stored in the Baan database. The data dictionary concept is that the Safari software can translate Baan data that can be used by anyone who doesn't want to create reports using Baan tools, but prefers to manipulate in a Windows environment. Safari is a product of Interactive Software and can be found at **www.intersw.com**.

Using the DEM Tools

Understanding Baan's Dynamic Enterprise Modeler

What is Baan's Dynamic Enterprise Modeler (DEM)? DEM is readily associated with the capability to define Enterprise Resource Planning (ERP), business processes, and using those processes to generate user-specific desktops for the Baan ERP system. Myopic as it may be, one of DEM's strengths lies in its capability to deliver a desktop environment that reflects the various roles currently assumed by the Baan user while maintaining session-level access control for every Baan ERP user. Powerful? Yes, but it pales to the power gained by widening its scope and integrating these operational strengths with the strategic planning components of a global corporation.

DEM enables executives to return to their war rooms by enabling them to define and execute long-term business plans that are integrated with a fully operational ERP information system. No longer are the strategic and business planning functions separated from an enterprise's daily business operations. Today they can be one and the same, pulling and pushing together in unison.

Executives can be assured of a quick, flexible, and integrated Baan implementation as they move forward using the Dynamic Enterprise Modeler. The DEM concept has three key objectives:

- Speed—DEM is based on a short and compact implementation cycle that minimizes cost through rapid implementation.
- Flexibility—DEM proposes optimization phases throughout the project period that enable smooth configuration changes due to market conditions without the need for time-consuming and costly reconfigurations.
- Integration—DEM is fully integrated with the Baan applications.

Baan's Dynamic Enterprise Modeler consists of three basic components:

- A framework
- Business reference models
- Editors

The framework defines DEM's working environment. It provides the relationships that are shared between the generic components of a business model and its operational elements. Using this framework, you can see how a business reference model provides the details that enable you to better understand a fully integrated Enterprise Resource Planning system. By understanding this framework and following a Business Reference Model as an initial roadmap, you can readily learn the Baan ERP system and the DEM Editors that empower you to better satisfy your ever-changing business requirements.

Understanding the DEM Framework

A framework sets the boundaries within which all points of reference to an object can be defined. To define a business model, DEM uses:

- Business functions to define what the business does.
- Business processes to define how they accomplish the business functions.
- Organizational structure to define where these business functions and processes are done.
- Phases to define when business functions are implemented.
- Roles to define who performs the business processes.
- Rules to define relationships shared between the what and how.

One boundary of the DEM framework identifies generic, project-level components. The other boundary represents a business model in terms of business functions, business processes, organizational infrastructures, and user-specific desktops.

To define, capture, and encourage the sharing of the generic components of a business model for a Baan company, DEM provides a Master Data Repository. Within this repository, editors are provided for the creation and modification of generic business functions and business processes used to define a business. The glue that binds the business functions with the business processes is also collected and maintained in the Master Data Repository. This glue includes, but is not limited to, business rules, roles, parameters, wizards, and utilities.

Moving from the repository to the next level, the Reference Level, the DEM framework provides an environment that groups the Master Data Repository components into generic business infrastructures, which best meet a business' specific requirements. To support this generic business model, an organization structure can be initially defined at this Reference Level. It is at this level where roles can be attached to any or all three business elements (function, process, and organization). Here is where the Baan Reference Models (Assemble-To-Order, Engineer-To-Order, Project Industries, Systems Management, and Finance) are defined.

The top level in the DEM framework represents the customer-specific/project-specific business model. This level is reserved for the specific business functions and processes that are going to be implemented over a specific period of time. It is at this level where the scope of the project is fully defined.

Implementing an entire ERP system is a tremendous project, but not all business functions are required initially. Business pressure points dictate which functions must be implemented initially and which can follow at a later time. These phases can be defined within the DEM project-specific business model. The scope of these phases is locked in only when two complete simulations of the implementation for a specific phase are completed. This provides the flexibility to pull in or push out business functions to better meet the market or corporate demands.

At the DEM Project level, the employees responsible for maintaining the Baan information systems are assigned to the various roles required to perform the business functions of their specific model. Recognizing that employees may accept different responsibilities over any period of time, business roles are assigned to a specific activity. These roles can then be assigned to specific employees. By associating a role(s) to an activity, the company has the flexibility to move employees from one role to the next without affecting the information system. This is a powerful capability for the employee, the manager, and the information systems operational support personnel.

Change will affect the business functions, processes, and organization. Within each DEM level (Repository, Reference, Project), the framework provides the ability to accommodate many changes. At every level in the framework, DEM provides an editor that creates or modifies the business functions and business processes. Because organization structure is specific for each company, no editor for the organization structure is found in the repository. The organization structure can be defined and modified at both the Reference- and Project levels within DEM.

To generate a user-specific desktop for a given phase of a project, the following must be completed:

1. A project must be defined.
2. A scope for each phase must be defined based on the business functions to be implemented.
3. Business rules must be evaluated.
4. Employees must be identified.
5. Roles must be assigned for each employee.

These desktops contain either the business processes for each role assigned to the employee or a simple menu browser with only those Baan ERP sessions associated with the assigned roles of the employee. For the new or temporary employees, the business process desktop is useful in leading the new employee step-by-step through the process. The user-specific menu browser desktop, however, is used by the experienced Baan ERP user who fully understands the business process and how the Baan ERP sessions relate to the process.

For the DEM modeler, the framework is an invaluable tool. It guides the modeler to the correct level to alter any component in a business model. The details of how and where to make these changes occur in the following "Using DEM" sections.

Understanding DEM Business Reference Models

Baan's Business Reference Models provide a roadmap into the Baan ERP system. Baan initially defined five generic reference models.

- Assemble-To-Order [ATO]
- Engineer-To-Order [ETO]
- Project Industries
- Systems Management
- Finance

Many corporations operate with one or more of these business models. The advantage of using a Business Reference Model during an initial implementation of a Baan ERP system is that it is comprehensive enough to set up a basic operating company. After a Baan company is operational, the corporation begins to learn how the Baan ERP system behaves in that specific environment.

A simple analogy answers this question: Why use a generic reference business model? A reference model represents a roadmap to a new city an experienced traveler chooses to venture. In this case, the new city is an ERP information system. A traveler knows of the many great opportunities that exist in this city, but is unaware where and how to take advantage of these opportunities. The roadmap shows the paths that can be taken to take advantage of specific opportunities. In the case of an ERP system, these paths show how to process a purchase or sales order, how to plan or release a shop order, or how to process an EDI acknowledgment.

Once the traveler learns the lay of the new city, he or she can try a different route, define new routes, or renovate one of the buildings to better fit the way he or she is accustomed to doing business.

The Baan Business Reference Models take full advantage of both DEM and the Baan ERP sessions that make up their integrated ERP application. The smart travelers take advantage of them whenever they enter into new territory.

Understanding DEM Editors

Simple and easy to use are the attributes that best define the Baan editors. The editors function to create and maintain the various components needed to support a fully integrated business model, which is interactive with an ERP system. Several editors are available and each deals with a specific area of the DEM framework. The following sections discuss specific editors in greater detail.

Understanding DEM's Business Function Editor

Business functions in Baan's business models are represented simply by bubbles, or circles. These business functions are only concerned with what the business entity does. To break down what a company does can be an overwhelming experience, but the Baan Business Function Editor provides the modeler with the ability to decompose any entity without cluttering the process with other extraneous thought. From the DEM business model perspective, even the decomposition structure of the functions has no bearing on the model. Decomposition is only provided as an aid to the modeler to assist in answering what the entity does.

The function editor is rich in features. Once the question of what each entity does is answered, the modeler has the ability to ask what roles are required to perform these functions. If a new role is identified, it can be added to the Master Data Repository through the main Baan menu browser. Again, the Business Function Editor aids in the thought process by focusing only on the business functions.

Critical success factors (CSF) are associated with many business functions. These CSF's can be monitored by creating a performance indicator within Baan's Performance module. These performance indicators can be assigned to functions within the DEM Business function model. As new functions are added to the business model, the need to define new performance indicators may also arise.

Another valuable feature found in the Business Function Editor is the capability to identify which project phase a specific function activates. This capability is invaluable in determining

Part
II

Ch
7

the scope of each phase and then controlling the correct flow of the business processes that support the functions being implemented. Not only does the modeler ensure that the correct process is being used, but it enables the modeler to display future changes within a process. The future flows are dimmed but are readable by the user, who can recognize that a change in their flow is highly probable. Change becomes acceptable because possibilities are introduced prior to actually being required.

Understanding DEM's Business Process Editor

"How does a business entity accomplish a business function?" The experience of building business processes to answer that question can be very complex. Many different means can represent a business process. Baan selected a modeling technique that was originally designed to meet the real-time modeling requirements for space exploration, which is called *Petri-Net modeling*.

The Petri-Net modeling technique was selected because it can reflect complex process flows by using only four constructs or *building blocks*. These four constructs are a natural state, a process activity, a controlled activity, and a nested process. Most users have the ability to maintain up to seven entities/relationships at any given point in time. Using this technique, Baan has more flexibility to add functionality to the process model.

Recognizing that a business model must represent the business processes that support the business functions and not just the processes to support their ERP system, Baan's Business Process Editor enables a process activity to be any of the following:

- A manual activity
- A process defined and bound by a Baan ERP application main session
- A process performed by another application outside the Baan ERP system

Combining these options for a process activity with a controlled activity or a nested process (which Baan calls a *business process*), any business process can be defined on a single sheet of paper. It's important to be able to capture the essence of the business process in a single glance. The actual business process may "drill-down" many layers, but it captures the flows and activities of all its subprocesses. Thus, the complexity is reduced for both the modeler who must design the process flow and the user who must interpret it.

Through the use of the controlled activities, logical and programmatic controlled routes can be defined. These conditional routings can be defined using standard Boolean splits, joins, and iterative loops, all of which can be represented using the four constructs found in the Baan Business Process Editor.

Understanding Baan's Business Organization Editor

Although the Business Organization Model plays a vital role in capturing the who and where relating to the business functions, the effort to maintain the DEM Organization Model exceeds its benefits. The modeler can capture who is assigned to the various roles and held responsible for those respective process activities in the DEM Business Process Editor at the project level.

The employees selected to use the Baan ERP system can be entered and their roles assigned using the Project-level Business Process Editor. Once these employees have been entered, their user-specific desktops can be generated.

To increase the value gained by using the DEM Business Organization Editor, Baan needs to reflect the asset and budgetary impact of changes made from one implementation phase to another for analysis and review. Until then, it is best to use the Project-level Business Process Model to capture the employee information.

The quickest and most effective way to implement Baan's ERP system is to use DEM and Baan's Business Reference Model(s). The implementation can be done in seven steps:

1. Select a Baan Business Reference Model.

2. Define and scope the implementation project. Working at the highest conceptual level, executives can choose the functionality that must be implemented in a specific time period using the DEM Business Function Model. This is achieved by doing the following:

   - Add or delete business functions to align to the company's current and future direction.

   - Transform the reference model's business function into their corresponding business processes.

   - Add or modify the business processes to fit the company's current and future requirements.

3. Define or assign roles to each process activity in the business model. Many roles are already defined and assigned in the Baan Reference Model.

4. Define and assign roles to employees authorized to use the ERP system.

5. Evaluate the business rules associated with the Business Reference Model.

6. Set the company parameters and create the Baan company.

7. Generate the Baan user-specific desktops.

Within these seven steps, DEM is being used as a planning tool, an implementation tool, and quality improvement tool. In the next section, you learn how to use DEM as an interactive business planning tool.

Using DEM as a Planning Tool

Rather than defining a new business model by showing how a business does a particular function, the DEM modeler should first define what functions the business does. Although this is a simple task and one that can be easily overlooked when faced with a short implementation time frame, defining both current and future business functions moves DEM from being an implementation tool into a powerful planning tool. As a planning tool, DEM enables the tight integration of the corporate business strategy with its daily operations.

The following sections explain how to develop an interactive business model that interfaces with the business' daily operations. You learn how to use the tools and methods necessary to effectively use the enterprise modeler.

Using a Baan Business Reference Models

Selecting a Business Reference Model is best done by determining a customer order decoupling point. If the customer order can be delivered directly from finished goods inventory, the Baan Assemble-To-Order (ATO) Business Reference Model can be modified to be a "Make-To-Stock" model by removing the Final Assembly business functions. If the customer order must be configured from existing sub-assemblies that can be pulled from a work-in-process warehouse and assembled to the customer's specification, use the standard Baan ATO Business Reference Model. If the ordered product must be engineered from a customer specification, use the Baan Engineer-To-Order (ETO) Business Reference Model. All other types of manufacturing companies should check with their local Baan representative to see if a partner-based reference model is available.

If a Business Reference Model can be selected, it should be imported into the Baan Company Business Model using the following menu selection: Enterprise Modeler/Master Data/Versions/Import Model. Most models are shipped in a compressed file format. These files normally end with a .Z suffix. Be sure to use the suffix if provided when importing the file. By importing a Baan Business Reference Model, the Master Data Repository and the Reference Level Business Model is loaded for a specific Baan company.

After the Business Reference Model has been imported into the designated Baan Company, a new project can be defined using the following menu selection: Enterprise Modeler/Maintain Project Model/Import Model. This moves all the information from the Reference level into a specific project where the business functions and business processes can be aligned to the target company.

With an implementation project initiated and DEM loaded with the various components of a generic business model, the modeler can now use the DEM Business Function Editor to align the Reference Business Function to the target company's business functions.

Using DEM's Business Function Editor

When working with the Baan Business Reference Models, it is important to look beyond the current business functions and align the functions in this new project with those that are required to meet the company's future business. With this being the case, many of the Business Reference Model functions remain, but their implementation are pushed out to later phases in the implementation. Because the time frame is unknown, it is advised to use the TEXT option to add any pertinent notes as to why this function may be of future importance.

If a function is not included in the Reference Model, they may be added by going back to the main menu browser under the Enterprise Modeler folder, within the Master Data folder in the Business Function Repository. From within the Master Data folder, open the Business Function Repository folder. Within the Business Function Repository editor, new functions can be added. After they're added to the Master Data Repository, return to the Enterprise Modeler folder found in the main menu browser, open the Maintain Project Model folder, and open the Function Editor. From the editor, you can follow these steps to retrieve the newly created function:

1. Select Model from the menu bar.
2. Select the Business Function Repository.
3. Locate the new function.
4. Select the new function.
5. Copy the new function.
6. Select the Model from the menu bar.
7. Select Function Reference Model.
8. Paste new function where best appropriate.

For all new business functions added, the business process that defines how to accomplish this new business function needs to be added to the business model. This task may range from simply adding a new activity within a process, to creating an entirely new business process that gets incorporated into a main business process. Creating and adding these new business processes is discussed in the section "Refining the Business Processes."

To delete a function, simply select the function and delete using either the Edit menu bar or the Delete icon from the toolbar. Deleting a function does not purge any associated business process or processes. If the function is associated with a business process through a transformation business rule, the associated business processes are not referenced on the Project level when the business rules are evaluated. If the business function is not associated to a business process through a transformation rule, the purging of the associated process activities may be done during the implementation phase review of the business processes.

With the business functions aligned with the company's current and future business requirements, they need to be grouped into their respective implementation phases.

Using DEM's Project Phasing

To elevate DEM above being just an implementation tool, Baan created a simple trigger mechanism that controls which Baan ERP sessions are operational and who has authorization to access those sessions. Baan does this by defining implementation phases and linking business rules to those phases that are affected by the business functions of other phases. This simple but effective mechanism enables DEM to merge the "as-is" and "to-be" business models into a single model. This minimizes any negative effects when pulling-in or pushing-out various business functions to meet changing business requirements over a longer planning horizon.

To use project phasing, each implementation phase needs to be defined with a start and completion date. DEM enables a user-defined color to be associated with each phase, thus allowing a clear visualization of which business function is operational in which implementation phase.

Part
II

Ch
7

To define and personalize each implementation phase, enter the Enterprise Modeler folder from the main menu browser. Open the Maintain Project Models folder and select Define Phases. After the phases have been defined, select the Color tab and set the colors associated with each phase by sliding one or more of the color slides to the right.

Once the implementation phases have been defined, return to the Enterprise Modeler folder, open the Maintain Project Models folder, and select Business Function Model. All the basic business functions require a phase assigned to them. Remember, "basic business functions" are the lowest level element in the function model; hence, those functions that are not shadowed need phases assigned to them. With the "as-is" and "to-be" business functions assigned to the various project phases, the DEM Project Model is ready to progress to the implementation stages.

Using DEM as an Implementation Tool

Following Baan's implementation methodology (Target Enterprise), an implementation is divided into three separate stages:

1. Mapping
2. Pilot
3. Migration

Each stage ends with a simulation of the business environment that is implemented at the end of the last stage.

In the first stage, Mapping, the business processes associated with the business functions for the current implementation phase are reviewed with the key users on the project team.

N O T E The project team members for each implementation phase may or may not be made up of the same key users. It depends on personnel availability and the business functions being implemented.

The key users alter those business processes found in the Baan Business Reference Model to reflect the specific process activities that are used when this phase is implemented. Once the business processes are aligned to the key user specification, the first simulation (SIM I) is done for management review. From this review, the requirements for the second stage on the implementation are specified.

With these refinements, the project team enters the second stage, Pilot. It is in this stage that the business processes and specific Baan sessions with their associated data requirements, roles, responsibilities, and affected employees are locked-in and agreed upon. This refinement is then presented by the key users to the management team during the second simulation (SIM II) for the second decision to proceed with the implementation.

During the third and final stage, Migration, the implementation team converts and loads the necessary data, trains the users in the use of the new information system, and performs the final system test before going live. The last simulation (SIM III) is completed by the project team and the new users of the current implementation. On completion of the last simulation, the system goes live. In the weeks following the go-live, the system is fine-tuned. A project review is conducted and all outstanding issues are incorporated into the next implementation phase requirements.

It is natural for changes to occur during an implementation. By limiting the duration of the current implementation, the number of changes that can occur is also limited. For changes that do come up, it is much easier to determine if they should be included in the current phase or if they can be pushed out and incorporated into the next implementation phase. A good rule of thumb is to target the duration of an implementation phase from three to nine months to minimize the negative effects of the changing business environment.

The following sections provide more details on determining the scope of each implementation phase. In addition, they discuss transforming and aligning the business processes of the generic business model to the business processes of the client for the functions included in the current implementation phase, refining those processes, and training the end-users of the information system based on the actual business processes.

Managing the Project Scope

Although driven to have a fully integrated Enterprise Resource Planning information system, most companies do not have the resources to implement an entire ERP system. Most are driven to correct or enhance a specific area within their operations, which is made much simpler through DEM.

At this point, the DEM Project Model contains those business functions that are required to meet both the current and the future business requirements for the company being implemented. To address the immediate business requirements, select only those business functions that are required to be implemented in the initial implementation phase. For all remaining business functions, choose whether they are required in the long or short term.

CAUTION

All business functions need to be placed into a project phase. If no phase is assigned, then it is assumed to be required for all phases.

To assign a phase to a business function, you must first select the business function. Follow these steps to select a business function:

1. Enter the Enterprise Modeler folder from the main menu browser. Then open the Maintain Project Models folder.
2. Select the corresponding Project Model.
3. Enter the Business Function Model.
4. Locate the lowest level business functions that support the immediate business requirements.

For each function located, determine if this function is required for all phases of the project. If it is, assign all phases to that function. The simplest way to accomplish this is to select the function, go to the Special menu, and select "Select All." This assigns all defined phases to the selected function. If the function is not required for all phases, select the Phases icon from the toolbar and select the phases applicable.

If other business functions exist, determine which phase they are required in, based on the requirements found in the company's business plan. Select the Phase icon from the toolbar and make the assignments. Continue this process until all low level business functions have been assigned an implementation phase.

Once all business functions have been assigned an implementation phase, the business processes associated with the business functions designated to be implemented in the initial phase can be captured by generating the user specific desktops.

Generating Business Process Desktops

The current status of the DEM Project Model is:

- A Baan Business Reference Model has been imported.
- Business functions have been removed or added to support the company being implemented.
- The remaining functions are associated to an implementation phase where the most critical functions are assigned to the initial implementation.

The model reflects what this company does and when selected functionality is implemented for this project. Given this information, DEM is ready to generate the user-specific desktops that support the roles of the business process activities associated with their corresponding business functions.

To generate these desktops, the Project Model needs to identify which employees are going to be assigned these roles. To do this, enter the Enterprise Modeler folder, and then enter the Maintain Project Models folder. Select the Project Model followed by selecting the Employee button or Employees by Project Model from the Special menu.

Once in the Maintain Employee Baan session, enter the employee information for the employees that are assigned roles for this initial implementation. Each employee added must have a system logon identification. If one is not entered, the person currently logged on to the system will have their system logon identification used as a default value. It is advised that all users have their own system identification with a password assigned.

If the employee does not have a Baan logon, one can be generated by using the Generate Users button or choosing Generate Baan Users from the Special menu. After the employees are successfully assigned to the Project Model, they must be assigned a role or roles. These roles should coincide with those assigned to the process activities that support the business function in the initial implementation.

With the roles assigned, the desktops can be generated by returning to the Maintain Project Models screen and following these steps:

1. Select the correct Project Model.
2. Select the User Dialog button or select User Dialog Generate from the Special menu.
3. From the Generate User Dialog Baan session, select the initial Optimization Phase.
4. Check the Process Flow Menus box (to obtain the business process desktop).
5. Check the Overwrite box (to overwrite the previous desktop).
6. Check the Enter Session Authorization box.
7. Select the Generate button.

This causes DEM to regenerate the desktops for all employees assigned to the initial implementation phase for this project model. Review all desktops generated and print those desktops for each role identified for the initial phase.

By following this procedure, the resulting business processes represent those designated for the initial implementation. These business processes are reviewed by the key users and refined to meet the initial phase requirements.

Refining the Business Processes

With the initial phase desktop business processes on paper, copies can be easily marked up to reflect the desired process flows. When a consensus is reached within the project team, those affected business processes can be modified.

The only changes that can be made to the business processes in the Project Model are limited to the following:

■ Deleting an entire business process
■ Altering the roles assigned to the process or the process activity
■ Adding or modifying the Specific Help for a process activity

All other changes must be made in the Master Data in the Business Process Repository.

When changing any element in the Master Data, caution is strongly advised. Although many elements found in the Master Data are bound to a specific version, they still represent commonly shared objects. What is changed in one version may cause a conflict in another and when objects that are commonly shared, a change control procedure must be enforced.

Deleting objects from Master Data demands the highest level of discipline. The reason is that DEM has made it very easy to permanently remove an object. With three clicks of a mouse, an object is removed. If the version is derived from a pre-existing business model, then the deletion of an object is not as critical because it can be recovered from the other version. Hence, it is advised to derive from an existing model whenever changes are going to be made.

Part
II

Ch
7

TIP If you are adding a new set of process activities, first look to see if a new business process can be used.

Many times a manual process activity is replaced with a number of other activities. It is advised to group these new activities into a new business process and then replace the old manual process activity with the new business process. This helps to protect the integrity of the original process model. The same is true when changing the process flow. Look to see if the old flow can be replaced with a new business process that contains the new flow. Making this extra effort will help if there ever is a need to upgrade the kernel reference model.

After all the changes have been made to the business model, it is time to train the new users. End-user training is now based on the roles these employees are expected to perform.

Training Baan ERP Users

DEM enables Baan ERP training to progress through an iterative learning process. The major hurtle that DEM-based ERP training must overcome is breaking the traditional training model.

Although it is not referred to as training, DEM-based ERP training begins in the first planning session where business functions are added or deleted from the Baan Business Reference Model. It is in this early session where the new ERP user begins to get a sense of how the various Baan ERP sessions are combined to accomplish specific tasks, such as processing a sales order or an invoice. This initiates the initial discussions of how Baan does a specific task without delving into every little detail of a Baan module.

During the mapping stage of using DEM and a Baan Business Reference Model, the project team exchanges and shares information that helps align the Project Model's business processes. Specific questions are resolved that pertain to specific operational or administrative issues as they arise during this alignment process. During the pilot stage, the key users may want additional detail training and opt to take the advanced training for specific modules. It is during this advanced training where the A-to-Z module training can take place.

Within the migration stage of the project, the Project Business Model reflects exactly what will be implemented. From this model, the actual desktops are generated and the Baan users receive their training based on the actual business processes as defined in the business model. Actual training material should be referenced through DEM's Specific Help capability.

DEM Specific Help is useful in conveying not only Baan ERP Session Help, but it is also a good repository for referring to any reference documentation or online support documentation, such as the training manuals. To add DEM Specific Help, follow these steps:

1. Enter Enterprise Modeler folder and then enter the Maintain Project Models folder.
2. Select the Project Model being used for this implementation.
3. Select Business Process Model from the Special menu or click the Process Model button.
4. Select the business process and enter the Business Process Editor.

5. Locate and select either the business process or the process activity where the specific help is to be added.

6. Enter the Text editor by selecting the text icon from the toolbar.

Information added in this text file appears as Specific Help for the selected business process or activity. If the activity is a Baan ERP Session, a zoom session exists within the Option menu where a hyperlink can be added to point to the standard Baan Help for a specific ERP session.

The DEM Specific Help feature is very useful for capturing all documentation that supports that business process. This includes Standard Operating Procedures (SOP), Work Instructions, and International Standards Organization (ISO) documentation.

Coupling this capability with the detail business process maps that graphically represent the business process, the training for the normal Baan ERP user is focused only on how the business processes that they support have changed, and not on the information system itself.

Using DEM as a Quality Improvement Tool

Recognizing that a high rate of change occurs in manufacturing, a design objective for Baan is to minimize the negative effects caused by this rapidly changing environment. DEM satisfies this objective very well.

In a single business model, DEM defines and maintains the following:

- What a business does
- How it does what it's supposed to do
- Who does it

If change occurs, a decision can be made to include this change immediately or to delay any action until a later time. In this section, you learn how DEM enables the business model to adapt to change and how it utilizes an iterative approach to incorporate change over a specific time frame.

Adapting to Change

DEM is designed to provide a layer of abstraction that buffers changes which occur in the business environment from changes that occur in the information systems development environment. This abstraction is achieved in DEM primarily through its use of business functions and to a lesser extent through its use of roles.

Recognizing that main process flows cross both functional and organizational boundaries and that the business functions change far less than a business organization, DEM uses the business function to link the main business processes to the business model. By using the more stable entity, DEM can focus the definition of the "as-is" (current) and the "to-be" (future) business model into a single model that spans a far greater time frame. To distinguish whether a function is active now or later, DEM uses a phase attribute for each function defined. By generating user specific desktops by phases, DEM can identify what functions are active.

By having an awareness of all the business functions in a generic manufacturing business model, business processes can be fully active at any given time, branches in a fully defined business process can be activated based on what business functions are active.

Given a specific set of business functions, business rules (static conditions) can be set to grant or deny access to a particular process path within a business process. In other words, access to process path A is only accessible if function A is active. If function A is not active, access to process path A is denied.

To help the users to recognize if the path is activated or not, DEM shows the process path for A as either highlighted or dimmed. It is highlighted if function A is active and dim if not. This enables the person using process A to see whether a change is most likely to come sometime in the future. Although a path in the business process may be dim, a person can still read what activities will take place, but they do not have access to that path at that time.

The phasing attribute also allows a large implementation to be scaled down into manageable projects that require less time to implement. A business user is more likely to push functions out as long as they know that they will be implemented at some later time. This helps to properly scope a phase of a project given the current time and resource constraints.

Roles also provide a level of abstraction that helps to minimize the negative impact of change. DEM chooses to generate user-specific desktops based on the roles assigned to process or process activity. Roles assigned to a process or process activity change far less than the roles assumed by individual employees. Thus, the employee may assume new roles as required without negatively affecting the information system.

Adapting to the changes in a business environment becomes much easier if the buffer reduces the number of changes that must be made. Although DEM allows changes to be made to any element of the business model, DEM attempts to focus all changes on people, roles, or business functions.

Using Iterative Implementation Phases

Defining phases for an implementation provides the opportunity to define much smaller projects. These smaller projects can be more easily controlled and typically can be fully operational in three to nine months.

With a shorter implementation cycle, changes that arise during a project can be evaluated based on the risk associated to implementing the change in the current project, or in three to nine months. Chances are that most changes will be incorporated in the next phase of the project. ●

CHAPTER 8

Getting to Know the Structure

In this chapter

Understanding the Baan Language

You will encounter many different words that you need to know in order to have a better understanding. The most important were outlined and the best definitions possible were given.

Using such a complete package as Baan requires you to be introduced to new concepts like Enterprise Modeling, which allows a quick understanding of the process used for any functions.

The following sections define some of the structure you need to know to manipulate the data; it also defines the different data elements critical to the software.

Knowing the Keywords

Introducing a new software also means introducing new terms, as well as many new acronyms. Many have been introduced with release of Baan IV. Both the new user, as well as the experienced user will benefit from knowing the meaning of the terms in Table 8.1.

Table 8.1   Baan Keywords

Keyword	Description
ATO	Assemble-To-Order. Used to qualify the process where manufacturers are following this specific process.
BShell	This is the layer between the Baan software and the operating environment. The BShell allows Baan to write software that can be ported on various environments without any modifications.
Customization	Change made to the software in order to fulfill a need at a site, when a session is customized it means that you no longer use the original Baan process, but a version modified to the customer needs.
DEM	Dynamic Enterprise Modeling, a new approach to adapt computer systems to business needs.
Enum	Enumerated field, predefined options to be selected for the value of a specific field. A good example is a field where the accepted answers are Yes or No.
ERP	Enterprise Resource Planning, the process of managing all the information related to an enterprise.
Form	Display screen to prompt for parameters or to show results of an inquiry.
GUI	Graphical User Interface, a Windows-like approach introduced with version IV.
Icon	Graphic representation of an option.
Localizations	This is a lighter version of a customization. Generally, localizations are made on site by the company information technology developers and are minor or cosmetic changes to original screens and reports.

Keyword	Description
Orgware	The business Organizer module offered by Baan to ease the implementation process.
Session	A session contains a form to display or prompt for parameters to run a report or to show an inquiry.
Source Code	Program scripts of the various Baan sessions. Can be maintained by the developer at a customer site if purchased or by a customization partner.
Table	Physical file that contains information.
Triton	The former name for Baan software.
Zoom	Process to search data in a file by opening a window.

Understanding Technical Terms

After you become familiar with the development tools, you can easily determine what tables are used in the different sessions thanks to the naming convention used in the software.

The developer or database administrator has to be knowledgeable of the following terms:

- Package code—A two-character designator for a set of programs. For example, tf is the package designator for all the programs, sessions, and tables related to finance.
- Table—A physical file that contains information. For example, the sales detail information can be found in the table tdsls041. This table name can be broken down this way:
- td   Indicates that the file is in the Distribution Package.
- sls   Sales module.
- 041   Tables Number.

In UNIX, the file is named:

- tdsls041150.dat—For data.
- tdsls041150.idx—For the index files.

Sessions are designated using a similar structure. For example, the session to be used to maintain the purchase orders is tdpur4101m000, which stands for:

- td—Indicates that the program is in distribution.
- pur—Purchasing module.
- 4101—Session number.
- m000—Program version.

All main sessions end with m000, where subsessions end with s000.

Version Release Control is the designator for your software version. Generally, every site has some modifications and this VRC indicator ensures that no change is made to the original code.

To summarize the structure of Baan, it can be said that sessions allow you to manipulate different tables and the software can be used at different levels, so you don't alter the software's original state when changes are made.

Navigating the Software

Depending on your user level, you may use Baan from a different aspect. There are three ways available for navigating Baan software.

As time goes by, you will become more experienced with the Baan software and may prefer one method over the others. In addition, the method of software navigation is also impacted by the method of implementation selected. Some of the following described features may not be available to you if the DEM tools are not used to implement. The need to access a multitude of sessions can also command the exclusive use of the menu browser.

Using the Menu Browser

The menu browser may be the most complicated way to access all the functions of Baan software, but it is also the fastest. This method is very efficient in the following situations:

- You have to use all the software's functions.
- You are a key user.
- You work in the Information Technology Department and you support the software.

Basically, the menu browser allows you go through the different menus using a tree approach; you first select a module and then choose a business object. From this menu object, you select either inquiries, procedures, maintenance, or reports, depending upon what you want to use. Within the session level, you select the desired session.

Using the Windows Desktop

The Windows desktop is a very good tool for the user who is not utilizing a large number of sessions. A user on the shop floor may be using only four or five different sessions. You will want to give them access to a menu with five icons, in which case he or she has to click the desired session. This is a very easy way to manipulate the software.

The desktop can be coupled with the menu browser. You can have some icons pointing to sessions on the desktop and also have an icon that points to a menu browser—if you are not using the contents of a module that contains too many items or is not used too often.

Using the DEM Flowcharts

The DEM offers an entirely different navigation approach. You can look at the flowchart and click on a Baan Process; when you select a process, you can drill down until you find a flowchart that represents the function you want to perform. The equivalent Baan session is activated when you click on the box that represents that action.

FIG. 8.1

This is an example of the steps to follow to access the Maintain Purchase Order Session.

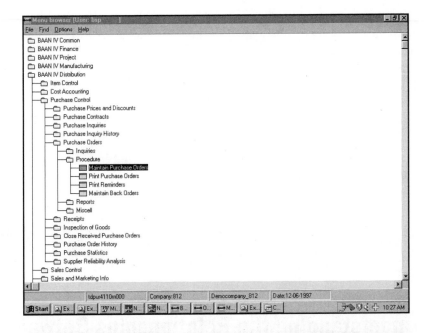

FIG. 8.2

Using a desktop is an easy way to access any session.

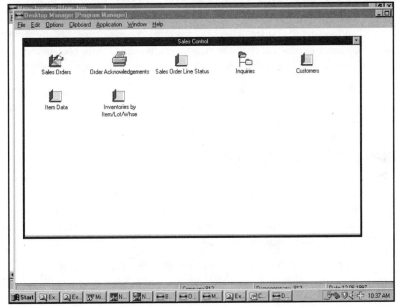

This DEM process is also geared to create menu browsers and Windows desktops from the models used.

The DEM tools really give an advantage to the Baan software over its competitor—it eases the use of the software and because you can benefit from models already developed in various industries, it also speeds the required implementation time.

FIG. 8.3

Finding the right session to use is easy when using the DEM flowcharts.

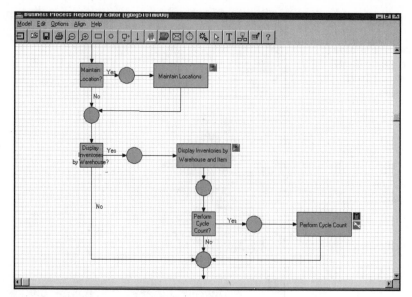

Understanding the Relationships Between Modules

Using integrated software implies that some of the modules communicate, and it is important to understand the relations between the different components of the Baan software. *Integrated software* means that all the software's components talk to each other; Inventory transactions-generated finance transactions, as well as a set of common tables, drive the use of a package.

When using Baan it is very important to understand the relationship between the various elements. You must know the fundamentals of the logistics and finance tables as well as have a good understanding of modules, such as Item Control.

Knowing the Main Modules

There are a few modules that support most of the operations in Baan. It is imperative that you have sufficient knowledge of the Common Data module; this module contains all files known as logistics tables, such as area and warehouses. This module also contains financial tables such as banks relations. A module equally important as that of the Item Control is where the Item Master will be maintained.

The Common Data module contains all of them. The information found for the different common files, such as Employee Master, Supplier Master, and Customer Master, are used in many modules. All the company's areas must agree upon the maintenance and use of those files. Finance and Operations must agree on how to create suppliers because Accounts Payable and Purchasing are sharing the same file.

When you utilize Baan software, most of the sessions make use of the common files. You should spend the appropriate time defining the content of each file. A proven approach is the creation of a databook that describes each file and the naming convention for all codes. By creating such a document with your key user team, you initiate discussions that benefit the implementation process.

Item Control is another module that is used everywhere. You find access to this module in Distribution, Manufacturing, and Service. A cross-functional team or an individual with knowledge of all operations within the company must maintain this module.

The Item Control contains all the information required by the Manufacturing, Distribution, and Service Package Departments. A good understanding of these packages is necessary before creating your items, because many of the fields found in the Item Master impact your use of those modules.

Understanding the Interaction Between Modules

Basically, Baan software can be viewed as generating two types of activities:

- Operation data generated by modules such as Distribution, Manufacturing, Service, and so on.
- Financial information generated from the different transactions.

Operation data helps you manage the inventory levels, the purchase, the sales, and the manufacturing of your products when the financial data tells you how much it cost you to perform those activities. It is possible to use only the operation data if you use an external finance package. The opposite is also true—you can use only the finance data. The data in Baan software can also be interfaced with any external package.

The interaction between the operation transactions and the finance package is mainly managed through the Financial Integration module. Every time a receipt is entered, Baan writes a transaction in a file. Then, at a desired interval, you can post the content of that file to the general ledger. Baan looks up how you built the relationship between the various elements, such as Item Groups and Warehouse, and then translates this in ledger accounts. You can refer to Chapter 27, "Understanding the Integration Between the Modules" to have a complete explanation of the structure. ●

Navigating the Baan Software

Understanding the Different Form Types

There are four different types of forms in the Baan software. The key to successfully using or teaching the use of this software is to be able to quickly recognize what kind of session you are using. Whatever function you try to accomplish, the keystrokes are the same, making the use of the software easier for everyone.

Because all of the programs have to manipulate data differently, Baan had to design ways to handle records the proper way. One of the successes of this software over the years is the fact that the screen types had been limited to four. Once you understand that you have a certain type of screen in front of you, it is easy to perform any function knowing how to use that screen.

The different types of screens have been developed for specific needs. Table 9.1 summarizes the use of the different screens or forms. Each of these form types is discussed in greater detail in the following four sections.

Table 9.1   Use for Different Forms

Form	Use
Form I	Handles single records.
Form II	Used when many records could be manipulated.
Form III	Handles files where two different actions could be done and the user must specify on what part of the file he wants to act.
Form IV	Accommodates print selection.

Using Form I

Form I, a single occurrence format, is generally used when you have to maintain or display an item with a unique key field and it is possible to see one item at a time. The Item Master Maintenance is a good example of a Form I. This is the easiest form to use. You just have to click the insert icon to create a new record or click search to find an existing record. When you scroll from one record to the other, the entire page is updated. Figure 9.1 shows the Item Master Maintenance screen.

Using Form II

Form II is a multi occurrence format in which you can see or maintain more than one record onscreen. A good example of Form II is the maintenance of Logistic Tables. It would be a waste of time if you had to scroll from one page to another to maintain the areas or any files where you only had a key field and a description.

When you insert a new record in Form II, a blank field appears and you just add to the existing records. The information posted previously remains onscreen and you keep adding to the existing list. This process is beneficial for long lists. When scrolling from one record to the other, you will see the cursor going up and down the page. You can also use the Windows arrows on the right side of the screen to locate yourself in the file. Figure 9.2 shows the Maintaining Areas screen, which uses Form II.

FIG. 9.1
The Item Master Maintenance is a typical screen using Form I.

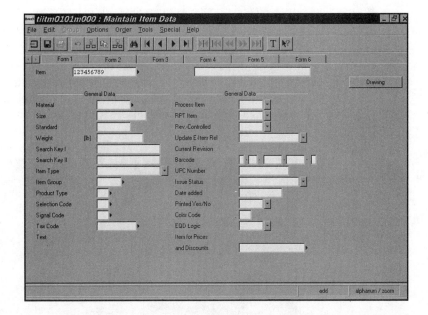

FIG. 9.2
Maintaining Areas is a good example of Form II; having one record on a page would not be efficient.

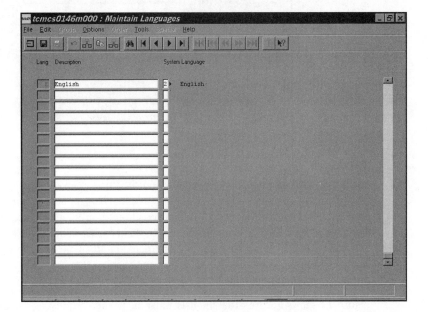

Using Form III

Form III was designed to allow users to maintain or display files in which more than one record is attached to a main field. When there is more than one transaction, you need to see multiple transactions. Through the use of the command keys, you can move from the main part or the sub-form part. A good example is an inventory display. You want to see all the locations. So, you need to move from item to item, which are part of the main form, but you also need a mechanism to move from line items in the sub-form.

When you scroll in Form III, you can either move to the next main record by clicking the single right arrow or move to the next field in the sub-form by clicking the right double arrow. It takes you a little longer to get used to that type of screen, but you will enjoy the capability of displaying information in a convenient format. Figure 9.3 shows a screen that uses Form III.

FIG. 9.3

In Form III, you may want to act on the header part or on the detail part.

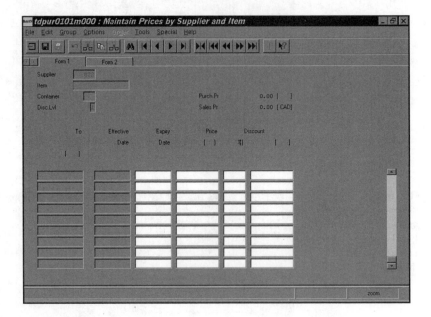

Using Form IV

Form IV is used as a selection screen for reports. This screen contains all the ranges to be filled in order to produce any reports. There is a mechanism built in most of the programs that eases your work using that screen. When you enter different information than the system default in a "from" field, Baan defaults the "to" field to this value. That is what you would type in most cases. Also, you can save time when processing that type of screen, if all values are correct, by going straight to the special option and clicking Continue. You don't have to fill in all the fields if values are supplied.

Figure 9.4 shows Form IV that the user must fill in when requesting a report. Any time a report is requested, this type of screen is presented.

FIG. 9.4

When asking for a report, the user has to fill in Form IV.

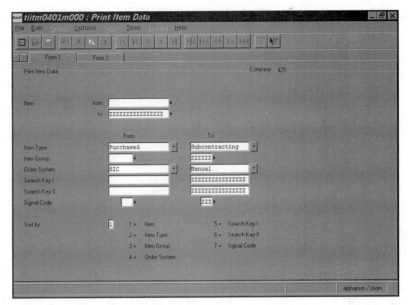

Using the GUI Version

Introduced with Baan version IV, the GUI version is a user-friendly interface that allows the user to use the Baan software in a Windows environment. The use of the icons in the GUI version is very intuitive and eases the process for users who don't like to remember command keys. Most of the commands of the previous ASCII version have been converted to icons. The experienced Baan user will not require too much time to get used to the change and the new user will be comfortable if he has used any Windows software before.

With the use of the special options, it is now easier to find other sessions attached to the main program. Also, the process is more consistent. You don't have to question yourself to see if you typed "Y" or "R" to activate a report, like in the previous ASCII interface. Table 9.2 lists the desktop icons and their associated commands.

Special options allow you to invoke sessions that are related to the current session. This reduces the time it takes for you to find a session in the menu structure and invoke it. For example, to define supplier postal addresses, you can invoke the session from within the supplier master screen instead of invoking it from the menu. Also, in this example, the current supplier code is automatically passed on to the postal addresses session and you don't have to search for the supplier code again. Special options are also used to trigger processes like process delivered sales orders.

Table 9.2   Desktop Icons

Icon	Command
	EXIT PROGRAM
	SAVE
	PRINT
	UNDO
	INSERT RECORD
	COPY
	DELETE RECORD
	PREVIOUS RECORD
	NEXT RECORD
	TOP RECORD
	BOTTOM RECORD
	FIND
	TEXT
	FIELD HELP
	GO TO (FORM TYPE III)

Icon	Command
◀◀	PREVIOUS RECORD (FORM TYPE III)
▶▶	NEXT RECORD (FORM TYPE III)
▶▶▌	TOP RECORD (FORM TYPE III)
▌◀◀	BOTTOM RECORD (FORM TYPE III)

Part

II

Ch

9

Knowing Keyboard Equivalents

Some users are more comfortable with keystrokes than icons. To accommodate that, Baan created the equivalent of certain icons in keyboard combination.

Those keystrokes are available in forms where the icons are available (see Table 9.3). You won't be able to use the insert keystroke combination in a Type IV form, as you would not be able to use the icon. The easiest way to know if the function is available is to see if the icon is in bold. If the icon is in light gray shading, this means the function is not available.

Table 9.3   Keyboard Commands

Command	Keys
Save	Ctrl+S
Exit	Alt+F4
Undo	Ctrl+Z
Find	Ctrl+F
Insert	Ctrl+Insert
Copy	Ctrl+Shift+C
Delete	Ctrl+Delete
Modify	Ctrl+E
Refresh	Ctrl+R
Text	Ctrl+T

Using the GUI Screen

The Baan graphical user interface, better known as *Baan GUI*, is quite impressive. Users who started with earlier releases, as well as new users, really appreciate this new screen, which really brings Baan to a Windows environment and makes it user friendly.

When defining this screen, Baan listened to the users' needs and tried to use a process similar to any software that operates in a Windows environment. Because most of the users are using software designed under the same standards, mastering that environment should not take long.

The GUI screen is less cumbersome to use. Now, all of the zoom processes and the continue options are stored under the special option. In the ASCII version, you have to either press Y, R, or sometimes CTRL+Z to have the available options. This is no longer the case. With the GUI screen, everything is consistent.

Introduced with the GUI screen is the Desktop Manager, which allows users to customize menus and have icons represent the various sessions. Even the Baan opening menu is under a desktop function now, as you can see in Figure 9.5.

FIG. 9.5

The look of all the screens in Baan are now similar to any Windows software.

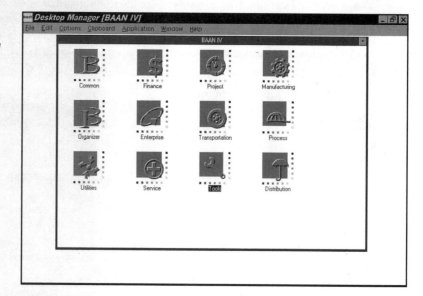

Zooming in GUI Mode

The zooming process used in Baan is very useful and prevents users from having to exit a program or start a second session to find additional information. Most of the sessions contain a zoom session—hidden under the special section—that is linked to the main screen used.

There are two different ways to access the various zooms in the GUI interface. The one used the most calls a zoom directly from a field. To do so, you click the triangle on the right side of the field. If you don't see the triangle next to the field, you cannot zoom. Figure 9.6 shows an example of a zoom.

FIG. 9.6

The sub-session display countries has been called from the main session maintain employees.

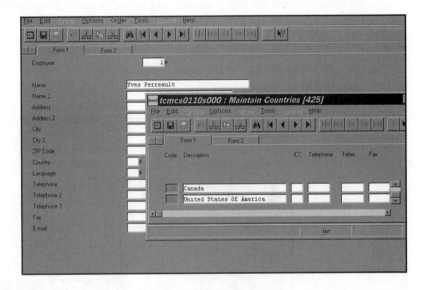

The second way to access a zoom under the GUI interface is to look under the Special option from the main menu. Most of the sessions contain zoom options that make the life of the user easier. Those are shortcuts to other sub-sessions. If you are doing a transaction, you may want to have a look into a sub-session showing the inventory for the item for which you are doing a transaction.

To select from a zoom window, complete the following steps:

1. Activate the zoom window by clicking the triangle or from the special options.
2. Mark the desired sub-session by clicking it.
3. Click OK.

Using Enumerated Fields

From a user standpoint, there is no difference between a zoom and an enumerated field, other than the process to select an item. The enumerated field process allows the user to select a variable from pre-defined options. It is impossible to add or to retrieve choices from the choice window other than accessing the database dictionary. In the zoom process, the user is always allowed to add or retrieve from various maintenance screens.

The enumerated field is used by Baan when a limited number of options that cannot be changed is offered. This process is mandatory to prevent the addition of an option that could not be handled by the system, like a new type of inventory transaction.

As much as possible, Baan gives the user access to a cross-reference table when the user could be adding options and then the zoom process is used to access the data. The screen to select an enumerated field will vary from the zoom fields. Figure 9.7 shows an example of an enumerated field.

To select from enumerated options,

1. Click the triangle to the right of the field.
2. Double-click the desired option.

FIG. 9.7
Click the desired option to go back to the main session.

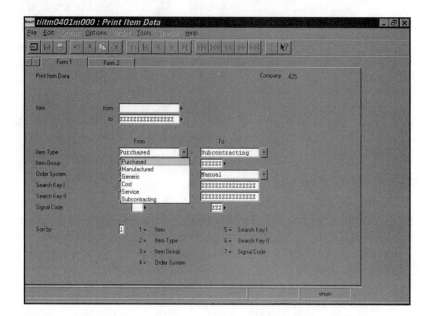

Using the ASCII Version

The ASCII interface had been around since version 1.0 of Baan. Experienced users like the comfort of using this interface, even if it is more difficult. After a few weeks of manipulation, you'll find that this interface is not that complicated after all.

This interface, which is a text-based interface, was first designed to accommodate the use of dumb terminals. Because more and more users are moving to a Windows environment, Baan decided to move to a GUI interface. If you use the ASCII interface or the GUI interface, there is no difference in the way data is stored. You could have a mix of users using both interfaces in the same company. Sometimes the hardware forces users to use the ASCII interface. Other than losing the ease of use of the new screen, they won't be giving up functionality. This may be the case if you install terminals on the shop floor.

Table 9.4 shows the keys and the commands that they are used for.

Table 9.4 Keyboard Commands for ASCII Interface

Command	Keys
Abort program	A
Go to bottom record in file	B
Change record, modify	C
Delete record	D
Exit	E
Activate text manager	H
Insert	I
Change index	K
Mark (within zoom)	M
Go to next record	N
Display available options	O
Go to previous record	P
Print Report	R
Search (Form III only)	S
Go to top record in file	T
Undo	U
Continue, activate process	Y
Go to bottom record (Form III)	Ctrl+B
Copy record	Ctrl+C
Find record	Ctrl+F
Go to top record (Form III)	Ctrl+T
Activate zoom	Ctrl+Z
Go to previous form	Right arrow
Go to next form	Left arrow

In ASCII mode, the zoom process is always activated by using Ctrl+Z. If you see the Mark and Zoom message using a zoom window, the process is very simple:

1. Activate the zoom by pressing Ctrl+Z.
2. Type **M** to activate the Mark mode.

3. Use the up and down arrows to scroll the screen. When you see the desired items, type **Y**.

4. Type **E** to exit and bring this data in the field from which you zoomed.

Using the Text Manager

The Text Manager is used in various sessions to allow users to add comments to different types of orders or files. The text format is always the same, regardless of where the process was called.

The Text Manager is a very handy function when you want to record information in a free format, such as a conversation with a customer that could be attached to a record in the Customer Master. This text can be printed on various documents. The Text Manager could also be used to record special instructions on production orders.

When you access the text mode and there is no text present, the system prompts you to create a new one. Just type **create** when you get this prompt. If you access text already created, you are immediately able to maintain the data already entered.

Under the GUI mode you have to click the T Icon. In ASCII, you must type **H** at Choice. You may know if text is present on the text field by looking at the value of any text field on screen. "Yes" means text is present and can be maintained. "No" means you are to create one. The Text Manager allows you to enter as many lines as you want and the system keeps all the created text under a different number that is tied to the file you are accessing.

Table 9.5 lists the keyboard commands for maintaining text.

Table 9.5 Keyboard Commands for the Text Manager

Command	Keys
Replace text	Esc+G
Delete character	Ctrl+C
Delete word	Ctrl+W
Insert character	Ctrl+E
Write and quit	Esc+E
Write	Esc+W
Restart Editor	Esc+R
Print text	Esc+O
Insert/overwrite	Esc+I
Exit without save	Esc+Q

Corporate Readiness

Preparing for an Enterprise Resource Planning Project

Prior to the actual task of installing and configuring the Baan system, before the project teams are assembled and trained an organization must conduct an assessment of its readiness to proceed with an Enterprise Resource Planning (ERP) project.

A software system as complex as an ERP system is not readily understood by most senior management. The ERP system's implementation touches on all parts of the business. No part of the business can be excluded. ERP bridges all the operational aspects of the organization. Although it may interface with several other subsystems that provide localized processing, the ERP system is the glue that holds the entire Order-to-Cash cycle intact.

In this chapter, you will review the issues that must be addressed prior to the work of installation, configuration, and training can begin. This is much like a marathon distance runner, who's successful performance will have less to do with the type of shirt and shorts worn than it will have to do with the body's fitness level to compete.

The greatest criteria for success is to know when it is achieved. This will be based on the ability of both senior management and the project leaders to have a clear understanding of the objectives and the measurements used to determine when the objective has been reached.

Performing a Corporate Assessment

Three distinct assessment processes must occur:

- Information Technology assessment
- Business Process assessment
- Corporate Readiness assessment

The first two issues are treated separately in further detail in this book, in Chapter 3, "Focusing the Information Technology Plan," and in Chapter 2, "Align the Order-to-Cash Business Process." They are presented here for continuity. The third assessment to estimate the readiness of the organization is the topic of this chapter. The Corporate Readiness assessment includes data gathered during the Information Technology and Business Process assessments. This is required to reach a conclusion on the organization's overall readiness.

The organization must decide whether to conduct the assessments with internal resources, external resources, or with a combination of the two.

Performing an Internal Assessment

An organization can conduct an assessment with internal resources if it feels it can remain unbiased in the process and the outcome. If the internal group conducting the assessment has a stake in the outcome, it is likely to be an assessment in the best interest of the organization. The internal group must possess a high level of credibility within the organization if it hopes to receive relevant information. Being credible usually translates into having experience in a particular part of the business. This is necessary because the data being gathered must be analyzed and determined to be a rare occurrence or a typical event. Having experience obviates the need to have every intricacy explained. It also provides a measure of camaraderie in having "been there."

In the case of the Information Technology assessment, an internal group can take advantage of existing inventories of hardware, software, help desk call logs, and so on.

The Business Process assessment will benefit from an internal group because there will be a level of understanding with existing processes as well as the methods that aren't well documented, which typically are those involved with expediting or product change.

In the same way, the Corporate Readiness assessment will benefit from the understanding of existing conditions and the history behind recent decisions. Organizations have various cultures, charters, and missions that help to explain the level the organization has currently attained.

Performing an External Assessment

The external assessment team brings no (or little) bias to the organization. Unless of course it is the same firm that stands to gain from the positive or negative assessment result. If an external assessment can be conducted without bias it will serve the organization well. However, an external assessor should possess experience in your organization's particular business. If the external assessor has little knowledge in your organization's industry, then too much time will be spent educating the assessor. Likewise, if an external assessor is too close to your specific industry, then there may be too much assumption in the assessment and not enough true analysis. Your organization might receive a boiler plate assessment with little insight into your current situation.

The option to combine an external assessor with an internal team is the optimum choice. The external assessor should act as the facilitator who can provide methods and tools to the team. Further, the external assessor can contribute industry knowledge and experience that the internal team can evaluate. This industry knowledge can be used to create benchmarks against which the internal team can compare its results.

Part
II

Ch
10

Determining the Type of Return Management Expects

The Corporate Readiness assessment must answer a very broad question. That is, what type of return does the senior management team in this organization expect to get from its investment in projects, in general? Further, how does the senior management team change its return on investment expectations when the project initiative is information technology related? This is not an uncommon occurrence. What was reasonable and hence the basis for approval in the general projects case does not hold the same approval weight for information technology projects.

Perhaps the lack of understanding of the benefits from information technology leads to this situation. Possibly, a less than exemplary success record with information technology projects has made the senior management wary of risk.

The discrepancy between senior management's understanding of benefit and the information technology's understanding of benefit exists for two reasons. First, there is a definite gap between how the senior management team will define benefit, usually as some type of value return to the business, and how the information technology team will define benefit, usually along some price/performance curve.

In the section "Defining Business Value," you will review the concept of business value. It is with business value that you will build a common definition of return on investment with which both the senior management team and the information technology team can agree. Agreement, of course, comes from understanding and the concept of business value builds on the two basic ingredients of business process and information technology investment.

Here you will look at two precursor opinions that must be understood. Before you can even discuss what the definition of business value is to either group, you have to define how the senior management team will consider an ERP project. It may be very different from the view of the project leaders. Even without considering the business value concept, both the senior management and the project team must have the same project vision.

The project or success vision is different from the return on investment definition. The return on investment definition utilizes a common understanding of business value. It can be an on-going discrete measurement. The success vision is used to bound the business value measurements. The success vision is the perspective on how you will look at the business value measurements.

Defining Delivery Focus

The delivery focus is driven by the completion date of the project. In this mindset, the success of a project is determined from whether the project was completed on or before the timeline completion date. The earlier the completion the greater deemed the success of the project. Likewise the later the completion date the less likely the project will be labeled a success. This is an all too typical information technology project team approach. Until recently, the information technology projects teams had little else on which to rely.

The completion date of a project measures success. There may be other implied success factors but the overriding measure is completion date. Unfortunately, senior management appears to hold this success metric in high regard as well. Both teams would like to disguise it with the addition of other success metrics. The problem is a result of the completion date being the only clearly definable and measurable metric that both teams have in common. Thus this metric is the one focused on most. The senior management team drives for earlier completion while the information technology project team pushes the date to accommodate new requirements.

In the case where the information technology project misses the completion date, it is usually caused by additional requirements being added that were not contemplated when the project duration was originally estimated. Although a superior solution may have been the ultimate result, the success metric of completion date was not met.

In the other case, the information technology project that is completed on time or earlier than the completion date may have been done so because specific requirements were dropped from the project. In this case, although the project has limited functionality, the project is deemed a success.

Obviously, the completion metric is not a reliable method to gauge success. You need to establish a new focus on profit to replace the completion date focus. This is not to say that completing a project on time is not important, but that delaying or expediting a project should include the benefit value increase or decrease. A current case in point is the year 2000 programming issue. Benefits aside, it is very important that these year 2000 projects focus on completion date as a major success factor.

Defining Profit Focus

If the senior management team and the information technology project teams could agree on a metric to measure project success other than the completion date, the benefits to the organization could increase.

The term *profit focus* is used here. Think of profit in a figurative sense—not in a literal sense. Profit could be replaced by any metric value your organization considers a good return on investment. As noted earlier, in the case of the year 2000 programming issue, the profit focus could even be replaced by the completion date metric.

Both teams must learn new skills to support the profit focus approach. The senior management team will have to take time to understand how particular technical systems produce or return value to the business. The information technology project team will develop examples to draw the connection between a particular technology and the benefit the business experiences. This will help condition the management team to perceive benefits from the technology that may not be traditional to their thinking. The information technology project team must learn the basics of return on investment. The organization is not investing in technology for the sake of technology.

The earlier success metric of completion focus has no place in this thinking. However, the decision to delay the completion of a project can be measured in terms of additional benefit to the organization. If the two teams agree on the definition of benefit then it's simply an exercise for the information technology project team to show the amount of increased benefit and the related cost. The management team will make a decision based on a clear cost/benefit calculation. Likewise, the early completion of a project can be measured to ensure that enough benefit has been returned to the organization. Otherwise it may be necessary to further fund the project until an acceptable level of return has been received.

The need to change the definition of the success metric is clear. The focus on project completion can be a poor indicator of success. On the other hand, the focus of project completion on the benefit returned to the organization is superior. However, it is the challenge of finding a common ground for the profit focus to work for both senior management teams and information technology teams that you will look at next.

Defining Business Value

You need to define a common success metric for information technology projects so you can begin to deal with the large number of projects that do not succeed. Organizations believe they are investing sufficiently in these projects. But do they understand how much is enough?

Part
II

Ch
10

In other words, what are the barriers to successful implementations? What will stand in the way of a successful Baan ERP system implementation?

Once you understand the investment strategy and the barriers to success, define your new profit metric, called business value. You move through a progression of defining information technology and business processes and then how the combination of the two produce business value.

Determining Information Technology Investment

The investment organization's make in information technology varies by industry, as shown in Figure 10.1. Investment varies by organizations within an industry as well. This is due to the fact that there is no standard to determine how and what constitutes an investment. For example, some organizations will include both operating and capital costs in the investment amount, while others will only include the operating expense and not the capital. Capital costs can influence the investment amounts considerably. In time, investment metric will include only operating expenses. This too, would create discrepancies. For example, an organization that leases certain technology would include this amount in the investment whereas another organization may capitalize the purchase and the investment would not reflect this amount.

FIG. 10.1

The investment in information technology varies across industries.

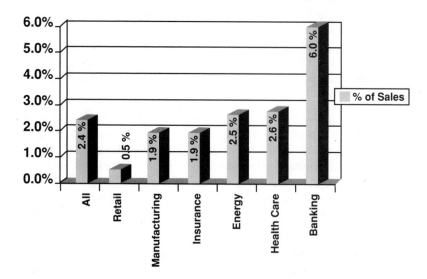

Even the operating expenses can vary widely. For example, a decentralized information technology department may have personnel that reside in business units and the business unit may actually be supporting the cost. Or the opposite may occur, where business units have personnel dedicated to support a particular application (like Baan) and charge the cost to the information technology department. An increasing number of information technology budgets attempt to classify and charge certain costs directly to the business units. These groups are trying to create a technology utility. As such the more you use the more you pay.

The most disturbing discrepancy is the fact that some information technology budgets may not account for all the expenses. Many of these costs may be buried in business units and may not be realized as a cost of technology. A close review of the general ledger accounts can reveal an interesting list of expenses that can be technology related but born by an unsuspecting business unit. A new financial model called the Total Cost of Ownership (TCO) has emerged to help capture these stray costs as well as implicit costs related to administration, support, and cost of capital.

Determining Why Benefits Are Below Expectations

Organizations make significant investments in the information technology used in their business. Although many organizations receive a good return on their investment, some still face many barriers to success.

In the section, "Determining What Type of Return Management Expects," you learned about the lack of correlation between the project team and the management team perception of project success. First you will learn more about those implicit issues specific to the senior management team. Next you will look at the more explicit technical barriers to success.

In some organizations there is still a belief that information technology is a necessary evil—that it must be tolerated as a cost of doing business. Nothing could be farther from the truth. You'll see in the definition of business value that the use of information technology can return value to the business. In other words, it is not a cost but an opportunity.

Senior management teams may have a low tolerance for lengthy projects. In the case of a comprehensive Baan implementation, the duration may take 18 to 24 months or more. Hardly a length of time that a management team will wait for results to appear while still investing a considerable amount of money. A related issue could be the lack of direct involvement by the management of the project, not from a steering committee role but from direct project management and leadership activity. Most organizations today realize this to be the case and regularly place business unit personnel at the head of large system implementations.

Just as there are management barriers to success there are several technology barriers to success, such as the following:

- Technology rate of change
- Lack of standards
- Staff turnover
- Dependence on legacy systems
- Outsourcing the problems

The technology rate of change is clearly evident to anyone who works in the discipline of information technology. Gordon Moore, of Intel fame, developed Moore's Law with the net effect being a doubling of computing performance approximately every 18 months. Regardless, large projects can fall victim to this pace of change. If, for example, a large scale systems implementation spans 18 months, the available computing performance of the original platform has depreciated to half. The converse is also true in that twice the computing performance can be purchased at the end of the project than could be purchased originally. However, the computing platforms are typically purchased early to support project development.

The lack of standards will create havoc. The ability to agree on and to document the standards that will be supported for the project implementation is critical to the success. If the client environment is non-standard, then trying to support multiple versions of client software will only detract from the real issues. This will also require multiple instances of training material. If the server environment is non-standard, then there will be issues with data integrity between databases. The version of the application may be different for each platform. The upgrades or patches to fix application problems may be released at different times for each platform.

The increase in staff turnover is a big problem with many organizations, primarily due to the rate of change of technology. Personnel are finding opportunities to learn different disciplines in different organizations. The ERP area is growing at a tremendous rate and many opportunities await the experienced team member in any number of different disciplines.

The dependency on legacy systems can impede the introduction of a new system. Clearly, if the business units are comfortable operating with a particular suite of applications then it is unlikely they will (initially) endorse a replacement application. Why would the business unit want to assume the risk to change unless there is an overwhelming reason to change? Personnel are comfortable with the legacy system; they know what and what not to expect. More often than not they can fix problems that occur and can get around the rest.

Outsourcing has been given an enormous amount of discussion in the information technology area. Unfortunately, not much of the reviews have been good. The first problem is a result of why most choose outsourcing in the beginning. Most organizations review outsourcing to do the following:

- Reduce technology costs
- Reduce staff costs
- Make otherwise invisible and fluctuating costs appear as operating expense
- Eliminate the responsibility to do non-strategic tasks

Most organizations outsource certain functions to let someone else take care of the problems. This is absolutely the worst reason to outsource. Any function that is to be considered for outsourcing must be completely understood by the organization (that is, to understand the real cost of what the function needs to operate). If an organization has any hope of breaking even on the outsourcing arrangement it must completely understand the cost. Second, the organization must completely understand the process that it will outsource. This will indicate how dependent the organization will be on the outsource partner. If the function it will outsource is a critical business process, it follows that the outsource deal must be contracted at a much more sophisticated level. The organization must be able to measure the outsource partner to ensure compliance. To that end the organization must fully understand the process steps, duration, and cost.

These issues reveal just some of the technology barriers to successful information technology deployment. They in turn become obstacles to major project implementations, such as the

Baan ERP. The information technology department needs to address these issues in support of its mandate to increase benefits and decrease costs.

Defining Information Technology

The first component in the business value equation is the information technology variable. This variability is a result of the virtually limitless number of permutations and combinations of ways in which technology is being implemented in various organizations. The difference in technology implementation is greater the closer you scrutinize an organization. The farther away you get the more similar the implementations begin to appear.

If you draw far enough back from an organization you begin to see a clustering of similar implementations, as shown in Figure 10.2. This technology alignment appears at the same rate as the business processes begin to align into specific models. Manufacturing the assemble to order (ATO) and the engineer to order (ETO) are just two examples of business process alignment. If you compare several ATO organizations to several ETO organizations you will begin to see a commonality between the technical implementations within each model.

Regardless of the alignment of technology implementation there exists common core technology groupings. You reviewed these in greater detail in Chapter 3, "Focus the Information Technology Plan." In this section, the concept is presented sufficiently to support the development of the business value equation.

Part

II

Ch

10

FIG. 10.2
There are four major areas within the information technology definition.

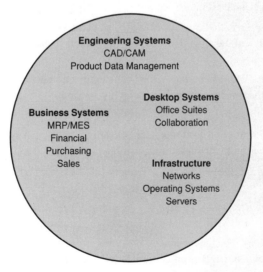

Defining Infrastructure Services The first group is considered classical information technology; it's called it the Infrastructure. In this group you find technologies dealing with the following:

- *Data management.* This includes such items as data warehousing and database systems, relational or otherwise. No applications are included at this layer.

■ *Operating systems.* This includes the operating systems that exist in the organization's server environment. It can also include client operating systems, although this classification does change more often than the server operating systems.

■ *Server hardware.* This is the platform on which the organization supports the application level groupings you will review next. These include the desktop tools, business production systems, and engineering production systems.

■ *Communication networks.* This is the lowest and most significant layer within the infrastructure. It includes the data, voice, and video communications technologies. It is the functionality required for the server platforms to communicate.

Defining Engineering Production Systems   The Engineering applications depend on the infrastructure in order to operate. The engineering function varies a great deal between manufacturing organizations but typically there are core requirements, such as the following:

■ *Computer Aided Design (CAD).* Even within the CAD application layer the needs and capabilities vary widely. For example, two-dimensional, three-dimensional, wire frame, solids, hybrid, and parametric features and functions are but a small sampling of what is available.

■ *Product Data Management (PDM).* A more recent entry into this area is the need to properly structure product and design information. PDM production systems can still find themselves more closely aligned with the ERP systems within the business production systems class.

■ *Manufacturing Execution Systems (MES).* The connection between the CAD systems, CAM systems, and the shop floor. Providing real time capabilities important to shop floor control.

■ *Computer Aided Manufacturing (CAM).* The connection between the automated design function and the machine shop floor. A highly specialized family of feature and functionality is available.

Defining Business Production Systems   The business production systems have features and functions that align with the business process model (ATO, ETO, and so on). Production applications are categorized within this class that might not typically be labeled business systems, including the following:

■ *Manufacturing Requirements/Resource Planning (MRP, MRP II).* Typically referred to as legacy systems, the MRP systems focused on the product bill of material.

■ *Financial systems.* The major financial systems include the accounts payable (A/P), accounts receivable (A/R), and general ledger (G/L) applications.

■ *Purchasing systems.* These systems evolved to compliment the MRP systems.

■ *Sales systems.* These include sales force automation applications, such as order configuration. Contact management is sometimes grouped here but is usually found within the desktop area.

■ *Enterprise Resource Planning (ERP).* Includes the Baan application. Includes most of the feature functionality found in the other areas of the business production systems area.

Defining Desktop Productivity Systems   Within the desktop productivity systems area are two major items:

- *Productivity tools.* Most of the desktop applications reside in this area. For example, integrated suites of presentation graphics, word processor, spreadsheets, and database.

- *Collaboration tools.* This area includes email, scheduling, video conferencing, and any tools that support communication amongst a group of individuals.

The desktop area is the fastest growing segment of the information technology portfolio. It has provided the most opportunity but has also created the most issues to control.

Defining the Business Process

The second variable in the business value equation is the business process itself. There are two parts to the business process definition:

- The Order-to-Cash process
- The Customer Order Decoupling Point

Defining the Order-to-Cash Process   Every business operates on some variation of an order-to-cash process, as shown in Figure 10.3. That is, at some point the organization receives an order (the Order point) and collects payment on the goods sold (the Cash point). Everything else an organization does is contained between the Order point and the Cash point.

In a typical manufacturing environment, the following functional departments can be defined:

- *Sales.* This department can include inside sales and customer sales. Inside sales supports the movement of goods between business units, it may also be referred to as technical sales, acting in support of the customer sales groups.

- *Engineering.* Responsible for the development of product designs requested in the sales order. Organizations can perform varying levels of product design from custom design, component design, to assembly.

- *Purchasing.* Responsible for acquiring the materials specified by the engineering design needed to manufacture or assemble the products.

- *Manufacturing.* Responsible for fulfilling the order request (from sales) by assembling or machining the components or raw materials provided by purchasing according to the design provided by engineering.

- *Finance.* Responsible for tracking, categorizing, and allocating the costs incurred by the organization throughout the Order-to-Cash process. As a result this department will summarize the financial performance of the organization.

Defining the Order Decoupling Point   Baan utilizes a concept called the Customer Order Decoupling Point, as shown in Figure 10.4. It is a succinct definition that explains the difference between various manufacturing models. The following manufacturing models are defined:

Part
II

Ch
10

FIG. 10.3

A typical Order-to-Cash process in a manufacturing organization includes the functional areas of sales, engineering, purchasing, manufacturing, and finance.

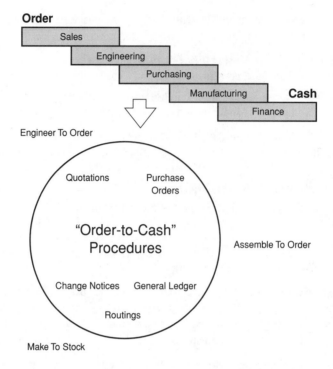

Make to Stock. In this model the organization produces goods destined not to fulfill an existing customer order, but to replenish a depleted inventory. Product sales are fulfilled from inventory. The products leaving the organization are considered finished goods.

Assemble to Order. In this model the organization utilizes existing sub-assemblies to produce its finished goods. The sub-assemblies are likely pre-engineered for specific combinations. The final product can't be assembled until a customer order is received to specify certain features.

Make to Order. In this model the organization does not produce a final product until a customer order is received. The order from the customer will indicate certain product features. The product is built from an inventory of pre-configured optional components. Each component has been engineered; however, there may still be some need to engineer a particular combination of these components.

Engineer to Order. In this model the product run length is one or a very few units. There is no pre-existing product to meet the customer requirement. The customer must specify explicitly the final requirements. There may be recursive attempts to reach an acceptable final product. The engineering function is the determinant factor in the product cycle.

Defining Business Value

The equation to derive business value is composed of the two variables previously described:

- Information technology variable
- Business process variable

FIG. 10.4

Baan's Customer Order Decoupling Point is a good template to help define the different manufacturing models.

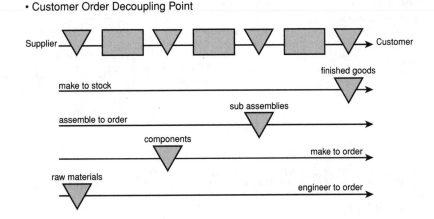

• Customer Order Decoupling Point

To determine the level of business value an organization receives from information technology investment, the degree to which information technology can be directly connected to the business process must be established.

First, you must review and understand the business Order-to-Cash process. Clearly, most management teams are closely aligned with the relative importance of the various parts of the business process. Based on the importance of any piece of the process the management team can declare a relative value of the process.

Next, the information technology that supports each piece of the process must be identified. The value of the information technology is then proportional to the value of the process it supports. The sum of these independent process values is the business value metric. The objective is to maximize the business value from information technology investment and thus tactical IT funding must dominate other funding of strategic and R&D initiatives, as shown in Figure 10.5.

This provides a mechanism to estimate the return on investment from information technology investment. A proposed investment can be evaluated by determining the value of the process step the technology will support.

The business value diagram provides a mechanism to illustrate where the information technology project investment will be allocated. The IT strategic plan should be attempting to apply technology to support processes not yet automated. The IT tactical plan should account for the resources necessary to support currently supported processes. This could be upgrades or replacement of legacy systems. Also, the daily needs of administration, operations, and support must be included. The IT research and development plan must support those initiatives that are investigating emerging technologies that can be used in the IT strategic plan.

Part

II

Ch

10

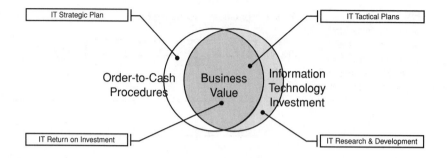

FIG. 10.5
Business value is the sum total of the individual process values the are supported by information technology.

Determining What Type of Project Management Expects

The time it takes to complete an ERP system implementation can vary widely between organizations. Early in the ERP project history it wasn't clear why this variation existed. Today, there is a good definition of two types of project implementation. Baan has called these two styles of implementations

- ▓ Comprehensive
- ▓ Compact

The following provides a comparison of the two types of implementations.

Using a Comprehensive Implementation

The comprehensive implementation is the most complete of the two. It includes both business process re-engineering and the implementation of the ERP system. The objective is to go live with an ERP system that is close to optimal.

This style of implementation is a challenge to manage and is proportional to the size of organizations and the extent to which the ERP is propagating. The business re-engineering process itself may take several months (or years) to complete. It is a highly complex and risky project.

The demand placed on the end users is much greater. Not only will there be a new ERP system installed but the entire business process (the way you do things) will change too. Because the organization will introduce new processes, the challenge to debug system problems increases. It won't be apparent whether the process has broken or the technology has broken (or both). The training programs will have to incorporate both process and technology information.

Probably the most difficult issue facing the comprehensive implementation is the duration of the project. Historically, these projects can be counted in years: two or more was not uncommon. Obviously, the tolerance of management teams to tolerate this type of duration is paramount. There will need to be a very clear communication channel that indicates positive progress. Otherwise the fate of such a lengthy project will be decided quickly.

Using a Compact Implementation

The compact or rapid implementation provides the management team with a more desirable duration. The focus of the implementation is on the technology and less on the process. The concept is to get the technology in place with the current business process. Improvements to the process and technology are assigned to an optimization phase.

The end users are free to concentrate on only new technology issues. The comfort connection is that they will use new technology but within familiar business processes. Training can focus on technology. System problems are attributed to the ERP system and not the process.

Management teams will appreciate the expeditious approach to completing the project. However, you must be very careful to draw out the fact that business processes will not change at this time. Compact implementations can occur within months.

> **CAUTION**
>
> Unfortunately, project leaders get caught in the trap of being expected to deliver all the benefits of a comprehensive implementation within the timeline of a compact implementation.

Determining Project Configuration

An ERP project will require substantial preparation to ensure sufficient resources are made available. It is best to make as many of the requirements visible before the project begins. Surprises along the way tend to slow the project and bring scrutiny that is a waste of an organization's energy. Done properly in the beginning, the project requirements stand on their own merits for the duration of the project.

To enable this preparation, Baan has provided within the Orgware family of products the Enterprise Implementer. It contains the Project Organizer suite of project tools. Specifically, the Project Organizer tool set was created to support the Target methodology. Within the Project Organizer there are the following four modules:

- *Software configurator.* A tool that will propose a software budget considering the Baan product pricing model.
- *Hardware configurator.* A tool that will suggest a hardware configuration appropriate to the software configuration an organization has chosen. However, this configuration will only be as reliable as the performance information provided by the respective hardware vendors.
- *Budget configurator.* A tool that will propose a budget for the project. It can allocate costs according to the Target milestones discussed earlier.
- *Schedule configurator.* Using the information created by the Budget configurator, this tool produces a standard project timeline that includes responsibilities of the project team members.

The Project Organizer tools provide a method to produce software and hardware configurations and project budget. Another benefit is that the tools help develop the Target milestones and project team responsibilities.

Determining Software Configuration

A software proposal is needed as part of the project requirements. It is fundamental to understand how many software components will be included in the project. Within Baan there are many modules from which to select. Issues such as your organizational structure will impact your selection of modules. For example, whether your company is multi-currency, has multiple financial centers, or has multiple logistical business units will effect the inclusion and exclusion of various software modules.

But also consider products required outside the Baan modules. Will any client software be required? This could be Baan products and protocol stacks to work with your specific database selection. The database application must be included. Other software components, such as operating systems, can be included within the hardware configuration.

Another consideration is the level of service and support your organization requires. Although this does not effect the module selection, Baan does consider the cost associated with service and support to be accounted for in the software configuration.

Determining Hardware Configuration

The hardware configuration will consider information about your organizational structure, your expected user environment, and the hardware you would prefer to operate. It will also require the output from the software configuration exercise. This information combined with commercially available benchmark information will propose a hardware configuration.

Some organizational issues to consider are whether you plan to run your server environment in a decentralized or centralized configuration. A centralized configuration will be the easier to manage of the two configurations. It may, however, not be practical. Consider an organization that has business units in different geographic areas or time zones. It may not be practical to depend on a single machine to be available all the time and leave no room for administration. The communication channels between sights may be inadequate to support remote users. Likewise, a decentralized model has issues. The need to replicate the database has communications issues and reliability issues. However, your organization likely has a preferred model in place today. It makes sense to first consider that model.

It follows that the preferred hardware will likely be the hardware your organization is currently trained to administer. It would require a great deal of justification to move away from your organization's standard hardware platform to a preferred Baan platform. Regardless, the options should be reviewed.

The number of expected users is another critical factor. The user load factor will determine the appropriate sizing for the application server(s) and the database server(s). Spin off requirements are that network bandwidth be sufficient to handle the expected user load factor.

You can combine this information with commercially available benchmarks and a preferred platform can be identified. There is risk with this approach in that the benchmarks are suspect as to the conditions under which they were achieved.

Determining Budget

The project cost will include more than the software modules and the hardware platform. There will be items such as the following:

- *Organizational structure*. Issues not mentioned previously are whether the project is for a single site or multiple sites. How will this effect the creation of project teams and project coordination? Will it be cost effective to have the teams located in the same place?

- *The available IT services*. Does your IT department have sufficient resources available to support a major application such as Baan? Will your IT department have to hire or train additional personnel?

- *Style of project*. You previously reviewed compact and comprehensive implementations. The costs of these projects are relative to their duration. In the comprehensive implementation, you will have to decide whether to include the costs of process reengineering.

- *Level of external involvement*. This area is usually where the budget deviates from the original. Industry has shown that the services cost to software cost is at best 1:1 but usually climbs in the area of 5:1 and can go higher in the area of 10:1. Be conservative in this area. You will need outside help—account for it up front.

- *Level of experience within your organization*. If your organization has already implemented Baan in another business unit and the same personnel are used on the new project the training costs will be less as will the external services cost.

The budget should be broken down into a capital portion and a recurring annual expense portion. It is usually the annual expense that is overlooked in the budgeting process. Annual expenses included all the maintenance and support costs as well as ongoing training and application development costs.

The cost of the project team members should be considered as part of the project cost. Although various business units are sponsoring the project staff, the cost could be recognized by the project.

Determining Schedule

The timeline is the culmination of the previous three steps: software configuration, hardware configuration, and budget. The timeline will utilize the Target milestone and responsibility definitions albeit modified to suit your particular implementation. Along with such information as available workload, internal and external rates and the required functions are part of the project timeline.

As with any timeline the project manager is to consider issues relating to milestones being met, the relationship between tasks, and the ability to allocate resources accordingly.

The schedule in the comprehensive implementation will be more susceptible to change than the compact implementation schedule. Recall that the basic premise of the comprehensive implementation is to review the business process and to realign or reengineer the processes to be more efficient. It will be unlikely that the project manager will be able to predict the variation that the process improvement work will introduce into the project timeline. ●

Setting Up a Company

Understanding Company Setup

This chapter details the steps that create a company in Baan. Those steps should be performed by a database administrator or an authorized person. Ensure that your Information Systems Department is aware of the impending operation, so they are ready to assist you if any problems arise.

Performing the Initial Steps

Before you perform any operations in the system, you must plan the structure of the company you want to create. You must decide if you will share tables with other previously created companies. This must be decided prior to performing any of the following actions.

When you have decided on the setup, you can perform the sessions shown in Table 11.1. The sessions in Table 11.1 are mainly found in the Tools module.

There is one session, Maintain Logical Tables, found in Tools. This session can save you time by linking existing physical tables to tables in another company. Use this option if you do not want to create all the physical tables in the new company. This option allows you to use only one version of a given file, like the Country tables, and have two different Baan companies using the same physical file. That reduces the maintenance required and ensures data integrity among consolidated companies.

To share a table, go to the Tools menu and select the Database Management Business Object. Select the Maintenance Business Object, Maintain Logical Tables.

Table 11.1 Sessions Necessary to Create a Company

Session	Description
ttaad1100m000	Maintain Companies
ttaad4111m000	Assign Tables to Database
ttaad4115m000	Maintain Tables Directories
ttaad4200m000	Conversion to Runtime Data Dictionary
ttaad4230m000	Create Tables
ttaad4232m000	Check Tables
tccom0100m000	Maintain Company Data
tcmcs0110m000	Maintain Countries
tcmcs0146m000	Maintain Languages
tcmcs0102m000	Maintain Currencies
tcmcs0108m000	Maintain Currency Rate
tfgld0103m000	Maintain Company Parameters

Session	Description
tfgld0101m000	Maintain Group Company Parameters
tfgld0105m000	Maintain Period Data
tfgld0107m000	Maintain Period Status

Understanding Logistic Tables

Logistic tables must be set up as well. Table 11.2 indicates the program that maintains each table. In addition, it supplies the table name, so it can be used for further referencing in programming.

Before populating files such as Item Master, you are required to populate all the Logistic tables detailed in Table 11.2. It is unnecessary to populate all those tables; you must populate only those that relate to your process.

Table 11.2   Logistic Tables and Their Sessions

Session	Table	Description
tcmcs0145m000	tcmcs045	Areas
tcmcs0110m000	tcmcs010	Countries
tcmcs1143m000	tcmcs043	States
tcmcs0147m000	tcmcs047	First Free Numbers
tcmcs0123m000	tcmcs023	Item Groups
tcmcs0146m000	tcmcs046	Language
tcmcs0131m000	tcmcs031	Line of Business
tcmcs0124m000	tcmcs024	Price Groups
tcmcs0115m000	tcmcs015	Product Types
tcmcs0144m000	tcmcs044	Statistic Groups
tcmcs0141m000	tcmcs041	Terms of Delivery
tcmcs0101m000	tcmcs001	Units
tcmcs0107m000	tcmcs007	Units by Language
tcmcs0106m000	tcmcs006	Units Sets
tcmcs0112m000	tcmcs012	Units by Units Sets
tcmcs0103m000	tcmcs003	Warehouses

Understanding Financial Tables

You also need to populate tables that the financial package will use. Currencies to be used, tax codes, and the payment terms are the main elements. The sessions are listed in Table 11.3.

Table 11.3   Financial Tables and Their Sessions

Session	Table	Description
tcmcs0102m000	tcmcs002	Maintain Currencies
tcmcs0108m000	tcmcs008	Currency Rates
tcmcs0155m000	tcmcs055	Invoicing Methods
tcmcs0153m000	tcmcs053	Rounding Codes
tcmcs0137m000	tcmcs037	Tax Codes
tcmcs0136m000	tcmcs036	Tax Codes by Country
tcmcs0113m000	tcmcs013	Terms of Payments

Understanding Common Data

The Common Data tables are used by various modules. Company Data, which contains the name and address to be printed on various documents, is the first element to define. You must also define the company's Currency during that session.

The other files to be created in the Common Data include Customer Master, the Supplier Master, and the Employee Master. Take a look at Table 11.4.

Table 11.4   Common Data Tables and Their Sessions

Session	Table	Description
Tccom0100m000	tccom000	Maintain Company Data
tccom0101m000	tccom001	Maintain Employees
tccom1101m000	tccom010	Maintain Customers
tccom2101m000	tccom020	Maintain Suppliers

Understanding Cost Accounting

The cost element is an important Item Master factor. In order to cost any items, you need to set up the Accounting module. You may want to plan the use of any elements, such as a Cost Component, to summarize cost elements.

Before you perform any transactions, you need to perform a cost calculation. It is very important to set up the Cost Accounting data with the sessions found in Table 11.5.

Table 11.5   Cost Accounting Tables and Their Sessions

Session	Table	Description
ticpr0110m000	ticpr010	Cost Price Components
ticpr0150m000	ticpr150	Operation Rate Codes
ticpr1101m000	ticpr100	Cost Price Calculation Code

Understanding Item Control

The Item Control module is the main driver for the Manufacturing and Distribution modules. You obviously need to create items in order to use most of the sessions in Baan.

The proper way to create items is to first define Item Default Data. This allows you to use default information and ensure that you don't have to fill all the forms found in the Maintain Item Data session. In addition, if any conversion factors are required, it is recommended you create them using the Maintain Conversion Factors session. You can find more information of the Item Control module's functions in Chapter 15, "Understanding the Item Control Module."

Create some items in the Item Master. Make sure that you perform a cost calculation on every item you create, so you can use these items with other modules. Table 11.6 shows the Item Control tables.

Part
II

Ch
11

Table 11.6   Item Control Tables and Their Sessions

Session	Table	Description
tiitm0101m000	tiitm001	Maintain Item Data
tiitm0130m000	tiitm100	Maintain Item Data by Item and Container
tiitm0110m000	tiitm002	Maintain Item Default Data
tiitm0120m000	tiitm004	Maintain Conversion Factors

Modules

Understanding the Common Data Module

In this chapter

Using Logistics Tables

The *Logistics tables* give you information needed when setting up your common data. Most of the fields in common data are coming from predefined tables (Logistics table).

Complete the following steps to access the Logistics tables:

1. Go to the main menu.
2. Select Common.
3. Select Tables.
4. Select Maintain Logistics Tables.

   Selecting Maintain Logistics Tables takes you to further submenus and sessions.

There are many Logistics tables that you can set up, but they may not all be used or needed by your company.

Logistics tables are used when master data such as Items, Suppliers, Customers, and so on, are defined. For example, the item groups you create in a Logistics table can be used during the creation of items. Usage of the Logistics tables is entirely dependent upon the mapping of your company's business process to Baan.

Using Areas

If you need to make some geographical groups, use the *Area* table. Area can serve to group customers, suppliers, and employees.

Complete the following steps from the Maintain Logistics Tables to create a new Area:

1. Select Maintenance 1.
2. Select Area.
3. Insert an Area Code and give it a description.

By creating areas, you have the ability to generate sales or purchase statistics grouped by area.

Using Commodity Codes

Commodity Codes are item groups used to collect import and export statistics. Create some of those codes if your business is in imports/exports and needs statistics on certain groups of items.

Complete the following steps from Maintain Logistics Tables to create new commodity codes:

1. Select Maintenance 1.
2. Select Commodity Codes.
3. Insert an Commodity Code and give it a description.

Using Countries

When you deal with other countries, you need to set them up in Baan. It's used, for example, in the suppliers' or customers' addresses.

Complete the following steps from Maintain Logistics Tables to create new countries:

1. Select Maintenance 1.
2. Select Countries.
3. Insert a country code and give it a description.

Using States

Just as you did for countries, states must be created for use in addresses. The *states* defined here are used for the electronic filing of 1099-MISC income; this is specific to the countries where 1099-MISC income reporting is used. The states defined here are used in the payer's 1099 details and also the supplier's 1099 details.

Complete the following steps from Maintain Logistics Tables to create new states:

1. Select Maintenance 1.
2. Select States.
3. Insert a state code and give it a description.

Using First Free Numbers

The *first free numbers* are the available numbers for a series of orders. The series are the default numbers for the different kind of orders (Purchase Order, Sales Order, and so on).

Complete the following steps from Maintain Logistics Tables to create new series and first free numbers:

1. Select Maintenance 1.
2. Select First Free Numbers.
3. With the Enumerated field, select the kind of order for which you want to create a series.
4. Enter the first (or first two) digit(s) of the series and provide a description.
5. For the series you just created, enter the first number that correlates to where you want the series to start.

    For example, if you select a series 22 for purchase orders and assign the first free number as 1, the default number to appear for you would be 220001 when going in session Maintain Purchase Order.

Part

III

Ch

12

> **CAUTION**
>
> Whether a single person or group of people is responsible for handling first free numbers, input must be gathered from many sources before these numbers can be established. For example, maintaining first free numbers affects purchasing through the issuance of purchase orders and sales through sales orders. All groups effected must agree on these numbers.

Using Forwarding Agents

The *forwarding agents* are the transportation companies with which you are dealing. You can assign a supplier number to each of them. They are used in modules like Sales and Purchasing as transportation companies.

Complete the following steps from Maintain Logistics Tables to create a new forwarding agent:

1. Select Maintenance 1.
2. Select Forwarding Agents.
3. Insert a forwarding agent and give it a description.
4. Insert what carrier type the forwarding agent is. Choices are listed in the Enumerated field.

You can assign a supplier number if the forwarding agent has an account with your company.

Using Item Groups

You need to classify items in groups for statistics, financial integration, or control. The item group is the most commonly used classification for items in Baan. You can group items based on their characteristics. Item groups can also provide a channel for you to post transactions originating from the Logistics modules into the general ledger.

Complete the following steps from Maintain Logistics Tables to create new item groups:

1. Select Maintenance 1.
2. Select Item Groups.
3. Insert an Item Group Code and give it a description.

Using Languages

You create different languages for external output such as reports in customer or supplier languages. You can even create different languages for an employee menu.

Complete the following steps from Maintain Logistics Tables to create new languages:

1. Select Maintenance 1.
2. Select Languages.
3. Insert a Languages and give it a description.

4. In the Enumerated field, select the number that belongs to the language you just created.

   This number is used in the Baan Tools module to link to the language of your choice. In the other modules, it's mostly the code that is used.

Using Lines of Business

The *line of business* is a group of customers or suppliers in the same sector or activity. It's used for statistical data or selection in certain reports or inquiries.

Complete the following steps from Maintain Logistics Tables to create new lines of business:

1. Select Maintenance 1.

2. Select Lines of Business.

3. Insert a line of business code and give it a description.

 TIP A line of business can be used to create purchase and sales statistics reports.

Using Price Groups

The *price group* is multiple items with the same price structure. It's used to link customers and suppliers to a price structure.

Complete the following steps from Maintain Logistics Tables to create new price groups:

1. Select Maintenance 1.

2. Select Price Groups.

3. Insert a price group and give it a description.

4. In the Enumerated field, select the price unit of the group you are creating.

Using Price Lists

Price lists are other levels of price structure that you can assign to customers.

Complete the following steps from Maintain Logistics Tables to create new commodity codes:

1. Select Maintenance 1.

2. Select Price Lists.

3. Insert a price lists code and give it a description.

4. Select the currency to which you want to assign the price list.

By defining price lists, you have the ability to define prices and discounts for suppliers and customers by price group and price list. As stated earlier, price groups are used to group customers or suppliers with similar price structure. Price lists can be used to further classify the customers/suppliers for defining prices and discounts.

Part
III

Ch
12

Using Product Types

Product type is another group of selection for items. It's generally used with item groups for statistical information on products.

Complete the following steps from Maintain Logistics Tables to create new product types:

1. Select Maintenance 2.
2. Select Product Types.
3. Insert a product type and give it a description.

Using Reasons for Rejection

The *reasons for rejection* consist of various reasons for rejecting products delivered by suppliers. This is used mainly in the Receipt module.

Complete the following steps from Maintain Logistics Tables to create new reasons for rejection:

1. Select Maintenance 2.
2. Select Reasons for Rejections.
3. Insert a reason and give it a description.

Using Routes

Routes enable you to set up pathways to sort printing of documents, including picking lists or shipping notes, in a convenient way.

Complete the following steps from Maintain Logistics Tables to create new routes:

1. Select Maintenance 2.
2. Select Routes.
3. Insert a route and give it a description.
4. You can also assign a day to the route. This is the day that an item should be delivered. It prints on Picking List for Sales Order.

Using Seasonal Patterns

If you have items that fluctuate during a year and want to use forecasting, this is where you create those fluctuation codes.

Complete the following steps from Maintain Logistics Tables to create new seasonal patterns:

1. Select Maintenance 2.
2. Select Seasonal Patterns.
3. Insert a seasonal pattern code and give it a description.
4. Enter a seasonal factor for each the period. The factor indicates the increase or decrease in demand for the period.

Manufacturing pesticides in the agricultural industry is a good example of a product that uses seasonal patterns.

Using Selection Codes

Selection codes are criteria that you set up to select items. You can then select items by size, length, weight, and so on.

Complete the following steps from Maintain Logistics Tables to create new selection codes:

1. Select Maintenance 2.
2. Select Selection Codes.
3. Insert a selection code and give it a description.

Using Signal Codes

Signal codes are mainly to block items from being purchased, sold, or manufactured. They are also used to display on-screen messages when an item is typed.

Complete the following steps from Maintain Logistics Tables to create new signal codes:

1. Select Maintenance 2.
2. Select Signal Codes.
3. Insert a signal code and give it a description.
4. For your signal code, select whether you want to block the item for the different module. Select Free if you choose not to block.

Signal codes can be useful, especially if a component becomes outdated or obsolete for the product you manufacture. You can block the item from being selected for purchase.

Using Terms of Delivery

The *terms of delivery* are the different agreements of delivery that your company has.

Complete the following steps from Maintain Logistics Tables to create new terms of delivery:

1. Select Maintenance 2.
2. Select Terms of Delivery.
3. Insert a term of delivery code and give it a description.
4. You can specify the kind of parameters you want to set with this delivery term. Such parameters include:
   - Cash on Delivery—Payment should be made immediately upon delivery of goods.
   - Carriage Paid—The freight is paid in advance by the consignor.
   - Point of Title Passage—Used by the Taxware system for destination sales tax. The sales tax is calculated based upon either Point of Destination or Point of Origin.

Part
III

Ch
12

Using Units

Units are the physical quantity of an item. You specify here whether that unit is weight, volume, piece, or something else.

Complete the following steps from Maintain Logistics Tables to create new units:

1. Select Maintenance 2.
2. Select Units.
3. Insert a unit code and give it a description.
4. Select the unit's physical quantity and give it a rounding factor.

Using Warehouses

Warehouses are your different company locations, or the different places you store goods in the same location. The warehouse is used for Inventory, Invoicing, Purchasing, as well as other Baan applications. It's important to have at least one warehouse set up, so that you can process orders.

Complete the following steps from Maintain Logistics Tables to create new warehouses:

1. Select Maintenance 3.
2. Select Warehouses.
3. Insert a warehouse code and give it a description.
4. Fill the other fields relevant to your warehouse.

Using Common Data

The *common data* are the data used in many other sessions for important information or sets of records. Complete the following steps to access the common data:

1. Go to the main menu.
2. Select Common.
3. Select Common Data.

Common data is accessible from all the modules, because you can limit access to the package, Baan Common, by all users for security reasons. You can make changes in common data to the Supplier Master, Customer master, your company data, and so on.

Using Company Data

You can specify different companies in Baan. Each company is attached to a set of data. An organization creates many companies for different projects, different entities, or as legal needs. Test companies are also very popular for program or customization testing. That way, none of your live data are modified by your test.

Specify each different company by a number. An address, language, and currency can also be specified when creating a new company.

Using Employee Data

You assign a number to your employees and enter all the information that concerns each particular person in the Employees file. Some of the items that might be tracked for an employee include:

- Name
- Address
- Email
- Birth date
- Hourly rate

The employee numbers are used as representative numbers in sales and many other places. To fill the table, assign a number to an employee name and enter all other fields relevant to the employee.

Using Customer Data

The *customer data* are the information used when entering an order, invoicing, doing a quote, getting a price, and so on. The Customer Master is very complete in regards to the amount of information you can fill out. It's important that you take your time making sure most of the fields are filled with the correct information. Different problems arise, if the information is incorrect, when it's time to enter an order or invoice a customer.

Certain information in the Customer Master cannot be changed (for example, financial customer groups). Various control accounts are defined in the financial customer groups and when you start entering transactions for a customer, you cannot change the customer group. These groups can also be used to print various reports such as aging, customer balances, and so on. Certain other information—order type, receipt method, and payment terms—are used as defaults and can be changed even after creating the transactions.

You can also create different delivery addresses and postal addresses for a customer. Create a delivery address if your customer doesn't always have goods shipped to the main address listed in its customer file. The *postal address* is an address where your customer wants paperwork sent. For example, a customer may have a street address, but prefer to get its invoice sent to its post office box. You can create a postal address for this customer, and the invoice program automatically prints that address on the invoice. If there is no postal address, the main address is used.

Using Supplier Data

The *supplier file* contains data that you can fill out for you supplier, similar to the way you can fill out customer data. This information is mainly used in the Purchasing module. You can also specify a postal address for your suppliers.

Part
III

Ch
12

Just as in the Customer Master data, financial supplier groups cannot be changed when trans-actions are entered for a supplier. Certain information that you enter here is used as default. Information such as order type can be changed during the creation of a purchase order. Other information, such as payment method and terms of payment, can be changed after invoice transactions are entered. ●

Understanding the Financial Tables and the General Ledger

Using Financial Tables and Parameters

The Finance module in Baan contains programs, processes, and reports required to produce the financial position of your company. This chapter explains the setup required, the processes, and the most important reports required for financial analysis. All information flows to the Finance module via the integration options (see Chapter 27, "Understanding the Integration Between the Modules"), making it critical that all areas of your company understand what information is required for financial reporting and analysis. Training your staff about requirements and the implication of transactions on the end results is imperative.

The Baan software is a tightly integrated system, which requires discipline of all your users. The result is accurate financial statements, flexibility in reporting, and transaction traceability throughout the system. Tables and parameters have to be set up for all the companies, including the consolidating companies you plan to set up in the Baan software. You may just have a single company or have multiple facilities world-wide.

The correct setup of the Finance tables and parameters is critical to the successful implementation of the Baan Finance module. These tables and parameters determine how the software reacts to the transactions you create and also ensures you the flexibility to create the reports that your company will need for its reporting purposes. This section explains the information that must be provided, which information is optional, and the significance of this information.

The Financial tables can be accessed in two ways:

1. Go to the Baan general/main menu.
2. Select Common, Tables, Maintain Financial Tables.

As an alternative, you can perform the following steps:

1. Go to the Baan general/main menu.
2. Select Finance, Tables, Maintain Financial Tables.

Like the Logistics tables, many Financial tables can be set up, but not all tables may be required by your company. Some companies can also opt to use the tables for different purposes. After you have read this section, you should be able to make the choices that are suitable to your company's needs.

Using Maintain Bank Addresses

Baan requires you to set up the name and address of each bank your company does business with. In the Cash Management Options, you can set up multiple accounts in multiple currencies against each bank address.

In order to set up the Bank Address tables, you must perform the following steps:

1. Go to Maintain Financial Tables, Bank Address.
2. Click the Insert icon and give the code a description.
3. Complete the remaining information, bank name, and address as required.

Using Maintain Currencies

Baan enables you to operate in multiple currencies. In order to do this, you must set up each of the currencies using the Maintain Currencies option. You are asked what description you will use to identify each currency you set up. Currency rates are also maintained from this option, as discussed in the next section.

In order to set up different currencies, you must perform the following steps:

1. Go to Maintain Financial Tables, Maintain Currencies.
2. Click the Insert icon.
3. Enter the currency description.
4. Fill in the long and short currency description forms.
5. Enter the *rounding factor* your company wants to use. This is the method that's used by the system to round off amounts in the currency concerned.

These steps can be repeated to set up as many currencies as your company requires.

Using Maintain Currency Rates

You have the option of changing the currency as frequently as you like by entering the effective date for each rate. You can set up different rates for use in the Purchasing and Sales modules if your company chooses to do business this way, or have them the same. These options enable each company to run their businesses in a fashion that suits them.

Complete the following steps to maintain currency rate changes:

1. Go to Maintain Financial Tables, Maintain Currency Rates.
2. Click the Insert icon.
3. Enter the effective date of the rate change and the currency rate to be used for purchasing and for sales.

Currency rates can be changed as frequently as your company requires. Figure 13.1 shows the Maintain Currency Rates screen.

Using Maintain First Free Numbers

First free numbers enable you to select which number you want to start with for numbering everything from purchase orders to sales orders to production orders to sales invoices. Different numbering series can be set up for each of your purchasing clerks or production control clerks. This feature allows unlimited flexibility in numbering.

You can set up the first free numbers in a different series, allowing different users to be identified by a designated number series. Perform the following steps to set up first free numbers:

1. Go to Maintain Financial Tables, Maintain First Free Numbers (see Figure 13.2).
2. Click the Insert icon to enter the type of number (Purchase Order, Sales Order, and so on).

FIG. 13.1

The Currency Rates screen is used to record the various changes in exchange for the currencies you use.

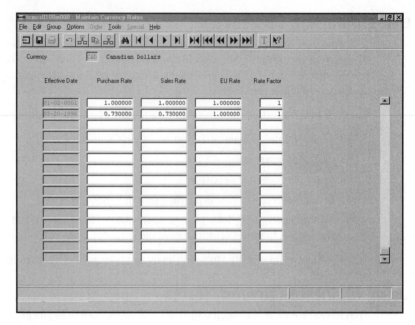

3. Select a series number and give the series number a description. Series 1 could have a description such as Purchasing Clerk #1 or John Doe, for example.

4. Enter the number at which you want to start.

 TIP You can block a numbering series from being used at any time. This is useful if an individual leaves your company or is transferred internally.

Using Maintain Invoicing Methods

This option enables you to set up what invoicing methods you will allow. When you set up your Customer Master, you are asked to select an invoicing method for your customer. Essentially, this determines whether multiple orders can be invoiced on one invoice or if there must be one invoice per order. Some of your customers may insist on one invoice per order and others may allow one invoice per shipment, regardless of how many orders are included.

Following are the steps you can use to set up the different invoicing methods:

1. Go to Maintain Financial Tables, Maintain Invoicing Methods.

2. Click the Insert icon to create a code for each method.

3. Set up the description based on your company's requirements.

FIG. 13.2
The First Free Number file records all the series number for each type of document.

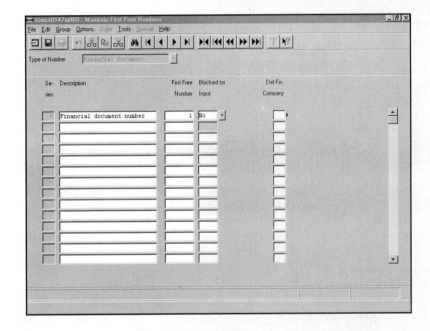

Using Maintain Late Payment Surcharges

This is where you can set up the late payment surcharges that you can charge customers for overdue invoices—this is optional. The codes you set up here are used in your Customer Masters.

In order to create late payment surcharges, you must perform the following steps:

1. Go to Maintain Financial Tables, Maintain Late Payment Surcharges.
2. Click the Insert icon to enter the assigned code.
3. Complete the remaining information as required.

Using Maintain VAT (Tax) Codes

You must set up codes in this section for the different tax situations that need to be applied against different purchased and sales items. Some items may be tax exempt, for example, and others may have city and state taxes applied. Still others may have only state taxes applied. You can set up 999 different tax options in the standard Baan software and these codes must be applied to the Item Masters as they are set up. Baan also has approved Alliance Partners available who provide add-on software to further enhance the capabilities in the standard software.

To set up VAT Codes, perform the following steps:

1. Go to Maintain Financial Tables, Maintain VAT Codes.
2. Click the Insert icon to create your user defined tax code.
3. Give the code a description.

Part
III

Ch
13

Using Maintain VAT Codes by Country

VAT codes by country enables you to further define your VAT codes by allowing you to specify code requirements for each country.

To maintain VAT codes by country, you must perform the following steps:

1. Go to Maintain Financial Tables, VAT Codes by Country (see Figure 13.3).

2. Click the Insert icon.

3. Enter the applicable country code that was set up in the Logistics tables.

4. Type in the VAT Code as defined in the VAT Code Option of the Financial tables.

5. Type in the remaining information as requested, including the VAT Ledger Account for Sales and Purchasing.

FIG. 13.3

You also have to create a record if no tax is applicable.

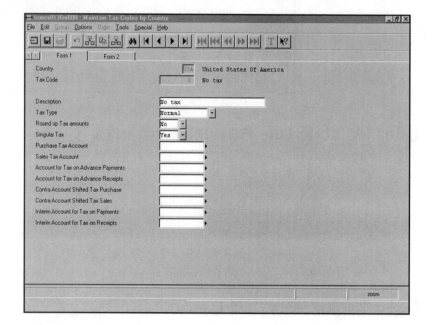

Using Maintain Terms of Payment

Your terms of payment codes are set up in this section. These terms can be applied to either Accounts Receivable or Accounts Payable. When the interest calculation is to be started if applicable is also defined in this section.

To create terms of payment codes, you must perform the following steps:

1. Go to Maintain Financial Tables, Maintenance 2 (at the bottom of the screen), Maintain Terms of Payment.

2. Enter the three-digit alphanumeric code you want to use.

3. Enter the description that applies to the code.

4. Enter the remaining information requested as is applicable to your organization.

Using Maintain Credit Insurance Companies

If your company uses credit insurance companies, they can be recorded appropriately in the Financial tables.

To set up credit Insurance companies in your system, perform the following steps:

1. Go to Maintain Financial Tables, Maintenance   2 (at the bottom of the screen), Maintain Credit Insurance Companies.

2. Enter the code you want to assign to the company.

3. Enter the name and address of the credit insurance company.

Using the General Ledger

In this section you learn how to set up the master data in the General Ledger module, including Ledger Accounts, Account Dimensions, and Company Data. You also learn how to perform the basic general ledger transactions, such as standard journal entries, recurring journal entries, account inquiries, and running general ledger reports. The Baan General Ledger options are almost endless, which makes it possible to meet almost any user requirement.

For purposes of this discussion, the general ledger section is divided into five sections:

- Master Data
- Transaction Processing
- Reports
- Financial Period Close
- Year-End Close

Using General Ledger Master Data

The Baan General Ledger Master data is where you define your periods for finance, tax reporting, your chart of accounts, dimensions, transaction types, and transaction schedules. The way Baan has created the software allows for much flexibility, making the software adaptable for almost any kind of business in any country.

It is very important to give a lot of thought to how you want to use the software for your business before you set up your master data in your company. You can use a test company to experiment with different settings until you find exactly what you are looking for. In addition, use the Baan Help text, as it is quite useful in describing the different options available.

Part
III

Ch
13

Using Maintain Group Company Parameters

The group company is the company that you use to perform your consolidation process, if possible. You can have many companies, all reporting to the group company. This is also where you set up the home currency to be used for the group company and the number of financial, reporting, and VAT periods you plan to use. Your company can opt to have, for example, 12 financial periods but only four reporting periods. These options largely depend on the type of company you have and what reporting regulations you have from your board of directors, government, or stock exchange regulatory board.

This is also where you indicate which dimensions your company will use. Dimensions are described in detail in the section, "Using Maintain Dimensions in General Ledger Master Data," later in this chapter, but it is recommended that you indicate all the dimensions to be used, because it is not feasible to turn the feature on after you are running your company live.

To maintain Group Company parameters, you must perform the following steps:

1. Go to Finance Module, Finance Parameters, Maintain Group Company Parameters.
2. Enter the name of the company you want to use.
3. Enter the country code from the Logistics Table.
4. Enter the currency you plan to use as the Home Currency.
5. Enter Yes against all the dimensions.
6. Enter Yes against the Reporting Periods.
7. Enter the number of financial, reporting, and VAT periods your company plans on using.
8. Save and exit to end in the Choice field to complete the entry.

Using Maintain Company Parameters

This is where you set up the company name and other information, including company address, current fiscal year, group company, name of the budget file being used, and so on.

To set up the above information in your system, you will have to perform the following steps:

1. Go to Finance Module, Finance Parameters, Maintain Company Parameters.
2. Enter your company name and address.
3. Enter your company's current fiscal year.
4. Enter the group company number and actual budget file being used.
5. Enter the Default Access by Batch option that is appropriate for your company. To see the list of options, press the space bar and they appear. For a description, click Help.
6. Enter the Default Finalization by Batch option that is appropriate for your company. To see the list of options, press the Spacebar and they appear. For a description, click Help.

TIP   If you want to get a printout automatically with each finalization run, enter Yes in this field.

If you have set up history company to use for archiving, you must enter the company number here. If you have not set one up, just leave it at zero.

In the next section, you have to set up the information required by the system to create the journal entries for currency differences. If you want a different account for each currency's differences to be charged, indicate Yes in this field.

To define these currency difference accounts, you will be required to do the following:

1. Enter the account number you want the system to use for recording currency differences.

2. Assign the transaction type that you want used for the Currency Difference journal entries.

3. Assign the account numbers you want to use for currency translations, rounding differences, and the interim closing account used by the system for processing the year end close.

4. Save and exit to end the input.

Using Maintain Periods in General Ledger Master Data   There are three types of Baan periods:

- Financial
- Reporting
- VAT (Tax)

The financial period is usually for defining in which period a transaction takes place. The reporting period is the one used for reporting the financial transactions. This could be monthly, quarterly, or any other period, but in most cases, companies have it the same as the financial period. The VAT (Tax) periods are used to coincide with the VAT or (Tax) period in which your company reports.

Periods can have a status of Open, Closed, or Finally Closed. A period that has been closed can be reopened, but no additional transactions can be posted to it once it has been closed. Once it has been Finally Closed, however, it cannot be reopened.

Complete the following steps to set up your company's periods:

1. Go to Finance, General Ledger, Master Data, Maintain Periods (see Figure 13.4).

2. Click Special and maintain the end dates for the year.

3. Click the Form Insert icon to enter the period type: fiscal, reporting, or VAT.

4. Enter the year.

5. Click the Insert icon to enter the periods and their descriptions.

6. Enter the start date for each of the periods.

7. Save and exit and record the data you have input.

Part
III

Ch
13

FIG. 13.4

The different periods must be defined in this table.

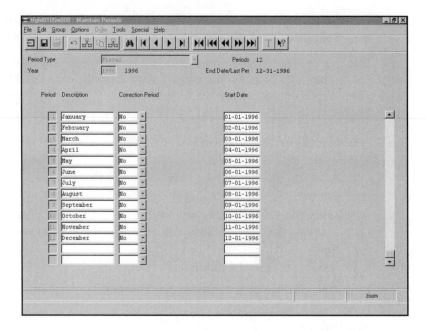

Using Maintain Chart of Accounts in General Ledger Master Data   The general ledger in this software is the key to being able to pull the financial information your organization will require to run and analyze the success of the business activity. When setting up the chart of accounts, you need to think ahead about what information you want to see and how you would like it sorted. If you set up your chart of accounts correctly, you will find that the Baan software is a powerful tool for reporting and analyzing financial data.

Baan works on a parent-child relationship where many child accounts automatically total up to a parent account. The parents can then total to a grandparent and so on. Always remember that in Baan a parent can have unlimited children but a child can have only one parent.

This parent-child relationship also exists when you are setting up your Dimensions, which is discussed in the next section, "Using Maintain Dimensions in General Ledger Master Data." A child account should be a zero sublevel, and you can only create entries to zero sublevel accounts. Any accounts with a sublevel greater than zero are strictly used as parent accounts, which are used for subtotaling.

Additional account numbers can be set up at any time and can also be restricted from manual input or totally restricted if the need arises just by entering that fact in the appropriate field of the master. The restriction can be time-limited also by entering the effective dates. Follow these steps to maintain your chart of accounts:

1. Go to Finance, General Ledger, Master Data, Maintain Chart of Accounts (see Figure 13.5).

2. Click the Insert icon to enter the account number for your first account.

FIG. 13.5

Each account must be created by using this function, you can specify whether the dimensions are applicable to this ledger account.

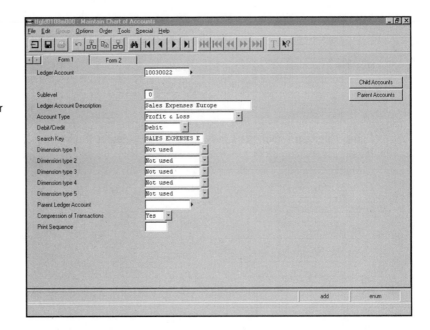

3. Assign a sublevel to the account, keeping in mind that a child account should be the zero sublevel and that you can only create entries to zero sublevel accounts. Any accounts with a sublevel greater than zero are strictly used as parent accounts, which are used for subtotaling.

4. Assign a description to the account.

5. Select the account type from the list of Balance Sheet, Profit and Loss, Inter-Company, or Text.

6. Select whether this account's "normal" balance is a Debit or a Credit.

7. Assign a Search Key description for the account.

8. Decide whether or not this account has a dimension attached to it. You can always add the dimension capability at a later date, but due to information that accumulates in the history, you can't remove the dimension capability from it. This is indicated by choosing Mandatory, Optional, or Not Used in the Dimension field.

9. Assign the parent account number to the account.

N O T E Set up your highest level of parents first and work backward to the child accounts. ▪

10. Select Yes for Compression of Transactions if you don't want to see all the detail in your general ledger.

11. On Page 2 of the Chart of Accounts input screen, indicate whether you want unit information to show on your inquiries. This is usually most applicable to sales and inventory accounts.

Part

III

Ch

13

12. Choose to have your account history stored in either Home Currency or in another currency by choosing the appropriate option in the Currency Analysis field.

N O T E The Blocking Status and Blocking Effective Dates enable you to block manual or all transactions for a given time range. ▪

13. Save and exit.

Using Maintain Dimensions in General Ledger Master Data The Baan software enables you the option of using up to five different dimensions to further define and classify data. You have complete freedom to assign the dimensions to whatever you want to. The following are some examples of what you can use them for:

- ▪ Cost Center/Department
- ▪ Projects
- ▪ Assets Under Construction

As mentioned previously, dimensions have the same structure as ledger accounts in that they have the parent-child relationship. You can also block transactions to certain dimensions by indicating that in the master file.

Accounts can be restricted for use with certain dimensions, which again enhances the flexibility of the Baan software. The account set up for audit expenses, for example, could only be charged against the dimension for cost center Finance, or the account set up for tooling expenses could only be charged to the cost center for Manufacturing.

If you decide that Dimension 1 is used for the cost center, then use a different dimension for projects and other dimensions. Remember that it is difficult to change your dimension setup once you are running live due to the history in the system. This means it is very important that you think clearly how you want to see your data to appear before going live.

Perform the following steps to maintain dimensions:

1. Go to Finance, General Ledger, Master Data, Maintain Dimensions (see Figure 13.6).
2. Click the insert icon to enter the dimension type for your first dimension. You have a choice of five dimension types.
3. Enter the dimension number you have assigned.
4. Assign a description to the dimension.
5. Assign a sublevel to the dimension, keeping in mind that a child dimension should be the zero sublevel and that you can only create entries to zero sublevel dimensions. Any dimensions with a sublevel greater than zero are strictly used as parent dimensions for subtotaling.
6. Enter the Parent Dimension. As with the chart of accounts, you must enter your dimensions starting with the highest level so that parents are already set up as you need them.

7. Assign the Search key for the dimension.

8. You have the option of assigning a person responsible for each dimension. This information comes from the Employee Master data set up in the Logistics tables.

9. If required, complete the Blocking Status information.

10. Save and exit.

FIG. 13.6

The dimensions can be used as departments, areas, territories, and so on.

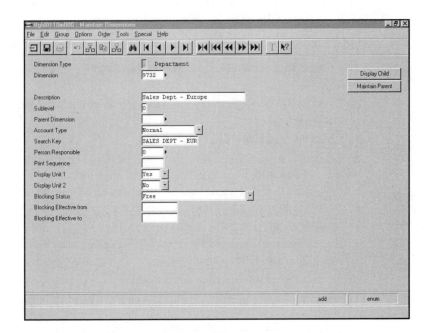

Using Maintain Dimension Ranges by Ledger Account   As indicated in the "Using Maintain Dimensions in General Ledger Master Data" section, you can assign certain ledger accounts to be restricted to use with only specific or specific ranges of dimensions. This is done via the Maintain Dimension Ranges by Ledger Account option. The default in the Baan system is that any ledger account is open to use by all dimensions.

In order to maintain dimension ranges by ledger account, you must do the following:

1. Go to Finance, General Ledger, Master Data, Maintain Dimensions.

2. Click the Form Insert icon to enter the ledger account to be restricted.

3. Enter the dimension type to be restricted.

4. Click the Insert icon to create the range of dimensions you require. You can enter single or multiple dimensions or ranges of dimensions.

5. Save and exit.

Part

III

Ch

13

Using Maintain Transaction Types Baan uses the transaction types for grouping like transactions. You can assign a transaction type for journal entries, for example, another for Recurring Journals, another for accounts payable invoices that link to purchase orders, and yet another for invoices for utility payments.

When setting up your transaction types, you must assign the series that defines the number all transactions of this type start with. You also have to assign Baan session numbers, so that the system knows what the intent of this transaction type is.

In order to maintain transaction types, you must perform the following steps:

1. Go to Finance, General Ledger, Master Data, Maintain Transaction Types (see Figure 13.7).

2. Click the Insert icon to assign three-digit alphanumeric name for the transaction type you are setting up.

3. Give the transaction type a description.

4. Select the transaction category by pressing the space bar once in the field and selecting one of the types that appears. The Help text gives a full description of each type. Some of the choices include Journal Voucher, Sales Invoices, Purchase Invoices, and Cash.

5. If you select Cash, you have to enter the Contra Account, which is usually your bank ledger account for that transaction type. This forces you to have different transaction types for transactions in each currency if you use separate bank accounts by currency. Doing this helps to keep your bank accounts easy to reconcile.

6. Define whether you will allow negative amounts to be keyed for this transaction type.

7. Define your series number, which is the digit or digits that begin your transaction number for each of the transaction types defined. After keying in the Default Series, the system gives you a message: Series is not defined for transaction type. Press Return. Press Return and continue.

8. In the Update Mode field, you have the option of Real Time, End of Session, and Finalization. It is up to your company to decide how they plan on using the Baan software. The Help text gives excellent information about the different options.

9. For sales and purchasing transaction types, you have to fill in whether negative amounts are allowed.

10. On Form 2 of the transaction type maintenance, you can use the predefined session links or can enter the main session and the next session number. These are the numbers that appear on the top-left corner of each screen. To find the correct session numbers for each transaction type, refer to the Help text.

11. Set up the series for the transaction type as indicated in Step 7. Zoom and complete the screen that appears.

12. Exit the screens until you are back to the Master Data screen. This process is complete.

FIG. 13.7

A transaction type is created for use with all the different set of transactions you use.

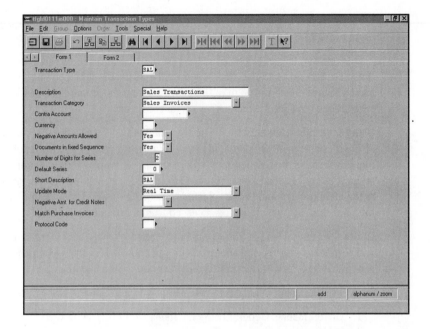

Using Maintain Transaction Schedules Transactions schedules are a tool that you can use to allocate standard amounts to a standard series of accounts/dimensions by percentage or by amount. These schedules can be used for journal entries or for accounts payable. These schedules are easily changed and maintained. A transaction schedule can provide a template for creating repetitive journal entries. The template can specify default account numbers and amounts to create an actual journal. The default values may be overridden at the time of the journal entry.

You must complete the following steps in order to maintain transaction schedules:

1. Go to Finance, General Ledger, Master Data, Maintain Transaction Schedules.
2. Click the Insert icon to create the three-digit alphanumeric code you have assigned.
3. Enter the description of the schedule to be entered.
4. Select Percentage or Amounts.
5. Click the Save icon to write the record to the system.

For a percentage transaction schedule, enter the details of the transaction by selecting the appropriate transaction schedule. To do this, click the record. A screen comes up, asking you for the Ledger Account, VAT code (if applicable), the percentage to be charged to the account, debit or credit, and a Reference field that enables you to enter a description of the entry.

For an amount transaction schedule, you would follow the same procedure. First, enter the details of the transaction by selecting the appropriate transaction schedule. To do this, click the record. A screen appears, asking you for the Ledger Account, VAT code (if applicable), Debit or Credit, and a reference field that enables you to enter a description for the entry.

Click the Insert icon to create the next line. Continue entering lines until the percentage at the bottom comes to zero. If it does not come to zero, it gives you a message at the bottom of the screen.

If you are entering a transaction schedule that is in amounts, you only have to enter the account numbers at this point in time. You can add the amounts as you know them. Then, save and exit to accept what has been entered so far.

Using Maintain Transactions   The General Ledger Transaction Processing Option is where all batches are maintained and finalized. All integration and finance batches flow through this menu, which can be restricted by user. You can set it up so that individuals can maintain transactions, but not finalize them. You can also set your system so that certain users are only able to maintain transactions using selected transaction types. These restrictions are set up using the Tools module, which can be accessed from the Baan main menu.

Under the general ledger, you can create regular journal entries, create recurring (standard and reversing) entries, and amend recurring entries. It is also possible to pull a transaction schedule (described earlier in this chapter) into a journal entry.

To access the maintain transaction sessions, you must do the following:

1. Go to Finance, General Ledger, Transaction Processing (see Figure 13.8).

2. Select Maintain Transactions.

FIG. 13.8

This screen enables you to create a batch for a General Ledger Transaction.

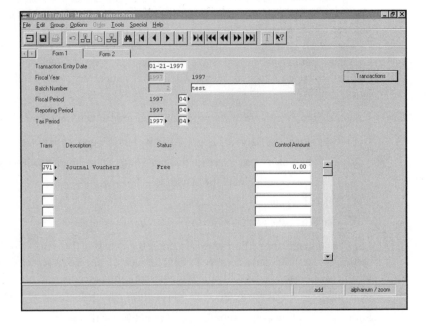

Now you are ready to create your journal entry. When setting up a journal entry, the transaction entry date is critical. The date determines which period the Journal Voucher will post to. To create a journal entry, you must perform the following steps:

1. Click the Insert icon to create the transaction type, then click Save to write the record.
2. Click the transaction type to be processed.
3. Enter the Document Number field.
4. Enter date (pulls date from batch screen), enter Currency for journal entry or take default, enter country or take the default, and enter VAT period.

At this point you have a choice of entering a regular journal, a journal using a transaction schedule, or a recurring journal. Each of the options is described in detail in the following sections. Figure 13.9 shows the detail screen.

FIG. 13.9

The detail screen for the ledger transactions is superimposed on the Header screen.

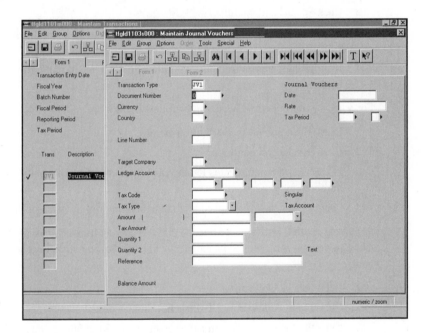

Creating Regular Journal Entries In order to create regular journal entries, you must complete the following steps:

1. Click the Insert icon to create the first line of the journal voucher.
2. Enter ledger account and dimension(s) if required.
3. Enter the amount for the line you are entering.
4. For reference, enter a description to explain your entry.
5. Take the defaults for all other fields.
6. Click the Insert icon to create the next line, and so on.

7. Before exiting Maintain Journal Vouchers, ensure that the balance amount at the bottom of the screen is zero.

Creating Journal from Transaction Schedule   To create a journal entry from a transaction schedule, follow these steps:

1. Click the special options to select Create Journal Option.
2. Click Create Transaction from Schedule.
3. Zoom and find the desired transaction schedule.
4. Click the schedule and the Save icon. This pulls it back to the screen for processing.

For a transaction schedule by percentage, follow these steps:

1. Enter the total amount to be distributed.
2. Click Special and continue.
3. When the system indicates Ready, click the Save icon. This pulls back the schedule for you.
4. If a rounding amount remains, you must adjust a line to make the balance amount come to zero.

For a transaction schedule by amounts, follow these steps:

1. Leave the amount for distribution at zero.
2. Click Special and continue.
3. When the system indicates Ready, click the Save icon. This pulls through the account numbers for you.
4. Line by line, click the record to change and enter in the value for each ledger account.

Recurring Journal Entries   To ensure that the correct transaction type has been set up in order to process this type of journal, perform the following steps to process a recurring journal entry:

1. Click Special Options.
2. Click Maintain Recurring Transaction Instructions.
3. Click the Insert icon to enter the creation date(s) of future entries. The date determines which year and period(s) in which the entries recur. Always use the same creation date for each period, such as the first day of each period.
4. In the Reversal column, enter:
    - Yes to reverse entries on the date indicated.
    - No for standard entries in the period(s) indicated.
    - E to end and the system returns to the Maintain Journal Vouchers screen.
5. Enter the journal entry as described in the section "Regular Journal Entries."

Select Batches for Finalization   Batches are not committed to the general ledger until they are finalized. The key to successfully finalizing batches is to finalize each batch individually and print out the report. It is important that you check that batches are posting to the correct financial/reporting/VAT periods. Also check summary totals and look for anything unusual that may have happened.

The system cannot finalize any existing batch errors. The system prints an audit list identifying the error. You can go to the batch in question, retrieve it, and correct it. If it states that the "Background Process Not Yet Completed," you have to "Invoke Background Process."

N O T E   It is a good idea to print non-finalized entries when you first start using Baan. It is possible to print to a printer or to display on the screen, and it highlights if there is a problem. You are able to correct any problems before you finalize the batch. ▪

Display/Delete Error Log   If a batch does not finalize, additional information is available in this inquiry by batch, line, and sequence number. To view error logs, follow these steps:

1. Go to Transaction Processing.
2. Click Inquiries.
3. Select Display Error Log.

N O T E   It is important to delete any error logs that have been resolved. This keeps only current errors on file. ▪

Display/Create Recurring Transactions   To view a list of the recurring transactions that have been created, follow these steps:

1. Go to the Transaction Processing menu.
2. Click Display Recurring Transaction Instructions.

It is possible for you to display by Creation Date which batches have recurring transactions associated with them. It indicates if the entry is a reversal or a standard entry and if the journal has been created. It is important to always use the same creation date for each period—the first day of each period. You cannot close a financial period without creating all recurring transactions for that period.

When creating recurring transactions for a period, ensure that you are using the correct creation date and batch number. Once the transaction has been created, you can go to Maintain Transactions and make the necessary adjustments (if required) to the batch. After the adjustments have been made, you can finalize the batch.

Change Access Mode by Batch   If you have set your Finance parameters in such a way that batches are restricted for access by the user who created that batch (Unique User), you need to use this option to retrieve a batch that belongs to another user. Before continuing, ensure that the batch has not been finalized.

Part
III
Ch
13

This option should be restricted to key users and should only be used to look at batches as the need arises. To do this, change the Access mode for batch from Unique User to All Users and click the Save icon to write record. You are now able to access the batch through Maintain Transactions.

N O T E If you find that a batch does not finalize and the error message says "Invoke Background Process not yet Complete," go to the Invoke Background Option and invoke by year, batch, and document. Click Special and continue to process the information. ■

Using Inquiries and Reports

The inquiries and reports available on these menus are very useful in financial analysis for your accounting staff and management. There are many ways of sorting information on the display options and the Zoom features are excellent for drilling down on transactions.

To access the Inquiries and Reports menu, go to Finance, General Ledger, Inquiries and Reports.

Display Ledger History   Always ensure that your default values are correct (year, period, budget). You have the option of including non-finalized entries in your inquiries.

After your defaults have been set, click Save and exit. Enter the ledger account and the system displays totals for the period selected (see Figure 13.10). Select from Options the function to list all transactions for that period.

FIG. 13.10

Ledger History is the fastest way to get at a glance all the information about a ledger account and the summary of the transactions entered.

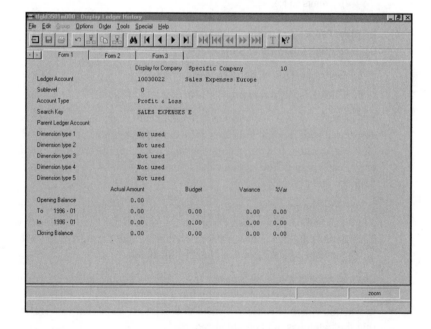

If you click the Special Options, you can select an option to specify how you want your information for this ledger account sorted. For example, if you select Dimension 1 for the sort and you are using that dimension to represent cost center, you see the detail for that ledger account by cost center. Click the line (Cost Center) you would like to see and the system lists the transactions. You can then zoom on a document to obtain additional information.

Display Dimension History   This inquiry is basically the same as Display Ledger History, except that it sorts by dimension. This option is excellent for management; they can view the costs for their dimension (cost center). Follow the previous steps—but this time look at dimensions for a particular period, and sorting possibly by ledger account (other options are also available).

Print Finalized Transactions by Ledger Account   This report prints the detail for ledger account(s), by transaction type, document, and financial period ranges. Take defaults or set specific ranges, depending on the kind of analysis you require.

Print Finalized Transactions by Dimension/Ledger   This report prints the detail for a dimension, ledger account, by transaction type, document, and financial period Ranges. Take defaults or set specific ranges, depending on the kind of analysis you require.

Print Trial Balance   This report prints ledger account balances for a particular period. Take defaults or set specific ranges. Print including or excluding the budget variance, and ensure the correct financial period and budget are selected.

Print Trial Balance with Dimensions   This report is useful for your management's review of dimension (cost center) and for your accounting staff to compare actual to budget by dimension/ledger account. Take defaults or set specific ranges. Print including or excluding the budget variance. Ensure the correct financial period and budget are selected.

Print Trial Balance by Currency   If you deal with multiple currencies, this report is excellent for totals in foreign and home currency. It is very useful to balance your bank accounts. Take the defaults or set specific ranges. Ensure the correct financial period is selected.

Using Periodic Processing

The Periodic Processing menu contains all the options required to process your financial period close. These are options that must be processed to successfully complete a period close. Go to Finance, General Ledger, Periodic Processing to access this menu.

Maintain/Display Period Status   Maintain period status is used if you are required to reopen any modules for a particular financial period. The first step is to ensure that your period type VAT for all modules is set to Open for the period to be reopened.

Next, ensure that the period type Fiscal for the module being reopened is set to Open. Click the Save icon to write. For example, to reopen GLD for period nine, first reopen period nine for the period type VAT for all modules (ACP, ACR, CMG, GLD); reopen period type Fiscal for GLD period nine. After the necessary adjustments have been made and finalized, reset all modules for Period Type—Fiscal and VAT to Closed for the period in question.

Close Periods   Close periods is used to close Accounts Payable, Accounts Receivable, Cash Management, and General Ledger modules. Always close period type Fiscal for each module as you are ready to close them. After all modules are closed for the Fiscal Period Type, it is then possible to close all modules for the period type VAT Before a period can be completely closed, each module must be closed.

N O T E   Final closing should always be set at No unless you are absolutely sure you will not need to reopen to perform any adjusting entries. ■

You can leave periods with a status of Closed until year end and perform the Finally Closed procedure during the year-end process. Do not close the period type Reporting until year-end processing is done.

Calculate Currency Differences   If you deal with multiple currencies, this process is required. Calculate Currency Difference revalues the balance of ledger accounts that have the Currency Analysis (option is located in Maintain Chart of Accounts) set to Required, Calc. Curr Diff at a particular date. This option is mainly used to revalue the bank accounts.

Before this process can be run, all batches must be finalized. Ensure that you are revaluing the correct financial period and that the transaction entry date and the financial/reporting periods are set correctly. This determines the exchange rate used and the period to which the entry posts. It is therefore recommended that all batches be finalized on a monthly basis.

Rebuild Opening Balance/History from Transactions   Occasionally, transactions can get posted and finalized to the incorrect period. Once they have been corrected and are in the proper period, a rebuild for the entire financial year must be processed in order to reset balances to Actual. Ensure that no one is working on the Finance module while this process is being run. ●

Understanding the Finance Sub-Ledgers

Understanding the Cash Modules

Baan's Finance module contains many modules to assist you with running your business. The previous chapter, "Understanding the Financial Tables and the General Ledger," reviewed Baan's Financial tables, Finance parameters, and the general ledger module. This chapter reviews the modules that control your business's cash functions: Accounts Receivable, Accounts Payable, and Cash Management. As with the general ledger, information flows from Sales and Receiving to Accounts Receivable and Accounts Payable via the Integration module.

The Baan Cash modules are very tightly integrated with the rest of the system and requires the discipline of all your users. The result is accurate financial records, flexibility in reporting, and transaction traceability throughout the system.

Using Accounts Receivable

The Accounts Receivable menu contains the tools you need to effectively monitor your company's cash receivable activities. This section explains the setup required as well as the processes and reports you need to analyze your accounts receivable.

All sales order invoices flow to the Accounts Receivable module via the Integration options. This makes it important that your Baan finance and sales personnel be well trained and understand the information required for financial reporting and analysis. Training is one of the elements central to your implementation's success.

▶ **See** "Integrating Sales Transactions," **p. 449**

Using Master Data for Accounts Receivable

You must create master data before proceeding with any of the Baan modules. This master data is the information the system uses to perform its functions. Every company has a slightly different set of master data, depending upon requirements.

Master data for accounts receivable consists of the following:

- ACR parameters
- Financial customer groups
- Problem codes (Optional)
- Problems references (Optional)
- Aging analysis data (Optional)

N O T E In the context of accounts receivable master data, ACR is an acronym for accounts receivable.

Each of these types of master data is explained in the following sections.

Using Maintain ACR Parameters   You are required to enter the information in the ACR parameters that the system needs to report your company's accounts receivable status correctly. You also need to use this section to set up the information the system needs to create the credit control letters. The use of these letters is optional. It is also important to define the invoice control account, as shown in Figure 14.1. Follow these steps to use ACR parameters:

1. Go to Finance, Accounts Receivable, Maintain ACR Parameters.

2. The first screen is where you must insert your transaction type for sales invoices (and the ledger control account and dimension account, if applicable). You must enter any payment surcharges information here, as well.

3. In the first screen's Miscellaneous section, you are asked to enter the level at which you are calculating your taxes. Some companies want to do this at the transaction line, others by invoice. The Payment and Currency Difference transactions types must be entered.

4. On the second screen, you are asked to enter the Credit Control parameters. These vary greatly from company to company. It is best to use the Help text, as there are far too many options to explore here.

5. End the data entry by exiting and saving.

These steps are critical to using Baan Accounts Receivable.

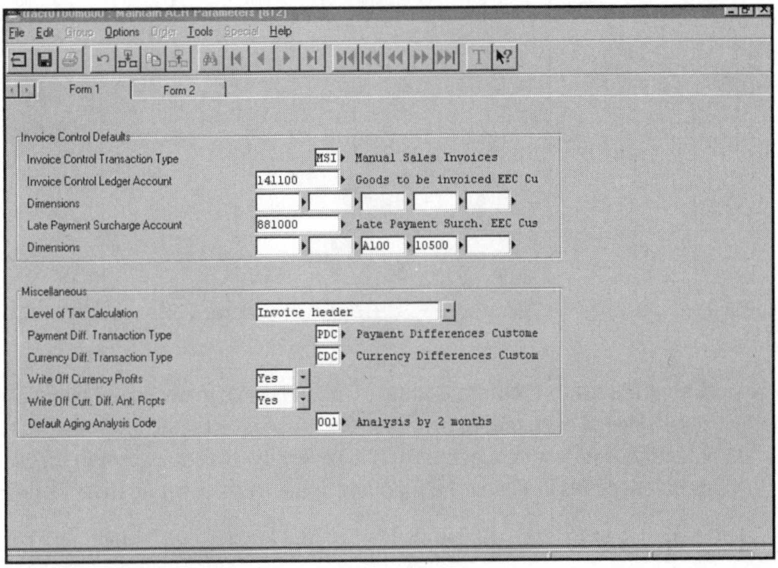

FIG. 14.1

In the Accounts Receivable Parameters session you must define in what invoice control account the accounts receivable information will be posted.

Using Maintain Financial Customer Groups   Baan software uses financial customer groups to define the currency in which a particular customer does business with your company. This is the section that allows you to set up the ledger accounts used by any transactions relating to each customer assigned a specific financial customer group (see Figure 14.2). Follow these steps to maintain financial customer groups:

1. Go to Finance, Accounts Receivable, Master Data, Maintain Financial Receivable Groups.

2. Click the Insert icon to insert the three-digit customer group code.

3. Click the Save icon to write the record.

4. Click the record to select it. This shows you all the control accounts that you need to assign to the customer group. Examples include the accounts receivable control account and the advance payment account.

5. Click the Save icon to write the record when all entry is complete, and click the Exit icon to quit the session.

Repeat these steps to set up all your required financial customer groups. Each organization requires different types of groups.

FIG. 14.2

Each customer must be assigned to a financial group. By doing so, you determine what ledger account is used by default.

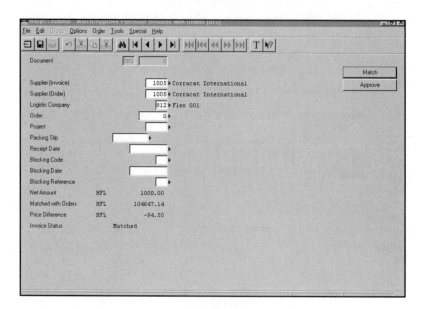

Using Maintain Problem Codes   One of Baan's many useful features include assigning problem codes to outstanding invoices. Their use is optional, but it makes these accounts easy to identify when your collection staff is reviewing overdue accounts. You see some examples of problem codes in Figure 14.3. Follow these steps to set up these codes:

1. Go to Finance, Accounts Receivable, Master Data, Maintain Problem Codes.

2. Click the Insert icon to create your alphanumeric problem code.

3. Enter the code's description.

4. Enter the problem reference code.

5. Either click the Insert icon to create another or exit the session.

Those codes can be assigned to any outstanding invoices to indicate why the customer did not pay the open balance.

FIG. 14.3
Problem codes are a good tool designed to explain why outstanding invoices are not yet paid.

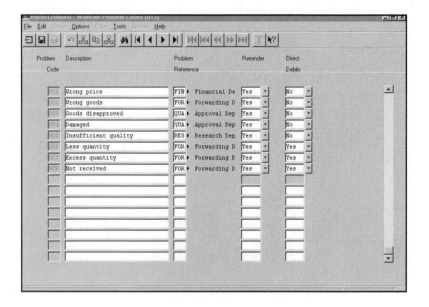

Using Maintain Problem References

As with problem codes, the use of problem references is optional—but can only be used if you are using problem codes. This feature allows you to assign a username to the problem code, which identifies who or what department is responsible for following up on the problem. Follow these steps to set up problem references:

1. Go to Finance, Accounts Receivable, Master Data, Maintain Problem Reference
2. Click the Insert icon to create your alphanumeric Problem Reference.
3. Enter the reference's description.
4. Insert another code or exit the session.

You have created your problem reference codes. You can add to this list whenever the need arises.

Using Maintain Aging Analysis Data

The aging analysis data is used to age your accounts receivable in a manner suitable to your company. You can define several methods of aging the open accounts receivable. For example, you could age your accounts receivable by 30, 60, 90, 120, 150, and 999 days, as shown in Figure 14.4.

N O T E The number of days and the interval for aging accounts receivable is at your discretion. These numbers do not have to be multiples of any other number, even or odd, nor do they have any other limitation. That makes the aging analysis work the way your company works—even if that means aging accounts receivable by 12, 23, and 108 days. ▪

As you run your accounts receivable aging reports, you can select any way you have defined in the aging analysis data to get different views of the same data. Follow these steps to establish your aging analysis criteria:

Part
III

Ch
14

FIG. 14.4

You can define various periods to analyze your accounts receivable aging periods.

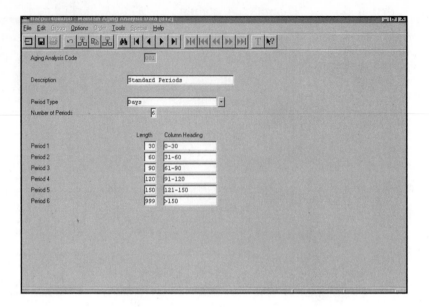

1. Go to Finance, Accounts Receivable, Master Data, Maintain Aging Analysis Data.

2. Click the Insert icon to create your desired code number (alphanumeric).

3. Enter the code's description.

4. Select the appropriate option: Days, Months, and so on. This period type relates to the number you select in the next two options.

   The Number of Periods is how many columns you can have. The maximum is six. The value you choose for the length of each period depends on how you have set up the previous options. An example is setting the Period type for Days, and the Number of Periods at 4. You could set the length of the first period to 30. That gives you all outstanding invoices in 30 days or less.

5. In the Column Heading field, you should enter the description that you want to see on the report heading for the column being defined.

6. Either click the Insert icon to create another code or exit the session.

Remember that you can set up different options, which offers you virtually unlimited reporting options.

Using Transactions Processing for Accounts Receivable

The transaction processing section of any module is used for performing any activities that update existing transaction information or add new transaction information to the module. In the case of accounts receivable, transaction processing is used to process invoices, cash receipts, and linking credit notes to invoices, thus reducing the open balance of the invoices.

A brief listing of some of the activities you can perform using the Accounts Receivable transaction Processing option in Baan follows:

- All cash receipts are maintained in this menu. Posting sales integration daily ensures accurate and up-to-date financial records. Sales order invoices do not appear in the Accounts Receivable module until the Process Delivered Sales Order option (located in the Distribution menu, Sales Order module) is complete and integrations are posted.

- It is possible to settle supplier invoices (for example, commissions payable to customers) by clearing off the accounts payable balance and creating a dummy cash receipt. Set the contra account on the transaction type to a Liability Clearing Account.

- If a cash receipt check is returned from the bank because of insufficient funds (NSF), it is possible to reinstate the invoice(s) allocated against that check.

- Internal miscellaneous sales invoice adjustments, allocating unallocated receipts, and sales credit allocations are also maintained in this menu.

- Always print nonfinalized reports and verify that the information is correct before finalizing any batches.

You must complete these steps to maintain transactions:

1. Go to Finance, Accounts Receivable, transaction Processing.
2. Select Maintain transactions.
3. The transaction entry date (deposit date) is critical when setting up an accounts receivable batch for processing. The date determines which period the receivable entries will post.
4. Click the Insert icon to create the Accounts Receivable transaction type.
5. Click the transaction type to be processed. Some of the options include:

   - Cash Receipts (Cash receipts can also be processed in the cash management area)
   - Allocation of Unallocated Receipt
   - Sales Credit Allocation
   - Miscellaneous Sales Invoice

These steps allow you to perform any type of transaction necessary to maintain your accounts receivable ledgers.

Processing Cash Receipts

If you selected the transaction type for cash receipts, you must perform the following steps to complete the transaction:

1. The Maintain Bank Balance screen appears if you are using control totals. Set the opening balance to 0 and the closing balance to the deposit total. You see a Cash Receipts screen.

Part
III

Ch
14

2. Enter the Document Number field. This automatically assigns a document number to the transaction. Enter the deposit date in the Document Date field. Click the Enumerated Field icon to get the different options at the Type of transaction field. Some of the commonly used options include:

   - Unallocated Receipt for a Customer Check
   - Journal for a Miscellaneous Check (A *miscellaneous check* is one that is unrelated to a customer account receivable.)

3. The system asks for the following if you choose an unallocated receipt:

   - Customer Number—Enter or zoom on this field to find the customer number.
   - Amount—Enter check value.
   - Reference—Enter the customer name and check number if you want detail to post to the general ledger and to the accounts receivable open entries.

4. Click Special, and then on Continue. This updates the cash receipt as an unallocated receipt to the customer account. The system goes into the Assign Unallocated/Advance Receipts to Invoices screen. This screen lists the customer's open invoices.

NOTE   Outstanding unallocated cash receipts do not appear in the Assign Unallocated/Advance Receipts to Invoice screen. ▪

5. Click the Customer Invoice line to change and match the cash receipt to the invoice(s) using either the manual or automatic method. Manual is used if you are partially allocating an invoice. Ensure that the correct amount is being allocated to the invoice. *Automatic* is used for allocating exactly what the invoice amount is.

6. If all of the check value is to be allocated, ensure that the balance amount is zero before updating. Click Special, and then on Continue to process the receipt allocation.

If the receipt is a prepayment or your customer sent more than they should have, you cannot allocate it all to an invoice(s). This means that an unallocated receipt is left on the customer account.

If you choose a journal in Step 2, the system asks that you perform the following tasks (see Figure 14.5):

1. Enter the check value in Amount. The system asks whether it's debit or credit.

2. Enter the description of what the check is for in the Reference field.

3. Click Special, and then on Continue. The system goes to the Maintain Cash Management transactions screen.

4. Enter the ledger account, dimension(s) you want to allocate the receipt.

5. Enter in the VAT country/code (if required), or enter past this field.

6. Enter the amount for ledger account. Enter to go to the Choice field.

7. Click the Save icon to write the record. If there are further allocations for the check, click the Insert icon to create another entry and repeat the previous steps.

8. Ensure that the remaining amount is zero before you end.

9. Exit from Cash Receipts after all receipts are entered.

N O T E If the total entered does not equal the closing balance when exiting cash receipts, the system does not allow you to end the batch. Either adjust the closing balance or adjust the cash receipts entered. ■

Those are the steps you need to know for recording your company's cash receipts for both accounts receivable and for miscellaneous cash receipts. In some instances, you will not be able to allocate these cash receipts at the time of receipt. The following section provides information you need to perform this task.

FIG. 14.5

This is how cash receipts are recorded to remove open invoices from the accounts receivable.

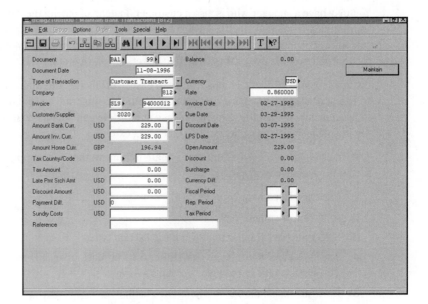

Allocating Unallocated Receipts/Credit Notes to Invoices

It is important, where possible, to keep updated records. Investigate regularly unallocated receipts and credit notes, and clear them.

Perform the following tasks when you need to allocate these unallocated cash receipts and credit notes:

1. Enter the customer number or zoom on the field to find the customer number.

2. Click the applicable unallocated receipt or credit note you want assigned.

3. Assign cash receipt or credit note values to the appropriate invoices.

4. Click the Special button, and then on Continue to update.

5. Click past the Maintain Document Numbers screen and the system automatically assigns the next available document number.

6. Click Exit to return to the main screen.

7. Click Exit to return to the Maintain transactions screen.

Allocating unallocated receipts enable you to remove invoices from the aged trial balance by assigning those amounts to existing open invoices.

Settling Supplier Invoices

You may have a supplier who is also a customer. Instead of paying the supplier, it may be more appropriate for you to settle the invoice by reducing the amount the supplier owes you on the customer accounts receivable ledger. When settling supplier invoices, it is important to remember that you process two entries, which in effect cancel each other out.

If you are using the control totals feature to ensure balancing, the Maintain Bank Balance screen appears after you have entered your Cash Receipts transaction type in the Maintain transaction screen. Set the opening balance and the closing balance to 0. The system goes to the Maintain Bank transaction screen when you exit.

The first step is to process a dummy payment to remove the outstanding invoice in the supplier accounts payable ledger:

1. Click the Document Number field.

2. Enter the document date.

3. Select Supplier transaction for the transaction type.

4. The system asks for the invoice. Enter the Purchase Invoice Document type and number. The system pulls in the invoice details and values.

5. Enter an explanation in the Reference field.

6. Click Special, and then on Continue to update the record. This allocates a normal payment to the supplier invoice.

The second step is to process a dummy cash receipt to show a credit on the supplier's accounts receivable record. It shows a reduced balance rather that making a payment to the supplier:

1. Click the Insert icon to create a new document.

2. Click the Document Number field.

3. Enter the document date.

4. Select Unallocated Receipt for the transaction type.

5. Enter the customer number or zoom on this field to find the customer number.

6. Enter the amount of the supplier invoice to be settled.

7. Enter an explanation in the Reference field.

8. Click Save icon to write the record.

9. The balance field in top-right corner of screen should be 0. If so, click Exit to end. If not, go back and look at the transactions you have done and make the necessary correction(s).

After these steps have been completed there is no longer be a liability on the account payable ledger for your supplier, but its customer record is reduced on the accounts receivable ledger.

Processing Nonsufficient Funds (NSF) Checks and Reinstating Sales Invoices

When you are reinstating sales invoices due to a customer's NSF check, it is important to remember that the closing balance is the negative check value. The Maintain Bank Balance screen appears if you are using control totals. Set the opening balance to 0 and the closing balance to the negative check value. Click Exit to end and the system goes to the Maintain Bank transaction screen. Complete the following steps:

1. Click the Document Number field.

2. Enter the date the check bounced in the Document Date field.

3. Select Customer transaction as the transaction type.

4. The system asks for the invoice. Enter the Sales Invoice Document type and number. The system pulls in the original invoice details.

5. Enter an explanation in the Reference field.

6. Click Special, and then on Continue. This updates the reinstated sales invoice.

If there is more than one invoice to be reinstated, click the Insert icon and repeat the steps.

Following these steps ensures that NSF checks are recorded correctly in your company's financial records.

Using Miscellaneous Sales Invoices

You can use this option when you need to create a miscellaneous invoice that does not require any inventory movement. In order to differentiate this type of sales invoice, you can use a different transaction type other than the transaction type(s) used for regular sales order invoices. Indicate on each Invoice line what ledger account should be used (see Figure 14.6).

You should perform the following steps to create one of these invoices:

1. Enter the Document Number field.

2. Enter the customer number or zoom on this field to find the customer number.

3. Enter the amount of the invoice.

4. Click Special, and then on Continue. The system goes to the Maintain Sales Invoice transaction screen.

Part
III

Ch
14

5. Enter the ledger account to charge the invoice.

6. Enter the value for the ledger account allocation.

7. Click the Save icon to write the record.

8. The remaining amount at the bottom of your screen must come to zero before you can exit from the document.

9. Click the Exit icon to go out of Ledger Account Distribution screen.

10. Click the Exit icon to terminate the batch.

Miscellaneous invoices can be used to record sales of assets and to invoice any amount not related to regular sales activities.

FIG. 14.6
When creating a miscellaneous invoice you must assign the general ledger account for use with this transaction.

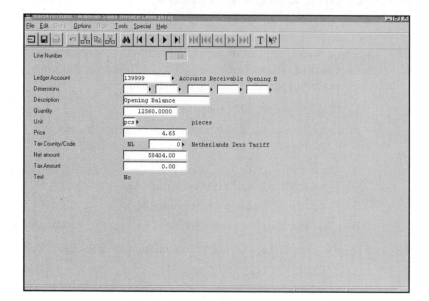

Using Customer Account Inquiries, General Customer Maintenance, and Customer Reports

All customer invoice/receipt history and open entry balance inquiries are located in these options. This is very useful for checking on the status of an account.

The Write Off Currency Differences option is critical if you deal with multiple currencies. Before a sales credit allocation, cash receipt, or period end can be processed, write off currency differences must be processed and finalized. This eliminates the possibility of leaving residual balances caused by changing exchange rates.

The aging analysis by customer is a balancing report. This report is critical for cash flow and financial position—it must balance to the general ledger. This report must be generated at a fixed point in time in order to balance to the general ledger.

Writing Off Currency Differences

This option is a required process if your company deals with multiple currencies. This process must be completed and finalized before a sales credit allocation, cash receipts, or period end can be done.

Press Enter all the way through and take the defaults. A sample of the Selection screen is shown in Figure 14.7.

N O T E It is important, at a period end, that the dates used are the last working day and that the financial period reflects the period on which you are working. This ensures that the entry produced posts to the correct financial period and reflect properly on the aging analysis by customer. ■

FIG. 14.7
The Write Off Currency session eliminates balances from Customer Account.

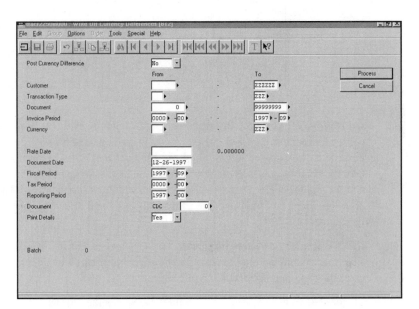

Using Display with Customer's Sales Invoices

This option gives you the outstanding customer balance in home currency. The outstanding invoices are listed in foreign currency.

If you need to see the receipt details on a particular invoice, click Special and then view all documents (paid and outstanding). Click the document in question and zoom in on it. It indicates the date the cash receipt was deposited.

If you need to see the invoice details on a particular invoice, click Special, and then view all documents (paid and outstanding). Click the document in question and then click Continue. The invoice information is listed in detail—due date, currency rate booked, taxes applicable, sales order if applicable, and so on. If you zoom the document when in the invoice details on Form 1-3, it is possible to get the transaction lines for invoice, as shown in Figure 14.8.

Part

III

Ch

14

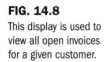

FIG. 14.8

This display is used to view all open invoices for a given customer.

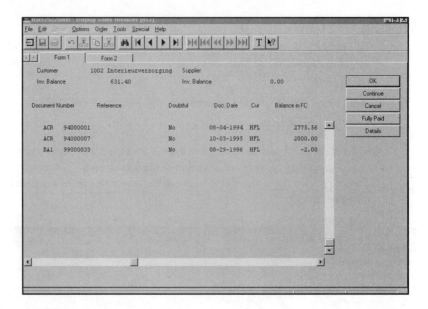

Using Write Off Currency Differences   This option is a required process if your company deals with multiple currencies. Before a sales credit allocation, cash receipts, or period end can be done, this process must be completed and finalized. Press Enter all the way through and take the defaults. It is important, at a period end, that the dates used are the last working day and the financial period reflects the period on which you are working. This ensures that the entry produced posts to the correct financial period and reflect properly on the aging analysis by customer.

Using Display/Print Sales Invoices   This display is useful if you have a cash receipt with a sales invoice number and no customer details. If you search by document, the document indicates the customer in question.

The print sales invoices report is useful if you are looking for what value and details have been processed for a particular customer. This report should balance to the aging analysis by customer. This is very useful if you need a straight summary of outstanding invoices.

N O T E   You print either to a file, the screen, or to paper when using the Print option in Baan. ■

Using Print Aging Analysis by Customer   This report is a useful balancing report. It states what is outstanding as of a certain period of time and how many days outstanding each invoice is. The report totals are in home currency. At a period end, it is critical that all sales invoices have been processed for the month and that write off currency differences has been processed and finalized. Ensure that no cash receipts are processed for the new period until the period you are working on is finished and this report balances to the general ledger.

When generating this report, the dates used must be the last working day and the financial periods must reflect the period on which you are working. Take the defaults on all other options. This report can be generated a variety of ways. The Selection screen for this report is shown in Figure 14.9.

FIG. 14.9

You can use various options when printing the aging analysis report.

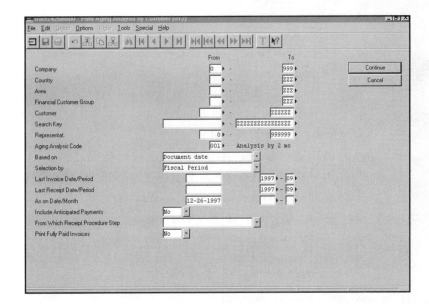

Using Invoice Control

This option is used to generate miscellaneous sales invoices (for example, sale of a fixed asset). It generates a paper copy of the invoice and posts financial data to account receivable open entries and general ledger.

To use the Invoice Control features, go to Finance, Accounts Receivable, Invoice Control. The options for the Invoice Control menu include:

- Maintain sales invoice header
- Print sales invoices
- Post sales invoices

Choose one of these options to continue. These menu choices are described in greater detail in the following sections.

Using Maintain Sales Invoice Header   This is where you enter the sales invoice details. For example, setting up the currency to be billed or the number of invoice copies required.

You must perform the following steps to maintain the sales invoice header:

1. Click the Insert icon and enter the customer number.
2. Enter the transaction type for your miscellaneous sales invoice and press Enter at the Document field.

Part

III

Ch

14

3. Enter the number of extra copies required.

4. Take defaults on all other options.

5. Click Special, and then on Details and the system goes to the Maintain Sales Invoice Lines screen for the invoice.

6. Enter the appropriate ledger account, description of what is being sold, unit, quantity, and unit price.

7. Click the Insert icon if there is more than one item being sold.

8. Click the Exit icon to return to the header screen.

9. Take note of the document number processed in order to print the invoice. Click the Exit icon to end.

A sales invoice has been created!

Using Print Sales Invoices   You must complete the following steps in order to post the sales invoice to the general ledger when you have generated the sales invoice.

1. Select to print by transaction type and invoice.

2. Enter invoice date to be printed on invoice.

3. Click Special and Continue to print sales invoices.

4. A proforma invoice prints. If details and amounts are correct, change Final Invoice to Yes and reprint. It prints the sales invoice.

Invoices do not get a status of printed unless you answer Yes to the Final prompt. This is an important consideration when printing invoices.

N O T E   It is impossible to make changes to the Header and Invoice line details after final invoice has been set to Yes while printing sales invoices.

Using Post Sales Invoices   This option posts details to accounts receivable, open entries, and the general ledger when the sales invoice has been printed.

1. Enter transaction type and document number to be posted.

2. Enter transaction entry date for posting and ensure that the year and posting periods are correct.

3. Click Special, and then on Continue.

After you have run this option, the invoices are posted to the general ledger, the cash management, and the Receivables module Then they are available for payment.

Performing the Month End Process for Accounts Receivable

Figure 14.10 describes the month end procedure for accounts receivable. It is important that all steps are completed in order, so you can avoid any problems in balancing the accounts receivable to the general ledger. You must be certain that all cash receipts and sales invoices have been posted prior to completing these steps.

FIG. 14.10
The process followed at month's end for accounts receivable.

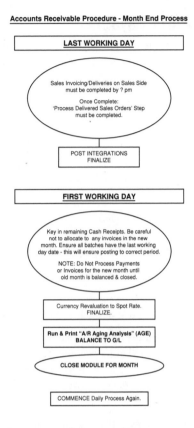

Accounts Receivable Procedure - Month End Process

LAST WORKING DAY

Sales Invoicing/Deliveries on Sales Side must be completed by ? pm

Once Complete:
'Process Delivered Sales Orders' Step must be completed.

POST INTEGRATIONS
FINALIZE

FIRST WORKING DAY

Key in remaining Cash Receipts. Be careful not to allocate to any invoices in the new month. Ensure all batches have the last working day date - this will ensure posting to correct period.

NOTE: Do Not Process Payments or Invoices for the new month until old month is balanced & closed.

Currency Revaluation to Spot Rate.
FINALIZE.

Run & Print "A/R Aging Analysis" (AGE)
BALANCE TO G/L

CLOSE MODULE FOR MONTH

COMMENCE Daily Process Again.

These steps must be completed prior to processing any accounts receivable cash receipts for the next month, or you will be unable to produce an accurate report. You must also be sure that all outstanding batches have been posted to the general ledger using the general ledger finalization process described in Chapter 13.

You can start your cash receipts processing for the new month when all these steps have been completed.

Using Accounts Payable

The Accounts Payable menus contain all options required to perform the AP functions and to monitor your company's cash disbursements. The following sections explain the setup, the processes, and the most important reports required for accounts payable analysis.

The Accounts Payable module is very dependent upon information from other modules, such as Purchasing, Receiving, and Manufacturing. Information from all these modules flows to accounts payable via the Integration options. The Accounts Payable options are probably the most complex of the Finance options, especially if your company uses multiple currencies. This makes the training of all those who affect this module a very important part of your implementation. Training ensures that you are using the software to its full advantage.

Part
III

Ch
14

Using Master Data for Accounts Payable

You must set up the master data in order to use the Accounts Payable module. This master data consists of information like the transaction types you want to use for the different types of accounts payable transactions, the financial supplier groups, and so on. The information to be set up in the master data consists of:

- ACP parameters
- Financial supplier groups
- Blocking codes (Optional)
- Blocking references (Optional)
- Aging analysis data (Optional)
- Tolerated price differences by user (Optional)

N O T E   In the context of accounts payable master data, ACP is an acronym for Accounts Payable. ■

Each of these types of master data are explained in the following sections.

Using ACP Parameters   You are required to enter information in the ACP parameters needed to apply your accounts payable to the correct ledger accounts, and to determine whether the system will use Baan software's automatic matching feature. You also use this section to set up what tolerances you will accept for price differences between the purchase order price and the supplier invoice.

Go to Finance, Accounts Payable, Maintain ACP Parameters. You are presented with four screens used to set the ACP parameters.

Screen one of four of the ACP parameters holds information particular to each individual installation. For example, you can choose to have taxes calculated by line or for a total order. You can have the system perform automatic matching between the invoice and the purchase order and or item receipt. For each field, click the Enumerated Field icon and choose the options that best fit your company. An example of Form 1 is shown in Figure 14.11.

Go to Form 2 by clicking the enter arrow. This is where you enter the transaction types you have assigned to each of the categories listed (Approval of Purchase Invoices, Currency Differences, and Payment Differences). The transaction types are three-digit alphanumeric codes. These must be set up in the general ledger master data before you can use them here.

Go to the final form by clicking the icon. It's here you set up your tolerances for matching. As stated previously, each company has a different requirement regarding what their tolerances should be for automatically approving an invoice. Baan software is very flexible; you can set the tolerances by percentage and by dollar value. The system gives you the flexibility to have a different percentage/dollar value for invoice totals that differ from the purchase order value (both under and over the assigned PO total).

FIG. 14.11

The Accounts Payable parameters must be defined before using this module. This is where you indicate whether an invoice will be matched automatically or manually.

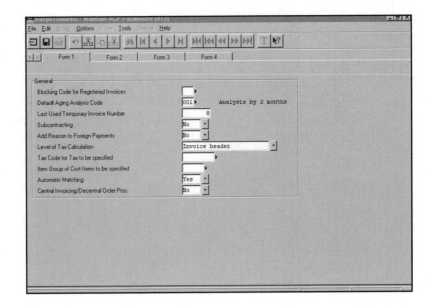

Using Maintain Financial Supplier Groups   Baan software uses financial supplier groups to define the currency in which a particular supplier does business with your company. You have to set up your ledger bank accounts and accounts payable accounts, which are used by any transactions relating to a supplier who has been assigned that financial supplier group. You see how Form 1 is maintained in Figure 14.12.

In order to create Financial Customer Groups you must perform a number of steps:

1. Go to Finance, Accounts Payable, Master Data, Maintain Financial Supplier Groups.
2. Click the Insert icon and enter the three-digit supplier group code.
3. Click the Save icon to write the record from the Choice field.
4. Click the record you want to select. Then click Special. This shows you all the control accounts that need to be assigned to the supplier group. Examples include the accounts payable control account number, the account number to be used for realized and unrealized currency profits and losses, and the payment differences. All these account numbers must be completed.
5. Click the Save icon to write the record when all entry is complete and exit the session.

You can set up as many financial customer group as apply to your business.

Using Maintain Blocking Codes   Baan offers a very useful feature for marking invoices that you do not want to pay. *Blocking codes* are user defined, so each company or user can define his or her own codes. Using these codes makes it easy to identify, at a glance, the reason an invoice is being held for payment. You find some examples of blocking codes in Figure 14.13.

These blocking codes are very easy to set up.

Part

III

Ch

14

FIG. 14.12

The ledger account to be used must be defined when setting up the supplier financial group.

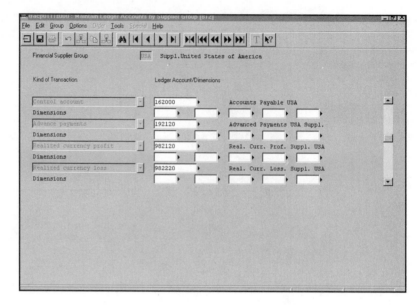

1. Go to Finance, Accounts Payable, Master Data, Maintain Blocking Codes.

2. Click the Insert icon to create your desired code number (alphanumeric).

3. Enter the description.

4. Select Yes for the Blocked for Manual Payment to ensure that the invoice can't be added manually to the check run selection. Select No if you want to allow a blocked invoice to be added manually to a check run without unblocking it.

5. Exit to end the session and enter the record, or click the Insert icon to create another code.

You can use any description that you feel fits the needs of your organization. It can be numbers, letters, or a combination.

Using Maintain Blocking References   This feature is also optional—as are the blocking codes. This feature allows you to assign a username to the blocking code previously described.

Blocking references are set up by following these instructions:

1. Go to Finance, Accounts Payable, Master Data, Maintain Blocking References.

2. Click the Insert icon to create your desired code number (alphanumeric).

3. Enter the code's description.

4. Click the Insert icon to create, or exit to end the entry.

After you have set up your blocking references, you have a quick and easy method of identifying the source of your transactions.

FIG. 14.13

The blocking codes must be defined to ensure that each reason an invoice cannot be paid is available to the accounts payable users.

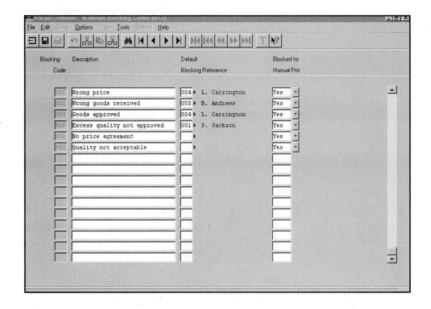

Using Maintain Aging Analysis Data The aging analysis data is used to age your accounts payable in a manner suitable to your company. You can define several ways of aging the open accounts payable. You can select any one of the ways you have defined in the aging analysis data to get different views of the same data when you are running your accounts payable aging reports. An example of the setup required is found in Figure 14.14.

Perform the following steps to set up your company's aging analysis data:

1. Go to Finance, Accounts Payable, Master Data, Maintain Aging Analysis Data.

2. Click the Insert icon to create your desired code number (alphanumeric).

3. Enter in the description for the code.

4. Select the appropriate option Days, Months, and so on. This period type relates to the number you select in the next two options.

   The Number of Periods is how many columns you can have. The maximum is six. The value you choose for the Length of each period depends on how you have set up the previous options. An example would be if you set the Period Type for days, and the Number of Periods at 4. You could set the Length of the first period to be 30. This would give you all outstanding invoices 30 days or less.

5. In the Column Heading field you should put in the description that you will want to see on the report heading for the column that is being defined.

6. Click the Insert icon to create another code or exit to End the entry.

Remember you can set up multiple options for aging accounts payable, which leaves you with virtually unlimited reporting possibilities. You can report your accounts payable using 30, 60, 90 or any other combination you deem useful for your organization.

Part
III

Ch
14

FIG. 14.14

Various periods can be defined to analyze the open accounts payable.

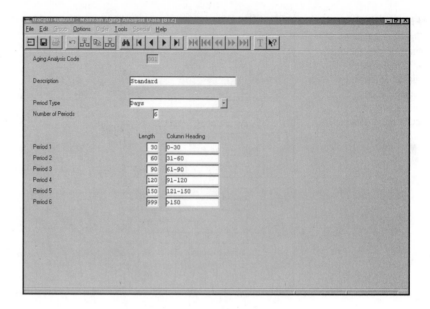

Using Maintain Tolerated Price Differences by User You can set up tolerated price differences by user in this section of the ACP master data. This information is used to prevent the invoice approvals by users not authorized to approve invoices that have price differences from the purchase order beyond what you have defined within this table. The tolerances are set by percentage and dollar value.

Perform the following steps to set up your tolerated price differences by user:

1. Go to Finance, Accounts Payable, Master Data, Maintain Tolerated Price Differences by User.

2. Click the Insert icon to create the user's login code as defined in the Tools module.

3. Enter the remaining information as indicated by the headings: invoice lower than percentage and dollar amount and invoice higher than percentage and amount.

4. Click the Insert icon to create additional users or Exit to end.

Because the tolerance allowed can be different from user to user, it is very important to use the Maintain Tolerated Price Difference by Users sessions.

Using Transaction Processing for Accounts Payable

All supplier invoices data entry is maintained in this menu. Supplier invoices fall into two categories:

- Linked invoices—Invoices for which a purchase order has been produced.
- Non-linked invoices—Invoices for which a purchase order is not required.

For the remainder of this chapter invoices are referred to as either linked or non-linked.

It is important that you match linked invoices correctly to purchase orders. If they are incorrectly matched, you are left with residual balances in your accrual accounts and cause incorrect entries. It is very important that your accounts payable, purchasing, and receiving staff understand the impact of their entries. Each entry has a direct effect on your accounts payable accrual and therefore, your company's balance sheet.

Using Maintain Transactions for Accounts Payable

Perform the following steps to process an account payable invoice into the Baan system:

1. Go to Finance, Accounts Payable, Transaction Processing.

2. Select Maintain Transactions.

3. The transaction entry date is critical when setting up an accounts payable batch for processing. The date determines to which month the invoices are posted. Click the Insert icon to insert the purchase invoice transaction type (purchase invoice non-linked, purchase credit non-linked, purchase invoice linked, purchase credit linked, or purchase credit allocation). This is demonstrated in Figure 14.15.

4. Click the Save icon to write the record.

Always print the non-finalized reports and verify that the information is correct before finalizing any batches.

FIG. 14.15

You must select a transaction type for accounts payable in order to enter accounts payables invoices.

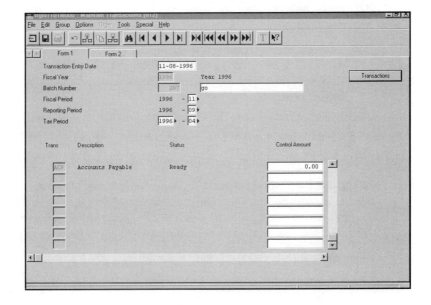

Using Non-Linked Invoices and Credits Non-linked invoices and credits are very straightforward. The only problem you may encounter are incorrect invoice details that you need to correct. If the invoice has not been finalized, the best way for you to make the corrections is to completely delete the invoice and start over. If you have finalized the invoice, you must create a credit note to delete the invoice. If you don't make your corrections this way, you find that the software tends to remember the original incorrect information (for example, incorrect exchange or currency) instead of the new, corrected information.

Do the following to enter an accounts payable invoice into the system:

1. Click the transaction type to be processed.
2. Click the Document Number field.
3. Enter the supplier number from the supplier master.
4. Enter the invoice date in the Document Date field. It is important to always use the invoice date, as that forces the system to use the correct currency exchange rate.
5. Enter the amount (invoice value).
6. Enter the VAT code. This creates the tax entry for you.
7. Enter the supplier invoice number.
8. Click Special, and then on Continue to confirm.
9. The system moves to the Distribution screen. Enter the ledger account and dimensions, if applicable.
10. Enter the VAT code if not entered in the previous screen, or press Enter past this field.
11. Enter the net amount for the ledger account.
12. If there is more that one ledger account for your invoice, click the Insert icon to create the next line for entering an additional ledger account. If not, click the Save icon to write the record. The remaining amount at the bottom of your screen must come to zero before you exit the document.
13. Exit to end your entry. The system returns to the Invoice Detail screen.
14. Click the Insert icon to create another invoice or Exit to end the batch.

You have entered an accounts payable invoice into the system.

Pulling In a Transaction Schedule You may have a fixed distribution of accounts for some supplier invoices (for example utilities or telephone bills). Baan has a feature that allows the set up of transaction schedules by percentage or by dollar value (see Figure 14.16). You can pull this schedule for use against these invoices each time you have one to process.

Follow these steps to enter an invoice using the transaction schedule:

1. Enter the invoice details as described in the "Using Linked and Non-Linked Invoices" section.
2. In the Distribution screen, zoom and click the Create Transactions from Schedule option.

3. Zoom to locate the required transaction schedule.

4. For a transaction schedule by percentage, enter the total amount to be distributed and click Special, Continue. Exit to end when the system indicates that it is ready. This pulls back the schedule for you. If a rounding amount remains, you have to adjust a line to make it amount to zero.

For a transaction schedule by amount, leave amount for distribution at zero and click Special, Continue. Exit to end when the system indicates it is ready. This pulls through the account numbers for you. Line by line, click the field to change and enter the dollar value for each ledger account.

Using the transaction schedules reduces the amount of accounts to be entered into the distribution, which reduces the chance of error and the time required to process repetitive accounts payable invoices.

FIG. 14.16
Transaction schedules can be used to split amount of any invoices according to percentages previously established.

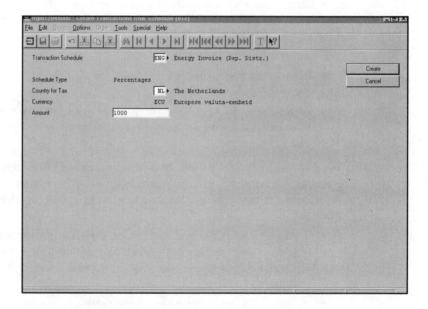

Using Linked Invoices and Credits   Linked invoices or credits are those associated with a purchase or return order. This type of invoice or credit is more complicated. It is very important that you match your invoices correctly to the item receipt. If any price difference is found when matching invoices, it is shown (see Figure 14.17). If you follow the necessary steps, you will have no problems processing these types of invoices and credits.

1. Click the transaction type to be processed.

2. Click the Document Number field.

3. Enter the supplier number from the supplier master.

4. Enter the invoice date in the Document Date field. It is important to always use the invoice date. That forces the system to use the correct currency exchange rate.

Part
III

Ch
14

5. Enter the amount (invoice value).

6. Press Enter past the VAT Code field.

7. Enter the supplier invoice number.

8. Enter the applicable purchase order number.

9. Click Special, and then on Continue to accept.

10. The system moves to the VAT Code screen. Enter the appropriate VAT code(s) and the amount(s) applicable. Exit to end.

11. Exit to end the Automatic Matching screen. The system moves to the Manual Matching screen.

12. You should always match the invoice for both value and quantity. You have the following options:

    - Match completely if the invoice quantity and value are exactly what the receipt quantity and value are.

    - Match partially if the invoice quantity or value are not equal to the receipt quantity and value.

    - If there is no Receipt line, it is impossible to allocate to a receipt. The invoice has a status of Registered.

    - Baan software does not allow a registered or matched invoice to be paid until it has been matched to a receipt and approved, if you set up your parameters for three-way matching.

13. You must ensure that the balance amount to be matched in the screen's top-right corner comes to zero before you exit the matching screen. If there was no receipt, the remaining amount is the net invoice amount. At this point you may experience one of two situations:

    - If quantities balance—Invoice to receipt, **Ctrl+A** to approve invoice. If within the price difference tolerances set up in the master data, the system allows automatic approval. If not, the system does not allow approval and the invoice must be investigated for the price difference.

    - If quantities do not balance—Invoice to receipt, do not attempt to approve the invoice. Investigate the quantity difference and make the necessary adjustments by either having the received quantity corrected or adjusting the invoice.

14. Exit to end. The system returns to the Invoice Detail screen.

15. You can exit to end the batch or click the Insert icon to create another document.

If you encounter any problems while linking invoices, you must ensure the invoice is unapproved, unmatched, and deleted to be able to reprocess at a later point.

Deleting Purchase Invoices Before Transactions Are Finalized   The invoice should be unmatched and deleted if it is realized that the invoice was incorrectly matched on the item, taxes, supplier, value, or quantity after an invoice has been approved.

FIG. 14.17

The price difference between the supplier invoice and the purchase order is calculated when performing the invoice matching operation.

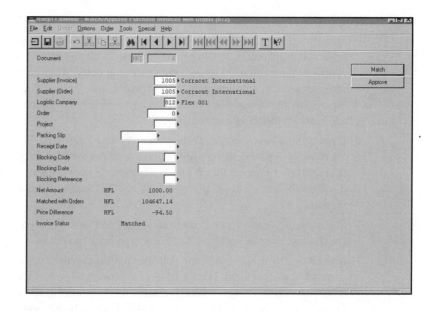

You must go to the accounts payable, transaction processing screens and click the correct transaction type in order to make the necessary corrections:

1. Pull up the correct document number, then click Special, Continue.

2. The Approval Information screen appears. Click Special and on the Reversing Approval.

3. The System goes to the Matching screen. Set the matching to No for all lines applicable to that invoice.

4. Click the Exit icon.

5. The invoice has a status of Registered. Enter a **D** at the Invoice Detail screen's the Choice field to delete the invoice. You are asked if you want to "Delete Y/N?"

6. Click Special, Continue.

7. Reenter the invoice with the correct information.

Remember, this option can only be used if the invoice has not been finalized.

Processing Linked Invoices More Efficiently   Here are some tips that help you process linked invoices efficiently:

- You should always match to what the invoice states in the Matching screen. This gives purchasing and receiving the ability to see how you were invoiced and what the problems were.

- Know what entries are expected. Check non-finalized reports. If you see anything unusual, large rounding differences for instance, go back into the batch and make the necessary correction by unmatching the invoice and making the adjustment(s) required (Delete invoice and reenter).

Part
III

Ch
14

■ Never attempt to approve an invoice with quantity differences. The system allows it, but the automatic accrual never clears correctly and causes problems with the ledger entries produced. If an item is over Received on the system, you have to do an adjustment on the purchase order and make an adjusting receiving entry. When corrected, unallocate what was matched and reassign including correction line. If under Received, you have to receive additional quantities and accounts payable must unallocate what was matched and reassign including correction line.

■ If you want to leave the responsibility of approving large price differences with the Purchasing Department, ensure that the tolerances for price differences is set up appropriately. Consequently, if a price difference is over the tolerance, the system does not allow the invoice to be approved by Accounts Payable. Purchasing has to approve on system.

■ Set up a paper or electronic form to send back and forth between Accounts Payable, Purchasing, and the Receiving Department to track problems.

■ If an invoice turns out wrong and you have not yet approved it, go to invoice and unmatch the full amount. Press **Ctrl+A** to approve the invoice. The system asks to what ledger account to charge it. Charge the invoice to a clearing account (liability account). Create a purchase credit for the invoice and charge it to the clearing account. Process a currency revaluation and have it finalized. Do a purchase credit allocation, allocating the incorrect invoice to the credit entered. Readjust the invoice to be paid, reenter and match to receipt, and approve.

Allocating Credit Notes to Invoices   If you deal with more than one currency, ensure that a currency revaluation is completed and finalized before doing this process. It is very important that where possible, you allocate any credit notes to the applicable invoices. This makes the check run process go smoothly.

After completing the currency revaluation and finalization, you are ready to start processing the allocation of credit notes. This is done by performing these steps in the Maintain Transaction screen:

1. Click the transaction type to be processed.

2. Call up supplier number from the supplier master data.

3. Click the credit note to be allocated.

4. Arrow to the appropriate invoice(s) and enter the amount to allocate against each invoice.

5. Click Special, Continue. A Document screen appears.

6. Click Document screen.

7. Exit to end and return to the main screen.

If you go into the inquiry screens and do an inquiry on the supplier, you find that the invoice and credit note no longer appear.

Using Match Purchase Invoices with Orders

This option is used for linked invoices that have already been finalized and have a status of Registered or Matched. These are the invoices that have no receipt booked or did not match to the receipt entered for either quantity or price. This option allows you to access the invoice and do adjustments pertaining to the way it was matched. In addition, you can change the purchase order number if necessary, if it has a Registered status. There is an example of this session in Figure 14.18.

Follow these steps to complete the matching process:

1. Go to Finance, Accounts Payable, Transaction Processing.
2. Select Match Purchase Invoices with Orders.
3. Search for the required document number.
4. Click Special, Continue to go into the Matching screen.
5. Check the purchasing result matching and receiving, by the quantity and amount.
6. Remember the balance amount to be matched at the top-right screen corner must be zero before exiting the Matching screen.
7. Click the Approve button if Purchasing has approved the price difference.
8. If Receiving approved and adjusted the item receipt, type **Ctrl+U** to unmatch and rematch, ensuring that the quantities now correctly match the invoice.
9. If Purchasing did not approve price difference or quantity difference, enter **Ctrl+U** to unmatch the full amount. Enter **Ctrl+A** to approve invoice. The system asks to what ledger account to charge it. Charge it to a liability clearing account.

After completing the steps, remember to create a purchase credit for this invoice and charge it to the clearing account. Process a write off currency difference. Do a purchase credit allocation, allocating the incorrect invoice to the purchase credit. Readjust the invoice to be paid; enter again, match to receipt, and approve as you have done when processing linked invoices.

The invoice should be correct and accurately reflect your company's liability, as well as ensure that the supplier is paid correctly.

Using Approve Price Differences

It is a good idea to have this option restricted to purchasing staff (or whoever has authority for approving price differences). They must go into this option if there is a price difference and Purchasing agrees to pay. The Maintain Tolerated Price Differences option was described earlier in this chapter. This option is the information Baan uses to determine the price differences that can be approved by each individual.

Complete the following steps to approve price differences:

1. Go to Finance, Accounts Payable, Transaction Processing.
2. Select Approve Price Differences.

Part
III

Ch
14

FIG. 14.18
This is the session used to match purchase invoices with purchase orders.

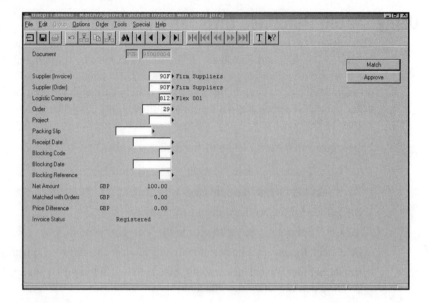

3. Enter the supplier number.

4. Click the document in question.

5. Change Approve to Yes.

6. Click the Save icon to write.

7. Exit to end the transaction.

The price difference is now approved.

Using Report Generation and Balancing for Accounts Payable

All data entry reconciliation reports against purchase orders are available in the Report Generation and Balancing menu. These reports are extremely useful for verifying several things: how a purchase receipt was allocated (quantities and values); how a linked purchase invoice was allocated against a purchase order receipt; what purchase order(s) were matched to a particular invoice; and the date an invoice was approved.

There are several other things in this menu: the balancing reports, the automatic accounts payable accrual report, and linked invoices that have been processed, but not approved (with a status of Registered or Matched). These reports are critical balancing reports for cash flow and financial position, and must balance to the appropriate ledger accounts in the general ledger. These reports must be generated at a fixed point in time in order to balance to the general ledger.

Using Print Purchase Receipts   This report is excellent for verifying how a purchase receipt was matched and as what purchase invoice document number it was processed. In the first two value columns, the report lists by line number on a purchase order what was received and the value driven from the purchase order. In the last two value columns, the report lists how the linked purchase invoice was matched to each receipt line. No data shows up on this report if a purchase order has not been received. The Selection screen is shown Figure 14.19.

Complete the following steps to print this report:

1. Go to Accounts Payable, Transaction Processing, Reports.

2. Go to Print Purchase Receipts.

3. Indicate supplier number or take defaults.

4. Indicate purchase order number or take defaults. Selection by purchase order is usually the most logical way to pull information required.

5. Indicate the receipt date of a purchase receipt.

6. Select No for print matched invoices if you do not require the purchase invoice document number. Select Yes if you require the purchase invoice document number.

This report can be run as many times as is required and can be either printed to display or committed to paper.

FIG. 14.19
This report indicates what purchased receipts have been linked.

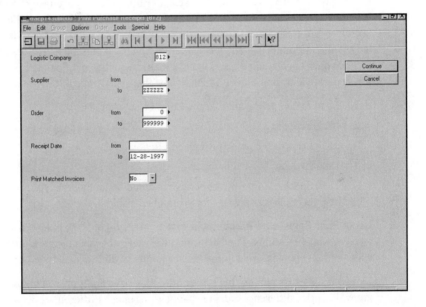

Using Print Matched Purchase Invoices with Receipts This report is excellent for analyzing which purchase orders have been allocated against a particular invoice. It lists quantity, price, price difference (if applicable) receipt and invoice, date approved, and financial period. To run this report, complete the following steps:

1. Go to Accounts Payable, Transaction Processing, Reports.

2. Print matched purchase invoices with receipts.

Part
III
Ch
14

3. Indicate the linked purchase invoice transaction type or take defaults.

4. Indicate the invoice's system generated document number or take defaults.

5. Indicate the supplier number or take defaults.

6. Indicate purchase order number or take defaults.

No data will show up on this report if an invoice has not been produced for a particular purchase receipt.

Using Print Receivable Specification Report   This report is the balancing report for the automatic accounts payable accrual. Any receipts for which invoices have not be processed and approved appears on this report. A linked purchase invoice can be processed for a receipt, but may have a Registered or Matched status. The accrual does not clear from this report until it has a status of Approved.

N O T E   The receivable specification report is generated in home currency. The system takes the currency rate from the purchase order header.

On the last working day of your Financial Period, when all purchase receipts and collect orders have been processed for the period, ensure the process delivered purchase orders step is performed. You can generate the accounts payable accrual report and balance it to the general ledger after accounts payable have entered the linked purchase invoices for the period, their batches have been finalized, and integrations are posted and finalized. The Selection screen for this report is shown in Figure 14.20. Follow these steps to run the report:

1. Go to Accounts Payable, Transaction Processing.

2. Click Reports.

3. Click Print Receivable Specification Report.

4. Take all defaults for this report.

5. Click Special, Continue. This report should be included in your month end routine to help reconcile the accrual for accounts payable.

Using Print Registered Purchase Invoices   This report lists linked invoices that have a Registered or Matched status. The balance on the receivable specification report less than the balance on this report is equal to the true accounts payable accrual.

Linked invoices remain on this report until they have an Approved status. It is important to know that price differences and exchange differences (differences between the purchase receipt and the linked purchase invoice value) do not adjust through the financial integration process and impact the general ledger until the invoice is approved and clears off this report. Therefore, it is important to keep current with any problem invoices to ensure accurate and timely financial data.

Generate this report and balance it to the general ledger on the last working day of your financial period, when accounts payable personnel have finished entering linked purchase invoices for the period and their batches have been finalized.

FIG. 14.20

This report indicates which receipt and invoices have not yet been linked.

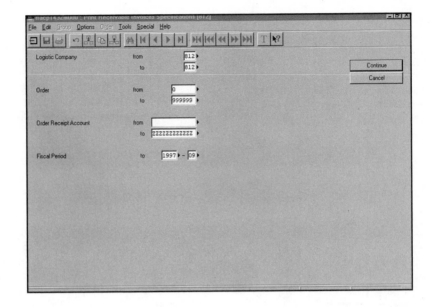

The Selection screen for this report is shown in Figure 14.21. The process printing this report is very straightforward.

1. Go to Accounts Payable, Transaction Processing.

2. Click Reports.

3. Click Print Registered Purchase Invoices.

4. Take all system defaults for this report.

5. Click Special, Continue.

As previously stated, it is important to look at this report on a monthly basis to clear any problem invoices.

Using Supplier Account Inquiries, General Supplier Maintenance, and Supplier Reports for Accounts Payable

All supplier invoice/payment history and outstanding balance inquiries are indicated in these options. These are very useful if a supplier calls to check on the status of his or her account.

From time to time you have to perform some maintenance type transactions. The following list provides some details:

■ Maintaining purchase invoice details is useful if you have to block an invoice for payment or change a due date on an invoice.

■ Write off currency differences is crucial if you use more than one currency. Write off currency differences must be processed and finalized before a purchase credit allocation, check run, or period end can be processed.

Part

III

Ch

14

FIG. 14.21

This is a reconciliation report. The balance on receivable specification report minus the balance on this report is equal to the accounts payable accrual.

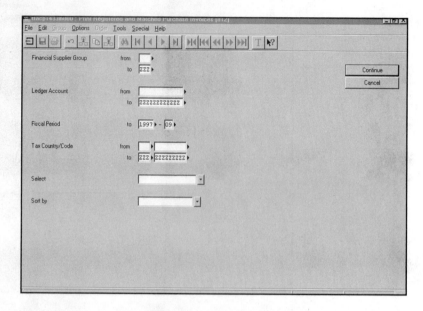

■ The aging analysis by supplier is a balancing report. This report is a balancing report for cash flow and financial position. You should verify that it balances to the general ledger. This report must be generated at a fixed point in time in order to balance.

Using those tools makes visibility to the amount outstanding for each supplier possible.

Using Display Suppliers Purchase Invoices   This option gives you the supplier's outstanding balance in home currency. The outstanding invoices are listed in foreign currency.

Press **Ctrl+A** to view all documents (paid and outstanding) if you need to see the payment details on a particular invoice. The date the check was issued is indicated if you click the document in question and zoom. If it indicates an anticipated payment only, the check has not been cashed. If it indicates an anticipated payment in and out, and a normal payment, the check has been cashed.

Press **Ctrl+A**, as shown in Figure 14.22, to view all documents (paid and outstanding). Click the document in question and press **Ctrl+E**. The invoice information is listed in detail—due date, currency rate booked, taxes applicable, purchase order (if applicable), document approval number (if applicable), and so on. It is possible to see the transaction lines for the invoice if you zoom when in the invoice details on Form 1-3.

Using Maintain Purchase Invoice Details   Logically, it is impossible to touch any values. There are various fields that can be changed, but the most important fields are Due Date, Supplier Invoice Number, and Payment Method. It is possible to block the invoice for payment on Form 2-2.

FIG. 14.22

This Inquiry screen is to be used when you want to have your account's status with a specific supplier.

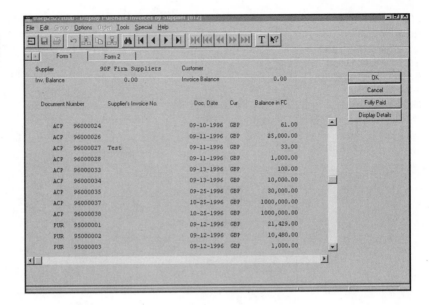

Using Write Off Currency Differences   This option is a required process if your company deals in more than one currency. This process must be completed and finalized before a purchase credit allocation, check run, or period end can be done. To do this, press Enter all the way through and take the defaults.

At a period end, you must use the dates for the last working day and be sure the financial period reflects the period on which you are working. This guarantees that the entry produced posts to the correct financial period and reflects correctly on the aging analysis by supplier.

Using Print Purchase Invoices   This report is useful if you are looking to see what value and details you have processed for a particular supplier. The purchase invoice report can be printed many ways. One way lists the outstanding invoices for a supplier. Another lists all invoices processed for the period specified. All the options are indicated on the Baan screens.

This report should balance to the aging analysis by supplier. This is also useful if you need a straight summary of outstanding invoices.

Using Print Aging Analysis by Supplier   This report states what is outstanding as a certain time, and how many days outstanding each invoice is. The report totals are in home currency. At a period end, it is important that all payable invoices have been processed for the month and that a write off currency differences has been processed and finalized. Ensure that no checks are issued for the new period until the prior period is finished and this report balances to the general ledger.

When generating this report, it is important to use the last working day of the period and ensure that the financial period reflects the period you are working on, as shown in Figure 14.23. Include Anticipated Payments should be Yes. Take the defaults on all other options.

FIG. 14.23

The aging analysis report can be printed for a specific date. Simply supply the desired date in the As On Date/ Month field.

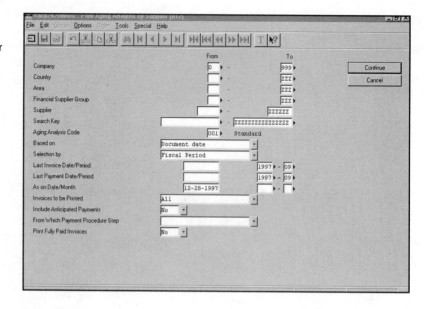

Reviewing Account Payable Daily Process

Figure 14.24 summarizes the process when processing accounts payable on a daily basis. The figure shows the flow of the accounts payable invoice from receipt of the invoice to payment of the invoice.

If an invoice is linked to a purchase order, you must register the invoice on the system, link it to the purchase order, approve or solve any price differences, and process for payment.

Reviewing Accounts Payable Month End Process

Figure 14.25 describes the account payable procedure for closing the period.

All collect orders and purchase receipts must be processed and the process delivered purchase orders step completed before starting the period close. All account payable invoices must be entered and finalized. The final integrations posting must be completed.

It is important to run all of the accounts payable balancing reports at this point, so that you can balance the account payable to the general ledger.

Using Cash Management

The Cash Management menu in the Finance module is used to assist your performing the cash activities required to run your business. The following section explains the setup required, the payment process, and the most important reports required.

FIG. 14.24
This diagram explains the daily process required for the accounts payable procedure.

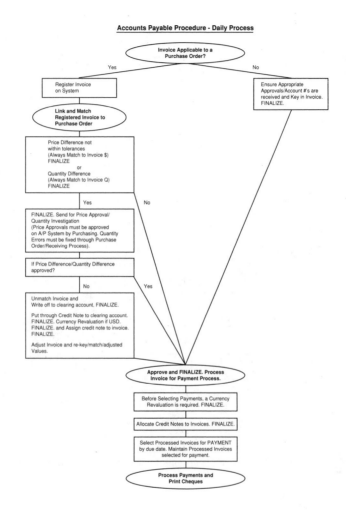

Accounts Payable Procedure - Daily Process

Invoice Applicable to a Purchase Order?

Yes

Register Invoice on System

Link and Match Registered Invoice to Purchase Order

Price Difference not within tolerances
(Always Match to Invoice $)
FINALIZE
or
Quantity Difference
(Always Match to Invoice Q)
FINALIZE

Yes

No

FINALIZE. Send for Price Approval/ Quantity Investigation
(Price Approvals must be approved on A/P System by Purchasing. Quantity Errors must be fixed through Purchase Order/Receiving Process).

If Price Difference/Quantity Difference approved?

No

Yes

Unmatch Invoice and Write off to clearing account. FINALIZE.

Put through Credit Note to clearing account. FINALIZE. Currency Revaluation if USD. FINALIZE. and Assign credit note to invoice. FINALIZE.

Adjust Invoice and re-key/match/adjusted Values.

No

Ensure Appropriate Approvals/Account #'s are received and Key in Invoice. FINALIZE.

Approve and FINALIZE. Process Invoice for Payment Process.

Before Selecting Payments, a Currency Revaluation is required. FINALIZE.

Allocate Credit Notes to Invoices. FINALIZE.

Select Processed Invoices for PAYMENT by due date. Maintain Processed Invoices selected for payment.

Process Payments and Print Cheques

The cash flow reports in this menu are extensive and can be easily customized to your requirements by following the information available in the online Help text included in Baan software. Training your staff, as in all other areas of the Finance modules, is a central element of implementing and taking advantage of all the Baan software has to offer.

Using Master Data for Cash Management

The purpose of the cash management master data is to set up all the information the system requires to perform your cash transactions, including direct debits/credits, actual cash receipts, and payments. As with the other modules, Baan offers many options that allow you to customize the software.

FIG. 14.25

This diagram details the steps to perform on the last working day of the month.

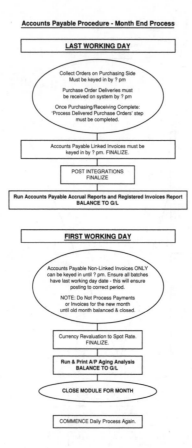

Accounts Payable Procedure - Month End Process

LAST WORKING DAY

Collect Orders on Purchasing Side
Must be keyed in by ? pm

Purchase Order Deliveries must
be received on system by ? pm

Once Purchasing/Receiving Complete:
'Process Delivered Purchase Orders' step
must be completed.

Accounts Payable Linked Invoices must be
keyed in by ? pm. FINALIZE.

POST INTEGRATIONS
FINALIZE

Run Accounts Payable Accrual Reports and Registered Invoices Report
BALANCE TO G/L

FIRST WORKING DAY

Accounts Payable Non-Linked Invoices ONLY
can be keyed in until ? pm. Ensure all batches
have last working day date - this will ensure
posting to correct period.

NOTE: Do Not Process Payments
or Invoices for the new month
until old month balanced & closed.

Currency Revaluation to Spot Rate.
FINALIZE.

Run & Print A/P Aging Analysis
BALANCE TO G/L

CLOSE MODULE FOR MONTH

COMMENCE Daily Process Again.

NOTE In the context of cash management master data, CMG is an acronym for cash management.

Using CMG Parameters Baan uses Cash management parameters to determine how to treat transactions used within the module. An example: You define whether you are using payments by company group, whether you allow the system to pay invoices that have not been approved, and what kind of aging terms you plan to use as standard when running aging reports. The first form of the Maintain CMG Parameters session is shown in Figure 14.26.

The CMG parameters are broken into the following sections:

- Payments
- Direct debits
- Advance payments/receipts
- Statistics/cash forecast
- Electronic bank statements

■ Receipt/Payments

■ Payment difference tolerances

To complete the information required in the CMG parameters:

1. Go to Finance, Cash Management, Maintain CMG Parameters.

2. Click the Insert icon.

3. Enter information as required by the system under the Payments section. You must define whether you allow payments by the group company. Other options to be defined include whether you want to be able to pay only approved and finalized invoices, and whether you want to be able to settle payments with sales invoices.

4. Continue to fill in all the required information, using the Help text to define the responses that meet your company's needs. Baan's Help text is adequate to assist you in this task.

5. Exit to end and move to the next task.

Use the system Help text for detailed descriptions if you are unsure of what parameters should be.

FIG. 14.26

The Cash Management parameters must be set before using this module.

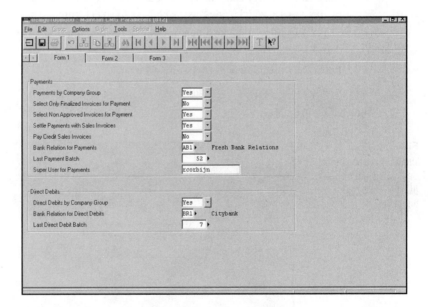

Using Maintain Bank Relations   The bank relations data is used to apply your banking transactions to the correct ledger accounts for the account and currency being used. Some of the required information comes from the codes set up in the Financial tables defined earlier in this book—Bank Address and Currency, for example. The transaction type also needs to be set up in the bank relations data, as shown in Figure 14.27.

Do the following to set up your bank requirements:

1. Go to Finance, Cash Management, Maintain Bank Relations.

2. Click the Insert icon.

3. Enter the bank relation code as you have defined (three-digit alphanumeric).

4. Enter the description of the bank relation you are setting up—bank name and the account currency.

5. Enter the bank, unless in Sweden or in the Netherlands, in which case you may opt for PostBank.

6. Enter the bank address as defined in your Finance tables. To do this, either enter the code or zoom to see what codes are available.

7. Enter your bank account number.

8. Select the code you have assigned in the Finance tables for the currency applicable to this bank relation. For example, if you are planning on using this bank relation for Canadian currency and you defined Canadian currency as CAD, enter CAD in this field or zoom to see which codes are available and select from the list.

9. Select transaction type by either entering it or zooming to select from a list of available codes.

10. Fill in the remaining fields per the Help text.

11. Exit to end to complete the entry and write the records.

Your bank relations are set up.

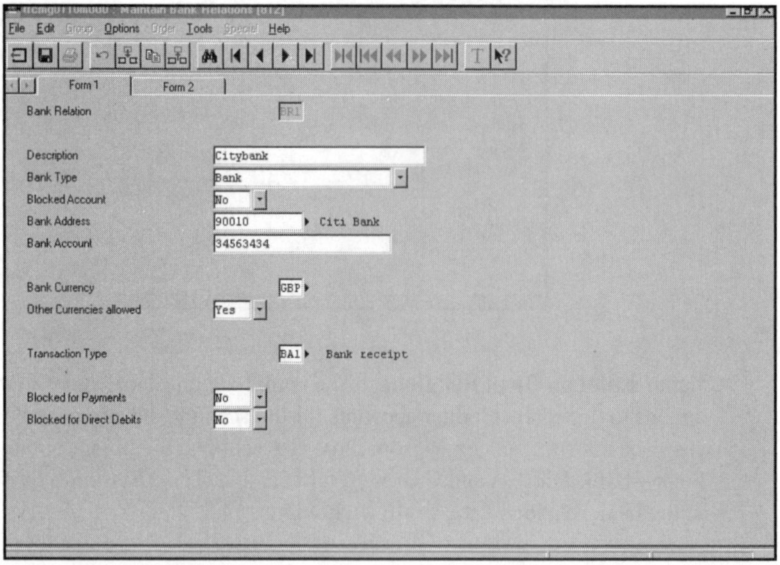

FIG. 14.27

The bank relations must be created and all assigned to a transaction type.

Using Maintain Payment Methods   Payment methods are used by Baan to determine how your payable invoices will be paid or how cash is received to settle sales invoices. Examples of payment methods include checks, bank drafts, direct debits, and so on.

Setting up the payment methods is straightforward. The maintenance screen is shown in Figure 14.28.

1. Go to Finance, Cash Management, Maintain Payment Method.

2. Click the Insert icon.

3. Enter the payment/receipt method code as you have defined (three-digit alphanumeric).

4. Enter the description for the method defined in Step 3.

5. Enter Yes or No in the Automatic Payment/Receipt field. If you answer Yes, you do not wait for the supplier to contact you to pay the invoice. Instead, you allow the system to generate the check according to the terms set up in your supplier masters.

6. Set up the maximum amount you will allow for a check.

7. Enter the rest of the data as prompted.

8. Exit to end the entry and save it.

Setting up the Baan payment methods is complete.

FIG. 14.28

The different payment methods must be defined using this session.

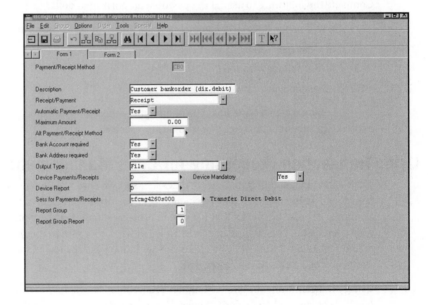

Part

III

Ch

14

Using Maintain Data by Bank/Payment Method   The purpose of this master data section is to link the payment methods to the appropriate banks to ensure that transactions are debited and credited to the appropriate ledger accounts.

You must complete the following steps to set up the data by bank/payment method in the system:

1. Go to Finance, Cash Management, Maintain Data by Bank/Payment Method.
2. Click the Insert icon.
3. Enter the bank relation and the corresponding payment/receipt code that you set up earlier in your cash management (CMG) master data.
4. Enter the transaction type you set up for anticipated payments and the ledger account for anticipated payments with dimension code (if applicable to your operation).
5. Exit to end to complete the entry.

You have created the necessary payment methods for each banks.

Using Maintain Payment Authorization   Payment authorization simply assigns a maximum dollar amount per supplier to each user authorized to perform check runs (see Figure 14.29). You can only assign a global dollar amount, which applies to all suppliers.

Complete the following to assign the payment authorization dollar levels:

1. Go to Finance, Cash Management, Maintain Payment Authorization.
2. Enter the user's ID.
3. Enter amount authorized.
4. Exit to end and complete the entry.

Your company may not have this type of limitation, therefore you should enter an amount that exceeds the amount of invoice you would ever process.

Using Transaction Processing for Cash Management

The Cash Management transaction Processing section is where the check master is maintained, and where completed or rejected checks are processed. The anticipated payment list is a summary report of checks that have been processed and their current status. This report is very useful as an outstanding check list, a list of what checks have been rejected (canceled), or to find the status of a check. The check master inquiry is very useful for determining a check status or when a check was reconciled.

Using Maintain Transactions   Maintain Transactions is where you process completed (cashed) or rejected (canceled) checks. It is a very easy process and the system creates the ledger entries for you.

When a check has been set to Complete, the system reverses the transactions created when the check was issued from the anticipated cash and anticipated payment accounts. It deducts the amount from the bank ledger account and clears it from the accounts payable ledger account.

FIG. 14.29

The example user, rkabbur, is allowed to pay any amount to any supplier. This is not the case for all other users.

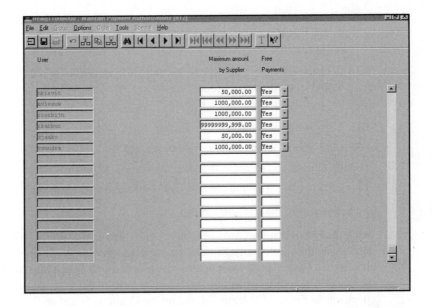

When a check has been set to Rejected, the system reverses out only the transactions created when the check was issued from the anticipated cash and anticipated payment ledger accounts. The invoice(s) issued against this payment are then reinstated on the accounts payable ledger. You can then re-issue the check; if the invoice is incorrect, a credit invoice can be entered and allocated to the invoice to clear the system.

Perform the following steps to change the status of a check:

1. Go to Finance, Cash Management, Transaction Processing.

2. Select Maintain transactions.

3. The transaction entry date determines to which period the checks are posted when setting up a batch for entering incomplete or rejected checks. This is important when you are trying to reconcile your bank accounts. Click the Insert icon to create the bank reconciliation transaction type and click the Save icon to write the record.

4. Click the transaction type to be processed.

5. The system pulls up the Maintain Bank Balances screen If you are using control totals. Click the field to change. Set the opening balance to zero and the closing balance to a negative amount (total value of checks being entered). Exit to end.

6. The system goes into the Maintain Bank Transactions Screen. Click the Document Number field.

7. Enter the document date. Take the same date as the previous transaction entry date.

8. Select supplier reconciliation for transaction type.

9. Take the defaults on the other options.

10. Click Special, Continue.

Part
III

Ch
14

11. The system enters into the Reconciliation of Anticipated Payments/Receipts screen. This screen lists the outstanding checks. Search through the screens or use Search to find the check.

12. Click the check or range of checks, and the system goes into the check's Reconciliation of Receipts/Payments screen.

13. Click the field. Select Complete for a cashed check or Rejected to cancel a check.

14. Take the defaults on the other options.

15. Click Special, Continue to update the record.

16. Exit to end and return to the Maintain Bank Transactions screen.

17. Click the Insert icon to create the next document or exit to end the batch.

You have changed the status of a check.

Using Maintain/Display Check Master   Before you can issue checks on the system, you must set up the check number master for each bank account in which you will be issuing checks. Use Cash Management options: Transaction Processing Maintain Check Master. Enter the bank relation and payment method used for that bank. Click the Insert icon to create the check number range. Click Special, and on the Continue to update. This sets up the check master, as shown in Figure 14.30.

N O T E   If you ever run out of check numbers while maintaining check master, simply insert more. ▪

The check master inquiries are very useful. It lists the check status by check number, supplier number and name, currency and amount, the date it was issued, and the date and document number under which it was completed or rejected on the system.

Using Display/Print Anticipated Payments   Display anticipated payments is very useful for verifying which purchase invoice(s) were paid on a check. A payment document is issued for each check issued. It is by this document that this inquiry is driven. Search to find the document in question and zoom. The system lists the purchase invoices to which the check was issued.

Print anticipated payments can be used as an outstanding check list if selected by Document Accepted/Sent. This lists checks that have been issued, but not cashed. This report is also useful if you want to see the status of a check.

Processing Inquiries and Reports for Cash Management Supplier Payments

It is possible to restrict the payment process to certain system users. The user can also be limited to a maximum dollar amount per check (see Finance parameters).

FIG. 14.30
The each check's status can be maintained using the Maintain Check Master session. That is where you can indicate that a check has been voided.

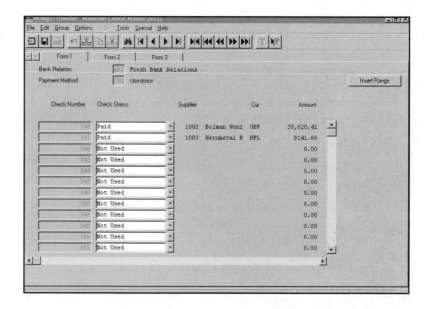

The Supplier Payments option is where you select invoices for payment, make necessary adjustments (add and or delete purchase invoices), and process and print checks. When selecting invoices for payment, it is possible to settle customer sales invoices and pay sales credit notes. You must set up the link between supplier/customer by entering the customer number in the indicated field in the supplier master, and the supplier number in the indicated field in customer master.

Using Display/Maintain/Print Payment Authorizations

This option is for setting which users can process supplier payments. There are also restrictions to set on the maximum amount that can be issued to a supplier per the user. The system does not allow them to process payments if the user is not set up under this option.

N O T E Remember to delete users from this option if they no longer have authorization to process payments. ▪

Using Select Invoices for Payment

If you deal with more than one currency, ensure that a write off currency difference has been processed and finalized. Ensure that all credit notes have been allocated to invoices where possible. This is the first step in the payment process. It is possible to select payments for a particular supplier, for a check run by due date and currency, payment method, and so on. Indicate the planned payment date; this is the date that shows up on the check, as shown in Figure 14.31.

Part
III

Ch
14

If you have suppliers who are also customers, you can settle sales invoices or pay sales credit notes. Occasionally, there may be a situation where a customer has requested a refund for a credit note or an accounts receivable overpayment. If it is for an overpayment, enter a sales invoice and credit note for the refund amount. Allocate the invoice to the overpayment; you are left with the credit note (see the Accounts Receivable module). Ensure that a supplier has been set up with the customer number for linking. The customer must also have the supplier number to complete the linking.

Complete the following to select invoices for payment:

1. Go to Finance, Cash Management, Supplier Payments.

2. Select Invoices for Payment.

3. Make selections required and enter on the payment batch. The system takes the next payment batch number available.

4. Click Special, Continue. Exit to end.

You have selected invoices for payment.

FIG. 14.31
When you want to select Invoices for Payment, you can use various options to narrow the range of the payment.

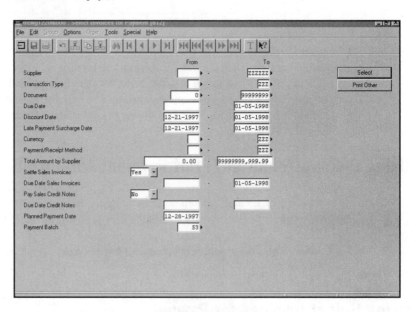

Using Display/Maintain/Print Payment Advice

The payment advice is a list, by supplier, of which invoices have been selected for payment. It is advisable to print a payment advice list and check what you are paying.

If an invoice you do not want to pay is on the report, go to Maintain Payment Advice and delete from the batch selection; you can also go to Maintain Purchase Invoice Details under Accounts Payable, Open Entries, Maintenance to see why it is on the report. It is possible the supplier's due dates are set up incorrectly.

If an invoice is not on the report, do not add to the batch selection without investigating it first. Go to Maintain Purchase Invoice Details under Accounts Payable, Open Entries, Maintenance to see why it did not show up on the report. If a linked invoice has a Registered or Matched status, it does not appear for payment because it does not have a status of Approved. Another possibility is that it may not be due yet according to the information entered into the system. An invoice that has been blocked for payment is not processed until it has been unblocked.

It is recommended, where possible, that all changes be made in maintain purchase invoice details. When all changes are made, reselect the Select Invoices for Payment option using the same payment batch number.

Using Process Payments

Process payments performs various steps. This process generates and prints the checks selected for payment (described in "Select Invoices for Payment").

Perform the following to generate the checks:

1. Go to Finance, Cash Management, Supplier Payments, Processing, Compose Payments. At each process, click Special, Continue, as shown in Figure 14.32.

2. The Payments screen appears, and it goes into the Print Check Run screen, where it asks for the printer to print the checks. It first assigns banks to payments and prints an audit payments report. This report indicates whether there are errors found. The system goes to the Post Payments screen if the message is No Error Found.

3. The Maintain Posting Data screen appears. Validate the transaction date and periods in which the check run posts to the general ledger.

4. The system generates a remittance advice report if a supplier has many invoices that are being paid.

You have now successfully completed a check run.

Using Display Batch Numbers for Payment Procedure

This option displays all payment batch numbers, the user who processed it, the date the payment was processed, and the payment batch status. If the status indicates Posted, then the payment process has been completed. If it still shows Selected, then the process has not yet been completed and should be investigated. If it shows Not Used, then the batch number has not been used. It also helps identify when check runs were completed. This information is very useful for audit and control purposes.

Part
III

Ch
14

FIG. 14.32

You must select the batch you want to process before you process your payment. You can zoom at the Batch field to see the status of all batches created previously.

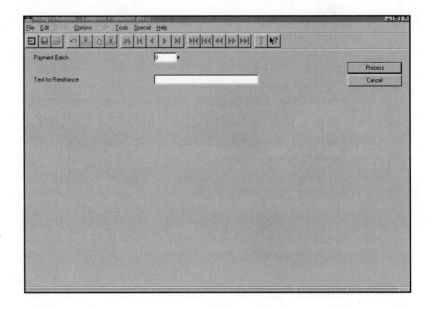

Understanding the Item Control Module

In this chapter

Understanding the General Section

The Item Control Module is the cornerstone for the integration of the various Baan packages at the functional level. Baan Item Control is divided into sections of similar information. Baan Item Control utilizes five different screens for the input of the item data. These five screens, also referred to as forms, are the following:

- Form1—General and Cost Price Data
- Form2—Inventory Data
- Form3—Purchase & Sales Data
- Form4—Order and Repetitive Data
- Form5—Production Data

The objective of populating these forms is to maintain standard item data, which will be used throughout the Baan packages. Apart from standard items, Baan also accommodates customized item data via the Project Control (PCS) module (see Chapter 23, "Understanding the Project Module").

You will review the different sections within the Item Control Module. In doing so, you will see the definite requirement to devote more "front-end" time to developing and loading quality data and well-defined parameters, rather than quickly loading this information and spending lots of valuable time correcting and analyzing after the fact. This chapter will permit you to review and understand the importance of each section within the Item Control Module.

Understanding the Item Code

Baan refers to Items as part numbers, material, or product codes. Within Baan, an item may represent component parts, subassemblies, semi-finished items, manufactured parts, end products, product variants, containerized items, or non-physical (administrative/resource/cost) items. In Baan, the Item is a string of 32 characters, which means that you can use either alphabetic or numerical characters, or a combination of both to represent the items. It is recommended that you plan ahead in order to determine the coding structure that best suits your business and its strategy. Some corporations prefer to use anonymous numbers and use the other functions of the software to find the items.

N O T E The standard version of Baan is not case-sensitive to the Item Code. So if you happen to use lowercase, it would automatically be converted to uppercase. ▩

The tendency in many organizations is to create part numbers that are fully descriptive, often making these part numbers unnecessarily long, hard to remember, and, in general, difficult to work with. In Baan the item does not require having a descriptive code or part number. The Item Control Module allows one to create simple non-descriptive part numbers identifying all item pertinent data through the populating of the five forms within the Item Control module. The proper loading of the fields within the Item Control module will result in ease of use and search capabilities of items throughout the Baan system.

Understanding the General Fields

The General (Form1) section is the area in the Item Control where you identify basic informative data and search keys pertaining to the item or part number. Here you will assign the item type, item group, and other general information for that specific item. Most of the fields in this section are informative and for internal reference needs. Table 15.1 details these fields.

Table 15.1   General Fields of the Item Control Module

Field Name	Description
Description	A 30-character long field that will accept letters and numbers. Always try to be consistent when creating the descriptions. To do so, you could supply a template for users so that all descriptions are created in a similar fashion.
Material	The material from which the item is made.
Size	The dimensions of the item.
Standard	The Standard is purely an informative field. It is used to monitor certain item specifications. The Standard applies to the production or purchase of the item.
Weight	The mass or weight of the item. This can be used as a sort selection.
Search Key I	Search keys are features that permit users to search for items throughout the Baan package. Search keys are extensions of the standard descriptions associated with the specific item in order for search capabilities. Search key 1 is used to retrieve items in various sessions. Other search keys are "item code," "item type," and "signal code."
Search Key II	This search key, like search key 1, is an extra option that is defined for retrieval of items in various sessions or reports.
Item Type	The item type places the item in a pre-defined group of items (for example, manufactured, purchased, generic, and so on).
Item group	The item group or family group enables you to define data for a group of similar items.
Product Type	The product type of the item (for example, purchased or manufactured).
Selection Code	The selection code enables you to select the item by extra features, such as history and statistical information.
Signal Code	The signal code causes a message to be displayed as soon as this item has been selected somewhere within the system. It also could be used to block items through signal codes. The blocking means that we could avoid the usage of the specified item for purchases, production, and so on.
Tax Code	The tax code that applies to this specific item.
Text	YES—A text is present with more general data about the item. NO—No text is present for this item.
Process Item	Manufactured item generated through a formula instead of a Bill of Material. A shop order would accept a by-product as an output for a process item order.

continues

Table 15.1 Continued

Field Name	Description
RPT Item	Manufactured item produced repetitively in large quantities.
Rev. Controlled	YES—The item is subject to revision control. The revision may impact the performance of the item. The revision number will follow through the shop floor process to avoid contamination. NO—Modifications to the process doesn't impact the performance of the product.
Update E-Item	YES—A new link is established with the originator (Engineering-Item). Rev Controlled has to be "YES." FREEZE—The link is kept with the originator (E-Item). Rev Controlled has to be "YES." BREAK—The link with the originator (E-Item) is canceled. Rev Controlled has to be "YES." NOT APPLICABLE—Default value when Rev. Controlled is set to "NO."
Current Revision	Display the actual Revision Control number.

Once Form1 has been populated, the item code, description, item type, and item group have been defined (see Figure 15.1). Baan now has the capability of grouping this item to specific item groups. In this area of the Item Control, several fields have been loaded with informative data, mainly used internally within the company's user community. The user can navigate and search for items throughout the system utilizing the search features created in the General section of the Item Control. The Cost Price Data section of this form is discussed in the Using Cost Information section of this chapter.

FIG. 15.1
The General Section of the Item Master is where you will create the item and record the Description.

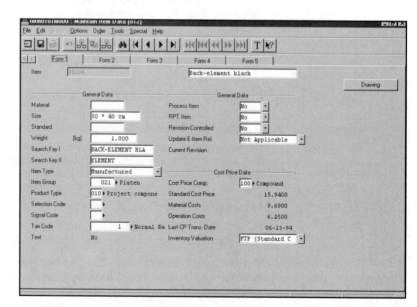

Understanding Inventory Data

The Inventory Data (Form2) is the area of the Item Control where you will define the data that will be utilized throughout the Baan package, mainly in the Distribution modules. Here you assign the units in which you want to store goods, identify the warehouse from which these goods will be transacted from and to, determine if this particular item is lot controlled or not, and establish inventory plans.

The inventory plans cover areas such as Safety Stock, Maximum Stock, Carrying costs, and the Expected volume to be sold or consumed on an annual basis. In this section, you also find a display of live data, such as status of on-hand inventory, if any of this inventory is blocked (temporarily non-usable), the ABC classification as well as the last counted date (based on cycle counting), the inventory on order, and the last transaction date. This data is coming directly from within the Baan system and is reflected in the Inventory Data section of the Item Control module. Table 15.2 shows a list of the fields used for inventory data.

Table 15.2 Understanding Inventory Fields

Field Name	Description
Unit Set	Grouping of units for a specific application.
Inventory Unit	Unit used for costing.
Storage Unit	The storage unit is the unit in which items are stored. The storage unit is useful, only if the "Inventory Location Control" module is used.
Warehouse	The warehouse that is shown for this item by default when issues and receipts are processed.
Lot Control	Lot control applies when the item belongs to a quantity of goods that are to be registered and traced with the "Lot Control" module.
Outbound Priority	The outbound priority applies if the Location Control module controls the item. The outbound priority determines from which locations and lots the item is issued.
Period for Shelf Life	The period for shelf life is the time unit in which the shelf life of the item is expressed. The "best before date" is relevant if a shelf life has been defined for an item.
Shelf Life (Periods)	The number of periods that the item may be held in stock and still retain its quality.
Floor Stock	Stocks of inexpensive production parts held in the factory from which production workers can draw without requisitions.

continues

Table 15.2 Continued

Field Name	Description
Service Level (%)	The service level determines in how far the item can be delivered directly from stock; it is expressed in percent. The higher the percentage, the smaller the chance of lost sales, consequently, the higher the safety stock will be.
Safety Stock	The safety stock of the item serves to buffer the difference between the expected and actual demand. as well as between the expected and actual delivery time.
Maximum Inventory	The planned maximum allowable inventory for an item. The maximum stock determines the quantity of items to be purchased or produced when the system recommends orders.
Seasonal Pattern for Safety Stock	The seasonal pattern for safety stock must prevent capacity problems during sales peaks and lessen the chance of unmarketable stocks.
Seasonal Pattern for Demand	This seasonal pattern is used to forecast the demand for the item in the upcoming periods.
Forecast Methods	The forecast method determines how the expected demand for the item in the upcoming period is predicted.
Inventory on Hand	The inventory on hand is the quantity of the item that is currently present in all warehouses, expressed in the stock unit. When stock transactions occur in the system, this field is automatically updated accordingly.
Inventory on Hold	The total amount of a particular item which is on hold, expressed in the stock unit. The "on hold" quantities are part of the on hand inventory.
Allocated Inventory	The allocated inventory is the quantity of the item allocated to production or sales for all warehouses. It is expressed in the stock unit and determines the economic stock.
Quotations Allocations	The "Quotation Allocation" is the quantity allocated for open sales quotations for a specific item. The system does not consider this quantity as actual allocations and will not be included in the "Allocated stock."
Last Inventory Transaction Date	The last transaction date is the date where physical stock transactions took place for an item, for a warehouse. Only changes regarding the on hand inventory will alter this date.

Field Name	Description
Last Counting Date	The last counting date is the date where an item was last counted. The data is updated after the items have been counted and processed in the session "Process Stocktaking Data."
Cumulative Issues	The cumulative issue is the quantity of the item which has been issued for sales and production orders from all warehouses.
ABC Code	The ABC code indicates the importance of the item for the turnover (sales). "A" items being important contributors to turnover, while "C" items contribute to a lesser extent.
Slow Moving percent	The slow moving percentage of the item gives an indication of its turnover rate. The higher the percentage, the lower the demand is for that item.
Inventory Carrying Cost	Cost of carrying inventory, usually defined as a percentage of the dollar value of inventory per unit of time (generally one year).
Expected Annual Issue	The expected annual issue is the quantity of an item that is expected to be issued per year.

In this section, you have populated the inventory related fields. Some of these fields, such as Safety Stock, Maximum Inventory, and Expected Annual Issue, will play a vital part for planning future requirements. This section is also very useful for live inventory data review. Keep in mind that the display data is the company totals for that specific item. If your setup has several warehouses, the inventory figures seen in this section show the total of all warehouse data for that particular item. To view individual warehouse inventory status, refer to the section "Maintain Item Data by Warehouse" in Chapter 17, "Understanding the Inventory Modules."

Understanding the Distribution Section

In the Distribution section of the Item Control, you will find the Purchasing and Sales data information. The purchasing and Sales Modules will link to the Item Master to obtain data such as pricing and margin information. Note that this information found in the item master can be overwritten within the Sales Module or in the Purchasing Module themselves.

You will also find fields such as Price and statistic groups, which are applicable to both the sales and the purchasing portions of this section. The currency in which the purchased item takes place in, the purchase price, supplier, buyer and planner who are linked to this item are also found in this portion of the Item Control module. Sales carry much of the same data, within the Item control. You have fields representing such areas as Suggested Retail Price, Sales Price and Upper and Lower Margins. Table 15.3 shows the fields used to track purchase data and Table 15.4 shows the fields used to track sales data.

Table 15.3   Purchase Data Fields

Field Name	Description
Purchase Unit	The unit in which the item is purchased.
Price Unit	The unit on which the purchase price is based.
Price Group	The purchase price group places the item in a group of items for which agreements about prices and discounts can be recorded.
Statistic Grp.	The purchase statistics group places the item in a group of items that can be grouped together in statistical reporting.
Currency	The currency in which the purchase or subcontracting of an item takes place. The currency is used when the cost price is calculated for purchased items in the session "Calculate Cost Prices."
Purchase Price	The purchase price of the item expressed in the currency as defined in the purchase data of the item. The cost price, which applies to production, purchase, and sales orders, is calculated from the purchase price. This purchase price is based on the price unit and the currency of this item.
Average Purchase Price	The system shows a price that indicates what has been paid on average for that purchased item.
Latest Purchase Price	The system shows the price that was last paid for the purchase of that item.
Last Purchase Price Transaction date	The system shows the day on which the purchase price of an item was last changed.
Supplier	The supplier from whom the item is purchased.
Buyer	The employee responsible for buying the item. Must be a valid employee in the employee table Code used to extract data from the purchase file Planner. The employee responsible for planning the item when the item is purchased must be a valid employee in the employee table.
Inspection	The field "Inspection" determines the arrival procedure of purchased items.
Purchase Text	YES—A text is present with more purchase data about the item. NO—No text is present for this purchased item.

Having populated the Purchase Data fields, the system now has a starting point for verification of such things as Purchase Price, Units that this item will be stored in, and the currency in which the item is purchased. You also have identified whether this particular item requires inspection.

The inspection field is related to Chapter 17, "Understanding the Inventory Module," where you will be able to see the link for proper transactions of items requiring inspection.

Table 15.4 Sales Data Fields

Field Name	Description
Sale Unit	The unit in which the item is sold.
Price Unit	The unit on which the selling price is based.
Price Group	The sales price group places the item in a group of items for which agreements about prices and discounts can be recorded.
Statistic Group	The sales statistic group places the item in a group of items which can be grouped together in statistical reporting.
Commission Group Field	Used to group items when a commission has to be paid for multiples items.
Rebate Group	Field used to group items when a common rebate agreement can be defined for more than one item.
Sales Price	The selling price of the item expressed in the currency as defined in the session "Maintain Company Data."
Suggested Retail Price	The recommended retail price is the selling price which you may charge to the customer. This price is non-binding.
Upper Margin	The upper margin is the allowable percentage of the actual selling price above the target price.
Lower Margin	The lower margin is the percentage that the selling price is allowed to be lower than the target price.
Last SP Transaction Date	The system shows the date on which the selling price of the item was last changed.
Direct Del. From	Economical order quantity for direct shipment. Ordered quantity has to exceed this value.
Sales Text	YES—A text is present with more sales data about the item. NO—No text is present for this item.

Once the Sales information has been loaded in the Item Control, the system now has the capability to refer, as a basis, to information such as Sales Price, Suggested Retail Price, and Margins. The user can overwrite the default data coming from the Item Control within the Sales module, while working with a specific order or at the line item.

Understanding the Order Section

Baan will require you to fill in this section of the Item Master. This section contains ordering data such as, lead times, first allowed order date as well as minimum and maximum ordering quantities. This information will supply various modules with data that would permit accurate computation of material requirements.

Understanding Order Data

When setting up order data, fields such as Order Policy, Order System, and Order Method must be given serious consideration. These fields play an important role in the ordering logic within Baan. Table 15.5 describes the fields used for order data.

Table 15.5   Order Data Fields

Field Name	Description
Order Policy	The order policy controls how the item is ordered, either anonymous or to-order. The choice of the order policy depends on the chosen item type.
Order System	In combination with the order method (among other things), the order system controls the way in which the system recommends purchase or production orders for this item. The choice of the order system depends on the chosen item type and the order policy.
Order Method	In combination with the order system, the order method determines the quantity of items which may appear on recommended purchase and production orders for this item. The choice of order method depends on the item type, order policy and order system.
Order Qty. Multiple of	This field is mainly relevant for items with the order method: "Lot for Lot," "Economic Order Quantity," and "Replenish to Maximum Stock." While generating recommended orders, the system checks whether the order quantity is a multiple of the quantity in this field, if this is not the case, the system advises you that an error has occurred.
Min. Ord. Qty.	The minimum order quantity prevents the purchase or production of this item in too small a quantity. When recommended orders are generated, the quantity of items to be purchased or produced will never be less than the minimum order quantity.
Max. Ord. Qty.	The maximum order quantity prevents the purchase or production of too many items for an order. The quantity of items to be purchased or produced will never be greater than the maximum order quantity, when the system generates a recommendation.

Field Name	Description
Fixed Ord. Qty.	The fixed order quantity is a quantity of items which appears as a fixed order quantity on recommended purchase or production orders if the order method is "Fixed Order Quantity."
Economic Ord. Quantity	The economic order quantity is the most favorable order quantity which appears for recommended purchase or production orders if the order method is "Economic Order Quantity."
Re-order Point	The re-order point is the average number of items which are sold during the item's delivery time plus the safety stock. The re-order point is used with a SIC re-order system.
Order Interval (Days)	The order interval is the minimally required number of days between two orders for the same item. Using an order interval may prevent too big and frequent a flow of recommended orders.
Order Lead-time (Days)	The order lead-time is measured in workdays. It indicates how long the purchase or production of the item lasts before it is available. It is a span of time required to perform a process.
Safety Time	An element of time added to normal lead time to protect against fluctuations in lead time so that an order can be completed before its real need date.
First Allowed Order Date	The first allowed order date indicates from which date an order may be created for the item. The system gives a warning when a purchase or production order is created before this date.
Update Inv./Order Data	A number of stock and order data is automatically updated by carrying out various sessions.
Commodity Code	Item identifier for export/import purposes. The code is listed on outbound document and could be used to retrieve data from the sales history.
Country of Origin	Identify the provenance of the goods. Used for export purposes.

Having populated the Order Data Fields permits the Baan system to assign the item to its proper ordering methodology. The system now applies the appropriate planning engine logic specified for this item for ordering purposes. These planning engines are Master Production Schedule (MPS), Material Requirements Planning (MRP), or Statistical Inventory Control.

Repetitive Data

The Repetitive Data section of the Item Control module allows the user to define specific fields relating to a *process* (large volume type manufacturing organization). Table 15.6 lists the fields used to track repetitive data. For greater detail concerning Repetitive Manufacturing within Baan, refer to Chapter 20, "Understanding the Manufacturing Module."

Table 15.6   Repetitive Data Fields

Field Name	Description
Schedule code	User defined code attached to an RPT (Repetitive Item) to identify the production rate (daily, weekly, and so on).
RPT item order period	SHIFT—Repetitive orders released based on the available capacity by shift. DAY—Repetitive orders released based on the available capacity by day.
Rate factor for planning	Ratio in percentage of the maximum output of a bottleneck work center to use to generate RPT orders.
Start day Pl. MPS order	First day of the period to release RPT order. The planner may want to give priority to "make to order" type order and process repetitive order at the end of the week only.
Min. remaining %	This percentage is used to determine if the system should generate a new order or add to the existing order when the needed capacity exceed the actual capacity.
MPS/MRP order system RPT	LOT for LOT—The quantity on the order equals the quantity needed. BATCH—The quantity on the order equals the production rate times the available hours.

N O T E   Master Production Schedule (MPS) and Materials Requirements Planning (MRP) are both planning engines. ▪

Once the Repetitive Data section of the Item Control has been loaded, the system will help manage the manufacturing organizations' high volume type production.

Understanding the Manufacturing Section

The manufacturing module will need parameters that are item specific. You will have to determine the unit to be used for the Bill of Material as well as how you want the MPS and the MRP to operate.

Understanding Production Data

The Production Data section of the Item Control module allows the user to identify the item as a Phantom item or not and the Time Fence associated with this item. You also define the Bill of Material and Routing units linked to this item as well as Scrap Factors and Order Costs. It is in this section that you will assign a planner to the specific manufactured item. This section is populated if the item type is manufactured. Table 15.7 lists the fields used to track production data.

Table 15.7   Production Data Fields

Field Name	Description
Phantom	An item is a phantom when it appears in the product structure but is not seen as a separate manufactured item in production. It is mainly applied in order to build up a modular product structure.
Bill of Material Unit	The Bill of Material (BOM) unit defines the number of manufactured items on which the product structure (BOM) is based. The BOM unit allows you to specify very small item quantities as BOM components.
Routing Unit	The routing unit defines the information detailing the method of manufacture of a particular item. It includes the operations to be performed, their sequence, the various work centers involved, and the standards for setup and run times.
Scrap Factor/Shrink	A percentage factor in the product structure used to increase gross requirements to account for anticipated loss within the manufacture of a particular product.
Order Costs	Order costs are handling and transport costs as well as the costs of the purchase and production planning and control departments, incurred for a production or purchase order.
Time Fence	The time fence is a period in which changes in planned production or purchase quantities for MPS items are only possible after you ignore a warning given by the system. This period, which is always calculated from the present date, may contain more than one planning period. The purpose of the time fence is to prevent disruption of the production or purchase by changes in orders that have already been released.
Round Off in MPS	In the MPS module, the calculated values of the forecast, the projected available and the planned production/purchase quantity of an item can be rounded off to whole numbers.

continues

Table 15.7 Continued

Field Name	Description
Critical in MPS	The planner has flagged this item as critical for his operation. YES—The system will calculate the number of unit needed to accomplish the production plan even on a what-if scenario to avoid shortages. NO—The requirement is not calculated until the planner firms the planned orders.
Net Change MRP	An approach in which the material requirements plan is continually retained in the computer. Whenever a change is needed in requirements, open order inventory status, or BOM, a partial explosion and netting is made for only those parts affected by the change.
Low Level Code	A number that identifies the lowest level in any BOM at which a particular component appears. Net requirements for a given component are not calculated until all the gross requirements have been calculated down to that level. Low level codes are normally calculated and maintained automatically by the system.
Order Qty. Dep. Rout.	YES—The production equipment used is dependent of the quantity on the order. NO—The system will default the standard routing for any quantity on the shop order.
Buyer/Planner	The employee responsible for planning the item when the item is purchased. Must be a valid employee in the employee table.
Quantity/Pull Note	Identify the quantity to release to shop floor. Pull Note is the document used for KANBAN type application.
Number of Notes	Number of container circulating in support of the operation.
Backflush Materials	The deduction from inventory records of the component parts used in an assembly or subassembly by exploding the BOM by the production count of assemblies produced.
Backflush if Material	The system will backflush (see previous description) if the item is identified as a component of an upper level backflushed item.
Backflush Hours	The system will backflush hours based on the quantity of unit reported completed for an operation at standard.

Understanding Process Data

The Process Data section of the Item Control module enables the populating of fields pertaining to activities within the Process module of Baan. The Process module serves a typical operation type. This type of operation produces products that involve the following:

- Mixing of raw materials in a certain composite
- Produce an end item using physical or (bio) chemical operations
- Packing of items in a variety of containers

Examples of these types of products would be paint, sugar, and so on. Table 15.8 lists the fields used to track process data.

Table 15.8   Process Data Fields

Field Name	Description
Containerized	YES—This field only applies to Process item. It identifies if the item is produced in multiple format (liter, 20 liter, and so on). NO—The item is produced only in one format.
Assayed item	The value of the item is influenced by the concentration of a critical component. The test value will be used to revise the cost of this produced lot.
Standard potency	Standard concentration for the critical component of this item (for example, Alcohol 40 proof).

Understanding Cost Price Information

The Cost Price section of the Item Control is the driver for the calculation of the Cost Price of an item. To calculate the cost price for a purchased item you must assign a cost price calculation code. Through this code the user must select the purchase price to be considered, the current purchase price, average purchase price, the latest purchase price, or a simulated price. Table 15.9 lists the fields used to track cost price data.

Table 15.9   Cost Price Information Fields

Field Name	Description
Cost Price Component	The cost price component of the item to which the material costs are usually posted.
Standard Cost Price	The standard cost price is the sum of material and operation costs and cost price surcharges for the item. The system shows what it costs to purchase or produce an item.

continues

Table 15.9   Continued

Field Name	Description
Material Costs	Material costs are calculated by adding the cost of the materials and any surcharges that may have to be paid on the materials for the item under consideration.
Operation Costs	Operation costs are calculated by adding the cost of the operations and any surcharges that have to be paid for the operations for the item under consideration.
Last CP Trans. Date	The system shows the date on which the cost price of the item was last changed. The last transaction date changes as soon as you have changed the cost price data in the session Update Cost Prices.
Inventory Valuation	The manner in which the stock for the item is valued.

N O T E   Manufactured items cost price calculation can only be carried out if the BOM and Routing have been defined and assigned to this specific item. The main reason for this is that the Routing will allow for proper operations to be included with material costs for a total cost price.

Understanding the Distribution Module

Using Purchase Control

A successful purchasing policy requires accurate supplier information—for example, data telling you which supplier can offer you the subassemblies you need with the correct specifications and against what terms. All the information required can be recorded using Baan. Your purchasing decisions will therefore always be based on the correct information.

The Baan Purchasing module provides the capability to modify agreements as quickly as market conditions change; to create specific contracts for individual suppliers and items; and to use historical data to evaluate suppliers.

Using Purchase Prices and Discounts

Baan allows you to control purchase prices and discounts. In order to purchase goods, you will have to make agreements with the supplier concerning the prices to be paid and the discounts that will be granted. Purchase Prices and Discounts deals with prices and discounts of a *normal* purchase order. Agreements of this nature can be stored in different ways.

The pricing hierarchy structure used in this module will also give you all the flexibility required to assign the right purchase price to each item under each combination of suppliers and agreements.

NOTE When purchase orders are created or generated, the system refers to the price files in order to determine the purchase price of and the discount on the items in the order. ▪

The system follows a specific path when searching for the purchase price and when creating a purchase order. The system will determine the pricing according to the following factors (in this order):

- Use of an existing purchase contract
- Prices by supplier and item (see Figure 16.1)
- Discounts by supplier and price group
- Discounts by supplier
- Prices by price list and item
- Discounts by price list and price group
- Discounts by price list
- Prices by item
- Purchase price from the item master

Using Purchase Contracts

Purchase contracts are used to record agreements that mainly relate to prices and discounts. These agreements are recorded for both items and price groups (see Figure 16.2). Apart from an effective period, you can also specify whether the minimum quantity to be purchased is binding. Both normal and special contracts can be created.

FIG. 16.1

This session allows you to assign a specific purchase price for an item purchased from a specific supplier.

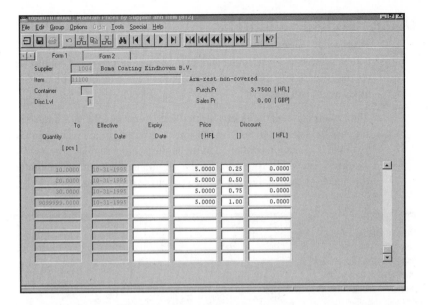

FIG. 16.2

This session allows you to maintain all the necessary information related to a purchase contract.

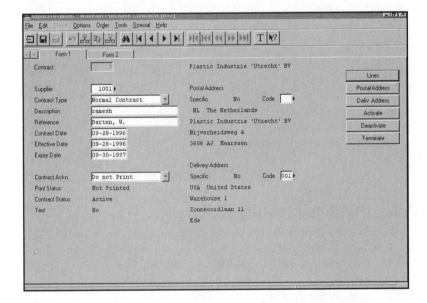

Other than prices and discounts, the purchase contracts are also used to record agreements on quantities to be purchased and on a delivery schedule. Using a delivery schedule, you can generate purchase orders that can be sent when goods are required.

It is also possible to activate or deactivate a contract as needed to prevent the generation of purchase orders using the Generate Purchase Orders session.

Using Purchase Inquiries

Purchase Inquiries allows suppliers to submit quotations for the delivery of goods. This inquiry can be printed and sent to the supplier. The quotations received in return (the inquiry results) can be entered into the system. This allows a comparison of the prices and discounts offered by different suppliers.

After you receive all the quotes from the different suppliers and have made your selection, the supplier to be used can use the session called Copy Inquiry Lines to Purchase Order to transform the information contained in the inquiry into a regular purchase order. When creating the inquiries, you will be required to enter all the necessary information that could be used later if you decide to turn that inquiry into a purchase order (see Figure 16.3).

FIG. 16.3

The Inquiries Contains session allows you to assign a specific purchase price for an item purchased from a specific supplier.

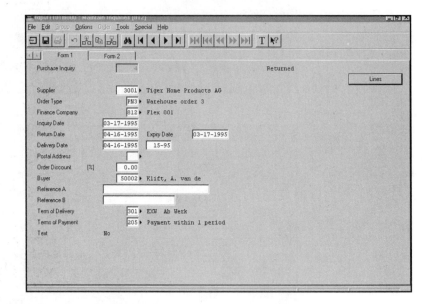

Using Purchase Inquiry History

Purchase Inquiry History allows you to view, print, or delete the history of purchase inquiries. This is useful if you want to compare quotes received with quotes previously sent by your different suppliers. You can also see which inquiries have been turned into purchase orders or see which inquiries have been deleted. All displays in the modules are sorted by supplier and item (see Figure 16.4).

The following types of history are available:

- Created inquiries
- Copied inquiries
- Deleted inquiries

FIG. 16.4

You can display all inquiries that have been accepted and turned into a purchase orders.

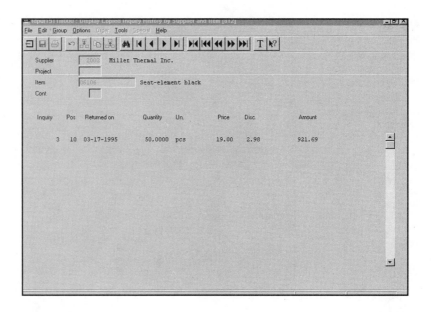

Using Purchase Orders

Purchase Orders allows you to create and modify orders for purchasing goods and services. A generated or manually created purchase order can be printed and sent to the supplier.

Like most purchasing modules of any ERP software, it is important that you control the steps to be taken from the time you place the purchase order to the time you pay the invoice.

In Baan, you will find order types and order steps that will control the next action to be taken on a specific purchase. For example, if you want to print a purchase order and a storage list every time you place an order, you need to use an order type that will contain those two steps. But if you place a purchase order and want to expedite the process, you may decide to use an order type that will require you to perform only a few steps. After you assign an order type to an order, you cannot change this selection.

Baan provides you a set of predefined order types. You might want to use them, modify them, or create your own. These predefined order types can be seen under Miscellaneous in the Purchase Order Business Object.

The Purchase Control module will have an impact in many other modules. For example, the MRP calculation will take into account how many parts you have on order. The receiving process will also be influenced by the creation of the purchase order.

This module will also allow you to maintain purchase orders that have been created by other modules, such as MRP, MPS, Inventory Control, and Project Control. Once created, the purchase orders can be maintained like any manual purchase order (see Figure 16.5).

FIG. 16.5

The Purchase Order Details form is used to record the item code, the delivery date, and the pricing information for each product ordered.

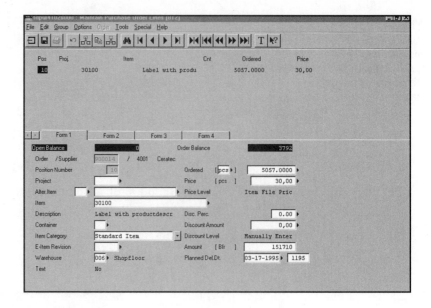

Using the Other Purchasing Modules

The Purchasing Control modules also contain a module to capture receipts of material. This module will use the information recorded in the purchase order and will allow you to enter the quantity received. That session will add the goods received to the inventory and decrease the amount of items on order.

There is an Inspection of Goods Business Object that will allow your quality control users to confirm that inspections have been done on items received if you indicate that inspection is mandatory for a specific item or a specific supplier.

The Close Received Purchase Orders is really self explanatory. After purchase orders have been received, there are a few actions you should perform. The Purchase Order Maintenance program will not allow you to change the purchase price when the goods have been received, but you will find a session in that business object to change prices when goods have been received. In this business object, you will find a session to print the purchase invoices for accounting needs. Finally, you can perform the Process Delivered Purchase Orders to write the statistical information to the history files.

The Purchase Order History Business Object contains various displays and reports to review created and invoiced purchase orders. Also, you can review the change code history for the header and the detail lines of the purchase order.

The Purchase Statisitics functions will require you to set up sort codes. Those sort codes will classify purchase statistics in the order you specify. You can use various predefined fields, such as Country or Item Group. The information gathered can be displayed through two different kinds of graphs, or it can be printed.

There are three interesting reports in the Supplier Reliability Analysis Business Object. You can print supplier reliability by Supplier and Item, by Supplier and Item Group, or by Item and Supplier. For this, Baan uses a reliability factor, which is a weighted factor that indicates whether the supplier delivered early or late.

Using Sales and Marketing Information

The Sales and Marketing Information allows you to record data in a flexible way. When used with the Sales Control module, this is a tool to support marketing needs. By using features that you will define in the Master Data section, you will be able to capture valuable information on your existing Customer Base.

Using SMI Master Data

The Master Data functions will enable you to build all the neccessary setup to capture the information required for the marketing department. It is very important to set up all the sessions related to the feature definitions in order to gather all the data. Those features are miscellaneous information you want to capture on your customers and prospects. You also have attribute regions for employees. You assign employees to various zip codes in the Maintain Zip Codes by SMI Employees (see Figure 16.6).

FIG. 16.6
You can assign all your customers and prospects to a responsible employee in your marketing department using this session.

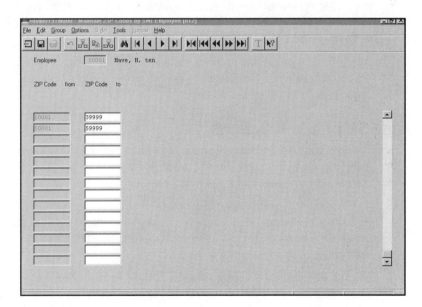

Using SMI Activities

The Activity Business Object of the Sales and Marketing Information module will enable the management of all activities related to marketing efforts. The possible activities to maintain are follow-up telephone calls, sales calls, registration of complaints, and the mailing of various documentation (see Figure 16.7).

FIG. 16.7

The activities of the Sales and Marketing Information module are in fact all the tasks you want your marketing department to perform, such as sending a multiple mailing to all your customers.

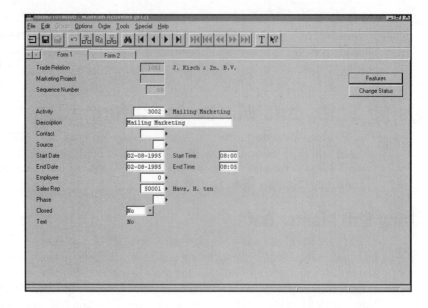

In this module, you will also be able to manage the appointments of all the SMI employees and your sales representatives. When you use this module, you must first set up an activity and then assign a description, a contact, a start, and end date. You also must assign an employee and a sales representative.

After you have created the necessary activities, you can assign appointments for your employees and schedule activities. Note also that when you create activities, there are two functions to create globally: activities and features.

Using SMI Trade Relations

The marketing department will be dealing with two groups of customers: existing customers and prospective customers. To ease the prospect, the Sales and Marketing Information module refers to the two groups as Trade Relations.

The Trade Relations Business Object contains various functions to manage the two groups of customers (see Figure 16.8). There is a session that will allow you to move a prospect customer to the status of normal customer. In this Business Object you will also assign contacts by relation and also by marketing project.

You also will maintain the letters that can be used for multiple mailing purposes. You first create the letter and then you use the selection process to indicate to which customers or prospects you want to send it. Various parameters will allow you to select Trade Relations. If you want to select all customers in the USA, you will have to create an expression statement that will read `tccom010.ccty = "USA"`. This is recorded using the Text Manager function.

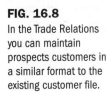

FIG. 16.8
In the Trade Relations you can maintain prospects customers in a similar format to the existing customer file.

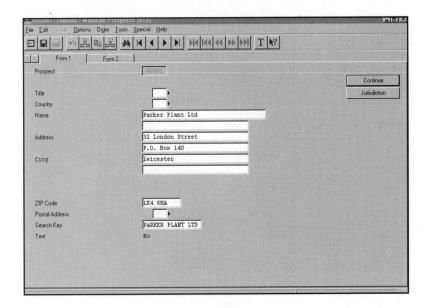

Using Replenishment Order Control

The Replenishment Order Control module is designed to help manage the flow of goods from one warehouse to the orders. Before the creation of this module, there was no easy way to control the replenishment of the various sites of a corporation. This module now gives you the visibility of movement and will let you track the material in transit between two sites.

Using the Replenishment Order Control is like placing a purchase order at the site requesting the goods and a sales order at the location shipping the goods. This process is completed by using a transit warehouse in which the goods are stored virtually until delivery.

N O T E Replenishment orders can also be used to effect the transfer of inventory between two locations in the same warehouse. ■

Using Replenishment Orders

When creating a replenishment order, you have to supply the three warehouses to be involved in the operation: the warehouse requesting the goods, the warehouse supplying the goods, and the transit warehouse. You have to specify the delivery date for the goods. Just like a regular sales or purchase order, you fill in the header form and then fill in the details form for each item you want to include in the replenishment order (see Figure 16.9).

Order steps are used as well in replenishment order to indicate the steps to be performed for shipment and receipt in each location.

FIG. 16.9

When creating a replenishment order, you have to indicate the destination warehouse, the replenishing warehouse, and the transit warehouse.

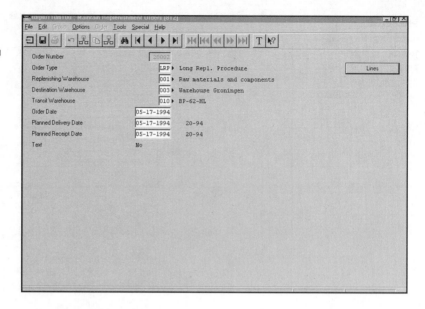

Using Replenishment Order Deliveries

The Replenishment Order Deliveries process is somewhat similar to the Regular Sales Deliveries process. You register quantity delivered against the planned quantity of the replenishment order. If the location control is implemented, you will have to maintain or generate the outbound data and release it to indicate that the goods have been shipped and that they must be relieved from inventory. Shipping documents can also be produced in the same manner as the regular sales documents.

When you performed all the steps indicating that the goods are shipped from the warehouse supplying the goods, then the goods are transferred automatically to the transit warehouse. If you look at the inventory of a particular item just shipped, you will see a quantity in inventory in the transit warehouse (see Figure 16.10).

Using Replenishment Order Receipts

When the goods are received at the warehouse that placed the request, you must move the goods from the transit warehouse to the demanding warehouse. Use the Maintain Receipts Session found in the Replenishment Control module (see Figure 16.11). This session is similar to the one used for regular purchase receipts. Information is recorded in the same way, and once again the sequence of events is based on the choice of the order type selected at the time of creation of the replenishment order. If location control is implemented, you will have to perform the inbound process to locate the goods in the inventory.

If you don't receive the entire quantity planned in the replenishment orders, this quantity will remain open and will be included in the amount of items you have on order for a specific product. Baan will reconcile the quantity shipped against the quantity received if you close the replenishment order.

FIG. 16.10
This display will allow you to track orders in transit between two warehouses.

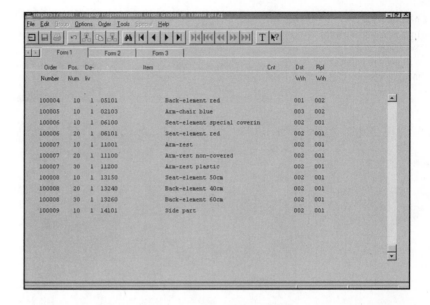

FIG. 16.11
The receipt process in the replenishment order control is similar to the process used in the Purchase Control module. Here you can see the display used to find the order status.

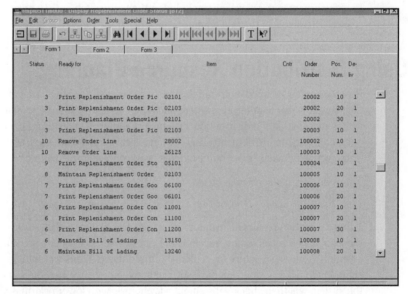

Using Replenishment Order History

The session found in the Replenishment Order History will allow you to display, print, and delete the history of replenishment orders. The system generates the Replenishment Order History when processing replenishment orders in the session Process/Delete Delivered Replenishment Orders. You might have to consult history to find information about transfers among the different warehouses (see Figure 16.12).

FIG. 16.12

This display summarizes the activity that occurred for replenishment orders.

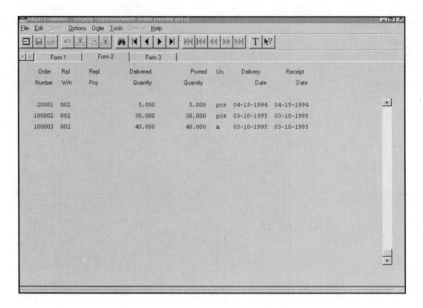

Replenishment orders are only included in the history when they have been completely processed. History data that is no longer relevant can be deleted.

Using Distribution Resource Planning

Based on an established distribution structure, also referred to as a *bill of distribution*, Business Objects allow you to determine where and when inventory is to be replenished. The system determines, within the distribution structure, whether the economic stock falls below the reorder point due to incoming demand. This demand is calculated from the higher of either the forecast or the actual demand (sales requirements or warehouse replenishment requirements).

The economic stock calculation is

```
((On hand+On order)-(on hold+ Allocated))=Economic stock
```

If this calculation results in inventory shortage, the system will check for inventory availability in the established replenishing warehouse. Priorities are assigned to specific warehouses within a given distribution structure for replenishing sequence. If this warehouse, the one with an assigned high priority, does not have sufficient inventory, based on the same calculation as above, the system will then check subsequent warehouses with lower priorities within that structure for replenishment.

After the system finds the warehouse that is capable of replenishing the warehouse-requiring inventory, the system generated a recommended order. The system not only considers the required inventory, but also the time it is needed in and the time to carry these materials. At this point the system simply generates a recommended order—this is only a system advice. The user can now review, modify, or even delete this recommendation. After the user agrees or modifies the system-generated recommendation, the next step is to confirm and release this recommendation into a replenishment order.

Due to the complexity of some distribution structures, it becomes important to have DRP review the optimal material supply flow on a regular basis (daily). The session Generate Planned DRP Orders will accommodate that specific need. This DRP session can be run in one of two ways: full regenerative DRP or net-change DRP.

Full regenerative DRP regenerates the entire file, not considering previously recommended orders, whereas a net-change DRP will only consider those items for which demand or consumption changes have occurred. The full regenerative DRP should be run as an overnight process because of the heavy load that it has to process (the entire file). The net-change DRP can be processed any time.

Using Bill of Distribution

A bill of distribution is a structure of several warehouses within a single logistical company. The warehouses on the higher level of the structure replenish the warehouses on the lower level of the structure (see Figure 16.13). In practice, the warehouses on the higher level of the structure are generally purchasing or manufacturing facilities, which are referred to as *nettable* warehouses. The nettable warehouses are planned by MRP and SIC planning engines.

FIG. 16.13
The bill of distribution indicates the orders, in which warehouses, that are to be selected to replenish a given site.

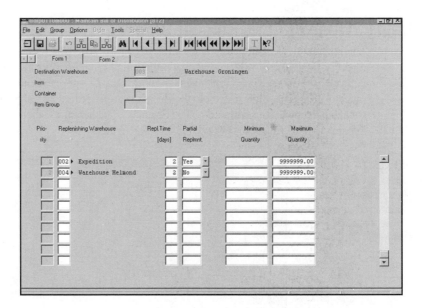

The warehouses on the lower level of the structure are generally regional distribution/sales sites, also referred to as *non-nettable* warehouses. The non-nettable warehouses are planned through the DRP planning engine. In DRP, the non-nettable warehouses are called *destination warehouses*. The non-nettable warehouses are replenished depending on the priority assigned to the replenishing warehouses and inventory availability. This structure determines which replenishing warehouse should supply the destination warehouse.

Using Distribution Requirement Planning

The Distribution Requirements Planning Business-Object allows an organization to manage the distribution of product between facilities. This tool (DRP) complements the user's ability to ensure that the warehouses within a defined structure (bill of distribution) are being replenished with the right product at the right time in the right quantities.

The DRP tool allows the user to anticipate which warehouse within the structure will require products by making use of the inventory and demand data within each facility of the structure. Organizations with multiple warehouses within one logistical company can use DRP to manage their inventory and calculate their future aggregated demand. DRP does not rely on historical sales data, but rather on future time-phased requirements. DRP is an extremely vital partner in safety stock level management. Safety stocks can be maintained centrally rather than unnecessarily increasing inventory levels, and possibly increasing the chance of non-usable lot sizes or obsolescence by having safety stock levels per distribution center (warehouse).

The DRP calculation output, in Baan, is Planned Replenishment Orders. Now the user can alter any of the data in these planned orders. After the order data is approved or accepted, it is then transferred to the Replenishment Order Control module.

Using Planned Replenishment Orders

The Planned Replenishment Order module allows the DRP planner to convert DRP orders to replenishment orders (RPLs). This can be accomplished either manually or automatically (see Figure 16.14). The planned replenishment orders can be approved and transferred, either by range of orders or single orders, to the Replenishment Order Control module. DRP orders are consolidated by destination warehouse. For more detailed information, refer to the "Using Replenishment Order Control" section of this chapter.

FIG. 16.14

Just like any other type of planned orders, the DRP planned orders can be maintained manually.

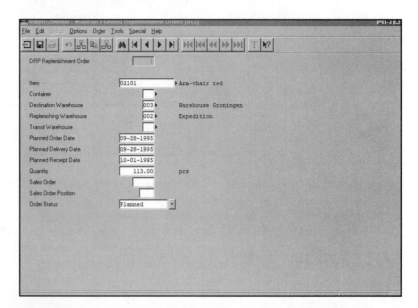

Rescheduling and Exception Messages

The system generates rescheduling messages during the DRP run. Examples of rescheduling messages are reschedule-in or reschedule-out. The system will advise the user when orders already exist for which actual requirement dates do not coincide.

Exception messages are also generated during the DRP run. Examples of exception messages are inventory above maximum inventory or inventory below safety stock. The system supplies the user with exception messages that identify differences with master data information.

Rescheduling messages and exception messages can be displayed onscreen or printed on hard copy. These messages are extremely useful tools for the user to optimally plan distribution of goods within the network. In the Display Planned Inventory Movements session, the DRP planner can review how the system arrived at the rescheduling advice or exception messages it generated (see Figure 16.15).

FIG. 16.15
When DRP orders have been generated, you can see what will be the impact on the inventory by reviewing the planned movements.

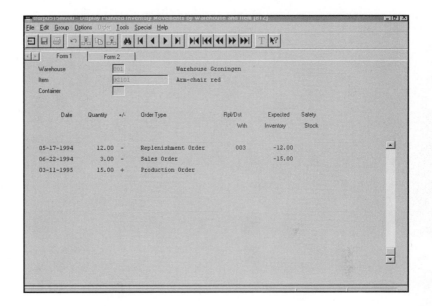

Understanding the Inventory Module

In this chapter

Managing Inventory

Baan offers the user two different ways to manage the inventory. This chapter covers in detail both the Inventory Control module and the Location Control module. You will be shown the functions of both modules, and you will be in a position to decide whether to use only the Inventory Control module or a combination of both the Inventory Control and the Location Control modules. These modules will serve as very useful tools for inventory managers to reach rational inventory decisions. These tools will allow the organization to view and manage inventories, not from a limited point of view (finance versus sales versus operations) but rather from an overall company standpoint.

Managing inventory is quite important in an integrated environment. Baan offers two different ways for managing one of the most important assets for any company. By reading this chapter, you will be able to set up your system in a way to control the inventory in alignment with the organizations' financial and operational objectives.

Using the Inventory Control Module

The Inventory Control module is built in such a way that you could use just this module to manage your inventory. In an environment where managing inventory by location is not a priority, this module can be used as a standalone. This module supplies the user with live inventory information that is received from the purchasing, sales, Master Production Schedule (MPS), Material Requirements Planning (MRP), and Statistical Inventory Control (SIC) modules. This data can be viewed in the Display Planned Inventory Transaction by item session, by order, or by item. The Inventory Control module also tracks all the historical transactions that have occurred for specific items within specific warehouses and by order.

Here in the Inventory Control module, you will be able to analyze the inventory through ABC classification reporting, Slow Moving Analysis, and Inventory Valuation. These tools are of utmost importance for superior inventory management.

Maintaining the Warehouse Information

The first step when you want to work with the Inventory Control module is to create a warehouse in the logistic tables. Warehouses are places where goods are stored. For each warehouse you can enter address data and data relating to its type. Different types of warehouses are

- *Normal.* A warehouse with or without locations where goods are stored.
- *Work-in-process.* Used to store intermediate inventory that is used to supply production lines and work centers.
- *Transit.* Warehouses used for registering inventory in transit.

The transit warehouses are used in the module Replenishment Order Control (RPL) to track inventory during transportation. Furthermore, you can define a warehouse to be *nettable* or *non-nettable*. A non-nettable warehouse is planned with DRP in the Distribution Requirements Planning module, and a nettable warehouse has its planned replenishment carried out through MRP and SIC. An exception is a nettable work-in-process warehouse because it can also be replenished by DRP.

Companies with a single warehouse; must define at least one warehouse, otherwise, orders cannot be processed. In order to create a warehouse, you must follow these steps:

1. Go to Baan Common.

2. Click Common Data.

3. Click Maintenance 3.

4. Click Maintain Warehouses.

5. Enter Warehouse Information.

The information contained in Form 2 of the Maintain Warehouses session is very important—that is where you define whether the components of this warehouse will be included in MRP calculations by making it nettable or non-nettable (see Figure 17.1).

FIG. 17.1
Define whether the components of this warehouse will be included in MRP calculations or not by making it nettable or non-nettable.

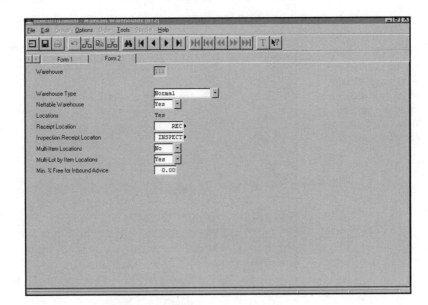

Maintaining Item Data by Warehouse

More than one warehouse can be linked to an item. For each item you can create an inventory record by warehouse. This will record the information for this item specific to this warehouse. This file will contain such information as the minimum and maximum to be kept in inventory as well as quantity on hand and quantity of goods allocated to sales orders. The default values are coming from the Item Control module (see Chapter 15 "Understanding the Item Control Module"). These values can be modified by warehouse. After you have set up the inventory and ordering values to suit that warehouses' specific needs, you can set the following parameters to avoid your data being overwritten by the Item Control values when the Global Update of Parameters is run. Set the following parameters to No: Use Item Parameters and Update Inv Parameters. This setup will allow for data in Maintain Item Data by Warehouse to remain as you have set it up or until you decide to manually modify the inventory and order data.

To maintain the item data by warehouse, perform these steps (see Figure 17.2):

1. Insert a new record, supplying item code, warehouse code, and container to be used.
2. If you use location control, enter a location for this item; otherwise leave it blank.
3. Specify if you want to use the main item parameters.
4. Enter safety stock for this item in this warehouse.
5. Enter maximum inventory to be carried in this warehouse.
6. Enter reorder point applicable in this warehouse only.
7. Specify order method. The usual choice is Lot for Lot.
8. Enter minimum, maximum, economic, and fixed order quantity.
9. Enter order interval in days. This will be accounted for when processing MRP functions.
10. Supply the date when transactions will be allowed for the first time in this warehouse.

FIG. 17.2

You can record specific warehousing information by product for each warehouse using the Maintain Item Data by Warehouse session.

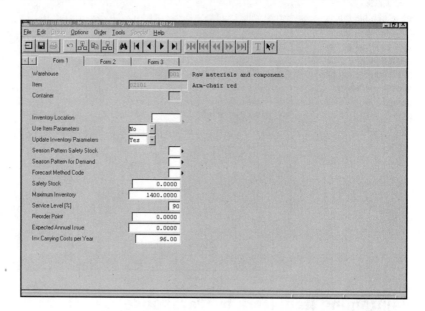

After this three-form session is populated (the third form displays information pertaining to the Items Inventory Status in that particular warehouse), the system can plan inventory replenishment for that specific item/warehouse. The system now has the data required to plan for inventory levels as well as ordering structures related to this item in this warehouse.

Using Inventory Transactions

In the Inventory Control module, it is possible to enter transactions to adjust or transfer inventory. If you are using the Location Control module, this function will be performed in this module, not in the Inventory Control module. Baan will advise you if you try to record a transaction in Inventory Control while you have the Location Control module activated. Baan IV supplies the capability to define that specific users be permitted to complete certain type of transactions only. This is done through the Maintain User Authorization for Inventory Transactions session. The different types of transactions that can be entered in both Inventory Control and Location Control are as follows:

- Production Receipts (not linked to a production order)
- Production Issue
- Purchase Orders (not linked to a purchase order)
- Sales Orders (not linked to a sales order)
- Inventory Adjustments
- Inventory Transfer

The Inventory Transaction section of Baan IV allows authorized users to conduct transactions relating to inventory movement or any modifications required to be done due to differences in inventory quantities. You can define reasons to identify why these adjustments occur. These inventory movements can be printed by different defining features, such as reason code date, transaction number, and so on.

Part

III

Ch

17

Using Allocations

Allocations are managed in two different ways in the system. There are *hard* and *soft* allocation types. All orders or demands going through the sales order modules will generate allocations automatically. Those allocations are often referred to as soft allocations. Baan reserves a quantity of goods but will not specify which lot are allocated to an order. This is done when you generate your outbound data, which is referred to as hard allocations. Outbound data is a procedure that allocates (hard allocation) a specific demand quantity to a specific item-lot-location warehouse. This basically assigns specific physical product to a specific order requirement for the fulfillment of that demand.

To complement this process, Baan inserted a new process called hard allocations that can be used if you don't have a location control system implemented. Baan will allow you to manually create hard allocations or to generate them automatically at the sales orders line level. Those allocations are updated when the sales orders are delivered or canceled.

Using Warehouse Cycle Counting

Even if you don't use a location control system, it is possible to use Baan to perform cycle counting in the Inventory Control module. Note that if you have the Location Control module implemented, Baan will advise you to use the business object located in the Location Control module to perform this function.

To perform cycle counting in the Inventory Control module, you first generate cycle counting orders for a range of items or locations. Then you print cycle count sheets to be used on the shop floor to do the physical counting, enter the results of the cycle count, and print a reconciliation report. When you agree with the numbers entered, the next step is to process those cycle count orders; then the new figures will be posted in your inventory, and adjustments will be created automatically. These processed cycle count orders generate stock adjustments automatically. As mentioned in inventory transactions, you are able to define specific reason codes for the adjustments relating to cycle counting and link them to a specific ledger account. It is important to categorize the inventory adjustment types for justification purposes. This enables better control over the total sum of adjustments. Delete your orders when the process is completed. Ensure that you are deleting only the orders that you have been working with. The open cycle count orders should be monitored because while the cycle count order is active, the inventory associated to it is blocked until the order is processed. This last step is part of the routine the user should develop in order to keep the system clean.

Using Warehouse Inquiries and Reports

There are various reports available in the Inventory Control module. You will use the Display Inventory by Item option the most. The main reason for using this display more often is that the user will search for a specific item at the aggregate level and have the capability to drill down to the exact location, warehouse, and lot of that specific item. This will be achieved through the zoom features within Baan in the Display Inventory by Item session. Of the eight different displays available, one of the most useful is the Planned Inventory Transactions by Item. This display will allow you to see all the live transactions, such as receipts, issues, and forecast for a given item over time, with cumulative available totals after each transaction specified for that item.

The reports provided in this module will allow users to print the total warehouse inventory, to print it by item, and to print the inventory by production bill of material. A very useful tool is the Planned Transactions by Items report. In it, you will indicate the inventory that is available to promise your customers over a certain period of time.

Using Inventory History

The Inventory History Business Object will allow you to archive all inventory transactions by items. You will also be able to archive issues either by period or by warehouse. This process must be planned ahead and will have you copy to a different company all the inventory transactions. Once archived, those transactions will be accessible for display or reports through that archiving company.

Archive once a year if the volume of your transactions allows you to wait for that period of time. Don't go beyond that period because you might have some performance issues producing inventory reports.

 TIP It is strongly recommended that you back up all your databases before performing the archiving function.

To archive Inventory Transactions by Item, you must perform the following steps (see Figure 17.3):

1. Enter the date up to which you want to archive the information.

2. Supply the company number to be used for archiving (always use the same number).

3. Answer Yes to overwrite any existing texts.

4. Click Special.

5. Click Continue.

FIG. 17.3
Supply the date up to which you want to archive, the company where the data is to be stored, and whether you want to keep the text information.

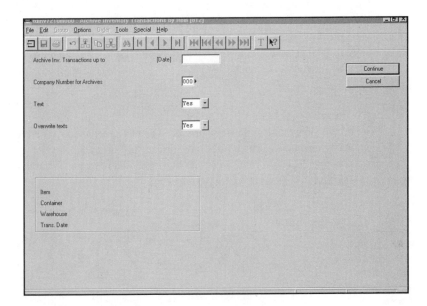

As previously explained, the user can now display inventory in various ways as well as print hard copies of the required data to obtain information pertaining to the desired item. You can now archive older data to enhance system performance. After the data is archived, you can still access it by extracting the selected data from the archive company.

Using Inventory Analysis

The Inventory Analysis will provide you three different reports to manage your inventory. These modules will serve as very useful tools for inventory managers to reach rational inventory decisions. These tools will allow the organization to view and manage inventories, not from a limited point of view (finance versus sales versus operations) but rather from an overall company standpoint.

The following are those reports:

- ABC Analysis
- Slow Moving Analysis
- Inventory Valuation

The ABC Analysis will classify all your items according to parameters you can maintain in the session tdinv0100m000, Maintain Inventory Parameters. Here you identify an item by ABC classification and rank that item in terms of importance within the entire inventory community based on overall turnover (sales or consumption). This classification can be used to determine the frequency at which specific items should be counted through the cycle counting module. In this session, you maintain what will be the ratio for A, B, and C items. This can be recalculated at any time after you modify those parameters. The basis for the ABC Analysis can be the cost price, the selling price, or the quantities.

The Slow Moving Analysis works the same way as the ABC Analysis. This tool allows the user to define the obsolescence of inventory as well as portions of that inventory that are becoming slow moving. To define the criteria for an item to become slow moving, go in the session tdinv0100m000, Maintain Inventory Parameters. Baan uses the following equation to calculate the slow moving percentage:

$$\text{Moving Percentage} = \text{Issues} / \text{Stock on Hand}$$

The Inventory Valuation will be an indicator of the value of your inventory. This report can be generated at any time and can be produced as of a specific date (see Figure 17.4). This is important when you want to get the value of your inventory for the beginning or the end of any given period. The different selection criteria for this report will enable you to narrow down to specific series of items or to item groups.

FIG. 17.4
This session will allow you to print the value of the inventory at any given date; this is very useful for reconciliation purposes.

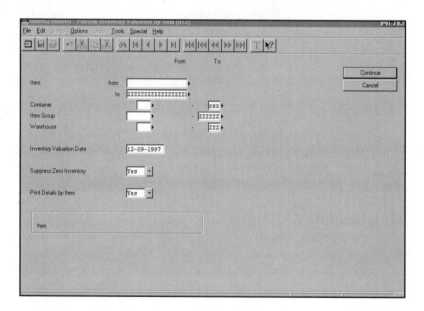

Understanding the Lot Control Module

The Lot Control module has been developed to allow the management of information for the items that require monitoring by lot. You might need to track the origin date of a manufacturing batch, or you might need to know specific features that can vary from one lot to the other.

The Lot Control module will ease the process of monitoring and will give you the tool to track information related to the lots in inventory or shipped to customers. This is an important feature that is vital to some companies to maintain quality standards that meet the requirements of the ISO 9001 certification.

N O T E In order to use the Lot Control module, you must first activate the Location Control module. ■

Using Lots

Before using the Lot Control module, you must specify in the parameters of this module how you want to generate the lot code (see Figure 17.5). It is possible to create lots manually to be used for production and inventory. The easiest way to use Lot Control is to let Baan assign lot number. You can go to the session called Maintain Lot ID Structure found in the Miscellaneous sessions and specify how you want to build the lot structure using such data elements as the manufacturing order number, the date, and so on.

FIG. 17.5

Using this session you can specify how you want the lot code to be automatically generated by Baan. You can specify what data element will be used; for this example, the year, the month, the date, and the item code are used.

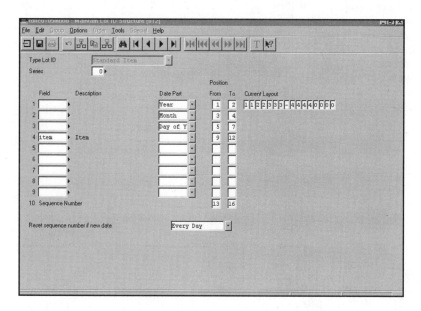

When you have specified that you want the lot code to be generated automatically, Baan will assign a lot code when it receives Finish Goods in Inventory or when you maintain receipts for purchase components. The lot code is created according to the specified parameters; if you use the manual process, you need to assign manually a lot code number.

The costing process is also easier for Lot Control. You might need to specify at the item level that your item is Valued per Lot Value instead of Item Standard Cost. Baan will then use the purchase price of the lot as the inventory value of the item.

N O T E For your item to be traceable by lot you need to specify that the item is lot controlled in the item data maintenance. ■

Using Variable Lot Features

The Variable Lot features have been designed to record information that can vary from one lot to the other (see Figure 17.6). For example, if you produce chairs and want to use only one item code for all chairs you produce, you first have to create a feature called color. After you have created a feature, you can then record a value for this feature for every lot of this product you have inventory by recording a Value by Lot feature. When you have recorded which lots contain blue chairs, you can get a display or a report of all the lots in inventory that are made of blue chairs.

FIG. 17.6

These are good examples of items defined as Variable Lot features. With this setup, you can record the color, diameter, height, and style of each lot in inventory.

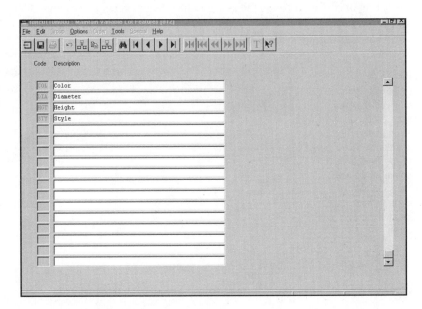

The features to be used are user-defined. You can create as many as you want, the only limitation being the management of information required to fulfill the feature values.

Using Lot Tracking

The Lot Tracking functions are used to trace the origin of the lots manufactured or purchased. You can find when the lots have been created and also where they have been used. The information can be extracted from production orders, sales orders, or service orders.

The Lot Tracking functions will also help you find the link between a supplier lot and the lot number equivalent in your inventory. It will also possible to find the origin of each lot by specific order.

There is a session that allows the deletion of the lots from the system (see Figure 17.7). This is only possible if the inventory for a given lot is at zero. You must be careful because if you run this session to delete a lot, the tracking information will no longer be available for this lot.

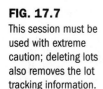

FIG. 17.7
This session must be used with extreme caution; deleting lots also removes the lot tracking information.

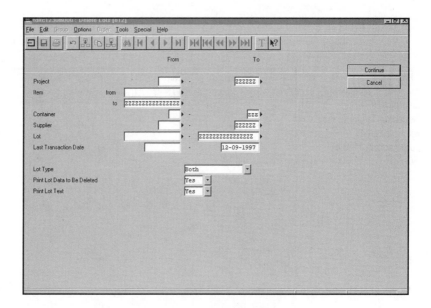

Understanding the Location Control Module

The Location Control module complements the Inventory Control module and allows users to segregate inventory by physical locations within specific warehouses. When you decide to implement this complementary module to the Inventory Business Object, you are enabling the tools to help keep track of your inventory accurately.

Generating a Location Control System

The first step to perform when you want to implement Location Control is to generate a Location Control system. To do so, perform the following steps:

1. Go to Location Control.
2. Click Inventory Locations.
3. Click Miscellaneous Options.
4. Select the option Generate Location System.
5. Enter the warehouse for which you want to generate a Location Control system.
6. Reply Yes to the validation prompt.

After you have decided that Location Control is the way you want Baan to help manage your inventories, you must implement a location setup. This process has been covered in the previous paragraphs. As stated, serious consideration must be given prior to the creation of your locations. Your shop floor or warehouse floor layout should be evaluated in order to load appropriate locations accordingly. This means that if you have defective storage areas, inspection areas, or receiving areas, this type of structure should be considered. Reporting by location will be enhanced by well-defined location structure setup.

It is possible to change a warehouse to use Location Control. This session is found under the miscellaneous functions on the Location Control Business Object (see Figure 17.8).

FIG. 17.8

You have to specify the default receipt and inspection location; they will be created automatically by the system.

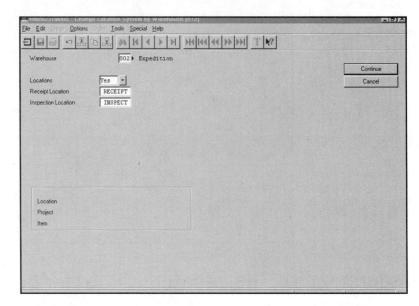

Maintaining Locations

Creating locations and specifying how they will be managed is a very important step in your implementation—spend the appropriate amount of time to map the process you will use to name your locations. The appropriate time is relative to the flow of your processes and general floor layouts. Use labels that are the same length, such as A0101 and A1015. This will make your life easier when you want to print reports sorted by locations.

In your numbering system, account for the row, level, and bin where the locations A1015 will be equal to row A, level 10, and bin 15. Although locations are defined as being broken down into aisle, row, level, and bin, it is not mandatory to create locations in this fashion. This example type facilitates the search for goods, depending on your floor layout. The location setup can be as personal as you want it to be, but remember the ease with which you want to deal with location reporting. Regular cycle counting and annual physical reporting could be facilitated if the locations had some logical sequencing, such as aisle, row, level, and bin. For example, if your defective area is one big location, you might want to identify it as DEFlocation. If you want to further define this defective area to reflect specific product types stored there, you might want to have DEF0101, DEF0201, and so on. Now you can print a report listing in quantities or in value for all goods in a specific location, such as DEF0101.

You can also assign specific items with specific locations, rendering the receipts and issues to locations more of an automated process. This depends on the volume of transactions per fixed period of time and availability of space for example. You can also use the specified process to help replenish fixed locations from bulk locations. An example of a fixed location could be a specific bin in a store, whereas a bulk location could be palettes in the store's stockroom.

Locations in Baan can be labeled with specific capacities and priorities in which the system will advise the user if that location is close to maximum capacity and which location should be filled first based on the mentioned priority.

Locations can be created to suit your specific needs. You should take the necessary time to develop a structure that will render your processes simpler.

To create a location, use the Maintain Locations option. Specify the following information:

- Warehouse
- Location
- Description of location
- Search key (alternative description)
- Row
- Level
- Bin
- Whether this is a fixed location for this item
- Whether this is an inspection location
- Whether more than one item can be stored in that location
- A code for the inbound priority
- A sequence for this location to be printed on the pick list
- Whether this location is an infinite capacity
- Total capacity and at what quantity Baan warns to stop filling this location (if not an infinite capacity)
- Whether this location is to be blocked for some transactions

When you create your locations in Baan, it is recommended that you use the Copy Locations function, which will ease your work. This creates several locations at one time rather than one at a time. To use this program, you must break down your locations into individual characters and increment each of them individually. An example of breaking down your locations would be A0101.

This following is a simple representation of the screen in Baan, Copy Ranges of Locations. It shows us the way to break down the location being copied (A0101); now you can create A0102 to A0109. When you process, you will have created eight new locations, copying the setup associated to A0101.

FROM	TO
A	A
0	0
1	1
0	0
0	9

Part

III

Ch

17

Using Location Cycle Counting

To perform cycle counting in the Location Control module, you first generate cycle counting orders for a range of items or locations. Then you print cycle count sheets to be used on the shop floor to do the physical counting. Enter the results of the cycle count and print a reconciliation report. When you agree with the numbers entered, process those cycle count orders. Then the new figures will be posted in your inventory, and adjustments will be created automatically. Delete your orders when the process is complete. This process is identical to the one specified in the Inventory Control module.

Using Inquiries and Reports

There are many options to display or print in the Location Control module. The first two displays are useful for seeing inventory level by items for standard items or for customized items. Every user prefers to display this information differently but the most popular screen is the Display Inventories by Item/Lot/Warehouse/Location. This display contains most of the information necessary to manage inventory. Add a few fields from the Item Master, such as weight, selling price, or cost. This will prevent the user from using another screen to make appropriate calls when it is time to pick an item.

The following are the various reports available:

- Print Inventories by Item and Lot
- Print Inventories by Item and Inventory Date
- Print Inventories by Item and Storage Unit
- Print Inventories by Item and Warehouse
- Print Inventories by Warehouse and Item
- Print Inventories by Production Bill of Material
- Print Inventories by Process Formula
- Print Inventories by on Hold
- Print Inventories by Item and Expiry Date
- Print Replenishment List

The previous list supplies the users with several options to print inventory data. The user generates or uses the reports she feels will supply the most information pertinent to her function. The user has the capability of printing a hard copy of the desired report or printing it to display, which will have the report print onscreen.

Using Location History

The Location History Business Object allows you to archive all inventory transactions by locations. This process must be planned ahead and will have you copy to a different company all the inventory transactions. Once archived, those transactions will be accessible for display or reports through that archiving company.

Archive once a year if the volume of your transactions allows you to wait for that period of time. Don't go beyond that period because you might have some performance issues producing inventory reports.

 TIP It is strongly recommended to back up all your databases before performing the archiving function.

To archive transactions by locations, you must follow these steps:

1. Enter the date up to which you want to archive the information.
2. Supply the company number to be used for archiving (always use the same number).
3. Answer Yes to overwrite any existing texts.
4. Click Special and on Continue.

You can now archive older data to enhance system performance. After the data is archived, you can still access it by extracting the selected data from the archive company.

Using Storage Conditions

Storage Conditions have been introduced to help users manage the warehousing operations in environmentally sensitive sites. If some goods must be stored in dry or humid areas or if any other conditions must be present, this is a good tool to use. The process is very simple. To use this feature, follow these steps:

1. Go to Distribution/Location Control/Storage Conditions.
2. Define storage conditions in Maintain Storage Conditions.
3. Assign conditions to locations using the Maintain Storage Conditions. When you define your location, you specify what condition types must be present and whether this condition is mandatory.
4. Assign conditions required by item. You can assign this by item in Maintain Storage Conditions by Item or by item group in Maintain Storage Conditions by Item Groups.

Storage conditions are mainly identifiers with specific conditions relating to specific items or locations. These conditions dictate where the goods can and should be stored (see Figure 17.9).

Part III

Ch 17

FIG. 17.9

You can specify what storage conditions must be present or not by item. In this example, the temperature must be between 1 and 7 degrees Celsius and there must not be any sunlight.

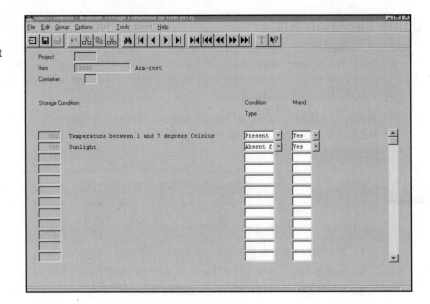

CHAPTER 18

Understanding the Sales Control Module

In this chapter

Using the Sales Control Module

The Baan Sales Control module can be compared to a box of wooden blocks. This toy does not come with instructions because a child's imagination makes possibilities endless. This is also true for the Sales Control module: Few parts or all parts can be used to design a system to fit business processes. In this chapter, you will learn how to open the Sales Control box and take inventory of its contents to begin to build a functionally rich Sales Control system that will meet your business needs.

You will see the relationship between Sales Control sessions and how these sessions operate together to provide functionality to enable sales business processes. The Sales Control module is the point of origin and the point of conclusion for all customer information. Mastering the operational parts for this module is imperative to the overall success of an order fulfillment process using Baan IV.

The Sales Control module is the point of origin and the point of conclusion for all customer information. Mastering the operational parts for this module is imperative to the overall success of an order fulfillment process using Baan IV.

Using Sales Prices and Discounts

Baan price and discount agreements can be recorded on a variety of levels. The filtering of price and discount structures is used to meet the pricing nuances of any business. The following are some of the functions available in this submodule:

- Effective and expiration dates
- Gross or net pricing
- Global editing by amount or percentage

The following sections will illustrate how the eight Baan price and discount levels work individually or in concert with one another.

If you do not want to define specific prices and discounts, the system takes the default sales price from the item master file. Hence the following eight levels of prices and discounts are possible:

I.	Prices by Customer and Item
II.	Discounts by Customer and Price Group
III.	Discounts by Customer
IV.	Prices by Price List and Item
V.	Discounts by Price List and Price Group
VI.	Discounts by Price List
VII.	Prices by Item
VIII.	Sales Price in the Item Master

Knowing Pricing Vocabulary

You will see how the pricing terms are defined and how they can be applied to the Sales Control module. The different terminology should be understood for the optimal usage of the pricing mechanism.

Before you study the pricing mechanism in Baan, you will need to understand a few reference terms. The following terms are important to know:

- *Gross*. Search additional levels to compound prices and discounts.
- *Net*. Stop searching after first hit at any level.
- *SLS parameters*. Price or discount by order date, system date, or delivery (ship) date.
- *Price and discount parameters*. Price or discount by order, line, or both.
- *Price group parameters*. Price or discount based on price list or price group.

These parameters are set in the Sales Control module. Some of the parameters, like the price and discount parameters, can be defined during the definition of the prices and discounts per price group and customer. Other parameters can be found in the SLS parameters.

Using Level 1—Prices by Customer and Item

In this first of eight pricing levels, prices or discounts can be set by item for a customer. This is the most specific level of pricing.

To access this price level, you must perform the following steps:

1. Go to Distribution Module.
2. Select Sales Control.
3. Choose Maintain Prices by Customer and Item.

In Level 1 pricing, you specify exceptions in pricing by items for each customer. Figure 18.1 illustrates the information recorded in this session. You can choose a customer and item for defining prices and discounts. After this you can define the method of calculating the discount, that is by order, line item, or both. You can also specify whether you want to define a discount based on the amount or the quantity of sale. If you choose amount, you can only define discounts if the total sale is up to a certain amount—for example, a discount of 10 percent for all sales up to $1,000.00. If you choose quantity, you can define a price and discount based on the number of units sold—for example, $2,500.00 and a 10 percent discount if the total quantity is up to 5,000 units. You can also have effective and expiration dates. This way you can track the history of your prices and discounts.

Using Level 2—Discounts by Customer and Price Group

In this second of eight pricing levels, discounts can be set by price group for a customer. A price group is a set of like items for which a discount applies. The item master determines to which price group an item belongs.

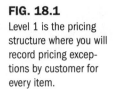

FIG. 18.1

Level 1 is the pricing structure where you will record pricing exceptions by customer for every item.

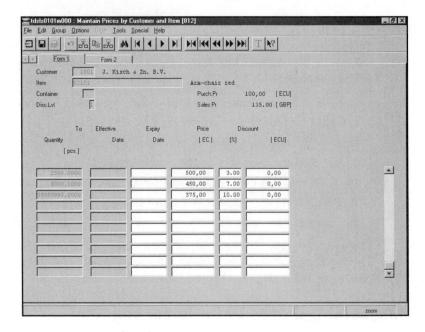

To access this price level, you must perform the following steps:

1. Go to Distribution Module.

2. Select Sales Control.

3. Choose Maintain Discounts by Customer and Price Group.

You can find an example in Figure 18.2. This level of discount calculation is similar to the previous level except the prices and discounts can be defined by customer and price group. Also, you can specify whether collective discounts are allowed; that is, it might be possible to calculate a higher discount based on the gross amount of the line items, as defined in the other levels—for example, discounts by customer or by price list.

TIP Using Level 2 is a very good way to establish pricing for customers with common status and helps reduce a lot of record maintenance.

Using Level 3—Discounts by Customer

In this third of eight pricing levels, discounts can be set for a customer. This allows you to use the same pricing for everybody except preferred customers, which can use a discount structure.

To access this price level, you must perform the following steps:

1. Go to Distribution Module.

2. Select Sales Control.

3. Choose Maintain Discounts by Customer.

FIG. 18.2

Level 2 pricing takes advantage of groups of customers.

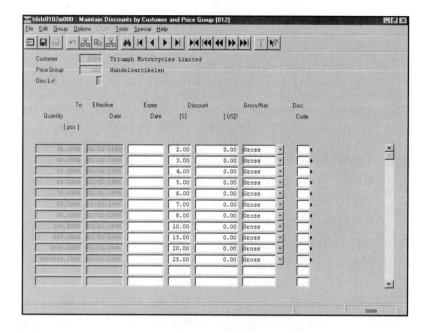

You can specify discounts based on quantity sold or order value. As in the earlier cases, you can either calculate line item discount, order discount, or both.

Using Level 4—Prices by Price List and Item

In this fourth of eight pricing levels, prices or discounts can be set by price list for an item. The customer master determines to which price list a customer belongs. A price list could be established for geographic area or for a specific industry. It could also be used to price items for customers who are members of a buying group.

In order to access this price level, you must perform the following steps:

1. Go to Distribution Module.
2. Select Sales Control.
3. Choose Maintain Prices by Price List and Item.

In this pricing level, you can set prices and discounts per price list and item. The price lists are linked to the customer and are used for grouping customers. Again, you can define this calculation by item line, order, or both.

Using Level 5—Discounts by Price List and Price Group

In this fifth of eight pricing levels, discounts can be set by price list and price group. As in Level 4, the customer master determines to which price list a customer belongs. As in Level 2, the item master determines to which price group an item belongs.

To access this price level, you must perform the following steps:

1. Go to Distribution Module.

2. Select Sales Control.

3. Choose Maintain Discounts by Price List and Price Group.

As in Level 2, you can specify whether a collective discount is applicable. Also, as in other levels, you can calculate discount at the level of item line, order, or both.

Using Level 6—Discounts by Price List

In this sixth of eight pricing levels, discounts can be set by price list. As in Level 4, the customer master determines to which price list a customer belongs.

To access this price level, you must perform the following steps:

1. Go to Distribution Module.

2. Select Sales Control.

3. Choose Maintain Discounts by Price List.

In this level of pricing, you can define discounts by price list. As in the earlier cases, you can specify a discount to be calculated at the level of item line, order, or both.

N O T E You do not have to alter your selling price using discounts to reduce the selling price for different groups of customers. ▪

Using Level 7—Prices by Item

In this seventh of eight pricing levels, prices or discounts can be set by item. This is an alternative way of maintaining selling prices if you do not want to use the price found in the item master. This could be useful if you don't want the sales department to maintain the item master file but you do want them to maintain selling prices. In order to access this price level, you must perform the following steps:

1. Go to Distribution Module.

2. Select Sales Control.

3. Choose Maintain Prices by Item.

This level is similar to Level 3. You can define the prices and discounts by item.

Using Level 8—Item Master Price

In this last of eight pricing levels, prices are set by item into the item master file. It is the simplest way to maintain selling prices. If you don't have a special pricing structure for any customers or items, you can use the item master price. If price list prices are used as points from which to calculate other level discounts, the item master price can be used as a reference-only field.

To access this price level, you must perform the following steps:

1. Go to Distribution Module.

2. Select Item Control.

3. Choose Maintain Item Data.

Even though item master is not part of the Sales Control module, it is used in the calculation of sales prices in the absence of the other seven levels of calculation of sales prices. Hence, you can consider the Sales Price in the Item Master as the eighth level.

Knowing the Pricing Hierarchy

The pricing hierarchy in Baan is quite simple. When a sales order is created, Baan first looks for an existing sales contract. If no contract exists, it then goes through the different pricing levels to find a possible price or discount "hit" (match). The price found is then used for the sales orders.

Say you define prices by item, for example, Level 7 for item A. If you create a sales order for item A, the system starts checking from Level 1 (Prices by Customer and Item) and keeps searching until it reaches Level 7. It uses the price defined to calculate the sales price. Again, for discounts, the system checks all the levels where discounts have been entered, and, in this example, when it reaches the last level, it takes the discount entered there.

Using Sales Orders

The Baan Sales Orders session has various functions. In addition to the order-taking functions, you will find options for the following:

- Multirelease of lines
- Automatic pricing calculation function
- Sales price simulation program
- Verification functions for available inventory and available credit

N O T E This module is linked to the MPS and the Replenishment Control module.

In the following sections, you will learn the fields used in entering a sales order header, sales order specific delivery address, and sales order lines, as well as the parameter options available to meet a variety of order processing needs.

Knowing Sales Order Vocabulary

The key to successfully completing a sales order entry is to understand the terminology used by Baan to identify certain key fields on the screen and their usage and application. The following will explain this more clearly.

Before you study the sales order mechanism in Baan, you need to understand the following terms:

Part

III

Ch

18

- *Order type.* Code used for defining procedures for processing an order.
- *Order step.* Each step refers to a Baan session use as a specific order procedure.
- *Sales order parameters.* Flags set in the Sales Order module to have it behave differently based on inputs.

Using Sales Order Entry—Header

The sales order entry is divided in two parts: header and lines. First you will see how to define the header and how you can capture information that will help you further process the order.

In order to access Sales Orders, you must perform the following steps:

1. Go to Distribution Module.
2. Select Sales Control.
3. Select Sales Orders.
4. Select Procedure.
5. Choose Maintain Sales Order.

The sales order header records all the customer-related information for your order such as customer number, delivery date, forwarding agent, and customer contact. There are two reference fields found on this screen. It is recommended that you use the Reference A field to record the customer purchase order number. The label for this field should be modified using tools to reflect the new use of this field. To create a new order, click the insert icon and then fill in the fields explained in Table 18.1. Figure 18.3 illustrates the steps involved in the order types order.

FIG. 18.3

The various steps that an order will go through.

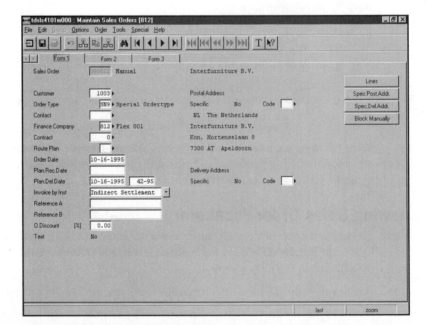

Table 18.1 Sales Order Fields

Field Name	Description
Customer	The number of the customer for whom the sales order is meant.
Blocked	Appears when the order has the exceeded the customer's credit limit.
Order Type	The code used to determine which of the sessions in Table 18.2 are part of the order procedure.
Contact	The code identifying customer contact.
Finance Company	The financial company number.
Contract	The contract number for special agreement link.
Route Plan	The predetermined route for shipping product.
Order Date	The date that an order was created.
Plan Receipt Date	The date shipment should arrive.
Plan Delivery Date	The date shipment should ship.
Invoicing by Installments	Indicates whether invoice can be paid in installments.
Order Discount	The additional percentage applied to the amount on each order line.
Postal Address	Bill to address.
Delivery Address	Ship to address.
Text	Indicates whether messages are attached to the order.
Reference A	Free field printed on external documents.
Reference B	Free field printed on order documents.
Currency	The currency in which the sales order should be expressed.
Terms of Delivery	Shipping terms code used to indicate term assignments.
Terms of Payment	Payment terms code used to indicate payment period, discount period, and discount percentages.
Sales Price List	See the section "Using Sales Prices and Discounts," for Levels 4, 5, and 6.
Direct Delivery	Indicator to authorize shipment directly from vendor.
Customer Prices	The parent customer used to retrieve price or discount data. If and Discount field is blank, customer on sales order is used for pricing.

Part

III

Ch

18

continues

Table 18.1   Continued

Field Name	Description
Customer Texts	The parent customer used to retrieve text data. If the field is blank, customer on sales order is used for text.
Forwarding Agent	SCAC code used for carrier assigned to ship the order.
Route	Indicates the route code used for the shipment of the order.
Tax	Indicates whether the sales invoice includes a tax amount.
Ship Complete	Indicates whether sales order lines can be back ordered.
Line of Business	Customer line of business code used for reporting.
Sales Rep	Sales representative responsible for a customer.
Name	Username processing sales order.
Area	Code to indicate where the customer is located.

You are now ready with the sales order header. The delivery date is used as a selection criterion during the shipment of the order. You can select a group of orders for shipment by specifying a range of delivery dates, and if the delivery date of your order is within that range, then it is selected for shipment. The order type cannot be changed after you start entering the lines, so make sure that the order type that you select is the one you need. The order steps are defined in the order type.

Using Sales Order Entry—Specific Delivery Address

The Specific Delivery Address is used when you do not want to ship the goods to the customer delivery address found in the customer master for just one order. To record a specific address for a shipment, you must enter the information from the Sales Order Header screen Special on the menu bar. Table 18.2 lists the fields and explains them.

Table 18.2   Sales Order Specific Delivery Address Fields

Field Name	Description
Sales Order	Order number
Position Number	Line number
Customer	Customer number
Name	Customer name
Address	Customer ship to address
City	Customer ship to city
Zip Code	Customer ship to zip code

Field Name	Description
Route	Route code to be used for delivery
Country	Customer ship to country
Tax Number	Customer's tax code number
Verification Date	Last date tax number was verified

You now know how to define a delivery address specific for a specific order without changing the customer master.

Using Sales Order Entry—Lines

All items on an order will be recorded separately in the details screen. To access, click Special on the Sales Order Header screen menu bar and then click Lines. (It will be your first choice from Special.) Each item will have its own position number. Usually, they are incremented in steps of 10. To create and maintain sales order lines, the fields in Table 18.3 are used.

Table 18.3   Sales Order Lines Fields

Field Name	Description
Sales Order	Order number.
Position Number	Line number.
Project	Project number.
Item Code System	Customer profile code for system containing customer/company item cross-reference.
Item	Company part number.
Container	Company container number. (A container is part of a set.)
Item Description	Company part description.
Item Category	Indicates if an item is standard or customized.
Engineering Item Revision	Code for controlling manufactured parts.
Product Variant	Base item used for configuring a customized item.
Warehouse	Ship from warehouse.
Delivery Date	Date order will ship.
Text	Indicates whether order line has a message attached.
Sales Unit	The unit in which the item is shipped.
Quantity	The quantity requested by the customer for delivery.

Part
III

Ch
18

continues

Table 18.3   Continued

Field Name	Description
Backorder	Difference between what was ordered and what was shipped. Back order can be created at Maintain Order or Maintain Delivery.
Direct Delivery	Indicates whether line can ship directly from vendor.
Sales Price Unit	The unit at which the item is priced.
Price	Unit price for the item.
Price Level	Indicates at which level the price for that line was found.
Discount Percentage	Discount percentage applied to that order line.
Discount Amount	The discount amount by unit.
Discount Level	Indicates at which level the discount for that line was found.
Currency	Indicates currency used for that order line.
Amount	Net order line amount. (Rounding is changed in maintain currencies.)
Open Balance	Customer's current open invoice balance.
Inventory Issue Status	Indicates whether main or component item will be shipped.
Lot Selection	Indicates whether any, same, or specific lots can be shipped.
Lot	Lot code used if Lot Selection is same or specific.
Standard Description	Indicates whether line text is printed below description or whether only created text manager text is printed.
Tax Code	Order line tax code.
Ship Complete	Indicates whether back orders are accepted by the customer.
Standard Cost Price	Cost price of the item.
Inventory On Hand	Quantity physically available in the warehouse.
Allocated Inventory	Quantity ordered out and on back order at a warehouse.
Quotation	Quantity ordered out and on back order needed for a sales quotation at a warehouse.
Delivery Address	Customer ship to address.
Name	Customer name.
Address	Customer bill to address.
City	Customer bill to city.
Country	Customer bill to country.

Field Name	Description
Route Plan	Predefined route for the transport of a line.
Order Date	Date order was taken.
Purchase Order	Customer's purchase order number.
Supplier	Supplier used for direct delivery.
Contract	Contract number to be used by the order line for price and discounts.

After entering the order lines (the items in Figure 18.4), you are now ready to proceed to the process of shipment. Make sure that the warehouse you want to ship out of appears correctly on the order lines.

FIG. 18.4

Each item on an order is entered as a separate line.

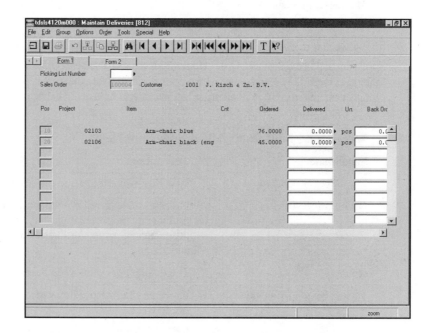

Part
III

Ch
18

N O T E Each item on an order gets a different position number to be uniquely identified.

Using Sales Deliveries and Invoicing

In the following sections, you will learn the fields used for all the steps following the entry of an order. These steps include printing an order acknowledgment and picking list; maintaining a delivery (shipment); printing a packing slip, bill of lading, and sales invoice; and processing a delivered sales order.

Note that the first processing step after order entry is Generate Outbound Advice, which is covered in Chapter 17.

Using Print Order Acknowledgments

An order acknowledgment is a confirmation of the customer's order received for processing. You will see how to print the acknowledgment and the different parameters associated with the selection of the orders.

In order to access order acknowledgments, you must perform the following steps:

1. Select Distribution Module.
2. Select Sales Control.
3. Select Sales Orders.
4. Select Procedure.
5. Choose Print Order Acknowledgments.

Many companies are now printing this document to a fax server in order to automate the transmission of this information. Order acknowledgments can also be printed on a regular printer and faxed or mailed to the customer who requested them. Note that order maintenance can still be done after this step. To print an order acknowledgment, use the fields in Table 18.4.

Table 18.4   Print Order Acknowledgment Fields

Field Name	Description
Enter Specific Orders	Indicates whether specific sales order will be printed.
Order Line Types to Print	Indicates all lines not printed, only lines added after last printing, all lines even if printed already, only lines printed and changed, or lines printed and changed or added.
Quantity to Print	The quantity of acknowledgments to be printed.
Variant Option Description	Indicates whether product variant option is to be printed.
Variant Sales Price Structure	Indicates whether product variant sales price schedules are to be printed.

Using Print Picking Lists

A picking list is a document you print to pull and load the goods necessary to ship an order from a warehouse.

In order to access picking lists, you must perform the following steps:

1. Select Distribution Module.
2. Select Sales Control.

3. Select Deliveries.

4. Select Procedure.

5. Choose Print Pick Lists.

It will show the following:

- Location of the goods
- When the Location Control module is used
- The lots to be picked
- When the Lot Control module is used

To print this document, fill in the fields in Table 18.5.

Table 18.5   Print Picking Lists Fields

Field Name	Description
Print Already Printed Documents	Indicator for reprints.
Enter Specific Orders	If Yes, a session for listing orders will begin.
Print Summary Picking List	If Yes, a summary by item, warehouse, or location can be printed.
Print in Order Language	If Yes, printing is done in order of language.
Print Shortages	If Yes, shorts will be printed.
Sort Sequence	Indicates whether sort is by location or sequence number.

With this list, you now have the ability to go directly to a warehouse or location (where location control is implemented) and pick the goods for shipment, without having to track down the goods in the storage area.

Using Maintain Deliveries

When you maintain deliveries in Baan, you indicate that the order has been shipped. This step will create the necessary information to be printed on the packing list and the bill of lading.

In order to access deliveries, you must perform the following steps:

1. Select Distribution Module.

2. Select Sales Control.

3. Select Deliveries.

4. Select Procedure.

5. Choose Maintain Deliveries.

Your shipping department can perform this step. They will have to fill in or reference the parameters in Table 18.6.

Table 18.6   Maintain Deliveries Parameters

Parameter	Description
Picking List Number	Number assigned to pick list.
Sales Order	Order number.
Customer	Customer number.
Name	Customer name.
Position Number	Line number.
Project	Project number.
Item	Company part number.
Item Description	Company part description.
Container	Company container number. (A container is part of a set.)
Order Quantity	Quantity requested to be shipped.
Delivered Quantity	Quantity actually shipped.
Sales Unit	The unit in which the item is shipped.
Backorder	Difference between what was ordered and what was shipped.
Delivery Date	Date order was shipped.
Warehouse	Ship from warehouse.
Confirmed	Indicates whether next procedure can be applied to line.
Order Number	Sales order number.
Standard Cost Price	Cost price at time of shipment.

At the end of this step, the goods have now been shipped out of the warehouse, and the inventory for the item that has been shipped is reduced by the quantity of shipment.

Using Print Packing Slips

The packing slip is the document used to pack the goods before shipment. This document will indicate how to load the products according to the customer's specification.

In order to access packing slips, you must perform the following steps:

1. Select Distribution Module.
2. Select Sales Control.
3. Select Deliveries.
4. Select Procedure.
5. Choose Print Packing Slips.

Many customers don't use this document; they use the picking list instead. If you want to produce this document, use the fields in Table 18.7.

Table 18.7   Print Packing Slips Fields

Field Name	Description
Print Already Printed Documents	Indicator for reprints.
Enter Specific Orders	If Yes, a session for listing orders will begin.
Print Summary Packing Slip	Indicates whether orders are printed together or separate.
Print Variant Option Descriptions	Indicates whether product variant options are to be printed.

Using Print Bills of Lading

The bill of lading is a legal document used to indicate to the carriers what they are transporting to the customer's site. Often this document must be customized to meet local regulations. The information printed summarizes the goods shipped and indicates the weight and the number of cartons on the shipment.

In order to access bills of lading, you must perform the following steps:

1. Select Distribution Module.
2. Select Sales Control.
3. Select Deliveries.
4. Select Procedure.
5. Select Forwarding Documents.
6. Choose Print Bills of Lading.

To print the bill of lading, use the parameters in Table 18.8.

Table 18.8   Bills of Lading Parameters

Parameter	Description
Bill of Lading Number	First free bill of lading number
Bill of Lading Line	Line number
Quantity	Shipped quantity
Packing Type	Packing unit expressed on bill
Description	Packing unit description
Weight	Line weight

Using Print Sales Invoices

Sales invoices are the most important documents generated in the shipping process. This document gives the customer all the details, such as the item shipped, quantity, price, amount due, payment terms, and so on (see Figure 18.5). Also if you have entered a specific bill to address for the customer, the invoice will be printed with this bill to address instead of the customer's address found in the customer master.

FIG. 18.5

The Print Selection screen requires you to specify whether the invoice is final or a pro-forma document.

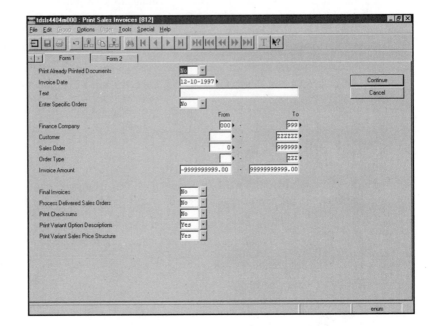

In order to access invoices, you must perform the following steps:

1. Select Distribution Module.

2. Select Sales Control.

3. Select Invoicing.

4. Choose Print Sales Invoices.

The sales invoices can be printed in a pro-forma mode for review and revision prior to finalizing the invoice. The pro-forma invoice is generated by leaving the field Final Invoice as No. If you are satisfied with the contents of the invoice, then a Yes reply will print the final document. When you finalize invoices, they are passed to the Accounts Receivable module. The information in Table 18.9 is used to run the Print Sales Invoices program.

Table 18.9   Print Sales Invoices Fields

Field Name	Description
Print Already Printed Documents	Indicator for reprints.
Invoice Date	Date invoice is printed.
Text	Text to be printed on bottom of invoice.
Enter Specific Orders	If Yes, a session for listing orders will begin.
Final Invoices	Indicates printing of final invoice.
Print Check Sums	Indicates whether invoice analysis should be printed.
Print Variant Option Descriptions	Indicates whether product variant options should be printed.
Print Variant Sales Price Structures	Indicates whether product variant pricing should be printed.

The invoice is now ready to be sent to the customer. Also, at this stage the invoice number generated by the system is used to post receipts from customers, and the invoice amount is used to post sales figures in the general ledger.

Using Process Delivered Sales Orders

The Process Delivered Sales Orders function is designed to create work files necessary for other Baan modules. The financial information and the statistical information is generated at this point. It is advisable that you are very careful with the parameter "delete orders." Ensure that you really want to delete the orders completely from the file.

Part
III

Ch
18

> **CAUTION**
> When orders are deleted, some details will not be accessible in history when the order is removed.

The parameters for this function are listed in Table 18.10.

Table 18.10   Process Delivered Sales Orders Parameters

Parameter	Description
Delete Order Data	Indicates whether order data should be deleted after processing.
Delete up to Date	Date up to which order data should be deleted.
Transaction Type	Transaction type to be linked to finance.
Invoice Number	Number assigned at invoicing.
Customer	Customer number.

continues

Table 18.10   Continued

Parameter	Description
Name	Customer name.
Sales Order	Order number.
Store Sorting Status	Indicates progress of process.

After this process is completed, the sales figures are posted as integration transactions, and, as mentioned earlier, the history tables are updated with the order and invoice information.

Using Sales Quotations

Baan designed the Quotation module using the same pattern used for the Sales Orders module. After a quote is accepted, it is relatively easy to turn it into a sales order. Sales quotations create inventory demand when entered, as well as a need for material to fulfill possible production orders. Demand is based on the success rate you enter for a quotation.

In the following sections, you will learn the fields used in entering a sales quote header, sales quote results, and sales quote lines. Sales quotations must be used in conjunction with product configuration or the project control.

Using Sales Quotation Entry—Header

You will learn to record sales quotations in Baan. Certain important parameters have been explained in further detail in the following steps.

In order to access sales quotations, you must perform the following steps:

1. Select Distribution Module.
2. Select Sales Control.
3. Select Sales Quotations.
4. Select Procedures.
5. Choose Maintain Sales Quotations.

The Sales Quotation process is similar to the one used for Sales Orders. Access is achieved by clicking the insert icon. The system will automatically assign a quotation number to the document (see Figure 18.6). You must then fill in the fields in Table 18.11.

Table 18.11   Sales Quotation Header Fields

Field Name	Description
Quotation Number	System assigned quotation number.
Customer	Customer number.
Order Type	Defines processing procedures for the quotation.

Field Name	Description
Company	Financial company number.
Success Percentage	Indicates the chance that the quote will result in an order.
Route Plan	The predetermined route for shipping product.
Quotation Date	Date quotation was entered.
Planned Receipt Date	Planned date for delivery of the item.
Planned Delivery Date	Planned date for shipment of the item.
Time of Delivery	Entered in calendar days, this time is added to the transfer date from quote to sales order to determine the actual ship date.
Expiry Date	Last valid date of the quote.
Order Discount	Order discount percentage applied to the net amount of each line.
Postal Address	Bill to address.
Delivery Address	Ship to address.
Text	Indicates whether text has been assigned to the quote.
Currency	The currency in which the sales quotation should be expressed.
Currency Rate Sales	Sales rate assigned to the currency.
Fixed Rate	Indicates whether the currency rate of sales is fixed or determined by the delivery or invoice date.
Terms of Delivery	Shipping terms code used to indicate terms assignments.
Terms of Payment	Payment terms code used to indicate payment period, discount period, and discount percentages.
Late Payment Surcharge	Indicates the late payment upcharge applied to item amounts.
Sales Price List	(See the section "Using Sales Prices and Discounts," Levels 4, 5, and 6.)
Price List for Direct Delivery	Indicates special price agreement for lines shipping direct from a vendor.
Customer Prices and Discount	The parent customer used to retrieve price or discount data. If field is blank, customer on quote is used for pricing.

continues

Customer Texts	The parent customer used to retrieve text data. If the field is blank, customer on quote is used for text.
Forwarding Agent	SCAC code used for carrier assigned to ship the order.
Route	Indicates the route code used for the shipment of the order.
Tax	Indicates whether the sales invoice includes a tax amount.
Ship Complete	Indicates whether quotation lines can be back ordered.
Country	Customer ship to country.
Language	The code for the language in which the quote is printed.
Area	Code to indicate where the customer is located.
Line of Business	Customer line of business code used for reporting.
Sales Rep	Sales representative responsible for the customer.

You are now ready with the sales quotation header. As you can see, much of the information captured here is similar to the ones on the sales order header that you saw earlier.

FIG. 18.6

The quotation screen contains fields to record confidence rate on this bid.

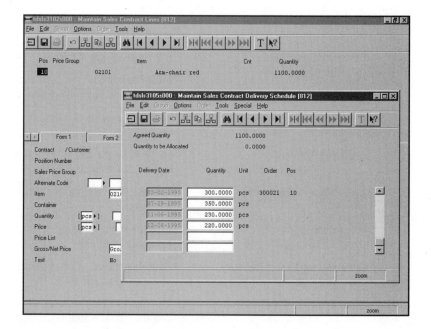

Using Sales Quotation Entry—Lines

Every item entered on a quotation is entered as a separate line. To access the line details, click Special on the quotation header screen menu bar and then click Lines. (This will be your first Special choice.) Use the fields in Table 18.12.

Table 18.12   Sales Quotation Lines Fields

Field Name	Description
Quotation Number	Sales quotation number.
Status	Indicates whether line is free, confirmed, processed, or canceled.
Position Number	Line number.
Budget	Code used if linked to budgets.
Item Code System	Customer profile code for system containing customer/ company item cross-reference.
Item	Company part number.
Container	Company container number.
Item Category	Indicates whether an item is standard or customized.
Product Variant	Base item used for configuring a customized item.
Warehouse	Ship from warehouse.
Planned Delivery Date	The date shipment would ship.
Time of Delivery	Entered in calendar days, this time is added to the transfer date from quote to sales order to determine the actual ship date.
Sales Unit	The unit in which the item will ship.
Ordered Quantity	The quantity requested by the customer for quotation.
Direct Delivery	Indicates whether line can ship directly from vendor.
Sales Price Unit	The unit in which the item is priced.
Price	Unit price for the item.
Price Level	Indicates at which level the price for that line was found.
Discount Percentage	Discount percentage applied to that order line.
Discount Amount	The discount amount by unit.
Discount Level	Indicates at which level the discount for that line was found.
Currency	Indicates currency used for that line.

Part

III

Ch

18

continues

Table 18.12   Continued

Field Name	Description
Amount	Net quotation line amount. (Rounding is changed in Maintain Currencies.)
Inventory Issue Status	Indicates whether main or component item will be shipped.
Standard Description	Indicates whether line text is printed below description or whether only created Text Manager text is printed.
Tax Code	Order line tax code.
Inventory On Hand	Quantity physically available in the warehouse.
Inventory On Order	Quantity on order from another warehouse.
Allocated Inventory	Quantity ordered out and on back order at a warehouse.
Sales Order	Order number.
Position Number	Line number.

Again, most of the fields are similar to sales order entry that you have already seen. At the end of this process, you are now ready with the order lines, that is the item code of the item that will be shipped, quantity, price, and so on.

Using Sales Quotation Results

The Quotation Results program will register all the information required to follow up on the status of a quote. You can record the fact that you have won the bid for an order or record the failure and the information pertaining to the reasons why you were not awarded the business.

In order to access quotation results, you must perform the following steps:

1. Select Distribution Module.
2. Select Sales Control.
3. Select Sales Quotations.
4. Select Procedures.
5. Choose Enter Sales Quotation Results.

All quotation result information can be analyzed at a later point from history. To create and maintain sales quotation results, the fields in Table 18.13 are used.

Table 18.13   Sales Quotation Results Fields

Field Name	Description
Quotation Number	Sales quotation number.
Customer	Customer number.

Field Name	Description
Position Number	Line number.
Budget	Code used if linked to budgets.
Item	Company part number.
Container	Company container number. (A container is part of a set.)
Ordered Quantity	The quantity requested by the customer for quotation.
Sales Unit	The unit in which the item will ship.
Planned Delivery Date	The date the shipment should ship.
Project	Project number.
Status	Indicates whether line is free, confirmed, processed, or canceled.
Reason for Blocking	Code indicating reason for quote success or failure.
Competitor	Competitor code for who got the business when quote failed.
Quotation Date	Date quotation was entered.
Item Code System	Customer profile code for system containing customer/ company item cross-reference.
Expiry Date	Last valid date of the quote.
Product Variant	Product variant code if generic item.
Sales Order	Order number.
Position Number	Line number.
Price	Unit price for the item.
Sales Price Unit	The unit at which the item is priced.
Discount Percentage	Discount percentage applied to that quotation line.
Discount Amount	The discount amount by unit.
Amount	Net quotation line amount. (Rounding is changed in Maintain Currencies.)

Part
III

Ch
18

By entering the quotation results, you can now convert the quotation into a sales order if the quote was accepted. Also, as stated earlier, the historical information can be tracked even if the quote was rejected, and it can serve as a tool to improve performance in the future.

Using Sales Contracts

The Sales Contracts session is designed to record contractual agreements reached with your customers on specific quantities or for specific periods of time. The information entered in the contract, like a quotation, can be turned into a sales order. Releases against the contract can be issued using the delivery schedule. Product demand and subsequent production plans to meet the contract requirements will be displayed on the Baan Master Production Schedule.

Using Sales Contract Entry—Header

You will see how to record a sales contract and the different parameters associated with it.

In order to access sales contracts, you must perform the following steps:

1. Select Distribution Module.
2. Select Sales Control.
3. Select Sales Contracts.
4. Select Procedures.
5. Choose Maintain Sales Contracts.

The sales contract header screen is similar to the sales order header screen. There are two types of contracts:

■ A normal type for a specific period of time.

■ A special contract that is created to record unique quantity and period agreements.

To create and maintain a sales contract header, use the fields in Table 18.14.

Table 18.14   Sales Contract Header Fields

Field Name	Description
Contract	Contract number.
Customer	Customer number.
Contract Type	Indicates normal contract (Lengthy Contract) or special contract (Short Exception Contract).
Description	Contract description displayed after contract number.
Contract Date	Date contract was entered.
Effective Date	Date contract starts.
Expiry Date	Date contract ends.
Contract Acknowledgment	Indicates whether an acknowledgment should be printed.
Print Status	Indicates whether contract has been printed or changed.

Field Name	Description
Contract Status	Indicates whether contract is free (created), active (available for sales order link), or terminated (deleted).
Text	Indicates whether text is assigned to the contract.
Contract Type Specific	Indicates whether the contract is bill to specific.
Postal Address	Bill to address.
Delivery Address Specific	Indicates whether the contract is ship to specific.
Delivery Address	Ship to address.
Terms of Payment	Payment terms code used to indicate payment period, discount period, and discount percentages.
Terms of Delivery	Shipping terms code used to indicate term assignments.
Currency	The currency in which the contract should be expressed.
Late Payment Charge	Indicates the late payment upcharge applied to item amounts.
Sales Rep	Sales representative responsible for a customer.
Forwarding Agent	SCAC code used for carrier assigned to ship the order.
Tax	Indicates whether the sales invoice includes a tax amount.

You have now recorded the header information of the sales contract, which has the customer information, validity period of the contract, terms of payment and delivery, and so on.

Using Sales Contract Entry—Lines

To access the contract lines you must click the Special option on the contract header menu bar and then click Lines. (This will be the first special choice.) The contract lines are similar to sales order lines. Most of this information will be copied to a sales order if one is generated. To create and maintain a sales contract line, use the fields in Table 18.15.

Table 18.15 Sales Contract Lines Fields

Field Name	Description
Position Number	Line number.
Sales Price Group	See the section "Using Sales Prices and Discounts," Levels 2 and 5.
Item Code System	Customer profile code for system containing customer/ company item cross-reference.

continues

Table 18.15   Continued

Field Name	Description
Item	Company part number.
Container	Company container number. (A container is part of a set.)
Sales Unit	The unit in which the item is shipped.
Agreed Quantity	Quantity to be shipped.
Sales Price Unit	The unit at which the item is priced.
Price	Unit price for the item.
Price List	See the section "Using Sales Prices and Discounts," Levels 4, 5, and 6.
Gross/Net Price	Indicates gross (discount granted) or net (no discount granted).
Text	Indicates whether the contract line has a message attached.
Called/Invoiced Quantity	Indicates called (total orders placed against contract) or invoiced (total orders invoiced against contract).
Discount Percentage	Discount percentage applied to that contract line.
Discount Amount	The discount amount by unit.
Contract	Contract number.
Customer	Customer number.
Quantity Binding	Indicates whether the contract should check min/max called quantities.
Minimum Quantity	Minimum amount for which a contract is accepted.
Maximum Quantity	Maximum amount for which a contract is accepted.
Tax Code	Contract line tax code.

On similar guidelines to entering a sales order, you have seen how to record a contract line item, specifying the agreed price and quantity for the item that you will sell to the customer.

Using Sales Contract Entry—Delivery Schedule

To create your Delivery Schedule, you most click the Special option within the order entry lines screen and select the Maintain Sales Contract Delivery Schedule option. The delivery schedule will indicate to other Baan modules when your customer requires the goods. Delivery Schedules are used to generate sales orders for release on a periodic basis to fulfill the customer needs. An example of a delivery schedule is shown in Figure 18.7. To create and maintain a sales contract delivery schedule, the fields in Table 18.16 are used.

Table 18.16 Sales Contract Delivery Schedule Fields

Field Name	Description
Agreed Quantity	Quantity to be shipped.
Quantity to be Allocated	Quantity to be ordered out of a warehouse.
Planned Delivery Date	The date shipment should be shipped.
Quantity	The quantity requested by the customer to be contracted.
Sales Unit	The unit in which the item is shipped.
Sales Order	Order number.
Position Number	Line number.

FIG. 18.7

This is an example of a delivery schedule used to generate sales orders on a periodic basis.

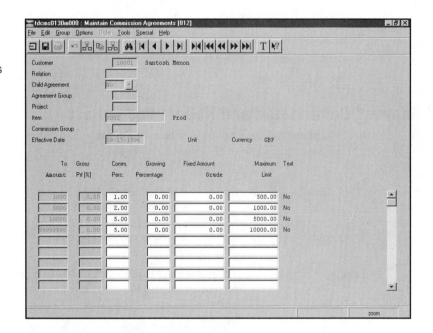

Using Sales Commissions and Rebate Control

The Baan commission and rebate control system can be used for payment of rebates to customers and commissions to suppliers or employees. This module is new in Baan IV and did not exist in the previous Triton releases of the software. This new functionality allows you to create and maintain commission and rebate agreements from the very specific (one item) to the very generic (many groups). Additionally, payment of commissions and rebates can be narrowly defined (one employee or customer) or broadly defined (sales or customer groups).

Commission and rebate considerations can be linked to all sales orders, only invoiced orders, or only invoiced and fully paid orders. These sales orders can be linked directly to a normal relation, to a relation team, or to a parent relation described below.

In order to access relations, commission/rebate groups, and default relations, you must perform the following steps:

1. Go to Distribution Module.
2. Select Sales Control.
3. Select Commission/Rebate Control System.
4. Select Master Data.

In order to access commission agreements and rebate agreements, you must perform the following steps:

1. Go to Distribution Module.
2. Select Sales Control.
3. Select Commission/Rebate Control System.
4. Select Agreements.

Knowing Commission and Rebate Vocabulary

Before you study the commission and rebate mechanism in Baan, you need to understand a few reference terms. Table 18.17 defines these terms.

Table 18.17   Commission and Rebate Vocabulary

Term	Definition
Agreements	The commission or rebate percentage defined for a customer, relation, project, or item.
Calculation Method	The method the commission or rebate is calculated. The option is for a percentage of the sales amount, or as a fixed amount per order.
Relations	The link between employee, supplier, customer, agreement group, parent relation, and period for processing.

In the following sections, you will learn about the fields used in entering a relation, agreement group, commission/rebate group, default customer relation, and commission/rebate agreement available to meet a variety of order processing needs.

Using Maintain Relations

A relation is a type of link used by the Commissions and Rebates system to determine if and how employees, suppliers, customers, groups, periods, and parent relations are connected. These relations tell the system what effect sales transactions should have based on the setup. Use the fields defined in Table 18.18.

Table 18.18 Maintain Relations Fields

Field Name	Description
Relation	Master record defining associations for linkage.
Relation Type	Indicates commission or rebate record.
Employee	Employee number used for commission.
Supplier	Supplier number used for commission or rebate.
Customer	Customer number used for rebate.
Postal Address	Bill to address.
Parent Relation	Higher relation in hierarchy. (For example, a parent relation could be a sales manager of the relation set for sales representative.)
Agreement Group	Code used to group set of employees, customers, or suppliers.
Period Table	Defines transaction frequency for commission or rebate.
Terms of Payment	Payment terms code used to indicate payment period, discount period, and discount percentages.

Using Maintain Agreement Groups

Agreement groups are sets of employees, customers, or suppliers linked together because of a common business factor, usually to detemine who should be paid. An example of an agreement group is all salespeople, customers, or suppliers who service one specific geography or market.

To create and maintain agreement groups, use the fields in Table 18.19.

Table 18.19 Maintain Agreement Groups Fields

Field Name	Description
Agreement Group	Code used to group set of employees, customers, or suppliers.
Type	Indicates commission or rebate record.

Using Maintain Commission/Rebate Groups

Commission or rebate groups are a set of items linked together because of a common business factor. A commission or rebate group couples for the purpose of grouping what is to be paid on. An example of a commission or rebate group is all items sold to one specific customer or manufactured with one specific material or process.

To create and maintain commission or rebate groups, use the fields in Table 18.20.

Table 18.20   Maintain Commission/Rebate Groups Fields

Field Name	Description
Commission/Rebate Group	Code used to group set of items.
Type	Indicates commission or rebate record.

Using Maintain Default Relations by Customer

A default relation by customer is a type of link used by the commissions and rebates system to determine if and how customers are connected to items and relations. These default relations by customer tell the system what effect sales transactions should have based on the setup.

To create and maintain default relations by customer, use the fields in Table 18.21.

Table 18.21   Maintain Default Relations by Customer Fields

Field Name	Description
Type	Indicates commission or rebate record.
Customer	Customer number.
Name	Customer name.
Item	Company part number.
Relation	Master record defining associations for linkage.

Using Maintain Commission Agreements

A commission is an allowance or payment made to an agent (an employee or supplier) for initiating or completing a certain type of sales transaction. Commission agreements can be expressed as a fixed or additional percent or as a fixed amount.

To create and maintain commission agreements, use the fields in Table 18.22.

Table 18.22   Maintain Commission Agreements Fields

Field Name	Description
Customer	Customer number.
Name	Customer name.
Relation	Master record defining associations for linkage.
Relation Type	Indicates commission or rebate record.
Child Agreement	Determines if the agreement is linked to the parent or child relation.

Field Name	Description
Agreement Group	Code used to group set of employees, customers, or suppliers.
Project	Project number.
Item	Company part number.
Commission/Rebate Group	Code used to group set of items.
Effective Date	Start date of the agreement.
Grade Unit	Unit in which grade (priority) is expressed if used.
Quantity or Amount	Quantity or amount for which the grade is applicable.
Profit Percentage	Profit percentage for which the grade is applicable.
Commission/Rebate Percentage	Percentage used for commission or rebate.
Growing Percentage	Growth percentage used in addition to normal commission or rebate.
Fixed Amount	Fixed amount used for commission or rebate.
Maximum Limits	Maximum commission or rebate allowed.

Using Maintain Rebate Agreements

A rebate is the return of part of a payment made by a customer for initiating or completing a certain type of sales transaction. Rebate agreements can be expressed as a fixed or additional percentage or as a fixed amount.

To create and maintain rebate agreements (see Figure 18.8), use the fields in Table 18.23.

Table 18.23   Maintain Rebate Agreements Fields

Field Name	Description
Customer	Customer number.
Name	Customer name.
Relation	Master record defining associations for linkage.
Relation Type	Indicates commission or rebate record.
Child Agreement	Determines if the agreement is linked to the parent or child relation.
Agreement Group	Code used to group set of employees, customers, or suppliers.
Project	Project number.

continues

Table 18.23 Continued

Field Name	Description
Item	Company part number.
Commission/Rebate Group	Code used to group set of items.
Effective Date	Start date of the agreement.
Grade Unit	Unit in which grade (priority) is expressed if used.
Quantity or Amount	Quantity or amount for which the grade is applicable.
Profit Percentage	Profit percentage for which the grade is applicable.
Commission/Rebate Percentage	Percentage used for commission or rebate.
Growing Percentage	Growth percentage used in addition to normal commission or rebate.
Fixed Amount	Fixed amount used for commission or rebate.
Maximum Limits	Maximum commission or rebate allowed.

FIG. 18.8

The relationship between the rebates agreement and the other Baan modules.

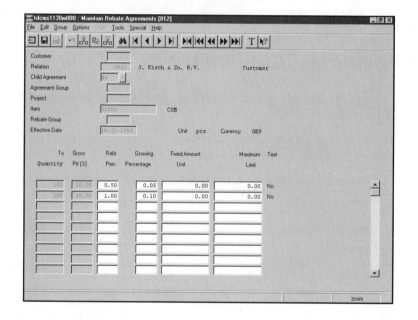

CHAPTER 19

Understanding the Transportation Module

In this chapter

Using the Transportation Module

To fulfill the needs of its large customer base, Baan introduced with release 3.0 a transportation package that is integrated with the software. The various components of this module will be helpful for the management of the transportation functions. This module is simple enough that it can be used by a company in distribution or in manufacturing to control shipment of their goods. It is complete enough that it can be used by a company that specializes in providing transportation services

The Transportation module is a module designed to allow users to manage their transportation fleet. Options found in this module will be useful to any company that specializes in transportation or to large companies that have to manage their fleets.

N O T E Evaluate the use of this module before making any decisions relative to the implementation of an external transportation component. This module covers the basic needs related to transportation; users can benefit from the integration to the other components. ■

The thrust of the Transportation module resides on generating transportation orders directly from distribution orders and then using consolidation and planning functions to manage the transportation aspect of the enterprise. In addition to the core functions, additional modules, such as Packing Control, Fuel and Fleet Management, Central Data Entry, and Integration to Finance, make this module a valuable add-on to the regular distribution functions of Baan.

Figure 19.1 shows a schema of the different functions that Baan created in this module.

FIG. 19.1

This module is designed to analyze your transportation activities.

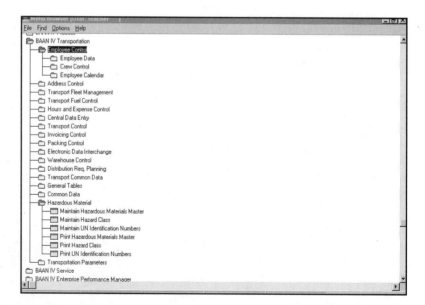

By using all the tools in this module, you will be able to ease the functions of planning shipments and you will be able to ensure that an optimal schedule is followed for the goods to be transported.

Different options are available to consolidate routes and to control the cost of the transportation linked with the Distribution module, the Electronic Data Interchange module, and the Finance module. The integration of the Transportation module within Baan is complete.

The additional functions, such as the fleet management, will help you control the equipment used for transportation and will help track fuel consumption. Other programs will help evaluate the distance between two points and how long it should take to reach point B from point A, as per the parameters you provide.

Using Transport Order Control

This section will cover the most important functions of this business object. The orders for transportation can be created manually using the following options or they can be imported directly from the Electronic Data Interchange module.

Using the Transportation Orders

The transportation orders are the means by which you create the demand in Baan for transportation of merchandise. By using the various fields of the order, you will indicate what type of equipment will be used and you will record information for the billing of the shipment.

The transportation orders contain all the necessary information required to manage the transportation functions. Table 19.1 describes the fields found in the transportation orders.

Table 19.1   Transportation Orders Fields

Field Name	Description
Order Procedure	The predefined procedure to be used for this order
Order	Unique order number
Principal	Customer number for the company who is requiring this order
Principal's Reference	Contact for the requesting company
Order Date	Creation date of the order
Loading Date	Baan will suggest a loading date according to the parameters in difference in loading
Transports Means Group	Fleet to be used
Transport Type	Type of transportation orders (used to manage the route)
Fixed Trip	Determines whether this order is to combine other stops with this trip
Order Acknowledgment Print Status	Specify whether you want the document
Contact	Customer's contact
Information	Additional information to be recorded against this order
Order Status	Status of this order

Part
III

Ch
19

From Table 19.1, the possible choices of order status are the following:

- Free
- No acknowledgment printed
- Print acknowledgment
- Acknowledgment is to be printed
- Acknowledgment printed
- Acknowledgment has been printed
- Invoice
- Lines are ready for invoicing
- Invoiced
- Lines had been invoiced
- Posted
- Process invoices lines had been run
- To history
- Releases for history and deletion had been performed

Once all the elements of the transportation orders have been defined, Baan is able to add this information to the existing orders giving the users the visibility of the demand helping the planning process (see Figure 19.2).

FIG. 19.2

The transportation orders record the necessary information to manage activities to be planned through the Transportation module.

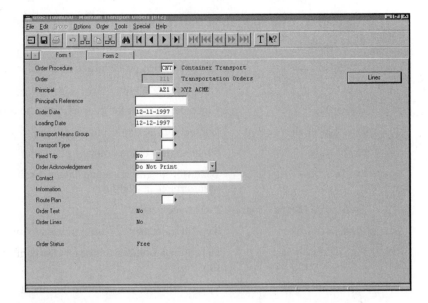

Managing the Transportation Orders

Now that the transportation order has been created, you need to process this order to calculate the value of the order. This process will also update various files like the employee calendar and the mean of transportation file.

In order to process your transportation orders, you have to perform the following steps:

1. Maintain the Transportation Orders.
2. Assign the Revenue Code to Transport Order Lines.
3. Collect the Logistic Units.
4. Perform the Calculate Transport Order Amounts Function.
5. Print Order Acknowledgments.
6. Update the Mean of Transportation and Employee Calendar from Order Control.
7. Release Transport Orders for Invoicing.
8. Release Transport Orders for History and Deletion.

Once you have completed these steps, a transport order has been created and fully processed. The transport order looks very much like a sales, purchase, or replenishment order.

Using the Transportation Functions

Baan created a series of other functions to complete the functionality required to manage the transportation aspect of your business. This will allow you to control the requirements of goods. It will also allow you to track the cost of moving them between your locations or to the customer site.

Using Address Control

The address control is designed to help you record all addresses needed to perform deliveries. First you will be able to generate an address file from the other modules, such as Common Data and Distribution. Then you can maintain transportation specific addresses using this module (see Figure 19.3). You can also build references tables in which you record everything from city name to zip code. You will also be in a position to maintain the printing sequences of address data that will be useful to plan routes.

At any time, addresses can be deleted. In order to keep the file clean, Baan created an option called Delete Unused Specific Addresses. Use this option on a permanent basis. This session gives you the ability to delete in batch or interactively.

A distance table is there to be maintained. In this file you will record the distance between two cities.

N O T E Baan can incorporate a conversion factor (in the distance table file) that enables you to indicate the average time it takes to go from one city to the other. Distances can also be recorded in another session by zip codes. ▪

A good example of a session using address codes is Maintain Transport Order Lines (trtoc1184m000). On each order line both a loading and an unloading address can be entered. To do so, you need only fill in the proper address code. The desired data (for example, name and address) will automatically be shown on the screen or printed on the report. If any defaults by zip code have been filled in, the system will fill a number of fields with the defaults once you have entered the zip code.

FIG. 19.3
This session records a specific address for transportation purposes for each customer.

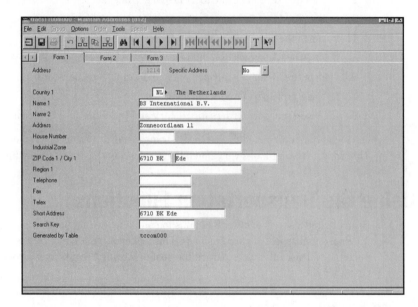

Using Distribution Requirement Planning

In this module you will find the bill of distribution that will indicate to Baan how to split the shipment per replenishing warehouses. The time it takes to move the items to the warehouse must be recorded as well as whether partial replenishments are allowed. The minimum and maximum level of items is also recorded in the bill of distribution. There is also a sales forecast module that will record the projected sales by item for the different periods of the year; this will be used to help plan your transportation needs.

Once the bills of distribution are loaded and the sales forecast is entered, you can generate distribution replenishment orders for each item. This generation can be regenerative, meaning that all calculations are redone eliminating previous needs or on a net change basis. After generation of the orders you must confirm them. Once this step is done you can transfer the orders. This step is copying your doers to the Replenishment Control module in the distribution part of the software to be manipulated as regular orders.

Using Employee Control

In the maintain employee session (see Figure 19.4), you will record the employee number, name, address, and hourly rate. You will link this employee to a department in order to categorize your employees within your organization. You will also record a job title for this employee. There is a field to record whether this employee is using the general employee calendar.

In this module, Baan allows you to use the concept of crews. You can assign employees to be members of a crew and a crew can be assigned for various routes. This will be used in the planning operations. You simply have to record the employee number and the crew to which you want to assign him.

The Employee Control module is where you will find the employee calendar, in which you can record an employee's available hours and dates. Those hours and dates can be recorded in a field. In order to speed up the process, there is an option called Global Update of Employee Calendar. Use this option to generate a basic calendar for many employees and then maintain each of them individually. Use the option Purge Employee Calendar to remove any unavailable periods for more than one employee.

Because a calendar of the crew's availability is maintained in real time, the issue of over-allocating or double scheduling of employees is now eliminated.

FIG. 19.4

You can create a crew or a team of employees to be assigned to specific tasks.

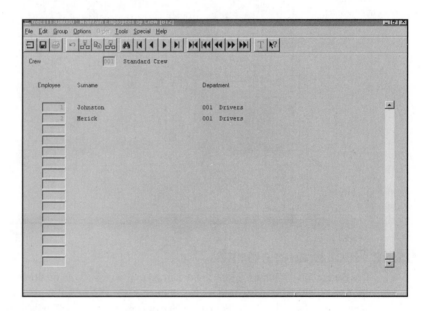

Part

III

Ch

19

Using Hours and Expense Control

This business object is designed to record all the financial activities related to the transportation. In order to categorize the expenses, you must maintain the various groups in the Maintain Expense Groups session (see Figure 19.5). You can record the ledger account to be used by expense group. If you use a payroll package, you can record a labor component code as well.

Expense codes must be defined also. Baan will allow you to record fixed amounts by expense code. This is used to account for tasks that are repetitive. The next step after that is to create activity groups. It is preferable to limit those groups to a few so you will not lose sight of the results given by Baan. Activity groups will help you analyze the activities done in the course of your normal operations. Overtime and bonus codes must be defined to help manage the hours accounting part of transportation. A session has also been added to enter the data related to your labor agreement. Take the appropriate time to study this file in order to save some valuable time while implementing the hours accounting for transportation.

All the operations done by the employees will be recorded in the Maintain Daily Reports session. You will enter per day how many hours were worked by the employee and you will report expenses. There is an option to enable you to copy daily reports from one employee to another if they performed similar tasks and had the same amount of expenses or to copy only one of the two data.

FIG. 19.5
Various expenses codes can be created to help track all the different expenses of operation.

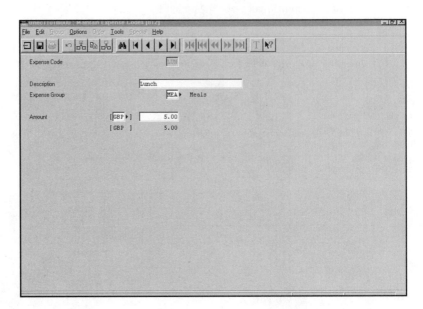

Using Fleet Management

The fleet management functions are designed to manage all the equipment used for transportation like the trucks and the trailers (see Figure 19.6). This will also manage the combination between trucks and trailers. For each piece of equipment you will be able to record the following:

- Loading capacity
- Fuel consumption
- Hours and miles driven
- Any specific characteristics proper to this unit

It is possible to calculate the cost price per hour or per unit for any given equipment. Equipment can be grouped in fleets, which enables you to group different equipment together. Having defined the previously mentioned criteria, the system can now advise whether transportation is available right at order entry. The system, from the master data loaded, can supply information pertaining to the maintenance requirements for specific pieces of transportation equipment.

FIG. 19.6

This session will record all the information related to your vehicles to be used in the transportation fleet.

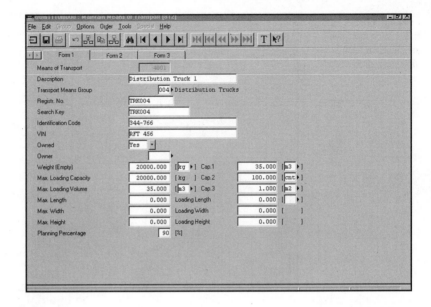

Using Invoicing Control

The invoicing control is built like the invoicing control in the Accounts Receivable module. You must first maintain a parameters table in which you will indicate the necessary information to produce invoices. In the financial parameters, you record the ledger account to be used for late payment surcharges and the accounts for line discounts. There is also a table to be maintained for revenue code indicating to the software where to assign the various revenue in the general ledger. You must also define invoicing types to be used. For this, refer to the Finance module instructions to get the proper way to set them up.

The invoicing options are as follows:

- *Maintain Invoices.* Allows you to change invoicing information before it is finalized.
- *Print Invoices.* Prints a copy of the invoices.
- *Print Invoices Check Report.* Allows you to verify the billing information and detect any inconsistencies.
- *Process Invoices.* Updates the customer balance, assigns a status of "posted" to the transportation order, and deletes the invoice lines if the parameter is specified when running the session.

In addition, you can check if every order has been invoiced by using the Display Invoices Lines session (see Figure 19.7).

FIG. 19.7

This session indicates the status for each transport orders.

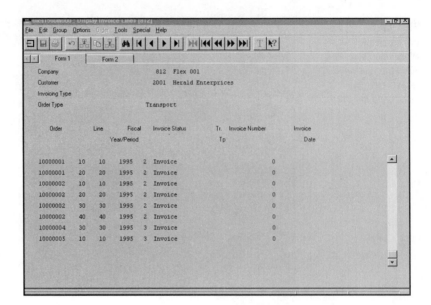

CHAPTER 20

Understanding the Manufacturing Module

In this chapter

Taking Advantage of the Manufacturing Module

Baan offers various options for planning and control of the manufacturing activities within an organization. Baan has powerful capabilities that address all the manufacturing environments, such as make-to-stock, assemble-to-order, make-to-order, and engineer-to-order.

Baan manufacturing can handle these scenarios in a seamless manner and is ideal for industries operating in multiple environments. This chapter acquaints you with Baan's ERPsystem's features.

Using Bill of Material Control

The Bill of Material Control module helps you maintain the product structure of your manufactured product. In other words, you can describe the parent-child relationships between the items. Such relationships, however, can only be maintained for an item described of the Manufactured type in the Item Control module. In the following sections, you see how to set up these relationships and various other facilities that the module offers.

Maintaining Bill of Material

Follow these steps to record the parent-child relationship for a manufactured item:

1. Go to Baan Manufacturing.
2. Click on Bill of Material Control module.
3. Click on Maintenance.

The Bill of Material business object offers to maintain the BOM data through either of the two forms. The two forms, though identical in nature, allow you to enter data in a slightly different way.

Often, when an item has a long lead time and has many components going into it at different operations, you might want to maintain the bill of material by operation. That is, you record components that go into an item at different operations. This facility allows effective time phasing of components and early ordering is avoided. Form 2 facilitates such entry of BOM by operation. Form 1 can be used if recording BOM by operation is not required.

Using Child Items

The child item for a manufactured item is recorded by means of two variables: position number and sequence number. A *position number* is like a serial number with a default step size of 10. The step size is designed to allow insertion of new items between two items. At the same position number, you might want to incorporate one more item that would become effective at some point in time. This can be achieved by using the Sequence Number field. Hence, for the same position number, you can record two (or more) items by using different sequence numbers.

NOTE The Effective and Expiry Date fields determine which sequence number is picked up from a position number while material planning. ▪

After you record the position number, sequence number, item, effective date, expiry date, and so on, record the net quantity of the item that goes into the parent item. You can attach a warehouse to the item (which could be different from the warehouse mentioned in the Item Control module), and the allocation is created for this item while material planning.

Routing

Routing can be described as a path taken by an item during the course of its manufacture. An item typically goes through various stages, or *operations*, as it progresses toward its manufacture. These stages and times are recorded in the Routing module. Some mandatory data needs to be set up before you can record such information. In the following sections you see how to set up this data and other details of the Routing module.

Defining Workcenters

A *workcenter* could be a physical location or some logical grouping of machines where one or more activity is carried out. A workcenter can be of the type Main Workcenter, Subworkcenter, or Subcontracting.

A workcenter could be broken down into subworkcenters if you need to have more detailed reporting or if you need to attach a different costing attribute, such as the operation rate code. It's here that you need to specify the main workcenter so that the reports and the capacity can be aggregated. It should be classified as subcontracting workcenter in case the workcenter is used to record subcontracting operations.

Each workcenter has a critical capacity type as either man or machine. There can be a number of identical machines or multiple employees in a workcenter. These form the *resource units* for the workcenter and are recorded in the workcenter information. Capacity per day and week is also recorded.

Defining Tasks

A *task* is an activity carried out during the manufacturing process. A task is carried out on a workcenter. Each task has two main attributes: set-up time and runtime. *Set-up time* is the time required during the initial setting up of the task; fixing tools on the machine or charge filling in the combustion chamber, for example. The time required per unit (to be precise, per routing unit) is recorded in the Runtime field after the setup is complete.

A task can be classified as Machine, Non-Machine, Indirect, or Absence. Machine and non-machine tasks can be included in the routing, whereas indirect and absence tasks are used for hours accounting purpose.

Part
III

Ch
20

You can define a man-machine ratio for a task of the type Machine. A *man-machine ratio* is the ratio of man occupation to machine occupation for a given task. For example, a task that requires two minutes of manual intervention for a runtime of six minutes has a man-machine ratio of 1:3.

You often encounter tasks whose runtime or production rate depends upon certain other variables like area, length, concentration, weight, and so on. For example, runtime for a gas cutting operation depends upon length and thickness of the plate. It would be very cumbersome to record all possible combinations as different tasks. Baan offers a facility by which you can define a task as generic in nature and define the runtimes or production rates based on two variables.

Defining Machines

A machine can be attached to a workcenter. Capacity by day and week can be included, as in the case of a workcenter. Machines are used to define routing, carry-out hours, accounting, and review load in capacity requirements planning.

Defining Routing

Having set up the data about machines, workcenters, and tasks, you can proceed to define the item routing. An item can have multiple routings and each routing is identified by means of a code. One can also define a standard routing, which can be used for any item.

You can enter number of operations for an item and a routing code combination. *Operations* are serial numbers in default steps of 10. As in the case of BOM, step size is designed to accommodate any operation that you want to add afterward. You have to specify a workcenter and a task in an operation. The system automatically picks up the task's details (such as set-up time, runtime, and so on), though you are at a liberty to make routing specific changes.

Production can be reported against these operations in the Shop Floor Control module. A task critical in nature can be defined as a count point operation. The significance of a count point operation is highlighted in the Shop Floor Control module.

Using the Company Calendar

Human beings follow one calendar. Organizations, by virtue of their nature of business, policies, and so on, have different holidays, working hours, number of shifts, overtime structure, and the like. The Company Calendar Business object allows you to define all these variables; therefore, you are able to configure a calendar for your company.

Company calendar serves as an input for production planning, capacity requirement planning, and hours accounting. Production is not planned for a holiday. The calender is used in capacity requirements planning to determine available capacity per time period (a day or a week, for example).

A few variables have to be set up to configure the company calendar as previously mentioned. You can specify the percentage of working hours and efficiency for each day of the week during those days. A half working day, for example, would be working for 50 percent working hours and 100 percent for efficiency, whereas during a holiday season, working hours would be 100 percent, the workcenter or the company might be working at 75 percent efficiency.

A company calendar would have either 52 or 53 weeks. While defining the company calendar, format for a week is prepared and is copied over for several weeks. For individual holidays, you can go to a particular year/week combination and set the percentage of working hours to 0.

The company calendar is defined for individual workcenters or for the entire company. In the latter case, a fictitious workcenter ZZZ is created and calendar is defined for this workcenter.

N O T E Remember that it is mandatory to run the Update Company Calendar session in order to see the changes in planning after making any changes to the company calendar. ■

Using Cost Accounting

The Baan Cost Accounting module allows you to calculate the standard cost of an item. This module also has simulation facilities, which allow you to see the effects of changes in price and order quantities. It also allows you to establish your sales prices. The following sections discuss how to establish the cost price structure of an item and various other features.

Setting Up Data

Some data set up is required for running the standard costing business objects. These data mostly pertain to breakdown of costs into various cost types, maintaining operation rates, and building the cost price structure.

The cost price components allow you to break down the cost into various cost types. The various cost types are material costs, operation costs, surcharge on material costs, surcharge on operation costs, and general costs. These cost price components are linked to items, operation rates, and subcontracting rates.

Using Operation Rates and Surcharges

Operation rates allow you to maintain charges in terms of labor, machine, and overheads for a task or a workcenter. Whether this information is recorded for a task or for a workcenter, it is determined by a parameter (?) in the CPR parameters. These rates are given against operation rate codes.

The machine, labor, and overhead rates that you specify are linked to the cost price components. These components, however, should be of type Operation Costs.

Surcharges can be added at item level or item group level, the former being higher in hierarchy. Surcharges specified as negative quantities act as discounts.

There are various ways in which you can specify the surcharges for an item or item group. A surcharge can be applied to total costs or added costs. Furthermore, you can specify whether you need to apply surcharges to selected lines in the cost structure.

You can enter a simulated price of an item in the Maintain Simulated Purchase Prices session for the purpose of simulation. You can choose to carry out cost price calculation by using these prices.

Using Cost Price Calculation

Cost price calculation is primarily driven by cost price calculation code. You specify, via this code, which purchase price to be considered out of current purchase price, average purchase price, latest purchase price, or simulated price.

The cost price calculated is stored in that cost price calculation code. Cost prices are updated only if the cost price calculation code that was used in generation process matches that in the CPR parameters.

TIP Cost price calculation can be carried out by using different cost price calculation codes. The results of these calculations can then be compared.

Using the Master Production Schedule

Master production schedule represents apex level plan of Baan MRPII. This plan is composed of the following three subplans:

- Demand Plan
- Production Plan
- Inventory Plan

Though linked, these plans can be worked upon independently, and the effects shall be passed on to the lower-level planning modules.

Master Production Schedule module allows you to create different scenarios for these plans and compare them. When you're satisfied, you can earmark one plan for your actual working. The following sections discuss how to form these plans and learn about this module's various aspects.

Working with Plan Codes

Different master production schedule scenarios are created through what are known as plan codes. A *plan code* basically defines the planning horizon and various other plan attributes. Plan items and plan periods are attached to plan codes.

Plan periods are time buckets within the planning horizon. To monitor a plan more closely, you might want to define smaller time buckets at the start of the plan and wider buckets toward the end. This strategy works more effectively with rolling plans. A *rolling plan* is one based on a reference date after which it regenerates itself.

Setting Up Plan Items

Analogous to the Bill of Materials, Baan allows creation of a product family tree. However, unlike the product structure, the product family tree comprises fictitious items and represents the business structure. For example, a company engaged in the business of manufacturing electrical appliances, which comprises motors and pumps. Motors manufacturers are in high horsepower and fractional horsepower sector. These, in turn, comprise end-manufactured (MPS) items.

Electrical appliances, pumps, or motors are not physical items. They are referred to as plan items in Baan. These form the product family tree. The MPS items are at the lowest level of the family tree. An organization can have a business plan that states that in a given period, they plan to manufacture 100,000 electrical appliances, of which 40,000 could be pumps and the rest could be motors. Thus, planning percentages can be attached to plan items, and a plan can be broken down to the MPS level.

 TIP After a product family tree is formed and planning percentages are attached, you can break down the business plan into the master production schedule for the end items by running the Generate Master Production Schedule session.

Defining Critical Materials and Capacities

Critical materials are typically those with long lead times and whose unavailability could jeopardize the project or production. Critical capacities are the resources that form the bottleneck for production.

Critical materials and capacities are defined in the Bill of Critical Materials and Bill of Critical Capacities. After the master production schedule is defined, these sessions help carry out rough material and rough capacity planning. It is mandatory to maintain bill of critical materials if you are using multilevel MPS.

Maintaining Master Production Schedule

After defining plan code, plan items, and plan periods, you should run the Generate Master Production Schedule session and keep all options set to No. This results in the generation of a matrix with the plans (demand, inventory, and production) on one axis and the time buckets on another. Figure 20.1 shows such a matrix.

NOTE Depending upon your plan code/plan item setup, you can opt to generate a demand plan, production plan, and inventory plan automatically or through manual intervention. ▨

FIG. 20.1

This is the matrix for the master production schedule.

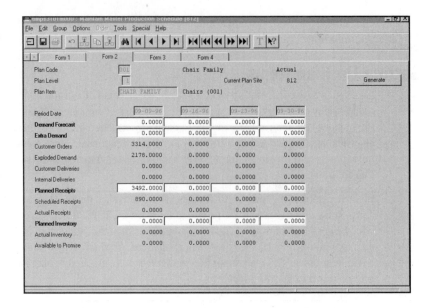

The concept of consumption is important in Baan's master production schedule. Suppose you have entered a demand forecast of 7,500 units in a future MPS time bucket. In that period, you receive customer orders of 800 units (till date). The customer orders eat away the demand forecast by 800 units. For that period, the consumed demand is 800 units and unconsumed demand is 6,700 units (till date). The system therefore generates orders for the demand forecast until the consumed demand equals the demand forecast. Orders are generated for customer orders as soon as customer orders exceed the forecast.

Generating the Master Production Schedule

The session for generating the master production schedule is the most important session in the MPS module. It has the following main objectives:

1. Generating the logistic plan constituting demand plan, production plan, and inventory plan

2. Planning and controlling plant goods flow between companies

3. Generating rough material requirements for the planning and control of critical materials

4. Generating rough capacity requirements for visualizing potential capacity bottlenecks

   A demand plan is generated if you have selected Yes in the Generate Demand Plan field and Yes in the Maintain Plan Items session for the Automatic Update of Demand Plan field.

   An inventory plan is generated if you have selected Yes in the Generate Inventory Plan field and Yes in the Maintain Plan Items session for the Automatic Update of Inventory Plan field.

A production plan is generated if you have selected Yes in the Generate Production Plan field and Yes in the Maintain Plan Items session for the Automatic Update of Production Plan field.

Planned orders are generated only if the Generate Planned Orders field reads Yes and the status of the master production schedule is Actual, not Simulated. The plan is made Actual by setting the plan code in the Actual Plan Code field in MPS parameters.

Using Material Requirement Planning

The Material Requirement Planning module primarily gets its requirements from the master planning. It does so through the master production scheduling, though it could come from other sources like sales order, projects, and so on. The requirement is broken down (*exploded*) into requirements for lower.

Using MRP Logic

Depending upon the quantity of the end products to be made, MRP logic calculates the resulting requirements for the constituent parts both in terms of quantity required and the requirement dates. The demand for the end product primarily comes from the MPS module. Sales forecast in the MRP module add to the demand originating from the MPS module.

The MRP logic, after obtaining the demand for the end item, refers to the BOM file for the demand's explosion. This gives the gross requirements. The gross requirements are broken down into net requirements by considering the inventory of that item. It also uses the Routing module to calculate the lead time required for manufacturing or purchase of that item. The lead time for a manufactured item is calculated from the routing file, whereas lead time for a purchased item is taken from the Item Control module.

MRP in Baan can be run three ways: regenerative MRP, net change MRP, and continuous MRP. Complete MRP run is carried out in regenerative type without considering the previous MRP calculations. Only changes of MPS and MRP items with respect to the previous run is calculated in net change MRP. Net change MRP requires a lesser duration than the regenerative MRP run. Continuous MRP is basically a net change MRP run that runs itself after a definite time period.

Generating Planned Orders

The Generate Planned MRP Orders session is used to generate the planned purchase and production orders. You can choose the type of MRP run (net change, regenerative, or continuous) in this session. As described earlier, sales forecast can be attached to MRP items, and the effective date for considering this forecast can be entered.

You also have an option to consider the sales quotations as a part of your demand. Each sales quotation can be attached with an expected success percentage. In the MRP run, you can specify that quotes above a certain success percentage should be considered on demand. You can specify whether firm planned orders should be deleted during the MRP run. There is also an option that allows you to automatically confirm orders if the planned start date for the order falls within the item's time fence.

Rescheduling and Exception Messages

Apart from the recommended (planned) purchase and production orders, MRP module produces two other outputs—rescheduling messages and exception messages. Rescheduling messages are of two kinds: reschedule-in and reschedule-out. *Rescheduling messages* are generated when the existing production or purchase orders do not meet the actual requirements date. *Rescheduling-in messages* are generated when the order is to be bought earlier in time; *rescheduling-out messages* are generated when the order is to be pushed out in time.

Exception messages are generated if the relevant advice cannot be made compatible with the master data or if there are any other exceptions.

 TIP   A smoothing factor can be applied during the MRP run if you want to do away with rescheduling messages or exception messages for minor changes in planning.

Using Capacity Requirement Planning

Capacity Requirements Planning module is designed to give the planner an insight into the use of his or her workcenters and machines based on the planning carried out. In principle, the required capacity is planned on the basis of infinite capacity. However, various reports and displays in this module highlight the projected bottlenecks. The planner has various options to avoid these bottlenecks, such as changing the order dates, routing, and so on.

This module also has facilities to perform financial analysis where it can reflect the projected profitability by week. In the following sections, you explore this module's various features.

Using Repetitive Manufacturing

Repetitive manufacturing scenario is characterized by high speed, large volume production typically on dedicated manufacturing facilities. The production is more rate-based than quantity-based and schedules rather than production orders are important.

Using Production Schedules

Because the environment is rate-based, bottleneck workcenter is calculated using the Routing Control module. Production orders are formed through the normal planning process. Production is monitored and reported in terms of schedule periods. A schedule period is analogous to the concept of MPS time buckets.

All the production orders falling within a scheduled period are consolidated and the production and rejection is reported against this consolidated quantity for that period. Internally, however, production and rejection is apportioned to individual production orders by means of a calculation logic.

Setting Up Data

The item that is manufactured in a repetitive environment should be set as **repetitive item** in the Item Control module. Schedule codes, which are linked to repetitive items and used to define the schedule periods, are then set up.

Dedicated production lines can be defined as scheduling areas. Scheduling areas can be linked to schedule codes. Therefore, a schedule code binds items, periods, and production line into one unit.

Using Repetitive Production Control

The production control concept is the same as that of the Shop Floor Control module described in the following section. The difference is that production is reported complete, and rejects are reported for a scheduling period instead of against an order. Material is generally backflushed in a repetitive environment. However, if material needs to be issued order-specific, you can do so through the Shop Floor Control module.

Operations and orders are completed through the session Report Completed Production Schedules by RPT Item. The reporting procedure is close to that of the Shop Floor Control module.

Using Shop Floor Control

Having accomplished the planning at the MPS, MRP, and PRP level, the next step is to monitor and report the operations at the shop floor level. This production control activity is carried out in the Shop Floor Control module.

Using Production Order Control

You have seen that the production orders are formed in theMPS and MRP modules. You have also seen how these orders are confirmed and transferred. These transferred orders form planned orders in the Shop Floor Control module. People in charge of micro-level planning are able to plan for these orders at the shop floor. Depending upon factors like material availability, capacity availability, and so on, they can release these orders on the shop floor.

Before releasing such orders, it may be important to print certain information or documentation to the shop personnel regarding these orders. These documents are typically the routing/operations sheet, material sheet, sawing list, and so on. Baan's Print Order Documents session provides standard documentation types. These can also be set in the Shop Floor Control parameters.

After the production order is created, the material required for execution of the order is calculated by the system. This is carried out by using the Bill of Material and is stored in the Maintain Estimated Materials session. If the planner expects changes in the material required, he or she can do so by making changes in this session.

Part
III

Ch
20

Material can be issued to WIP using the Enter Material Issue session after the production order is released. If a partial quantity is issued, the rest of the material is treated as subsequent delivery. Any material shortage can be tracked by using the Print Shortages by Production Order session. If the company is location control, outbound procedure needs to be carried out after the material issue.

You can start reporting the operations and the hours spent on the order after the material is issued from inventory. Operations reporting can be done by using the Report Operations Complete session. The system reports all preceding operations complete until it encounters a count point operation. A count point operation is not completed automatically and must be reported.

To transfer goods to the finished goods inventory, use the Report Orders Complete session. While reporting partial completion, keep the Order Complete parameter as No. Only when the total order quantity is complete should this parameter be set to Yes.

Each production order carries a status with it that helps in two functions:

- It allows the planner to monitor the order very closely.
- It allows the planner a varying degree of flexibility per the status of the production order.

As a production order is transferred from the Planning modules to the Shop Floor Control module, it attains a status of Planned. At this stage, various changes like item, routing, order dates, warehouse, estimated material, and the like can be done on this order.

The status becomes Order documents printed after the necessary documents are printed. Modified order documents can be printed if any changes are carried out at this stage.

After the released status, material can be issued against the production order, and operations and orders can be reported completed. When you start posting hours against the order, its status changes to active.

When you transfer all goods to the finished goods inventory, the status changes to completed. When you close the production order, financial transactions are posted to the general ledger.

Using Production Order Planning

Planning a production order is a process wherein the start and the end times of each operation for a production order are defined. Ideal conditions are taken into account while planning; however, you often find that small changes have to be made (in terms of adding operations, changing the capacity, and so on, for example). These are carried out in this module.

Sometimes, the entire production schedule has to be shifted for a day or so. This can be done using the Shift Production Planning session. If major changes are made to planning—routing changes of, workcenter capacity, or parameters, for example—you need to replan the production.

NOTE   Planning can also be viewed and modified in the form of a Gantt chart. This can be done through various sessions in Planning Board.

Understanding the Concept of Backflushing

Backflushing is the automatic issue of estimated materials or accounting for hours after an operation. This is typically used when it is either tedious or trivial to issue exact material to a production order. This occurs normally in cases of bulk issue or C class items.

To use backflushing for material, set the Backflush Material and Backflush if Material fields to Yes in the Item Control module. For backflushing hours, set the Backflush Hours field in the Item Control to Yes. For backflushing of individual operations, the Backflushing field in Maintain Tasks can be used.

Backflushing is carried out at the completion of an operation or order. It can be carried out three ways: interactively, automatically, or separately. Interactively means that the system asks, after order/operation is completed, whether to backflush the material. Automatically carries out backflushing without consulting the user. Separately can be carried out using the Backflush Materials and Hours session only.

Using Kanban—Pull Notes

The kanbans are referred to as pull notes in Baan. They can be applied to a JIT kind of manufacturing environment. The pull notes are used to "pull" the following:

- Materials to the shop floor
- Subassemblies from one operation to the next
- From the shop floor to the main item warehouse

There are four types of pull notes:

- From shop floor—These are used to govern the flow of material out of the shop floor.
- Inter-operation—These are used to govern the flow of material between the operations.
- To shop floor—These are used to govern the flow of material into the shop floor.
- Replenishment order—These are used to govern the flow of material from BOM warehouse to WIP warehouse.

Handling Subcontracting

Subcontracting in Baan is treated as purchase of service from the subcontractor and hence, no physical transaction of material takes place.

Items of the subcontracting type denote these services. These items are linked to tasks in the Maintain Routings session. Workcenters of the subcontracting type are added to the routing of manufactured items.

A normal production order is created for the manufactured item. For purchase of subcontracting services, a purchase order for the subcontracting item (against the production order) is generated using the Generate Subcontracting Orders session and is transferred to the Purchase Control module. When these purchased services are received by the Purchase Control module, further (in-house) operations are carried out for the manufactured item.

Sometimes, due to unforeseen circumstances, operations have to be subcontracted dynamically. Such unplanned subcontracting operations are handled through the session Maintain Subcontracting Operations. The operations to be subcontracted and the subcontractor is mentioned and the rest of the procedure is the same as mentioned above.

Using Production Order Costing

In Baan, production cost is monitored by comparing the actual cost versus the estimated cost. The estimated cost is available when the production order is planned. The estimated materials and hours are taken into account.

The actual cost is obtained after closing the production order. Material cost is computed by the product of standard cost and material issued against the order. Operation cost is computed by using the operation rates or man and machine rates (depending on parameter setup) and the actual hours spent. The difference between the actual and the estimated costs is treated as "production result."

N O T E   No financial transaction can be posted against an order if its status is Closed. However, the production order status can be reverted to Completed and the entries can be passed.

Using Hours Accounting

For carrying out actual costing of a production order, it is essential that actual time spent on the production order be recorded. The Hours Accounting module helps you enter the time spent by an employee and a machine for a particular workcenter. In the following sections, you see the formats in which you can enter this data.

Setting Up Data

Before being able to use the hours accounting module, some data setup is required. Baan allows you to maintain various working time tables. Each working time table is designated a code. A working time table allows you to assign working hours for each day. These times are maintained through the Maintain Working Hours session where the start and the end times for the day could be mentioned. Any breaks in the working hours can also be indicated.

Hourly labor types are used to indicate normal and overtime hours. You can attach various surcharge rates, either positive or negative, to the labor, machine and overhead costs. These surcharges are added to the rates mentioned in the operation rate codes in the cost accounting module.

Processing Hours Accounting

Hours can be accounted for production, projects or service. The hours transactions can be carried for a day or a week. For each hours transaction, you enter a start time and an end time. When you enter this data the system automatically calculates the machine hours if the task involves both employee and machine. Again, hours are broken down into different hourly labor types (basically normal or overtime hours) depending upon your working time table definition.

Hours can also be accounted for indirect tasks and absence tasks. Absence tasks are recorded, but financial entries are not passed in Baan finance.

Using Project Control and Project Budgets

Several companies are engaged in selling products that are manufactured based on customer requirements. The volumes are so small that it does not justify the need for making these items as standard items. The whole process of planning, costing, and execution is carried out for an item based on customers' requirements or, in other words, for a customized item. Baan PCS Projects module meets the requirements of such organizations.

Putting the PCS Module in Perspective

This module is designed for companies that work in the made to order environment. A project is an identifier that helps in storing the demand, planning, costing and execution information of customized items separately with respect to the standard items. The customized items are stored in a different database than the standard items. A project structure consists of customized items with its own bills of material and routings. Special project rates and surcharges can be defined and estimated costs are calculated by using these rates. You can carry out activity oriented network planning where the emphasis lies in determining the critical path.

In projects of long duration, material planning becomes critical and activity based material planning can be carried out by Module Planning. For large assignments, main projects and subprojects can be defined wherein the subprojects are defined within the timeframe of the main project. The project structure is translated into the production, purchase and warehouse orders by using the project requirement planning (PRP) functionality.

Common data for projects, such as project type, customer name, and so on is entered in the Maintain Projects session. A project type could be main project, sub-project or single project. A main project is made of several sub-projects. Total costs of sub-projects are aggregated to the main project. No items can be linked to main project. Sub-project is a subset of a main project wherein customized items could be manufactured. The start and the end dates are calculated using the network planning module. A single project is never a part of main project. Its purpose is to manufacture customized products. It is generally not necessary to use network planning for single projects. Project structure defines the relationship between main project and sub-projects.

Using Network Planning

The primary function of the Network Planning module is to coordinate activity dates between main project and sub-projects. Planning of material based on activities and linking rough capacity requirements to them can be carried out through this module.

It is important to define what is known as "activities" for network planning. Activities are the steps that must be performed to complete the project. By creating the links between the activities, a network can be created. The raw materials and capacity requirements are planned through the activities. Activity relationships are maintained in the session Maintain Activity Relations. Float can also be defined while maintaining the relationships.

If a required capacity must be distributed over the duration of the activity, capacity load tables can be defined. By linking different percentages of capacity to different percentages of the lead time, the capacity load table is described. This is only required when the capacity-load relationship is not linear.

Using Module Planning

Module planning business object is used for activity controlled project requirements planning. A module can be any number of customized items which, during an activity, must be delivered by production or purchase.

A safety time can be defined, which is related to the activity duration, to determine the desired delivery time of the customized items. If a safety time is used, the desired delivery time can be defined as a percentage of the activity duration.

Using Project Engineering

In this business object, customized BOMs and routings are defined for customized items. The data can be entered manually or can be copied from the standard modules, generic data or other project structure.

You maintain customized items in the project engineering module. A customized item may be purchased or produced for a customer order. A customized item always belongs to a project. A customized item could be derived from a standard item. In such an event, if there is a demand for a customized item and stock is available for the standard item, a PRP warehouse order is generated for this standard item to satisfy the demand for the customized item.

Using Project Calculation

Special project rates and surcharges can be defined in the project calculation at Maintain Operation Rates by Project. Subcontracting rates are maintained in Maintain Subcontracting Rates by Project. If no project rates are entered, the system takes standard rates from Cost Accounting module. Although it is possible to define project rates at different stages in a project, they are best defined after the project structure has been defined.

Estimated and actual costs are calculated in the Calculate Cost Prices by Project session. The actual costing data is obtained from Shop Floor Control and Hours Accounting module.

Using Project Planning

A project planning can be generated when there is a demand for a customized item. This demand can originate from sales order or from a *planning module*. Demand is translated into recommended purchase, production or a warehouse order by means of Project Requirements Planning (PRP) functionality. The PRP calculation is a material requirements calculation for customized items. This implies that, based on demand for a particular item, recommendations are made to purchase the required parts and produce the subassemblies in a certain time. PRP uses the economic stock to determine whether enough stock is available for a linked standard item or interchangeable alternative item.

It is also possible to do a capacity check while generating PRP. Different utilization reports for workcenters and machines are available. It is hence possible to detect any potential bottleneck at an early stage. Load profile for active and simulated projects is displayed.

Using PCS Budgets

PCS Budgets module is used if an organization wants to make multiple calculations for various project components. Cost simulations are based on rates, BOM and routing variations. The calculations are called *budgets* and can be used to generate sales quotations.

The first step in making a rough calculation for customized items is maintaining common data for budgets, such as customer information and the quantity of products asked for. These products are called *budget parts*. Within these, calculation parts, which are manufactured or purchased items specifically entered for the request, and its structure (material and routing sheets) are entered. Rates and structure of the calculation part can be changed using different "budget calculation codes" and different codes can be compared.

To calculate a price for a budget when a quotation must be issued, the structure of the parts must be defined. The structure consists of materials that must be used and the operations that need to be performed. The rates and possible surcharges belonging to the budget are defined. If no budget specific rates are defined, then the rates in Cost Accounting module are used. The cost and the selling price is calculated. The selling price is determined by applying the surcharges to the calculated cost price of each calculation part of the budget structure.

Having been satisfied with the calculation and the budget being approved, a budget can be copied onto a project. Likewise, a previous project can be copied on to a project. In such an event, project number is copied as budget number, project part is copied as budget part, customized items as calculation parts, customized BOMs as material sheets, and customized routing is copied as routing sheet in budget.

Using Product Classification

The product classification allows you to control family and family group data. A *family* is a collection of items with common features. You can define a structure with which to classify each family according to level.

A family structure is defined by attaching family groups and families to a main family group. The family groups are of types Main Family Group and Family Group. You can record family groups under the main family group. ●

Part

III

Ch

20

CHAPTER 21

Understanding the Production Management Module

In this chapter

Controlling Production

So far, the overview of the Baan Process package has focused on the setup of basic or master data such as product units of measures, formulae, and routings. This section outlines the use of this data in the Baan Process Production Management module. It is more an overview of production management concepts, however, than a step-by-step work instruction.

You can use the Production Management module to apply some controls over production such as the recording of rejected quantities, the reporting of completed quantities, and the monitoring of production costs, material usage, utilities, and so on. This information is stored under a *production batch*. The production batch can be seen as a control number used to verify production operations, runtime, and costs based on a standard quantity, a time period, the availability of a raw materials, and so on.

Defining Production

Production batches can be monitored with manufacturing software in a number of ways, and the Baan Production Management module is fairly flexible in this regard. Users should not get bogged down by the variety of tools available to oversee their production, however, and should try to narrow down the functions that will help them manage the entry, processing, and analysis of production data most efficiently.

Before users proceed with the setup of the Production module, some issues regarding your company's production environment should be addressed. This is done in the following sections. After these issues (among others) have been addressed, companies can have a better handle on which functions in the Production Management module will best suit their needs.

Determining What Drives Production

If production processes are work-order driven, a production batch is entered for each production run. Operations are typically reported as completed for the entire batch (instead of reporting for each individual routing operation). In this case, product routings should be created with few or no count points so that the system can update all operations in one step. Users will indicate that a production batch is completed and post the quantities to inventory using the session *Report Batch Complete*, or *Report End Items Complete* if the product is produced in different packages and variations. Co- and by-products can also be received at the end of the production batch.

If production quantities need to be reported for each operation, some operations should be defined as count points in the product routings. Also, some of the operations need to be qualified as restrictive. This method could apply to companies that process precious metals or pharmaceuticals, and also to where close monitoring of scrap or rejected quantities is required. In this case, completed operations are entered using the sessions *Report Operations Complete* as well as Report Batch Complete after all operations are closed.

For each operation, users can enter the completed quantities as well as the rejected quantities. If an operation that is not a start operation is reported as completed (for example, operation 5 in a series of 10 operations), the system asks whether you want to close all previous operations. If you choose to do so, all previous operations that are not count points will be closed. If some count points are present, the system does not let the user enter a quantity greater than that reported in previous operations. If no quantities have been reported and users try to report quantities for an operation that is past a count point, a message appears indicating that only a quantity of 0 can be reported as delivered/received. Also, note that co- and by-products can be reported at a specific operation.

If production is a continuous process, a production batch is entered for a longer time period. A production batch for pulp in a pulp and paper mill can be a continuous process, for example, where conditions do not change for several days. Users will report operations quantities completed for specific time intervals (after several days, after a week, or after a month), and then the batch will be closed so that production costs (materials used and labor hours reported) can be stored for that given period.

Producing and Containerizing Finished Goods in the Same Process

Are finished goods produced and containerized in the same process? If so, a production batch is entered for the main item and quantities are reported in the number of containers, end items, or product variations specified in the session *Maintain Estimated End Items*.

A process item can be produced and stored as an intermediary item to be reprocessed and packaged at a later time (presumably as a component of another product code that has end items), or it is just kept in bulk form. In this instance, the container field in the session *Maintain Production Batches* is left blank, and quantities are reported in the item's inventory unit, not in different types of packaging. (The session Report End Items Complete is not used.)

Monitoring Resource Usage

An estimated usage of utilities such as water, natural gas, or electricity can be recorded in a product formula using the session *Maintain Materials*. (For example, for each 100 pounds produced, 10 kilowatts of electricity are required.) The inclusion of resources in the product formula will help companies keep track of utility costs. Thus they can build utilities usage into the cost of the finished good.

To do so, resources must be entered in the item master as cost items (Item Type = Cost). If resource usage has been included in the product formula, the session *Enter Cost Resources for Production Batches* is used to report resource/utilities costs for a production batch.

Rescheduling Production

Companies might be subject to a long production cycle with significant wait times between operations. Thus the rescheduling of individual operations can often occur, and it will have more of an effect on the overall production capacity. If a lot of moving around happens in terms of specific production operations and the machines and work centers used, it might be preferable to set safeguards to avoid bottlenecks. You can do this with the session *Maintain Production Data by Item Group*. This function is used to indicate what should happen to specific operations (those that precede or follow the operations that are moved) when changes are made to the production schedule.

N O T E   The reschedule options (Do Not Move, Move All Operations, When Overlap Occurs, When Overlap > 100%) selected here are defaults that can be changed at batch entry. ▪

If production operations are generally interdependent, sequential, and are performed using specific machine or work centers, the entire series of operations for a batch should be moved when changes are made to the schedule. (The option Move All Operations would be selected.)

These reschedule parameters are verified by the system when operations are moved in the session *Maintain Estimated Batch Planning*. Fixed Planning Dates, another parameter set in the session Maintain Estimated Batch Planning, also affects the rescheduling of operations. If this is set to Yes for a specific operation, rescheduling of the previous or next operations do not change the start and end date for this "fixed" operation.

Reporting Material Usage and Employee Hours

Companies might keep a strict account of work hours and materials used. In some cases, raw material quantities might be adjusted continually in the production process. (Users might know the quantities used only after the finished goods have been processed.) As well, production personnel might be asked to report specific hours spent on a production batch. In this case, the raw materials are generally issued to a production batch using the session *Issue Materials*.

N O T E   Because the Baan Process package can only be implemented if the Location Control has been activated, the Issue Materials step is done in conjunction with the Outbound Data function in the Location Control module. Quantities to be issued are entered in the Issue Materials screen, and the session *Generate Outbound Advice* is run. ▪

Employee production hours are recorded using the session *Enter Hours Accounting*. Depending on the batch status, users can report work hours for a specific production batch and operation.

If materials and hours are backflushed after a specific operation or for an entire production batch, some backflushing parameters must be set so that all elements of the production batch are included in the backflushing process. First, the item produced must have the parameters Backflush Materials and Backflush Hours set to Yes in the session *Maintain Item Data*. Second, the materials used in the formula must have the parameter Backflush If Materials set to Yes in the same session. Third, the work centers used in the product routing must be tied to an employee. (Employees are linked to a work center in the session *Maintain Employees* in the Baan Common Data package.) Fourth, the field *Backflush* must be set to Yes in the routing operation where the backflushing should occur. Finally, in the session *Maintain PMG*

Parameters, users need to specify the backflushing method to be used. The following options are available:

- *Automatically*. As operations or batches are reported complete, the system automatically backflushes hours and materials (in the background).

- *Interactively*. When operations or batches are reported complete, the system displays a message prompting the user to backflush immediately (Yes/No).

- *Separately*. If this option is selected, users can only backflush hours and materials by using the session *Backflush Materials/Hours*. Therefore backflushing cannot be done from the sessions Report Operations Complete or *Report Production Batches Complete*.

Again, backflushing of materials and hours can be done for specific operations or for an entire batch. Also, backflushing can be done for a range of batches, items, or work centers via the session Backflush Materials\Hours. This session can be used if the backflushing method specified in the PMG parameters is not Automatically.

Assigning Lot Numbers

If lot numbers need to be tracked for quality and regulatory purposes, products need to be defined as lot-controlled in the session Maintain Item Data. (The Lot Control field is set to "By Lot.") The lot number can be generated automatically or entered manually, depending on the LTC parameter settings in the Distribution package. You can apply additional quality controls by implementing the Quality Management system. Inspection orders tied to product specifications can be performed during production operations or after a batch is complete. This is done by using the session *Quality Combinations* in the QMS module.

Issuing Rework Orders for Finished Goods

Additional costs and production planning time for finished goods that require further processing (because of poor quality or additional customer specifications) can be captured using rework batches. Users will specify that a finished good will be reworked by switching the Rework field to Yes in the session Maintain Production Batches. The system will also recognize a batch as a rework order if the routing field is left blank in the session Maintain Production Batches. Users then need to enter a rework task to be performed (for either a main or end item). This is done on form 2 of the Maintain Production Batches session.

In a rework batch, the substandard finished good serves as a component to the "refurbished." If needed, other materials can be added to the rework batch in the session *Maintain Estimated Materials*. You can also include additional operations in the *Maintain Batch Planning* session.

Reporting Material and Operations Costs for Production Batches

The Baan Production Management module records the following three types of production costs:

- Standard
- Estimated
- Actual

For standard production costs, the batch raw material quantities and production run time are based on the product formula and routing. The values are initially brought in when a batch is entered.

For estimated production costs, changes can be made to the raw materials used, the material quantities required, and the production operations. This is done via the sessions Maintain Estimated Materials and Maintain Estimated Batch Planning. After this is done, Baan refers to the batch raw materials and production planning as estimated. This often occurs because raw material quantities are frequently adjusted and materials substituted. As well, batch planning will be changed because production may be moved to another machine, machine efficiency/ capacity may fluctuate, and so on.

Actual production costs are the actual raw material quantities used and production time elapsed for a specific batch. Raw material quantities actually issued from inventory for a given batch may differ from the estimated quantities. (In some instances, these quantities are not entirely known until the batch is completed.) Actual production time will only be known after all hours have been accounted for. This is done either through backflushing or "manual" hours accounting using the session Enter Hours Accounting.

N O T E Backflushing hours will provide a theoretical number of production hours. These hours are based on the ratio between the total quantity to be produced over the quantities reported complete at time of backflushing. Therefore, if half the batch quantity is reported complete, half the production time will be posted.

The actual values are finalized after a production batch is closed.

Actual costs can be compared with either the standard or estimated material quantities and run time. A number of reports are available that compare actual costs to standard or estimated costs. Users can define which type of cost will serve as a basis for comparison in the session Maintain PMG Parameters (see the Default for Comparing Actuals field).

Entering and Processing Production Batches

Production batches are created in the Baan Process Production Management module, in the submodule Production Batch Control. After the item to be produced has been entered, the system pulls default information from the formula and routing records for that product. This default information can be modified if needed. The following three basic types of production batches can be entered:

- Main item production batch
- End item production batch
- Rework batch

For a main item production batch, a batch is entered for a noncontainerized process item. A production batch can also be scheduled for a main item, which is *containerized* in the same production run. In the latter case, the containerized output of the batch is specified using the session Maintain Estimated End Items. In both cases, the Container field is left blank on form 1.

For an end item production batch, a batch is entered for a main item that will be packaged in a specific container. In this case, the packaging type is specified in the Container field on form 1.

A rework production batch involves the further processing of a finished good that has either been damaged or deemed below established quality standards. In this case, the "to-be-reprocessed" finished good serves as a component to the "refurbished" finished good. For rework batches, the Rework flag on form 2 is set to Yes.

In the production cycle, a batch will have the following status:

- Planned
- Documents Printed
- Released
- Active
- Complete
- Closed

The following sections discuss each of these statuses.

Understanding Planned Status

A planned batch will soft allocate raw material quantities, add the batch quantity to the On Order inventory of the production warehouse, and use up capacity for machines and work centers. Raw material quantities can be modified as well as the production batch planning (operation run time, start and end dates, and so on). Figure 21.1 shows how you maintain the information related to production batches.

Understanding Documents Printed Status

For a batch with a status of Documents Printed, a batch ticket has been printed using the session *Print Batch Documents*. This can be made a mandatory step by setting the parameter Print Batch Documents Mandatory to Yes in the session Maintain PMG Parameters. Figure 21.2 shows how you can print the batch documents.

Understanding Released Status

Batches can be released individually or collectively. A released batch can be considered as in progress. This should be done after batch material quantities and the batch operations have been confirmed. Raw material quantities cannot be changed after a batch has been released, although the batch operations can be modified. When a batch is released, raw materials can be issued, and work hours can be reported. A released batch can only be canceled using the session *Cancel Production Batches*. Figure 21.3 shows how you can release a batch.

FIG. 21.1

You can enter and maintain production batches in the session Maintain Production Batches.

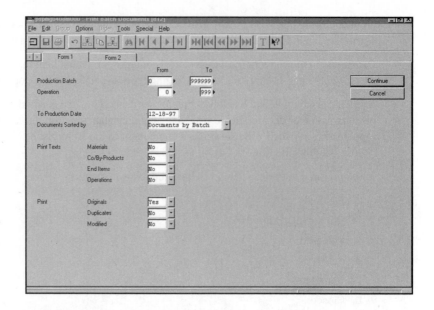

FIG. 21.2

Documents can be printed and issued to the shop floor by using the session Print Batch Documents.

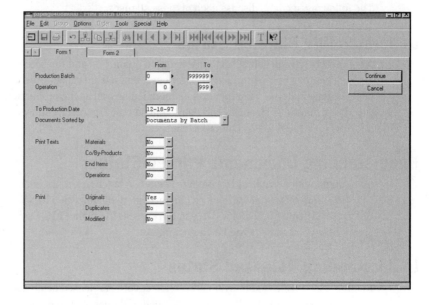

FIG. 21.3

You can release a batch by accessing this session from the Production Batch Control menu and from the Maintain Production Batches session (via the Special option on the menu bar).

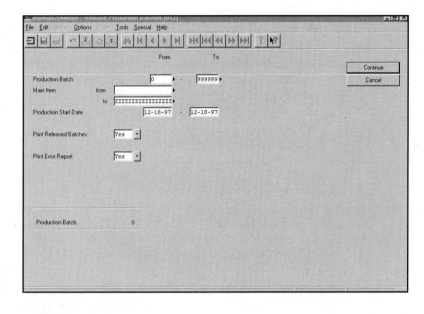

Understanding Active Status

An Active batch is one that has been released and for which some or all work hours have been reported. Figure 21.4 shows the status of a batch.

FIG. 21.4

After production hours have been reported, either through backflushing or the session Enter Hours Accounting, the batch status changes to Active.

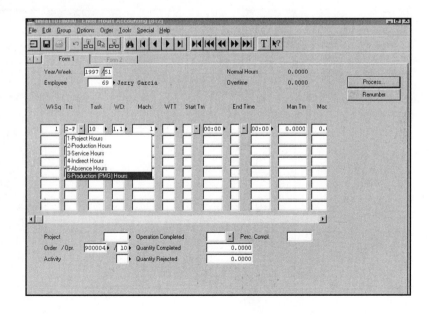

Part
III

Ch
21

Understanding Complete Status

When a batch has a status of Complete, all operations for the batch have been reported as complete, and the entire batch has been completed by setting the Completed field to Yes in the session Report Batch Complete. This can be done if all operations have been closed, end items (if any) have been posted to inventory, and co/by products have been accounted for. Thus a batch can have the Complete status after all goods have been received in inventory.

N O T E   You can still post hours and issue materials for a completed batch. ■

Finished goods will be received using the session *Maintain Production Receipts* (ILC). This session pops up if the user answers Yes to the question Post to Inventory. If the finished good is lot-controlled (this is specified in the item master), the system requires that a lot number be assigned to each receipt. From the Lot field, you can zoom to the session *Maintain Lots*. A lot number is assigned after all the mandatory fields in the lot record have been filled. Users can specify a storage unit of their choice (such as case, pallet, drum, and so on) if the item is stored in something other than the inventory unit (zoom on the storage unit field). Finished goods are received in the default warehouse receipt location (see the Receipt Location code in the session *Maintain Warehouses*). They are then stored in their proper location by using the functions Generate Inbound Advice, Maintain Inbound Advice (optional), and Release Inbound Advice. Figure 21.5 shows the details contained in the session Report Production Batches Complete.

FIG. 21.5

Total quantities that have been received from a production batch are entered in the session Report Production Batches Complete.

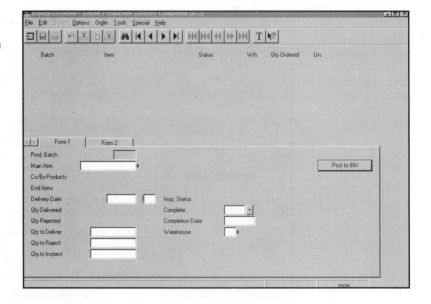

Understanding Closed Status

Users can close a batch if all raw materials have been issued, all work hours have been reported, all finished good quantities have been reported and put away using the Inbound Data module (see the section on Location Control), and co- and by-products have been processed. Closing a batch finalizes both the material and operation costs. After the batch status has been set to Closed, it can be reset to Completed to post additional hours and raw materials usage. This is done by using the session *Reset Production Batch Status*. Figure 21.6 shows the session used to close production batches.

FIG. 21.6

Production batches can be closed and actual costs can be captured after all batch elements have been accounted for.

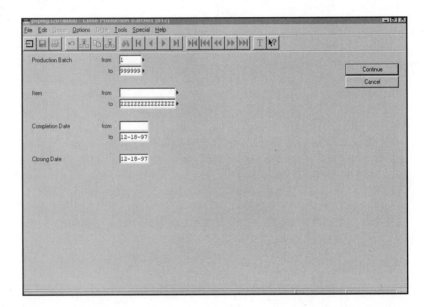

> **N O T E** If the Quality Management system has been implemented, all inspection orders generated following the creation of this batch must have a Closed status. ▪

After batches have been processed, Baan provides a number of production reports and batch costing analyses that can be used to oversee production activity for a given period. Additional reports can be created by using the Baan Tools Report Writer. ●

Understanding the Service Module

Controlling Installations

Baan's Service module allows users to service their customers. By helping you manage installations, contracts, and warranties, this module integrates the service aspect with the software's other functions. This module also takes care of planning your technicians' workload for dispatch to perform repairs or maintenance calls.

Managing the various customer sites' installations is important to service-related users; this business object is designed to record all the existing installations to be serviced. It is also through this module that the periodic maintenance to be performed is scheduled.

Managing Installations

The Installation control lets you record various information regarding installations performed at customer sites. You can create bill of materials to record the contents of the installation and necessary information, such as serial numbers. This is the base to record the history for all maintenance of the installed parts.

Other valuable information can be recorded. The original supplier of any components can be entered as well as customer information for billing. Every installation can be prioritized to help you manage service calls. If you get a contract agreement for this installation, a link with the Contract module is made.

Creating an Installation

The Installation screen is quite easy to fill. You can find an example in Figure 22.1. Follow these steps to create an installation:

1. Click the Insert icon.
2. Enter the installation Description (for example, Injection Machine at Plant #1).
3. Enter a Search Argument. This is a keyword to search on this installation at a later point. Don't use the serial number; it is already stored in the item master.
4. Enter an Installation Type. You can create various installation types that match your needs. The type must be created up front. Use IM, for Injection Machine, in this example.
5. Enter the original Project number (where this installation was performed).
6. Enter the Item code of the part installed, which could be either a standard item or a customized item defined in the Project module.
7. Supply the Location where the installation was done.
8. You can add additional information on that location if necessary.
9. Enter the Customer code.
10. You can record a customer reference number, the customer purchase order, or any valuable information related to the customer for this installation.

11. Go to Form 2 and enter a value for the counter reading. This helps in planning the preventative maintenance. In your example, the counter reading value could be the number of days of the Injection Machine's operation.

12. Enter a warranty code. This code must be created in the warranty file.

13. Enter a priority code. This is used to sequence all your service calls. The priority code for your production facility is set to 001 in order to get serviced first.

Part
III

Ch
22

FIG. 22.1
In the Installation screen, you record the details that relate to the installation done at the customer site.

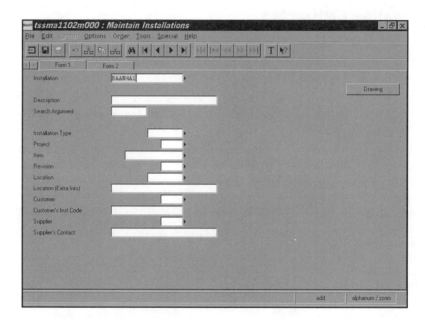

Performing Periodic Maintenance

The Periodic Maintenance function allows you to create schedules for preventative and maintenance work. You can assign a type of maintenance by which this task is done one time, is repeated, or is performed at fixed periods. Baan stores the following information for you:

- Rate
- Standard maintenance hours to perform the task
- Items the technician needs to inspect or repair

N O T E You can also create a checklist that can expedite the work done by your employees. ▧

When all the tasks are entered, you can generate a schedule that takes into account all the types of tasks you already entered. You can join some tasks to get the best efficiency possible after generating the schedule.

Using the Contract Module

Contracts can be created and maintained for any type of service call. You can record in a contract all the pricing information that is of use at the time of the service order's creation. This function can also be used to create quotations that can be turned into contracts if the customer agrees to the proposal.

Creating Contracts

Perform the following steps to create a contract:

1. In the Service module, select the Maintain Contract session from the Contract Control Business Object (see Figure 22.2). The fields in that session are detailed in Table 22.1.

2. Record all the necessary header information and then click the Installations button to attach installations to this contract. You have to supply the start and end date of each installation.

3. When you are done entering details, click the Save and Exit icons. Click the Special option from the menu and select the appropriate session to record contract installments or contract budget.

FIG. 22.2

The Maintain Contract session records all the installations to be grouped under the same agreement.

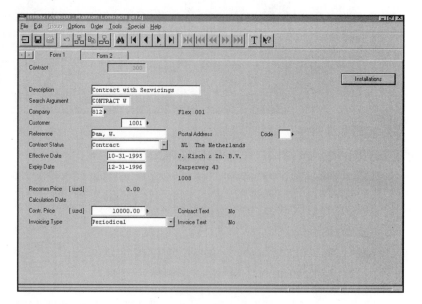

Table 22.1   Fields Used When Creating Contracts

Field Name	Description
Contract	Contract's number.
Description	Description to identify the contract.
Search Argument	An alternative key field that enables you to search the contract.
Company	Enter the financial company to be used.
Customer	Record the customer for which the report is created.
Postal Address	Record the customer's postal address, if different.
Reference	Enter any additional information such as Contact, Blocked, or Canceled.
Effective Date	The first date for which the contract is effective.
Expiry Date	Date when the contract is no longer effective.
Contract Price	Enter the price to be used for the contract.
Invoicing Type	None; the contract is not invoiced. Once; the contract is invoiced one time a year. Periodical; the contract produces over different periods. After execution; only possible when completed.
Servicing Amount	Servicing amount is billed only after the service had been executed and a cost is estimated by Baan.

T I P   Baan calculates the price for you if you zoom on the Contract Price field.

Managing the Contracts

You can perform various tasks after a contract is set up. You can have a block done on all service calls for a customer if one is late with payments; the costs of servicing this customer can be spread in different periods. If a budget had been created, you can compare to actual figures.

There are other functions such as copying the contract and logging history per customer. You can also renew the contract when it expires.

Using the Service Order Control

There are two ways to create service orders. First, you can generate service orders required through the Periodic Maintenance function. Second, create service orders by using the Service Calls Entry screen, which captures all the information required to perform a service call at a customer site. Select the option that is appropriate to your operation from the Service Order Maintenance menu.

Creating a Service Order

There are two screens on which to record service orders. The other screen (the Telephone screen) is not that different, but it is a little more user-friendly, which eases the process of taking orders while having the customer on the phone. You can find an example of a Service Order screen in Figure 22.3.

Follow these steps to create a service order:

1. Select the Maintain Service Order session from the Service Order Control Business Object. Record all the necessary header information.

2. When the header portion is completed, you can use four buttons to activate subsessions: The first allows you to print a service order, the second allows maintenance of the customer delivery address, the third records information about the work site, and the last records information about the technician who performs the service order tasks.

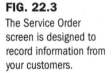

FIG. 22.3
The Service Order screen is designed to record information from your customers.

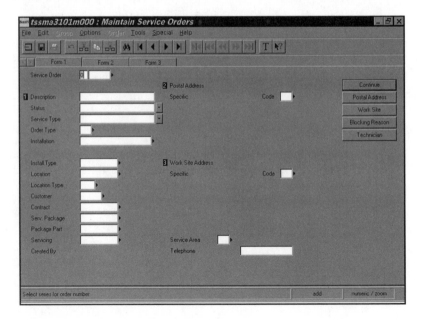

Processing Service Orders

You can perform the following functions when the service orders are created:

- Maintain the service orders.
- Delete the service orders if the status is at Free or Canceled, the order is not planned yet, and no outbound data exists for it.
- Report completed service orders to modify the status of the orders and record transactions against them.
- Maintain actual service order costs and revenues to maintain the financial transactions related to the order.
- Issue inventory to relieve all components necessary for the orders from the inventory.
- Close service orders to modify service orders' status.
- Print service orders invoices.
- Post services orders to history.

Using the Analysis Control

The Analysis control allows you to get valuable information regarding how the service calls were performed. This also links the Service module information to the Statistics module. The information highlights the repetitive problems, symptoms, and fixes often performed.

Using the Analysis Control Functions

The Analysis functions gather information for you on the various calls performed by your employees. Financial data can be gathered so that you can evaluate better ways to perform the next calls. Using this module, you can also track the redundancy of problems per customer and find ways to prevent them in the future.

 T I P Analysis control functions are also a way to see how the service aspect of your business affects your bottom line.

The Analysis control can also be linked to the Statistic control, so you can get service information stored in an analytical way. The link is done by maintaining the symptoms, problems, and fixes in the service orders. Those codes are created in the Analysis tables and are used to categorize the information.

Interpreting the Analysis

You must print the service analysis in order to interpret the information available in the Service module. The available ranges include

- Fiscal Year
- Service Orders

- Order Type
- Customer
- Contract
- Installation Type
- Installation
- Location
- Symptom
- Problem
- Fixes

All this information can be sorted by service order, installation, installation type, and location. ●

Understanding the Project Module

Using Baan Project

Baan offers various options to control project items. Baan Project gives the integrated project management tools necessary to meet project requirements today and anticipate the needs of tomorrow. It provides immediate visibility of status and costs, as well as early warnings about potential problems—hence, it ensures the profitability of projects. Because Baan Project provides real-time project information, projects can be managed proactively. This enables you to make better decisions and perform more timely actions.

Creating a Project Budget

After the project is awarded, all tasks that must be accomplished to complete that project must be clearly defined at a detailed level. A budget can be based on elements, activities, or both. The elements are detailed as budget lines; activities are detailed as actions. Budget lines are used to enter detailed information for material, labor, machine, subcontracting, and sundry quantities required to make the element. Actions are only used to enter the labor quantities.

Using an Element Budget

The elements are used to define a project's structure. The number of levels in a structure is unlimited. Based on the parent/child principle, relations are defined between elements, and in the case of generic elements, the system allows the use of multiple parents by child. Each element and its relation has a status (Free, Actual, or Final) and a relation quantity.

When the elements in a project have been recorded, their contents' detailed information is recorded in an element budget. The cost and quantity information for the material, labor, equipment, and subcontracting requirements are entered in a budget. This data forms the basis for project execution and control in the other modules.

An element budget has information about its cost objects in a detailed form. It is neither necessary nor practical to control the costs of the project at this level. The cost-related data for the elements and cost objects are generated. This data is then used by the Project Progress and Project Invoicing modules for an easy and efficient control of project costs without changing the detailed nature of an element budget.

Using an Activity Budget

The activity budget's role is very similar to that of the element budget. The only difference is that the detail lines in the activity budget are for the activities maintained in the project planning. After the activities in a project have been recorded, the contents' detailed information is recorded in an activity budget.

Using a Purchase Budget

A typical project has purchase items with long purchase periods, and quantities that are to be purchased are uncertain. Instead of waiting, the procurement of such items needs to be initiated well before the project's actual initial execution. This is achieved in purchase budget. The details of resources that need to be purchased are entered or picked directly from the actual budget to create a purchase budget. This does not disturb the actual budget.

Using Extensions

A typical project is usually unique and spread over a long period of time. This makes it difficult to anticipate future uncertainties. Extensions, which are linked to a project, are used in order to make a budget flexible to uncertainties in quantities, price, and invoiceable variations of work. These extensions are assigned to budget lines.

Analyzing Budget Cost

Different kinds of costs that make up this project can be analyzed from the project budget. Cost analysis of the actual budget can be created or updated, and hence, the reports of the total costs, the total quantities, and the total amount of time for budget lines at any time of the project. Overviews into budget are available by project, cost component, cost object, element-activity, extension, and coding system.

Planning a Project

Proactive planning is a must in order to succeed and complete any project in the required time. Baan Project facilitates integrated project planning. This module is completely graphics-oriented, and is a tool vital in defining the relationships between project activities, their duration, and the critical path of all activities. This information can be integrated with budget information. Projects can be planned manually or in a network, specifying all possible delays and displaying the critical path.

The available resources and their constraints, which are the basis for planning the work content and activities of a project, are recorded. Teams and their resources can be composed based on the employee or equipment files. This enables planners to allocate teams and assign tasks to teams.

N O T E Standard markers, meant to indicate possible bottlenecks, required actions, or checks, are recorded and can be copied to project plans. These markers appear on the planning board. ▨

Using Lay-Off and Calendars

Because a project can be phased over many months and seasons, some seasons can disrupt the project work onsite. This loss can frequently be anticipated and thus can be budgeted. A lay-off forecast can be recorded by company, area, or project.

It is necessary to know what resources are available on that day in order to allocate resources when planning a project on a particular day. The availability of a resource is based on whether it is a full, partial, or nonworking day. Such days are recorded as *calendars*.

Using Multiple Project Plans

Multiple project plans and versions can be developed and stored to enable tracking of the project plan's evolution by version or to compare different ways of executing the project. Based on teams, team resources, general planning data, and the relevant calendars with their lay-offs, a network plan can be generated for a set of related activities.

There can only be one actual project plan. The progress is defined in this. The project plan can be rescheduled based on the percentage of activities that have been completed.

 TIP A plan can be frozen or locked to prevent its being rescheduled.

Using Capacity and Financial Analysis

The capacity utilization of the labor and equipment resources used in the project are made available in graphical form. This shows whether rescheduling the project plan or activities is required. The information is available by project plan and for all actual project plans on the company level. Capacity analysis is available on a planning board by employee, trade group, team, and equipment code. The changes can also be made online on the planning board.

Financial analysis is used to view the various cash flows, both for one project plan and for all actual project plans on the company level. Planned, actual costs, and revenues can be shown by time unit or cumulatively; any one of those can be shown singularly. This information can be supplemented with the actual costs and revenues. Simulations can be made regarding expected customer and supplier payment terms.

Using Execution Planning

When executing a project, one needs to concentrate on a shorter time frame to plan in detail. This is for short-term planning and usually contains information derived from the total project plan. Execution plan consists of firm planned budget detail lines without relations. Actions (that is, budget detail lines) are divided into cost types (labor, material, equipment, subcontracting, and sundry costs). Because of short-term philosophy, the planning of employees, teams, and equipment is the main task.

Identifying Project Requirements

After a project has been awarded, a budget can be defined as a basis for project control. All material, labor, equipment, subcontracting, and sundry costs needed to complete the project are specified in this budget. In addition, a time planning for project execution is made. The planned orders are generated in project requirements from the planning data. Purchase orders and warehouse orders are generated based on planning information and budget. These orders result in deliveries of material, equipment, and subcontracting on the project.

Generating Planned Orders

To reiterate: The purchase and warehouse orders are generated based on the budget and the planning data. Present inventory, confirmed orders, and released orders are considered during the generation of the orders. Planned orders and rescheduling messages are also generated based on this data. These rescheduling messages appear when changes are made in the planning and the delivery dates are changed.

Using Planned Purchase/Warehouse Orders

The generated planned orders are only recommendations based mainly on the budget and the delivery dates. If needed, these planned orders can be maintained and can be transferred to the Purchase or Warehouse module. It also provides the ability to convert the planned orders directly into actual orders.

Tracking Project Progress

A project's stages can be registered for all cost types on various levels. These stages are used to determine the quantities and costs allowed and can be used for invoicing. Actual costs and commitments are registered. Every issued order or registered receipt is a commitment, and is recorded in the commitment accounting system until the corresponding invoice is entered. All a project's revenues are registered. If quantities, prices, or time spent for specific projects vary, the Project Progress module can control this information and generate the basis for invoicing the fluctuations. It provides the ability to handle project forecasts.

Tracking Progress

This is used to determine the quantities and costs and for project invoicing. The project progress for elements, activities, and extensions on different levels are maintained. Either element progress or activity progress is maintained. The progress is recorded for elements and activities. Installments can be released for invoicing after registering the element progress.

Tracking Costs

The actual costs and commitments are registered. If costs and commitments are the results of actions in Baan finance or distribution, the integration of these transactions take place automatically. Invoicing can take place after processing the costs.

Tracking Revenues

The project revenues can be entered. Project revenues are automatically available when the invoicing is printed in the Project Invoicing module. After processing the revenues, they can be monitored in the Project Monitoring module.

Using Financial Results

The financial results can be inspected while the project is ongoing. Financial results refer to interim results determined during the execution of a project. The profit or loss postings at the end of a financial year can be examined.

Using Fluctuation Settlement

A project contract's variations are controlled and invoiced, if needed. A percentage of the contract price can be settled according to price indexes. Items in the budget that contain a specific material can be settled while accounting for possible price fluctuations of that material. The differences between the actual quantity and the budgeted quantity of cost objects can be settled. The difference between the budgeted provisional amount and the actual costs can be settled. Fluctuations are processed after they're registered.

Monitoring a Project

Projects are controlled during execution using project monitoring details. After the project is awarded, a budget is defined in order to form the basis for project control. While the project is executed, planning is carried out, orders are generated, costs are booked, invoices are sent to customer, and revenues are recorded. The actual progress regarding the project is also tracked. The data regarding these activities is combined and presented in such a way that it is possible to see how the projects are coming along.

The budget, budget adjustments, budget extensions, costs, revenues, commitments, actual progress, and forecasts for final results are used to generate control data. When the control data is generated, it can be used in all project control inquiries, reports, and project monitoring reports.

Invoicing for a Project

Invoicing for a project provides the functionality for invoicing a project's principal. This supports five types of invoicing:

- Installments
- Cost Plus
- Unit Rate
- Advances
- Extensions

Installment invoices containing predefined partial contract amounts are sent at certain intervals. Cost plus invoicing of a project is based on actual costs of the project. Unit rate invoicing is based on the unit rates and the actual quantities. Advances are used in combination with the three invoicing types (installments, cost plus, and unit rate). Extensions such as variations of work, provisional amounts, and price/quantity fluctuation settlements can be invoiced.

Using Advances

Advances are amounts paid by the customer before the project's execution. These are used for making investments needed for the project. Advances can be created for installments and cost plus jobs. The advances can be invoiced to the customer.

Using Installments

The use of installments implies that invoices containing predefined partial contract amounts are sent at certain intervals. Installment schemes can be based on fixed amounts, percentages, or points charts. An installment can be invoiced when a milestone is reached or when an element or activity is completed within the project planning. Progress invoicing is done by invoicing partial contract amounts at a number of predefined intervals. Progress invoices are generated based on the recorded project progress and the sales amount by element.

Using Cost Plus

Cost plus invoicing is based on actual costs. The contract price is not fixed. This means that all actual costs can be invoiced to the customer.

Using Invoices

Invoices can be generated, maintained, and printed. Invoices are generated on the basis of data recorded in the advances, installments, and cost plus business objects. Revenues appear in the Project Progress module, and open entries are created in Baan finance's Accounts Receivable module after the final invoices are printed. ●

Understanding the Formula Management Module

Manufacturing Products Using a Process Formula

In the process industry, the product formula is the blueprint where information on ingredients, standard production quantities, and packaging configurations is stored as a guideline for production. Chemical, food and beverage, metal companies, and other sectors of the process industry combine these elements into a basis for product development, material requirements, production directives, and cost control.

The Baan Process Formula and Routing modules are designed to help you manage the information needed to manufacture process items. Discrete products (typically handled in the Baan Manufacturing package) are assembled from a set quantity of components included in a production bill of material. On the other hand, process manufactured goods are the outcome of a series of mixing operations, chemical reactions, extraction, and so on, which transform raw materials into a sellable product.

Part of the materials used in the formulation may get lost through evaporation, spillage, and so on. The processing of the ingredients can also yield goods other than the finished product; these can be either reused, sold at a profit, or disposed of at cost. In this same process, the processed good may go through other transformations where it is packaged in various types of containers and later inventoried as such.

Before users can see the ultimate application of formula and routing data—that is scheduling and issuing an actual production *batch*—they must go through a number of steps. This chapter explains those steps.

N O T E Baan enables you to determine whether process items are handled differently depending on how they are packaged. ■

Entering Basic Process Data in Item Control Module

Before entering new products using the Baan Process package, some basic information is required.

First, the logistics company in which the process items are to be managed needs to have the parameter Location Control Implemented set to Yes. This is done by running the session Generate Location System (tdilc0230m000, Distribution/Location Control/Inventory Locations/Miscellaneous menu). You can view this parameter in the session Maintain ILC Parameters (tdilc0100m000). Second, it is preferable to have the parameter Lot Tracking Implemented set to Yes as well. This enables users to track the movement of lot-controlled items.

Other data include the following:

- *Units*. Standard units of measure used by a company. Units are identified by a one-to-three character code.
- *Unit sets*. A set of standard units linked together by a common code.

- *Conversion factors.* Factors used to convert between a base inventory unit and other units of measure.
- *Formula and routing parameters*
- *Item data.* Product master file used to record information on standard finished goods and materials.

Entering Units of Measure

Baan enables you to determine whether process items are handled differently depending on how these are packaged. Most process items are packaged, stored, and sold using different types of containers. As for bulk products, these can be purchased in pounds or gallons and later sold in kilograms or liters. A company's standard unit of measure used to value inventory, establish formula quantities, and so forth must be linked to other units via a conversion factor. In Baan, all units of measure are stored in the system's Logistics tables. To enter new units, perform the following steps:

Part

III

Ch

24

1. Go to the main menu of the Baan Process package.
2. Choose Tables.
3. Select the Maintain Logistics Tables option.
4. Choose the Maintenance 2 menu item.
5. Select the session Maintain Units.

Baan has the following six types of units of measure:

- Weight
- Length
- Volume
- Piece
- Time
- Area

The unit types are specified in the Physical Quantity field of the session Maintain Units.

Creating Unit Types For the entry of process data, this discussion is concerned with the unit types Weight, Volume, and Piece because these are the most relevant to the process industry. To start, you will use the Maintain Units session to enter the base units for the company. Base units are the basic units of measure against which all units will be converted. Users need to establish a base unit for all unit types except the Piece unit type. In this introduction to the Maintain Units session, you will create five units that will be used as your base units. In the Maintain Units session (see Figure 24.1), create the following units:

Enter a unit code **lb** with a description **Pounds** and a **Weight** Physical Quantity.

Enter a unit code **gl** with a description **Gallon** (U.S.) and a **Volume** Physical Quantity.

Enter a unit code **ft** with a description **Feet** and a **Length** Physical Quantity.

Enter a unit code **hr** with a description **Hour** and a **Time** Physical Quantity.

Enter a unit code **sqf** with a description **Square Foot** and an **Area** Physical Quantity.

Set all rounding factors to the sixth decimal or **0.000001**. When these units are used, the system rounds the values at the sixth decimal.

FIG. 24.1

Units of measure are created in the Maintain Units session.

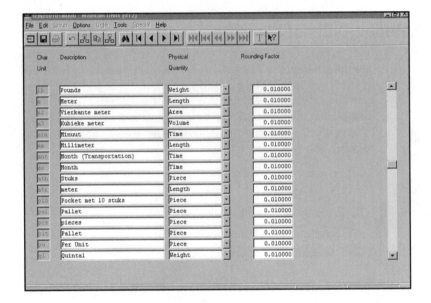

Save these records and exit the session. You now enter these units as your base units.

Entering Base Units   To enter the base units, follow these steps:

1. Go to the main menu of the Distribution package.
2. Choose Distribution Parameters.
3. Select the option Distribution Parameters 1.
4. Choose the Maintain Base Units menu item.
5. Enter the units **lb**, **ft**, **sqf**, **gl**, and **hr** as your base units (see Figure 24.2).
6. Save your data and exit. Return to the Baan Process package.

Creating Additional Units   You will now enter additional units to be used in a formula for margarine. These units will be used for the storage, valuation, and sales for the finished product, raw materials, and co/byproducts. Assume that the inventory unit for your product is pounds. You must then create alternative units for purchasing, packaging, and storage.

FIG. 24.2

The Maintain Base Units session records all the units to be used as default for the Process module.

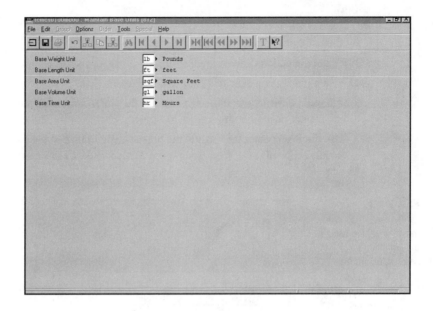

Return to the session Maintain Units and enter the following units (see Figure 24.3):

> Unit code **kg** with a description **Kilogram** and a **Weight** Physical Quantity
>
> Unit code **tn** with a description **Ton** and a **Weight** Physical Quantity
>
> Unit code **g** with a description **Gram** and a **Weight** Physical Quantity
>
> Unit code **2lb** with a description **Two-pound Container** and a **Piece** Physical Quantity
>
> Unit code **5lb** with a description **Five-pound Container** and a **Piece** Physical Quantity
>
> Unit code **hlf** with a description **Half-pound Container** and a **Piece** Physical Quantity
>
> Unit code **2gl** with a description **Two-gallon Container** and a **Volume** Physical Quantity.

In setting up the units that will be used as containers, it is preferable to use a different *type* of unit than that used as the inventory unit (for example, a Piece type container unit for a Weight inventory unit). Baan, as a rule, will not allow same unit type conversions such as a "weight-to-weight" conversion if it is applicable to a specific item (for example, setting up a pound-to-kilo conversion factor for plastic). Same unit type conversions are only allowed in regard to the base unit (kilogram to pound, liter to pint, centimeter to inch). In these examples, the inventory units for the products will be pounds and you will convert against different type units such as Weight to Piece, Weight to Volume, and so on.

Setting Conversion Factors Because the unit Pounds will be both your base unit and your product's inventory unit, first set the conversion factor between this unit and other weight units such as kilogram, gram, and so on. This ensures that a proper conversion is made between the company's base Weight unit and suppliers' and customers' weight units. To set conversion factors, follow these steps:

1. Go to the main menu of the Process package.

2. Choose Item Control.

3. Select the option Conversion Factors.

4. Select the session Maintain Conversion Factors.

5. After you have accessed the session, use the Go To command and enter base unit (**lb**) in the header portion of the screen.

6. Use the Insert command to add the other weight units and the conversion factor to the detail section of the screen (see Figure 24.4). Table 24.1 describes the fields for this screen.

FIG. 24.3

All the units to be used must be created using the Maintain Units session. You must record the Unit Code, the Description, and the Rounding Factor.

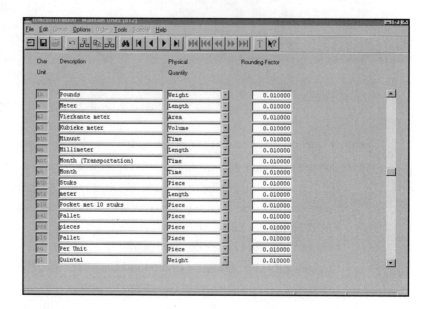

N O T E Just remember this rule of thumb when entering the conversion factor; the calculation works as follows:

base unit X conversion factor = alternative unit

Put simply, the unit in the *top* portion of the screen multiplied by the conversion factor equals the unit in the *bottom* portion of the screen. ■

7. Save your data and exit.

FIG. 24.4

This example shows how you can convert kilograms to grams and also to tons.

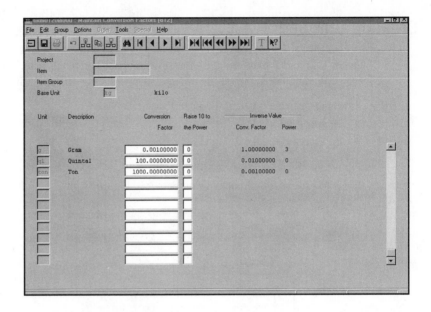

Table 24.1   Conversion Factor Fields

Field Name	Description
Base unit	If fields item and item group are left blank, the base unit refers to the logistic company's base unit as set in the session Maintain Base Units (Distribution/Distribution Parameters/Maintain Base Units). If the conversion factor is set for a specific item or item group, the base unit refers to the product inventory unit.
Unit	The unit that is different than the company base unit or a product inventory unit for which you need to set a conversion factor. If your base weight unit is pounds and you need to set a conversion from pounds to kilograms, enter the Kilogram unit code in this field.
Conversion Factor	The conversion factor between the base unit and alternative unit.
Inverse Value Conversion Factor	The conversion factor between the alternative unit and the base unit.
Power	If the conversion is between, for example, a unit representing a very small quantity and a unit representing a very large quantity (such as milligram to metric ton), the conversion factor can be set with an exponential factor.

Creating Unit Sets

Units sets are groups of units linked to various types of products. A unit set for raw materials (such as bulk items) may be different from that of finished goods, which may have more packaging configurations. To access the Maintain Unit Sets screen, follow these steps:

1. Go to the main menu of the Baan Process package.
2. Choose Tables.
3. Select the option Maintain Logistics Tables.
4. Choose the Maintenance 3 menu item.
5. Select the session Maintain Unit Sets (see Figure 24.5).

FIG. 24.5

To allow units per type of products, unit sets must be created.

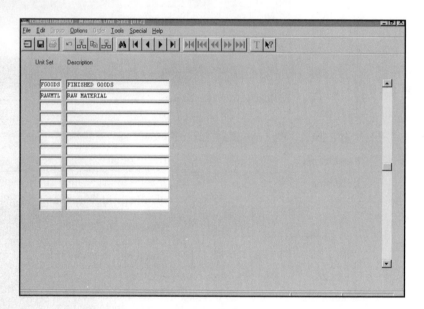

First you must enter a unit set code. Use the Insert command and enter these two unit set codes:

- **RAWMTL** for raw materials
- **FGOODS** for finished goods

Go to the session Maintain Units by Unit Sets. You can add the units that were recorded in the Maintain Units session to the units sets RAWMTL and FGOODS.

Use the Go To command and enter the unit set code **RAWMTL**. Insert the following units: **lb**, **kg**, **tn**, **g**, and **gl** (pound, kilogram, ton, gram, gallon). You must determine for each unit included in the unit set which Baan package or tables will make use of it. Indicate for each of the units whether they will be used as any of the following:

- Inventory units
- Distribution units (quantity units)

- Manufacturing units (production units)
- Price units
- Storage units (location control)
- Containers

This is done by entering the values Yes, No, or Stop. The Stop value allows all open transactions using the "stopped" unit to be completed. However, new transactions cannot include the stopped unit. You will assume that the raw materials are not containerized, so set the Container fields to No and all other fields to Yes, as shown in Figure 24.6.

FIG. 24.6

In this setup, you could use only the unit of measure ft with all the products using the unit set named FGOODS.

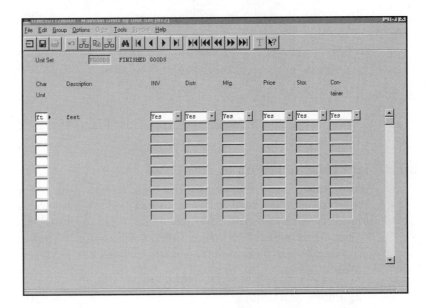

Next, use the Go To command to enter the units for the unit set FGOODS. Insert the units **lb**, **kg**, **tn**, **g**, **2lb**, **5lb**, **hlf**, and **2gl** (pound, kilogram, ton, gram, two-pound container, five-pound container, half-pound container, two-gallon container). Set the units 2lb, 5lb, hlf, and 2gl with value **Yes** in the Container field. For all other units, set it to **No**. After your first finished good product is entered in the item master and set as a *containerized* item, Baan creates item/container records for all units that have the container field set to Yes (see Figure 24.7).

N O T E If changes are made to the value of the Container field for the units included in the unit set, the session Update Containerized Items (tiitm0230m000) should be run so that only valid records are stored in the Item/Container file. ▪

When you are finished, save your data and exit.

FIG. 24.7

The Process Items field must be set to Yes in the Item Master Data for this item to be used in the Process module.

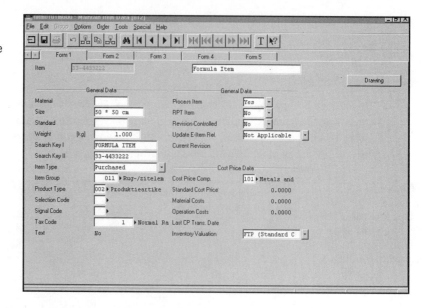

Entering Process Items in the Item Master

Before creating formulae for your finished good, the item master records for the raw materials, finished product (main item), and co/byproduct need to be added to the item master. This section focuses on item master data that pertains to process items. For more information on the item master, see the Item Control section in Chapter 20, "Understanding the Manufacturing Module." Follow these steps to access the Maintain Item Data screen:

1. Go to the main menu of the Process package.

2. Choose Item Control.

3. Select the option Item Data.

4. Choose the session Maintain Item Data.

You will enter the item code **MARG** with the description **Processed Margarine**. Define the item MARG as a **Manufactured**, **Process Item** that is **containerized** (Process Item field and Containerized field = Yes). Figure 24.8 shows the screen after this data has been entered. People in the margarine business will quickly notice that this is by no means a realistic item and formula. However, this exercise will give users a better handle on the formulation module. As far as actually producing this formula, don't try this at home.

Setting the Containerized flag to Yes generates item/container records that can be maintained in the session Maintain Item Data by Item and Container. The records listed in Table 24.2 should be created after the MARG product has been saved. In Figure 24.9, you will find an example of a record created of your product.

FIG. 24.8

The process information of the item master is grouped in Form 5 of the Item Data session.

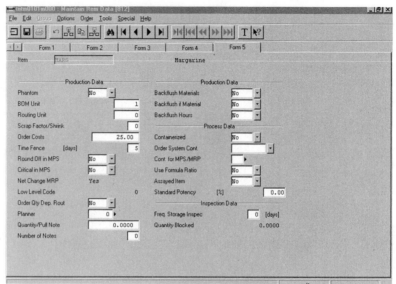

Table 24.2 Margarine Containers

Item	Container
MARG	2lb
MARG	5lb
MARG	hlf
MARG	2gl

These records are called end items. You will refer to the item MARG as the main item.

Because the product MARG is containerized, a conversion factor must be set between its base unit (lb) and the various packaging configurations tied to it. This information will be required when you define the container output for the product formula. You can access session Maintain Conversion Factors by clicking Special on the menu bar. Select Zoom and a list of sessions appears. Click the Maintain Conversion Factors session. When it is highlighted, click on OK. Figure 24.10 illustrates an example of conversion factors.

Enter the raw materials as **Purchased**, **Process Items** that are **not containerized** (Process Item fields = Yes, and Containerized fields = No). Table 24.3 lists the raw material codes to be added.

FIG. 24.9

The Item Data record has been created for an end item called Margarine. You will later create end items attached to this product.

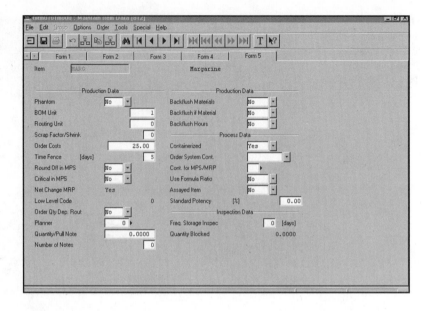

Table 24.3 Raw Material Codes

Item Code	Description	Inventory Unit
H2O	Water	gl (gallon)
CLBENZ	Calcium Benzoate	lb (pound)
SOY	Soybean Hydrogenated Fat	lb
BUTTERFL	Butter Flavor	lb
LECITH	Lecithin	g (gram)
MONOGL	Monogluceate	g
SODIUM	Sodium	kg (kilogram)

Enter another product record called **SOYOIL** (description: soya oil co-product), which will be used as a co-product in your formula. Assume that during production of processed margarine, a quantity of soya oil is generated and can be reused or sold. Enter the item SOYOIL as a **Manufactured**, **Process Item** that is **not containerized** (Process Item field = Yes and Containerized field = No). Enter SOYOIL's inventory unit as pounds (**lb**).

In the Item Type field for this example, set raw materials as **Purchased Items** and the finished good MARG as a **Manufactured Item**. Table 24.4 lists Item Type and the other key Item Master fields that relate to process items.

FIG. 24.10

Conversion factors can be specific to a given item, like in this example.

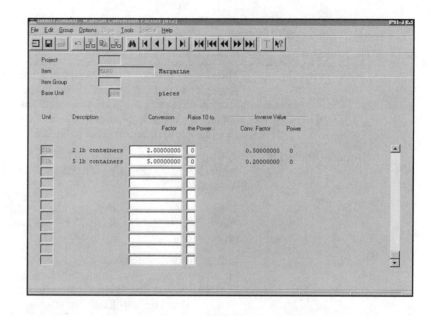

Table 24.4 Item Master Fields That Relate to Process Items

Field Name	Description
Item Type	The item type determines how an item is handled by the Baan application. Formula items need to be defined as Manufactured items. Raw materials can be set as either Purchased or Manufactured items.
Process Item	Indicates whether the item can be used in the modules Formula Management, Process Routing, and Production Management.
Unit Set	The set of units of measure allowed for this product. Units that need to entered as either inventory units, storage units, price units, and so forth in the item master must be included in the selected unit set.
Inventory Unit	The base unit for this product. This is the unit.
Storage Unit	A default unit used for storage. This unit can be changed at time of receipt. Any unit included in the selected unit set and for which a conversion factor has been entered can be used as a storage unit.
Lot Control	This parameter determines whether the product will be lot-controlled. Available options are By Lot (multiple units will make up a lot), By Unit (serialization, that does not usually apply to process items), and Not Applicable.

continues

Part
III

Ch
24

Table 24.4 Continued

Field Name	Description
Outbound Priority	The module Location Control can recommend inventory pick strategies based on a lot date, a receptor inventory date, or location code assigned to an area within a warehouse. Available options are LIFO (last in first out), FIFO (first in first out), or by location where recommendations are sorted by location code.
Period for Shelf Life	The time period that will be used to define a product's shelf life if applicable. Available options are Days, Months, Years, or Not Applicable.
Shelf Life	The product shelf life in days, months, or years. This field can only be accessed if a shelf life period has been entered in the previous one.
Phantom	Indicates whether this product is only assembled, mixed, and so on at time of production. A phantom item is not usually held in inventory. The materials that make up a phantom item will appear on a batch material sheet, although the item itself will not be listed.
Routing Unit	The standard quantity that can be produced in the runtime that has been specified in the product routing.
Container	Indicates whether the product is managed in the different types of containers. If so, an item /container record is created for each container unit that is part of the item's unit set. These records can be viewed in the session Maintain Item Data by Item and Container. Each item /container record can have its own cost, sales price, and so on.
Assayed Item	Switch this parameter to Yes if the product comes in different potencies or concentrations. Baan can be set to value or assess inventory quantities differently based on a product's potency.
Standard Potency	The standard concentration for an item expressed as a percentage. The value or usage of a product will be affected by how much its actual potency deviates from the standard. If standard potency is 90 percent, for example, a greater quantity of product will be required if the available inventory is at a potency of 75 percent.

This completes the data setup for process items. You should have enough information to enter a product formula.

Creating a Product Formula in the Formula Management Module

The formula management module includes all sessions that pertain to product formulae such as Maintain Materials (mandatory), Maintain End Item Containers (mandatory if the main item is containerized), and Maintain Co/Byproducts (optional).

N O T E Maintain Materials, Maintain End Item Containers, and Maintain Co/Byproducts can all be accessed from the Maintain Formula session itself. ▦

Two other sessions, Maintain Primary Application and Maintain Product Base, are used to create codes that can be tied to the formulae and used for various reporting or mass maintenance functions such as the session Replace Yield in Formula (Baan IV Process/Formula Management/Maintenance). After all formula elements have been entered, you must activate the formula so that it can be used in production. The formula activation is like an internal checklist that the system uses to make sure that all mandatory elements have been entered, raw material quantities add up to 100 percent, and so on.

To add a new formula for the finished good MARG, follow these steps:

1. Go to the main menu of the Process package.

2. Choose the Formula Management module.

3. Select the option Maintain Formulas.

4. When you have accessed the session, use the Insert command and type in the item code **MARG** (see Figure 24.11).

Part
III

Ch
24

FIG. 24.11
Every element of the formula must be defined using this session.

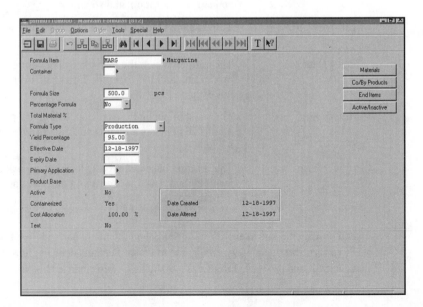

Table 24.5 describes all the fields in this screen.

Table 24.5 Maintain Formula Fields

Field Name	Description
Formula Item	The main item to be produced using the elements of the formula.
Container	The container in which the formula item will be packaged. The field can be left blank if the formula being created is for the main item or the process item is not containerized (this is determined by the Containerized field in the item master). If the process item is containerized, a formula for the end items must be created as well.
Formula Size	The default quantity of the formula item to be produced. In this example, the standard formula size is 500lb.
Percentage Formula	Identifies how the ingredients or materials of the formula must be entered. If this field is set to Yes, some materials can be entered as percentages. (Raw material quantities must equal 100 percent.) If No, raw materials can only be entered as absolute quantities.
Formula Type	Indicates whether the formula is ready for production (Production) or if it is in its test stage (Model). Model formulae cannot be used in the Production Management module.
Yield Percentage	The yield percentage is the ratio of usable output from a process to its input. If the yield percentage is 95 percent, for example, you can assume that usually 5 percent of a batch will be lost to spillage, evaporation, and so on.
Effective Date	The date on which the formula will become active. A production batch for this formula cannot be entered before this date.
Expiry Date	The date on which the formula can no longer be used for production and has expired. If this field is empty, the formula will not expire.
Primary Application	The most important area of application of a particular formula item. The field is used for reporting purposes and to categorize formula types.
Product Base	The product base is the basic form or the main ingredient of a formula item. Used for reporting purposes and to categorize formula items.

To add or maintain raw materials, click Special on the menu bar and then select Maintain Materials. If you are entering a new formula, the message Formula does not have any materials pops up. Just click OK and proceed. Table 24.6 lists the fields described in this Maintain Materials screen.

Table 24.6 Maintain Materials Field Details

Detail Field Name	Description
Position	The position number in the list of materials. The system will usually increment this value by 10. It is possible to enter a different position number than the one that is defaulted by the system.
Sequence	For each position number, the sequence number enables you to define more than one raw material. Each material listed under a different sequence number can have its own validity period (effective and expiry date).
Item	Enter the raw material item code (that is, LECITH, CLBENZ, and so on). The product must be a purchased or manufactured item (This is defined in the item master).
Cnt (container)	The container in which the material is packaged. This field can only be filled if the material is a containerized item. In this example, all raw materials are not containerized.
Mat. Perc. (material percentage)	Indicates whether the material is defined as a percentage of the formula size. This field can only be modified if the field Percentage Formula in the session Maintain Formulas is set to Yes. In some instances, some raw materials can be entered in percentages while others may not (such as packaging materials, resource-type materials). In a percentage formula, Baan enables you to enter both percentages and absolute quantities. Note that all lines that have the Mat. Perc. field set to Yes must add up to 100 percent, otherwise the formula cannot be activated.
Net Quantity	The raw material quantity to be issued in the production of the formula item. When a production batch is planned, the actual material requirement is adjusted based on the shrinkage factor.
Un. (unit)	The unit used for entering a quantity of a material. The system defaults to the product's inventory unit that was assigned in the session Maintain Item Data.
Shkg (shrink factor)	The percentage of the material lost because of evaporation, absorption, and so forth. You can prevent shortages in production by recording a shrinkage. Based on the shrink factor, the system will recommend to use greater material quantities. (If the shrink factor is 5 percent, for example, 5 percent more than the net quantity will be allocated to production.)
Op. (operation)	The routing operation or step in the production process where this raw material is required. After the routing for this formula has been set up (see the following section on formula routing), you can enter an operation number (for example, 10, 20).

continues

Table 24.6   Continued

Detail Field Name	Description
Wrh	The warehouse from which the raw material will be issued. This is a default warehouse that can be changed at time of production.
Phantom	Indicates whether the raw material used is a phantom product. If so, only the raw materials that make up this product (not the product itself) will be listed on production batch documents.
Quantity-Dependent	Indicates whether the material requirements are affected by the size of the production batch. If a batch quantity is changed, the system asks whether the material quantities have to change proportionally.
Scalable	Baan can readjust the batch size if a change is made to the quantity of a scalable material (Scalable = Yes). If a scalable material is increased by 10 percent, for example, the batch size will be adjusted accordingly, as well as the quantity for raw materials that have the scalable flag set to Yes.
Effective Date	The first day of the validity period of the material.
Expiry Date	The day on which the validity of the material expires. If the field is empty, the material will not expire.
Co-Products	Enter the Co-Product item (SOYOIL) and quantities to be generated from the production of the main item. Note that a co-product may also have its own formula if it is further processed after it has been generated from the main item.

Maintaining Co/Byproducts

It is necessary in the Process module to define the co- and by-products. This is done using the session called Maintain Co/Byproducts found in the Formula Management Business Object. Table 24.7 lists all the fields to be entered.

Table 24.7   Maintain Co/Byproducts Fields

Field Name	Description
Position	The position number of the co/byproduct in the list of co/byproducts generated in the processing of the main item.
Sequence	For each position number, the sequence number enables you to define more than one raw material. Each material listed under a different sequence number can have its own validity period (effective and expiry date).

Field Name	Description
Cnt (container)	Depending on whether the co-product is containerized (and in this example, SOYOIL is not containerized), the container in which the material is packaged.
Co/By	Indicates the type of secondary item that results from the production of the main item formula. A co-product is generally one that can be reused or sold; a byproduct is usually production waste.
Quantity	The co- or byproduct output based on the formula size of the main item. Here you assume that a 500lb batch of MARG, will yield 55lb of SOYOIL.
Unit	Unit in which you express the co/byproduct output quantity.
Cost All. (cost allocation)	The percentage of the total cost of the formula allocated to the co- or byproduct. The cost allocation can be negative or positive.
Opr (operation)	The routing operation to which this co- or byproduct is linked.
Wrh (warehouse)	The warehouse where the co- or byproduct is stored after it has been received. This is a default warehouse that can be changed at time of production.
Recurrent	A co- or byproduct is recurrent if the same item is used a an ingredient in the main item formula. Ten percent of a raw material, for example, does not dissolve when it is mixed with other ingredients. This quantity is recovered at a later stage in production and received as a co-product.
Recurrent Position	The value of the field Position in the session Maintain Materials where the material recovered as a co- or byproduct is included in the main item formula.
Yield Percentage	The percentage of the recurrent material anticipated to be returned from production as recurrent a co- or byproduct.

A co-product will usually have a positive cost allocation because it can be sold or re-used. Therefore it can assume part of the formula cost. (Based on the benefits of this co-product, the main item costs 10 percent less or it bears only 90 percent of the cost). If costs are incurred in the disposal of a by-product, however, the cost allocation can be negative. (Based on the cost of disposing of this by-product, the main item costs 10 percent more to produce or it bears 110 percent of the cost).

Maintaining End Item Containers

The item MARG is a containerized item. In this section, you will specify the production output in terms of packaging quantities. In a previous section, you defined four types of containers or end items (2lb, 5lb, hlf, 2gl) for the main item MARG. Now you must determine which quantities of the main item will be packaged in each container—that is, how much of the 500 pounds of the main item will go into each container. The total units for the end items (number of containers × conversion factor) must equal the formula size displayed in the upper portion of the screen. If not, the main item formula cannot be activated. In this example, you are merely setting up a default combination of containers; this combination of containers and the packaging quantities can be changed at time of production. Figure 24.12 demonstrates how you can maintain the end items' containers. Table 24.8 lists details of every field of this session.

FIG. 24.12

End item quantities must be maintained in the different packaging quantities.

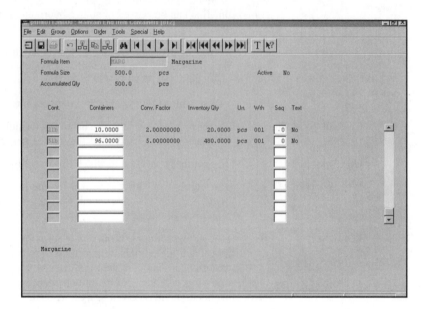

Table 24.8   Maintain End Item Containers Fields

Field Name	Description
Formula Item	The main item in this formula.
Formula Size	The formula quantity for the main item.
Accumulated Quantity	The formula quantity allotted to the containers entered in the lower portion of the screen. If 50 two-pound containers (2lb) are entered in the field Containers, for example, the accumulated quantity will be 100 pounds.
Cnt (container)	The container code in which (a part of) the formula is packaged. Enter the packaging units that were defined previously (2lb, 5lb, hlf, 2gl).
Containers	Enter the quantity of each container that will be used for this formula. Note that the system will "use up" the main item formula quantity (in this case 500lb) based on the conversion factors that were set up for the end items. Watch the value in the field

Field Name	Description
	Accumulated Quantity (in the header portion of the screen) increase as you add container quantities. You can only activate the main item formula after the quantity of the end items equals the quantity of the main item.
Conversion Factor	The conversion factor between the main item inventory unit and the container unit as set in the session Maintain Conversion Factors.
Inventory Unit	The end item quantity expressed in main item inventory unit (container quantity × conversion factor).
Seq (sequence)	Identifies the sequence in which the end items are to be packaged. (If you need to package the two-pound container first, enter a 1 in the sequence number field.) If the sequences are all defined zero, the packaging will be done in parallel. After all formula elements have been entered correctly, the main item formula can be activated from the session Maintain Formula.
End Item Formulae	For containerized process items, a formula must be created for the end items. Please note that the system will not prevent you from activating the main item formula if you do not have formulae for your end items. However, end item formulae are required for the entry of a production batch for containerized main items.

The end item formula is set up based on the production of one container. The system will default the raw material quantity for the end item formula to whatever conversion factor exists between the inventory unit of the main item and the container unit. The conversion factor between the MARG inventory unit and the container unit 2lb (two-pound container), for example, is 2. Therefore if an end item formula is set up for MARG 2lb, the formula size will default to 2 pounds.

Also, when you access the session Maintain Materials, you will see the system has defaulted the first material line with 2 pounds of MARG. You can then enter other components such as packaging materials, as shown in Figure 24.13.

In this example, the packaging items twolb (Two-Pound Plastic Container) and twolblid (Two Pound Plastic Lid) have been added as components to the end item. (These non-process items need to be added to the item master prior to being included in components.) The quantity for both packaging items is set to 1. This means that for each two-pound container produced, one two-pound plastic container and one lid are required. After having entered the material quantities, return to the Maintain Formula screen and activate your formula.

FIG. 24.13

All the elements of the formula are detailed in the Maintain Materials session.

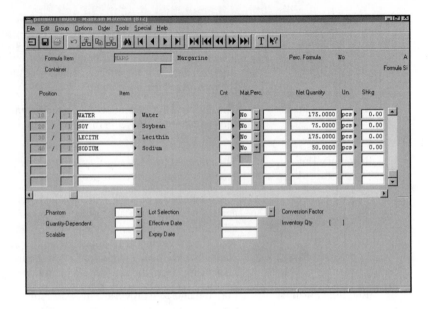

Understanding the Process Module

Manufacturing Process Items

For process items, the series of manufacturing operations do not generally stop once production lines have yielded a mixed, distilled, or melted good. Following production of the main process item (beverage, petroleum, metal), mixed beverages are then contained in bottles and cans, distilled chemicals are poured into drums and totes, and metals are molded into rods and bars. This is different from the discrete environment, where routing operations often result in an assembled product that is then received in inventory in its "final" form. Also, the additional packaging steps required for process items can be done simultaneously. After a beverage has been mixed, it can then flow to three production lines, where it can be packaged in three different size bottles. The three lines can have their own operations (capping and labeling on production line 1, for example, but capping only on production line 2), and they can operate simultaneously.

In addition to a network of packaging operations, the production of process items can also generate co/byproducts which are processed further (for example, paper roll trimmings turn into paper bales, excess cream poured into containers and refrigerated) on a secondary production line that trails off the main production line.

In Baan IV, the capability to create a network of routing operations is virtually exclusive to the Process package. Users can generate a series of complex operation relations for a product-specific or standard/generic routing. These operations come together as a network after a production batch has been created.

In this section on process routing, you continue with the example from the preceding chapter—the margarine item, its co-product, and the margarine end items (two-pound container, five pound container, and so on).

Entering Basic Data in the Routing Module

Before assigning a set of routing operations to a process item, users need to enter basic data such as that listed in Table 25.1.

Table 25.1   Basic Data for Routing Module

Data	Description
Process Routing parameters	A number of parameters that indicate the standard company routing code (the one used by Baan to calculate operation costs) and how capacity will be measured.
Work centers	A work area or production line to which machines or production tasks are assigned. A work center will have a certain production capacity (expressed in hours) and it can be tied to a specific work center calendar where production shifts, downtime, and so on can be recorded.
Machines	Production machines set up with default production rates or runtime.
Task	The operation performed by either a machine or worker.

Entering Process Routing Parameters

To enable the Routing module to use the Process module, you must set parameters in the module use part of the Routing module. To maintain the Process Routing parameters, you must perform the following steps:

1. Go to the main menu of the Baan Process package.

2. Choose Maintain ROU Tables.

3. Select the Process Parameters option.

4. Choose the Maintain ROU Parameters menu option.

Figure 25.1 shows the screen that appears. In this screen, you must designate the routing code that will be used as your company's standard routing. The standard routing code is used to calculate the standard cost for all manufactured items. The routing parameters will also indicate which type of plant calendar will be used. Table 25.2 lists the Routing Parameter fields.

FIG. 25.1

Routing parameters indicate which routing is used to calculate costs and how production time will be calculated.

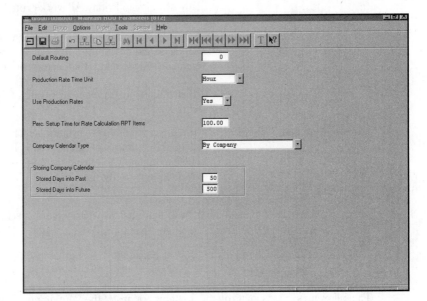

Part
II

Ch
25

Table 25.2 Routing Parameters

Field Name	Description
Default Routing	The routing that appears as a default when a production batch is planned. (Assuming the item is not tied to quantity-dependent routings, this is specified in the item master.) This routing is also used to calculate operation costs that are part of the item's standard cost.

continues

Table 25.2 Continued

Field Name	Description
Production Rate Time Unit	The time unit used in defining the production rate for an item (number of inventory units per hour or minute). Users can select hours or minutes.
Use Production Rates	Indicates whether the system is to use the production rate (number of inventory units per hour or minute) or the operation runtime in calculating the production lead time.
Perc. Setup Time for Rate Calculation RPT Items	This is not applicable to process items.
Company Calendar Type	The basic plant calendar for the logistics company. Options include: *Five Days a Week*—all facilities within the company operate only Monday to Friday. All work center capacities are extrapolated to five days. *Company Calendar*—a calendar with weekends, shifts, holidays, and downtime, which applies to the entire company (stored under a master work center identified as ZZZ). *Work Center*—capacity is maintained for each individual work center.
Storing Company Calendar	As a means to optimize system performance, users can specify the number of calendar days that must be stored in internal memory to execute various sessions related to production capacity.

After parameters have been defined, basic data such as work centers, machines, and production tasks must be added in the Routing module. To enter this data, perform the following steps:

1. Go to the main menu of the Process package.

2. Choose Routing.

The following sections focus on the first four options of the Routing menu (Work Centers, Machines, Tasks, and Operations). These are explained in relation to the example—production of the item MARG—outlined in Chapter 24, "Understanding the Formula Management Module."

Using Work Centers in Routing

A *work center* is a facility where a series of related operations are performed. A work center can represent a group of production areas (that can be defined as subwork centers), a production line comprised of several machines, a single machine, and so forth. Each work center is assigned a capacity, defined as a machine or labor-driven facility, linked to an operation rate (operations costs per hour). Figure 25.2 shows the work center type Work Center Maintenance.

FIG. 25.2
The work center file holds information on capacity and operation costs.

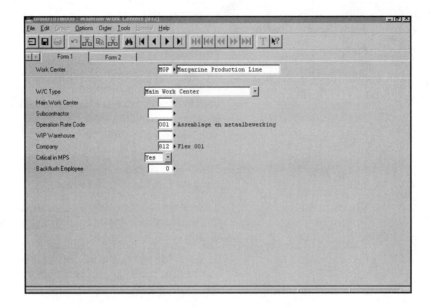

Table 25.3 lists the fields found in the Maintain Work Center session.

Table 25.3 Work Center Routing Fields

Field Name	Description
Work Center Type	A production area or facility can be designated as a main work center, a subwork center, or a subcontracting work center. For a main work center, users can link a series of subwork centers that have their own capacity and characteristics (if this situation applies). If a facility is defined as a subwork center, it must be tied to a main work center via the Main Work Center field. If a company outsources some of its production operations, outsourcing lead time and planning can be monitored using subcontracting work centers.
Main Work Center	If a work center is defined as a subwork center, enter the work center code for the facility that is considered the main or parent work center.
Subcontractor	The supplier that provides the service for outsourced operations.
WIP Warehouse	If you need to monitor the allocation of materials to work-in-process, you can specify the WIP warehouse in this field. The warehouse must be defined as a WIP warehouse in the session Maintain Warehouses. As well, the Use of WIP Warehouses parameter must be set to Yes in the session Maintain PMG Parameters (see the Process parameters option in the main menu of the Process package).

continues

Table 25.3   Continued

Field Name	Description
Operation Rate Code	The operation rate code where the hourly rate for labor, machine usage, and overhead are specified. These rates are used in the calculation of the product standard cost and they are entered using the sessions Maintain Operation Rate Codes and Maintain Operation Rates (see the Cost Accounting module).
Company	The financial company linked to this work center if a multi-company financial structure exists.
Critical in MPS	If this is set to Yes, rough cut capacity can be calculated for this work center in the Master Production Schedule module.
Backflush Employee	The employee code that will be used for backflushing. The backflushing function makes use of the employee's hourly rate and work schedule in calculating labor costs.
Critical Capacity Type	The capacity type can be either machine or man capacity. This designation affects the link to capacity resources. The system looks at the machine or labor resources tied to the work center—either the number of machines and their capacity or the employees and their work schedules.
Number or Resource Units	Depending on critical capacity type, the number of machines or employees linked to this work center. (This field can be filled manually or calculated by the system.)
Basic Capacity per Resource Unit	The basic capacity expressed in weekly hours for the machines or employees connected to this work center.
Basic Capacity per Resource Unit	The estimated number of daily hours that each machine or employee linked to this work center are available for production.
Wait Time	The waiting period (in days) between the operation performed in this work center and the operation performed in the next work center. This is usually due to the set up time required for the next operation (for cleanup, getting materials ready, quality tests, and so on).

Continuing with the example from the preceding chapter, enter a work center file that represents a margarine production line. The work center should be a main work center and the critical capacity type should be Machine Capacity; you are assuming that most of the operations are performed by machines. This work center should be available 112 hours a week (16 hours per day) with no wait time.

Create a second work center called Packaging Work Center; it should be a subwork center tied to the first work center (enter the code of the first work center in the Main Work Center field).

The packaging work center should also have Machine Capacity as its critical capacity type and should also have the same number of hours of production capacity.

After you have created those work centers, you can record operations and eventually calculate the capacity required to produce all the required products.

Using Machines in Routing

Production equipment information such as capacity, production cost, and operation rates can be recorded in a Machine file. Machines can in turn be linked to a work center. Figure 25.3 shows an example of a Machine file.

Table 25.4 lists all the fields that the Machine file contains. In that file, you define the Machine Rate, the Capacity, and also the Man/Machine Ratio.

FIG. 25.3

Machines also include production capacity information cross-referenced with a work center.

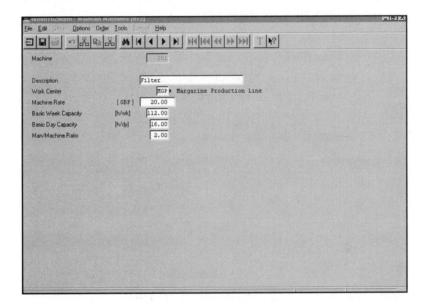

Part

II

Ch

25

Table 25.4   Machine Fields

Field Name	Description
Work Center	The default work center where this machine is used.
Machine Rate	The hourly cost of operating this machine. When actual operation costs are calculated in the Production Management module, the system uses this rate in this calculation. For the standard cost calculation, Baan makes use of the standard machine rate specified in the Cost Accounting module (see the sessions Maintain HRA Parameters and Maintain Operation Rates).

continues

Table 25.4   Continued

Field Name	Description
Basic Week Capacity	The number of hours per week that this machine is available for production.
Basic Day Capacity	The number of daily hours that this machine is available for production.
Man/Machine Ratio	The number of employees that usually work this machine. If two employees operate four machines, this ratio—which is also used in calculating labor costs—should be 0.5.

Using the session Maintain Machines, enter the machines listed in Table 25.5. All the machines should have the following attributes:

Machine Rate: $20.00

Basic Week Capacity: 112 (hours)

Basic Day Capacity: 16 (hours)

Man/Machine Ratio: 2 (persons per machine)

Table 25.5   Example Machines

Machine	Description
101	Blender #1
201	Filter #6
301	Pressurizer #2
401	High-speed mixer #2
501	Packaging Line 1
601	Packaging Line 2
701	Packaging Line 3

The first four machines should be linked to the first work center that was entered earlier (the one used in producing the main item). The last three machines should be tied to the second one (the packaging work center).

By setting up those machines, you have recorded all the necessary information to capture the manufacturing costs and also to calculate the capacity necessary for the production of the products.

Using Tasks in Routing

Standard tasks are the actual operations performed by workers or machines. Task records can be assigned a series of default attributes such as production rate, runtime, or machine used to perform the task (for machine tasks only). These defaults appear whenever these tasks are entered in the routing of a specific product, and they can be changed if needed. Figure 25.4 illustrates how to set up tasks.

FIG. 25.4

Tasks indicate which function is performed using a machine or work center.

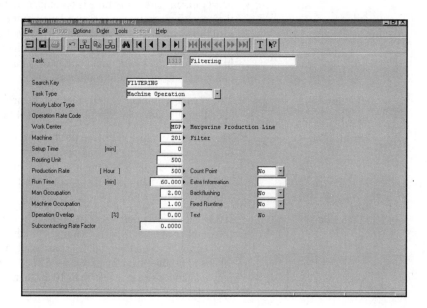

Table 25.6 lists the fields pertinent in the entry of process operations.

Table 25.6 Tasks

Field Name	Description
Search Key	A series of characters that can be used to search for task records (short key). The search key defaults to the task description, although this can be changed if users prefer another search option.
Task Type	Machine and non-machine operations are generally applicable to the production of process items. Non-machine operations can be entered, including such things as machine clean up, laboratory testing, and so on. If the task type is Machine Operation, the capacity of the machine linked to this task (see the field Machine) will be depleted when production batches are planned.
Work Center	The work center where this task is usually performed.

continues

Part

II

Ch

25

Table 25.6   Continued

Field Name	Description
Machine	If this task is of the type Machine Operation, specify which machine will carry out this task
Setup Time	The time required (expressed in minutes) to prepare a machine or work area. The setup time is optional and it will be added to the operation runtime in the calculation of the total production lead time. Note that the setup time is always fixed and will not be affected by changes in the production batch quantity. Variations in the setup time based on batch quantity can be addressed by using quantity-dependent routings.
Routing Unit	The standard number of units that will be produced in the specified runtime (for example, 100 units/4 hours).
Production Rate	The number of units produced per hour or minute. (This field can only be accessed if the routing parameters indicate that production rates are used.) The time unit (hours or minutes) is specified in the session Maintain ROU Parameters. The unit used is the product inventory unit.
Count Point	If this operation is defined as a count point (Count Point = Yes), the number of units reported complete in the next operation (if any) cannot exceed the quantity completed in this operation. If 100lbs of product have been reported in operation 1, for example, only a quantity equal or less than 100lbs can be reported in operation 2.
Extra Information	A free form field that can be used to enter additional information on this task.
Run Time	The number of hours or minutes required to produce the quantity entered in the field Routing Unit.
Fixed Runtime	This field indicates whether the runtime for this operation will be affected by changes in the production batch size. If a batch size is doubled, for example, the system will plan for twice the operation run time. If this flag is set to Yes, the runtime will not change if the batch size is increased or reduced.

Enter tasks that will be used for the routing of the main item and end items. Create the following tasks:

Main Item Tasks

- Mixing
- Filtering
- Whipping
- Pressurizing

Co-Product Tasks

■ Containerizing (for example, pour SOYOIL co-product in a container)

End Item Tasks

■ Packaging

■ Labeling

■ Shrink wrap

To create those tasks, you must perform the following steps:

1. Go to the Routing Business Object in the Process module.

2. Select the Tasks option.

3. Choose Maintenance, and then select the Maintain Tasks session.

4. Click the Insert icon and enter a code for your tasks. This task code can be up to four characters. Then fill in all the fields found in Table 25.6.

Link the tasks for the main item and co-product to the first work center created in the previous example (margarine production line). Link the tasks for the end items to the packaging work center.

By setting tasks, you can record all the information found in the routing. Each task represents an operation performed during the manufacturing process.

Creating Routings for Main Items, End Items, and Co/Byproducts

After the basic data has been created, the routings for the main item, end items, and co-products can be entered. Routings consists of the following three principal elements:

1. *Routing codes* (per formula). The code that identifies the series of operations required to produce an item.

2. *Routing operations.* The individual operations and their attributes, such as the setup and runtime, the performed tasks, the work centers and machines used, and so on.

3. *Routing operation relationships.* The links between production operations. These relationships will determine the complexity of the routing network.

N O T E Operation relationships indicate the operation sequence and operation overlap. ■

After these elements have been entered properly, it is possible to validate the routing code—a mandatory step prior to using it in the Production Management module.

Entering Routing Codes

Access the session Maintain Routing Codes by Formula. In this first step, you enter routing codes and their basic attributes such as the routing code description, the routing quantities (routing codes can be quantity dependent), and so on. Enter a routing code **001** for the main item (where the Container field is left blank) and end items (where the Container field has been filled with, for example, 2lb, 5lb). Figure 25.5 illustrates how to assign routing codes to each formula.

FIG. 25.5

Routing codes are entered using the session Maintain Routing Codes by Formula.

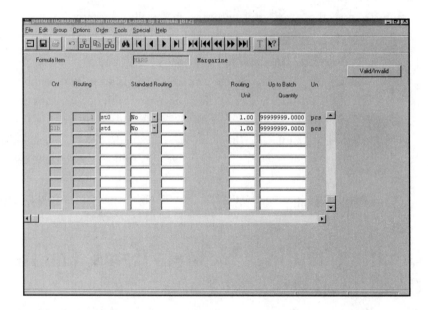

N O T E   Routing codes can be assigned to main and end items and set as quantity-dependent. ▦

Table 25.7 lists all the fields that you must fill in to set up routing codes.

Table 25.7   Routing Codes

Field Name	Description
Standard Routing	If the option Yes is selected, users can link a generic routing (a routing code not product specific) to the formula. This generic routing must be predefined.
Standard Routing Code	The code for the standard routing used for this formula.
Up to Batch Quantity	The maximum quantity for which this routing is applicable. The system can assign a specific routing based on the quantity and the parameter Quantity Dependent Routing, which is set for each product in the item master.

Field Name	Description
Routing Unit	The standard production quantity on which this routing and its production time is based.
Valid	Indicates whether the routing has been validated.

Because complex relationships can be created using the Process Routing module, the system performs a validation check on the routing operations and the operation relationships. After the four basic elements of process routings (the first four fields in Table 25.7) have been entered, a routing validation check can be done by using the session Validate Routings. This validation check can also be called using a special function in each of the routing sessions. Note that an invalid routing cannot be used in the Production module. If a routing cannot be validated, the system displays a message indicating the reason. Here are some examples of potential reasons:

- Only manufactured process items can have a routing.
- Item exists as a byproduct in a formula.
- Routing operations do not exist for [operation number].
- Operation [operation number] improperly linked.
- Non-main operation [operation number] has subsequent operation(s).
- Non-main operation [operation number] has more than one preceding operation.
- Operations for containers of end items and co-products must be sequential.
- All operations of a containerized routing must be "Restrictive" and "Main Operations."
- Non-main operation [operation number] must be restrictive.

After entering and saving this information, mark the first record by clicking it. Then click the Special option on the menu bar. Select the option Maintain Routing Operations. Each of the tasks required for production will be assigned an operation number, a runtime, and other characteristics. Figure 25.6 shows an example of how you should set up Maintain Routing Operations.

Entering Operations

When operations are entered, the system first requires a task number. Choose the appropriate task number from the list of tasks created in the preceding step. Most of the field values for the operations (such as work center, machine, set up time, runtime, and so on) default to those entered in the task record entered previously. These values can be changed if needed. Information on the "default" fields can be reviewed in the section on routing tasks.

Table 25.8 lists all the different fields you will find in the Operation file. You must define in that file whether the operations are restrictive—this indicates the relations between the various operations.

FIG. 25.6

Operations for the main process item.

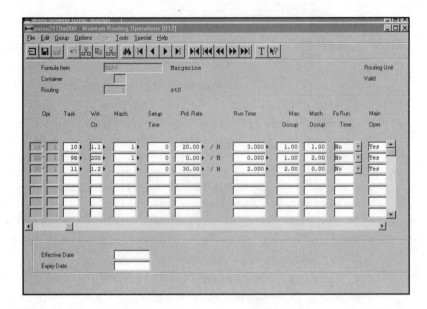

Table 25.8 Operations

Field Name	Description
Operation	The number that identifies this production operation. By default the system increments the operation numbers by ten, although users can enter these manually. More than one line can have the same operation number (although the combination of operation and sequence number must be unique) because these can have different effective periods.
Sequence Number	If the same operation number is used for several operations that have different effective periods, the sequence number is used as another identifier.
Restrictive	Indicates whether the following operation's reported quantity is validated against the quantity reported in this operation. If a quantity of 100lb is reported at the end of this operation, for example, the quantity reported in the next operation must match that quantity. (It should not exceed that quantity; if it does or if it is less than that, losses must be accounted for using the Rejected Quantity field.) These rules apply for restrictive operations: All operations that follow a restrictive operation must also be restrictive; all operations for end item containers are restrictive.
Main Operation	Indicates whether the operation is tied to the main product and its end items. This field is usually set to No when defining operations for a co/byproduct.

Co/byproduct operations are called *dangles* because they come out or result from a main operation. When the margarine is filtered at operation 20, for example, soya oil is produced and further processed or containerized. These co/byproduct-specific operations are known as dangles and are not main operations.

N O T E The operation number tied to a specific co/by-product needs to be entered in the Operation (Opr) field in the session Maintain Co/Byproducts. ▨

The number of operations and the production time may vary by end item depending on the complexity of the packaging process. You can enter the routing operations for both the main and end items as shown in Figure 25.7.

FIG. 25.7

Operations for one of the end items.

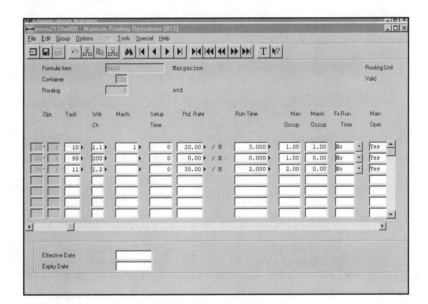

Defining Relationships

After all the operations have been entered, you must define the relationship between each operation. This mainly has to do with the sequencing of operations and the overlap between each operation. You must do this for the routings of the main items and end items.

N O T E More than one "next operation" may be entered per production operation. In other words, multiple operations can start simultaneously after a single operation and vice versa. ▨

The first three fields to the left (operation number and the two sequence numbers) identify an operation linked to another. Three operations—30, 40, 50—start simultaneously after operation 20, for example, and these will be performed in parallel. In this case, you need to use a setup similar to that shown in Table 25.9.

Table 25.9 Relationships

Operation	Seq.	Sequence	Next Operation
20	1	10	30
20	1	20	40
20	1	30	50

Enter the operation relationship as in the example in Figure 25.8.

FIG. 25.8

Routing operations relationships for a main item where the co-product operation is tied to operation 20.

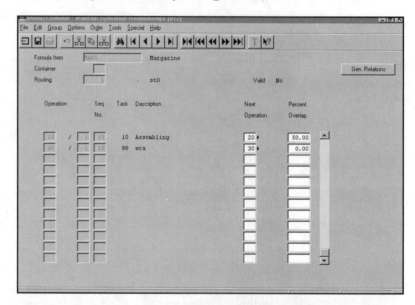

FIG. 25.9

Users can experiment with operation overlaps and see how these affect the production time.

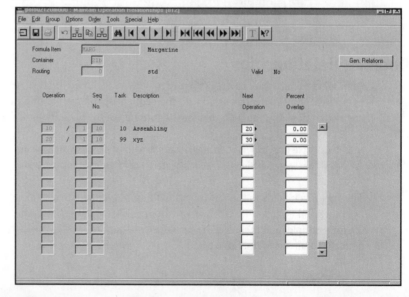

Validating Routings

The next step is to validate the routing. This can be done from the Maintain Routing Operation screen by clicking the Special option on the menu bar and selecting the function Validate Routing. The system may validate your routing if some information is erroneous or missing. A message will appear indicating why the routing cannot be validated. After the routings for the main and end items are validated, the routing scheme should look like that shown in Figure 25.10.

FIG. 25.10

Routing operations for main and end items.

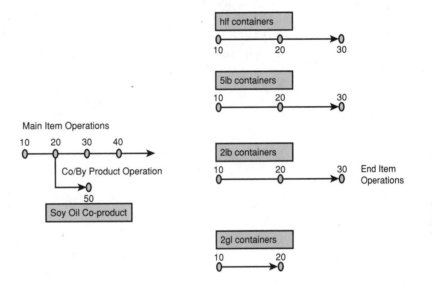

Viewing the Results of Routing

To view the combined result of main and end item routings, a production batch can be entered in the session Maintain Production Batches. (If any information is missing, this screen advises you of it and tells you to go to Production Management/Production Batches module.) After entering the batch, the final result displays in the session Display Batch Planning. (This is accessed from the Maintain Production Batch session by clicking the Special option on the menu bar). Figure 25.11 shows an example of the combined routings.

Hopefully this example of a process item routing has provided a helpful overview of the Baan Process Routing module. Users can now experiment with the various routing features to better reflect reality on the production floor. The following chapter outlines the application of these features.

Part
II

Ch
25

FIG. 25.11
Main and end item
routings are combined
in the Production
Management module.

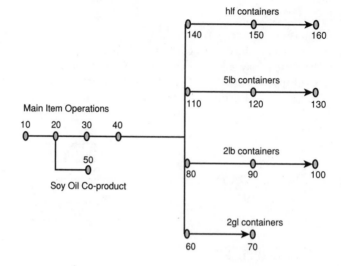

CHAPTER 26

Understanding the Tools Module

In this chapter

Using the Tools Package

The Tools package is designed to allow users with special skills, like system administrators or programmers, to set up a new company in Baan, create a user environment, and set up the database. You can also create new packages, modules, menus, forms, and sessions.

The following pages should be used as a textbook if you have to set up Baan for a new customer. You learn something about the Baan philosophy and, after this chapter, you should be able to understand the connection between a package combination, the Package Version Release Customers (VRCs), and a company. You also get an overview of the basic tools of Baan, like User Management and Device Management.

Using the Package Software

The Package VRC and the package combination are the most important pieces for setting up a new customer in Baan.

The version and release management of Baan offer a comprehensive solution to dividing different versions of the same program into different environments. This is a great advantage, because it is now possible to develop the software in one Package VRC while the user is working with the old release until everything is tested and released.

Using Package VRC

Package VRCs are customized versions of a previous package. A Package VRC should be derived from an existing Package VRC. The new Package VRC includes all changes that have been made for a specific customer. These changes can be the creation or modification of the following items.

- Tables
- Menus
- Forms
- Program Scripts
- Report Scripts
- Sessions

By using a version release control approach, Baan stores the changes in a different directory. This allows you to delete a change and revert back to the original menu, form, or report if you want to discard the change later.

Working with Standard Packages   All functions found in the Baan Software have been split into different packages. A package will group all sessions and files related for a specific area like Finance or Distribution. The software comes with standard packages and you can create your own to complement it. The standard packages are listed in Table 26.1.

Table 26.1 Standard Baan Packages

Package Abbreviation	Description
ps	Process—The Process package is used to manage production for items produced using formulas.
tc	Common—The Common Data package is used to manage company data and customer and supplier information.
td	Distribution—The Distribution module contains the sessions related to movement of material like purchasing, inventory, and sales.
tf	Finance—All the sessions related to the finance area like General Ledger, Accounts Payable, and Receivables.
tg	Organizer —The Organizer package contains all the sessions related to enterprise modeling.
ti	Manufacturing—The Manufacturing Package contains shop floor control-related functions from Bill of Material to Hours Accounting.
tp	Project—This package contains all the sessions necessary to manage jobs controlled as projects.
tr	Transportation—The Transportation package groups all functions related to the management of fleet and the control of transportation orders.
ts	Service—The Service Module manages all sessions designed to schedule service calls on equipment installed at a customer site and work contracts and warranties.
tt	Tools—All the sessions designed to maintain applications, users, and devices within the Baan software.
tu	Utilities—This is for the exchange utilities that allow the import and export of information with the Baan software.

Part
III

Ch
26

The standard packages will be stored under a specific path defined as the standard path. Then each modification done under a specific level will be stored under a different path that is proper to each version.

For example:

$BSE/application/tdB40_a   Standard Baan
$BSE/application/tdB40C_a_mi01   Customized Baan

N O T E A package combination, explained in further detail in the "Using Package Combinations" section later in this chapter, can be linked to several companies and different users. ■

Working with Software Components   For every package VRC directory there are sub-directories for each software component. The software components are the following:

- Forms
- Menus
- Program Scripts
- Report Scripts
- Include Files
- Program Objects
- Report Objects

For example a form for the sales package would be found under

```
$BSE/application/tdB40_a/ftdsls2
```

The system is searching for an executable from the highest level (in the example this would be td B40C_a_mi01) to the lowest level (td B40_a). If a program is found, the system tries to execute this session. If this is not possible (for example, if the object is expired), the system searches in the next level.

Using Package VRC Structure

Each package VRC should be derived from an existing one to ease the understanding of the structure when you want external resources to work with your system. This might be the case when you want to install a patch or upgrade to a higher release of the software. Figure 26.1 shows an example of the structure used to manage VRC.

FIG. 26.1
This is a powerful tool to control changes to the software.

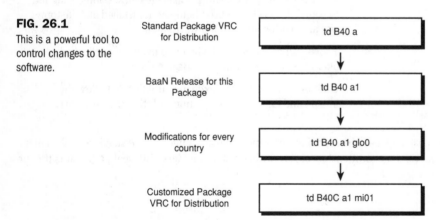

Standard Package VRC for Distribution	td B40 a
BaaN Release for this Package	td B40 a1
Modifications for every country	td B40 a1 glo0
Customized Package VRC for Distribution	td B40C a1 mi01

The package VRC td B40C a1 mi01 is derived from the package VRC td B40 a1 glo0, which contains customizations for a certain country. This package VRC was derived from the package VRC td B40 a1, which contains the new release from the Baan standard package.

Using Package Combinations

The term *package combination* is used to group different package VRCs. A company must be linked to an existing package combination. This means that you can group the customized Distribution Package and the standard Finance Package together, and every company that has a link to this package combination can use the modified sessions of the package distribution and the vanilla finance package.

Creating Examples

In this section, you will learn how to setup an environment for a new customer. In this example, the customer, Miller Inc., wants to have modifications in the distribution area. This company doesn't want to use a relational database. Baan has already installed the standard software on the machine, and the standard is working fine. After that, you will learn how to set up a company that already has a database created for it.

Creating the Miller Inc. Example

The first step is to create a new package VRC for the Distribution package. Follow these steps to do so.

1. Double click the Tools icon or folder.
2. Select the Application Development folder.
3. Select Packages and Modules.
4. Select the Maintenance folder.
5. Select the Maintain Package VRCs option.

At this point you can create a package VRC where all the changes done to the software will be stored. Make sure you follow a certain logic in creating your VRCs, and that you use a naming convention that is easy to follow for any external resource that may have to work on your system at a later point. There is an example of a created VRC in Figure 26.2.

Click the Insert button to insert a new package VRC. Now, you must fill in the fields to define the package. The fields are described in Table 26.2.

Table 26.2   Example Values for Maintain Package Fields

Field Name	Value	Description
Package	td	The package must exist.
Version	B40C	This is self-defined.
Release	a	You should use the same release of the package from which you want to derive it.

continues

Table 26.2 Continued

Field Name	Value	Description
Customer	mi01	Take a two-character abbreviation from the customer name, followed by a two-digit sequence number.
Description	" "	20 character, free-form field.
Status	Developing	Choose from three possibilities.
Version (derived from)	B40	Choose a value from an existing one (ZOOM).
Release (derived from)	a1	Choose a value from an existing one (ZOOM).
Customer (derived from)	glo0	Choose a value from an existing one (ZOOM).

The last three fields listed in Table 26.2 are very important. You have to say which package VRC should be used, if no changes are found in the new package VRC.

FIG. 26.2
Every developer must maintain the package VRC used to prevent them from making inappropriate changes and protect the original version of Baan.

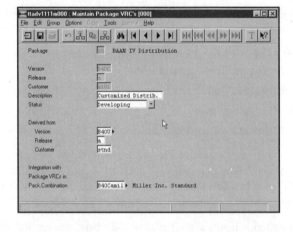

Integrating Package VRCs into Package Combinations At this point there is no package Combination for the new package VRC. That is the reason why you will have to come back to this session later. The next step is to create a new package combination for your customer, Miller Inc. To accomplish this, follow these steps:

1. Double click the Tools icon or folder.
2. Select the Application Development folder.
3. Select Packages and Modules.
4. Select the Maintenance folder.
5. Select the Maintain Package Combinations option.

At this point you have to create a package combination to be attached later to the different existing packages. A package combination will bundle various changes made to the software together, easing the management of customizations and applying patches. An example of package combination is found in Figure 26.3.

FIG. 26.3

You must define the different package Combination to be used.

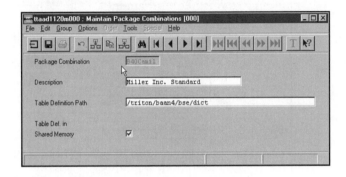

Insert a new package combination by completing the following steps.

1. Click the Insert button. The cursor is now waiting in the field.

2. Click the Insert button to create a new package combination. Now, you must fill in the fields listed in Table 26.3.

Table 26.3   Example Values for Creating a New Package Combination

Field Name	Value	Description
Package Combination	B40Cami1	Choose a unique name.
Description	" "	30-character, free-form field.
Table Definition Path	/triton/baan4/ bse/dict	Default value can be overwritten to store table definitions in a different directory.
Table Definition in Shared Memory	Yes	Determines if table definitions are stored in shared memory.

TIP If you have enough memory in your machine, storing the table definitions in the shared area can improve performance.

Inserting Directories for Software Components   To define the directories for the software components, perform the following steps:

1. Double click the Tools icon or folder.

2. Select the Application Development folder.

3. Select the Maintenance folder.

4. Select the Maintain Directories of Software Components option.

At this point you must assign directories for software components as indicated in the example in Figure 26.4. In this step you tell the software where to get the files for menus, forms, scripts, and reports.

FIG. 26.4

An example of the Software Component Directory.

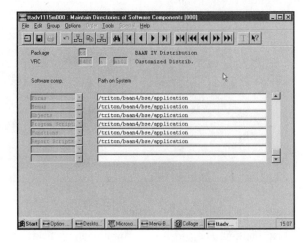

Click the Insert Group button. This is necessary because you have to enter all software component paths for a specific package VRC. After you have entered a new group you can insert multiple lines for this group. To do so, click the Insert button. The cursor is now waiting in the Software Components field. Select all values (Forms, Menus, Objects, Program Scripts, Functions, Report Scripts) from the pull-down menu. You must also enter a path for every component. For this example, enter **/triton/baan4/bse/application**.

Linking Package VRCs to the New Package Combination   To create a link from the package VRCs to the new package combination, complete the following steps.

1. Double click the Tools icon or folder.

2. Select the Application Development folder.

3. Select Packages and Modules.

4. Select the Maintenance folder.

5. Select the Maintain Packages by Package Combinations option.

At this point you are ready to assign the different package combination to all the different packages of the Baan software. These steps indicate what release level you want all the different components of the software to use. You will find an example in Figure 26.5.

Click the Insert Group button. This is necessary because you have to enter all package VRCs to an existing package combination. Enter **B40Cami1** as your group.

After you have entered a new group you can insert multiple lines for this group. Click the Insert button. The cursor is now waiting in the Package field. From the pull-down menu, select all values (ps, tc, td, tf, tg, ti, tp, tr, ts, tu) you want to use for the company.

FIG. 26.5

The various Baan packages must be linked to a package combination.

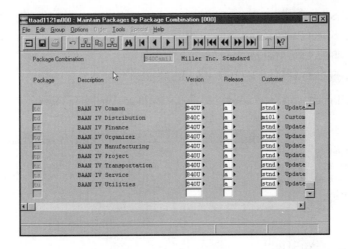

For every package, you have to enter the Version Release Customer. You have to select the VRC from existing ones, or you can enter the values manually if you know the exact name.

Creating the Data Dictionary   After this procedure you have to create the Data Dictionary. Complete the following steps to do this.

1. Select Special from the Menu bar.
2. Select Create Data Dictionary from the pull-down menu.

The system will automatically create the Data Dictionary for this new package combination. The Data Dictionary includes table definitions, domains, enum descriptions, and sessions. All components, even those that have not been changed, will be converted to runtime. By converting to runtime, you are writing all changes to the Data Dictionary. This step is required after most of the sessions found in tools; it is how you tell Baan to activate the changes you just made.

The table definitions, domains and enum descriptions are stored in the directory $BSE/dict/ddB40Cami1/d*-files, where ddB40Cami1 represents the package combination name. The runtime definitions for the sessions are stored in the table ttadv999 in the Master Company 000.

N O T E   If this session is finished, you will get a message like Data Dictionary Created. Now you can leave this program. ■

Linking the Package Combination to the Package VRC   To link the package combination to the package VRC, complete the following steps.

1. Double click the Tools icon or folder.

Part
III

Ch
26

2. Select the Application Development folder.

3. Select Packages and Modules.

4. Select the Maintenance folder.

5. Select the Maintain Package VRCs option.

At this point, you are ready to create the package detailed in Figure 26.6.

FIG. 26.6

This is the maintenance screen where you can maintain all the various VRCs per package.

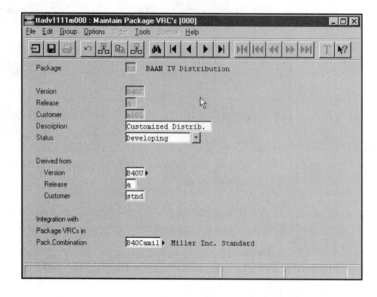

Click the Change button and go to the Integration with Package VRCs in Package Combination field. Now you have to enter or select the new package combination.

N O T E   If you want to have all Help information in your new package combination, you have to run the Create Runtime Help session. This session creates all available Help texts for selected VRCs.

Now you are ready to create the company for your new package combination.

Setting Up a Company

In this section, you will learn how to set up a company. This section only shows what you have to do to create a company for an existing database. Complete the following steps to begin setting up a company.

1. Double click the Tools icon or folder.

2. Select the Application Configuration folder.

3. Select the Maintenance folder.

4. Select the Maintain Companies option.

You are now ready to enter the information required to define the company information. An example of this session is found in Figure 26.7.

FIG. 26.7
This information is used in various reports and the parameters are used in various calculations.

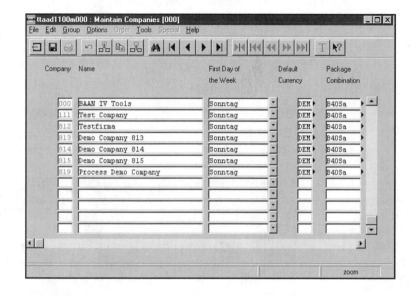

Click the Insert button. Now, you must fill in the fields. Table 26.4 gives example values for you to use and describes each field.

Part III
Ch
26

Table 26.4   Maintain Company Data

Field Name	Value	Description
Company	111	Type in your three-digit company number. You should start with 001. For demo companies you should use numbers greater than 900.
Name	Test Company	Free for your imagination (30-character space available).
First Day of the Week	Sunday	This day indicates the first day of the week and is used in some applications by a day number between 1 and 7. For that reason, the day sequence numbers can be converted into calendar days.
Default Currency	DEM	This currency will be the generic unit for that company.
Package Combination	B40Cami1	This package combination will be used for the new company. If you want to change the package combination, you have to call the Change Package Combination by Company session.

After making these entries, you have to run the program Convert to Runtime Data Dictionary. You can execute this session by selecting Special from the menu bar and clicking the field Convert to Runtime Data Dictionary from the pull-down menu.

The next step is to create tables for the new company. To do so, complete the following steps.

1. Double click the Tools icon or folder.
2. Select the Database Management folder.
3. Select the Miscellaneous folder.
4. Select the Create Tables option.

Now you have to fill in all the parameters required to create a table. You will find an example of this session in Figure 26.8. Table 26.5 gives example values for you to use and describes each field.

FIG. 26.8

When creating a table, you must physically create the file by using this option.

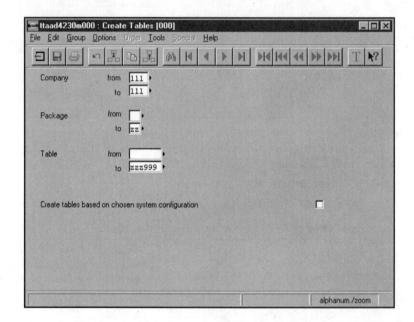

Table 26.5 Create Tables

Field Name	Value	Description
Company	111 to 999	Type in your three-digit company number. Only create the tables for one company at a time.
Package	" " to "zz"	Enter the whole range (this is the default).
Table	" " to zzz999	Enter the whole range (this is the default).

Start this session by selecting Special from the menu bar and then Continue from the pull-down menu.

Now you have to link a user to this new package combination and company. After that, you are able to start a new Baan session with your new environment.

Understanding User Security

One of the most important things a system administrator has to do is to set up every user or a group of users. Baan makes a distinction between a so-called *super user* and a *normal user.*

A super user has full access to each and every part of the Baan software. This includes authorizations for all packages and modules and for table and data manipulation, whereas a normal user has no permissions for anything. The next section explains how to set up the security for a normal user.

N O T E   There are still a few password-protected sessions that even the super-user doesn't have access to unless he or she knows the password, like the general table maintenance session.

Before you can announce a user in Baan, you have to define this person in your current operating system. The user must have a valid user ID and login code. The user must have additional environment variables in his or her Operating Environment User Profile, such as the following:

- The BSE variable—You have to define the directory where the Baan software is located (for example, BSE=/triton/baan4/bse).
- The BSE_TMP variable—This variable is used to store all temporary files from Baan (for example, BSE_TMP=/triton/baan4/bse/tmp).
- The PATH variable—This variable has to include the directory where the executable for Baan can be found (for example, PATH=$BSE/bin:$PATH).

These variables have to be exported to be available for Baan. In your user profile, you will need to have a statement that will allow those variables to be used by Baan. In order to do so, you must include a statement that does the export of variables. This statement is

```
export BSE BSE_TMP PATH
```

After this procedure you can start the setup in Baan. Complete the following steps to do so.

1. Double click the Tools icon or folder.
2. Select the User Management folder.
3. Select the General User Data folder.
4. Select the Maintain User Data option.

A profile is required for each user in order to define how each user will interact with the Baan software and communicate with the operating eEnvironment. Figure 26.9 details the first form of the Maintain User Data Session.

Part
III

Ch
26

FIG. 26.9

Every user must be defined in order to use the software.

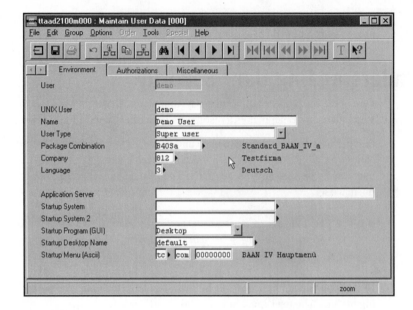

The first form of the Maintain User Data Session includes basic information used to link the Baan software and the operating environment. Table 26.6 describes the fields in the Maintain User Data session.

Table 26.6   Maintain User Data—Form 1

Field Name	Description
User	In UNIX, equals the environment variable USER.
Unix User	In UNIX, equals the environment variable LOGNAME.
User Type	Super user or normal user.
Package Combination Company	The default company, whenever this user starts Baan. Here you must define the package combination in use for the specific company to be used by this user.
Language	The language code in which the user starts the application.
Start Program	Desktop or Menu Browser. In this field you indicate if the user will first see a specific desktop at startup or use the standard Menu Browser.
Startup Desktop Name	If you have chosen Desktop in the previous field you have to select an existing Desktop from the Inquiry screen.
Startup Menu ASCII	The reason why you have to enter a valid information into these fields is so you can start Baan also in the ASCII version. (Default: tc com 00000000)

For each user, you will need to create a Baan profile so the software can communicate with the operating environment. Figure 26.10 details the first form of the session used to create user profiles in Baan.

FIG. 26.10
This is one way to set up users, which is very convenient and will save you time.

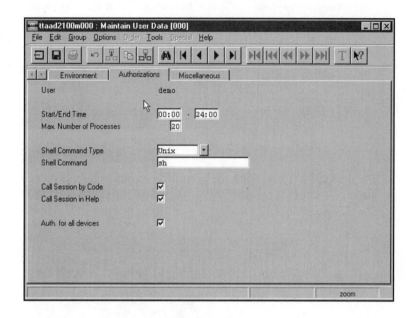

The Authorizations form includes the basic permissions. Table 26.7 describes the fields in this screen. To get to this screen simply click the Form II tab.

TIP Spend the appropriate time to set up your users properly, you will spend more time fixing files if you let users in areas with which they are not familiar.

Table 26.7 Maintain User Data—Form 2

Field Name	Description
Start/End time	The time during which the user is allowed to work with Baan.
Max. Number of Processes	This is the number of processes this user can run at a time. The value 0 indicates an unlimited number of processes.
Shell command Type	No / UNIX / Session.
Shell command	Only accessible if the Shell command Type is UNIX. (default is sh).

continues

Part
III

Ch
26

Table 26.7   Continued

Field Name	Description
Call Session by Code	In Baan, you have the opportunity to call a program by its name without going through all menus. To enable this you have to switch this Enum field to Yes. In GUI, you have to mark the button.
Call Session in Help	If this button is activated, the user is allowed to startup a process in the help viewer.
Auth. for all devices	This field specifies whether the user should be authorized to print from all devices (different printers, displays, kinds of files).

The third and last form (click the Miscellaneous form) contains the rest of the common information, like the time required before temporary information (reports) is deleted. Table 26.8 describes the fields found in form 3. This screen is shown in Figure 26.11.

FIG. 26.11

In the third screen of the user maintenance you can specify for how long the reports will be kept.

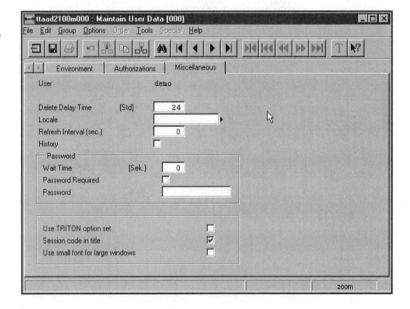

Table 26.8   Maintain User Data—Form 3

Field Name	Description
Delete Delay Time [hr.]	Default is 24. After this number of hours, the temporarily stored data for print jobs is deleted.
Locale	This field contains a so-called Baan Super Set. A locale is a collection of the TTS character set definition (The default is empty).

Field Name	Description
Refresh Interval [sec]	This field is only useful if the programmer allows the user to refresh a screen. If this occurs, the refresh is made automatically by the system. Default value is 0. This value indicates that no refresh is made automatically.
Use TRITON option set	You should switch this field to Yes if the majority of the users have never worked with Baan before. This option changes the key stroke set for Baan globally.
Session code in title	If you want to see the session code (for example, tiitm0101m000 Maintain Item Master) in each window, you have to switch this button on.
Use small font for large wind	If you want to have a smaller font for windows that are larger than 132 columns, you have to switch the field value to Yes.
Wait Time [sec]	This field is only useful in the ASCII version. The system waits this period of time without a keystroke from the user until the screen will be locked.
Password Required	This field is only useful in the ASCII version. This field will automatically be switched to Yes if you enter a value greater than 0 in the field Wait Time.
Password	This field is only useful in the ASCII version. The user has to type in this password, if he or she wants to unlock the terminal.

N O T E At this point it is important to perform the conversion ro runtime data dictionary. After this step is done you must log out the software and then log in again to have those changes activated. ■

Using Authorizations

This section can be very important to system administrators and should be read carefully. After you have entered the user profile into Baan, you are able to define the user security for this user. You can give the users access for special modules, sessions, tables, and even data. These changes have to be converted to runtime. After this setup, the user has the authorizations for the software and data the he or she is allowed to use. You distinguish between the following types of authorizations.

- Session Authorization
- Database Authorization
- Company Authorization

Part
III

Ch
26

N O T E   You can include and exclude authorizations.   ▓

To set up session authorization, complete the following steps.

1. Double click the Tools icon or folder.
2. Select the User Management folder.
3. Select the Authorizations folder.
4. Select the Session Authorizations folder.

You can enter the authorizations by module or session. If you want to give a user full access for a package, and the only things he or she shouldn't use are 5 to 10 sessions, it is much easier to enable all modules for this package and then exclude the 5 to 10 sessions. An example of the required setup is found in Figure 26.12.

N O T E   There is no rule that defines which session you have to use if you want to give a user certain permissions. You have to find the easiest way for you. Spend sometime planning which approach is best for you in order to save time.   ▓

FIG. 26.12

Various ways are used to define session authorizations.

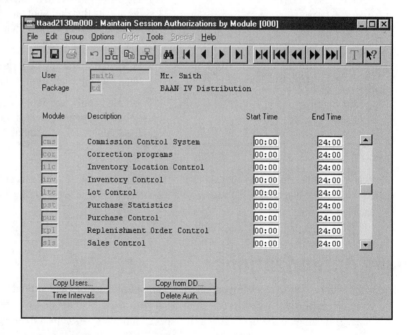

In this example, you want to give the user Mr. Smith full access for package distribution but he shouldn't be allowed to enter sales orders (`tdsls4101m000` and `tdsls4102s000`).

Select the Maintain Session Authorizations by Module option. Click the Insert Group button. This is necessary because you have to enter all modules for a specific user and package. The combination user smith, `package td` is your group.

After you have entered a new group, you can insert multiple lines for this group. Click the Insert button. The cursor is now waiting in the Module field. Enter all values (cms, cor, ilc, inv, ltc, pst, pur, rpl, sls, smi, sql, sst) or choose the Copy from Data Dictionary button. This button copies all modules for a specific package.

If you select Copy from Data Dictionary, the system automatically inserts the Start Time 00:00 and the End Time 24:00. If you want to enter the modules manually, you have to enter these time values also.

 T I P Say that you have a group of users that should have the same permissions. You should enter the whole security for one user, test everything with that User Id, and, if all works fine, you can copy the permissions to all other users.

Select Option Maintain Session Authorizations by Session. This step is critical because, at this point, you allow users to use all the various sessions in the Baan software. Figure 26.13 details how to authorize sessions by users.

FIG. 26.13

Maintaining session Authorizations by Session is another important step in planning your system security.

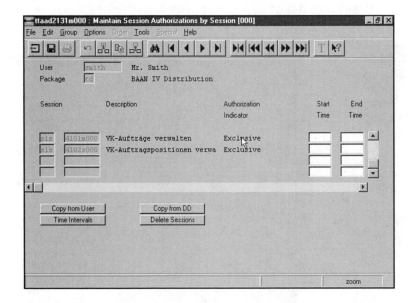

Click the Insert Group button. This is necessary because you have to enter all modules for a specific user and package. The combination user smith, package td is your group.

After you have entered a new group, you can insert multiple lines for this group. Click the Insert button. The cursor is now waiting in the Session field. Enter all session names for which the user shouldn't have access or choose Copy from Data Dictionary. This copies all sessions for a specific package.

If you have given the user the access for the module sls and are now entering the session sls4101m000, the system automatically switches the authorization indicator to exclude. If you enter a module that wasn't entered in the session Maintain Session Authorizations by Module, the system automatically inserts Include as the Authorization indicator and sets the values for the Start Time to 00:00 and the End Time to 24:00.

The next authorization possibility is by Database.

1. Double click the Tools icon or folder

2. Select the User Management folder

3. Select the Authorizations folder

4. Select the Database Authorizations folder

You can enter the authorizations by module or session.

N O T E   If you do not specify database authorizations, the user has Delete, Modify, Insert, and Read permissions in all the tables. ▪

In this example, you want to give the user full permissions for all tables except the Sales Order Header table (`tdsls040`) and Sales Order Line table (`tdsls041`). You can see how tables can be authorized or removed from users in Figure 26.14.

FIG. 26.14

All tables can be controlled and access can be removed for certain users.

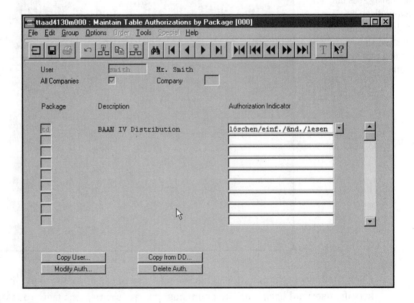

Select the Maintain Database Authorizations by Package option and click the Insert Group button. This is necessary because you have to enter all modules for a specific user and package. The combination `user smith`, `All Comp. Yes` is your group.

After you have entered a new group, you can insert multiple lines for this group. Click the Insert button. In the Package field, enter **td** and in the Authorization Indicator field, select the values delete, insert, modify, and read from the Enum field.

You will find an example of how easy it is to prevent users from using specific tables in Figure 26.15.

FIG. 26.15
This is how to exclude some tables for users.

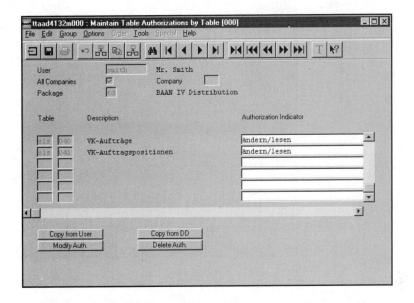

You are now able to exclude tables you don't want a user to have access to. Select Option Maintain Database Authorizations by Table and click the Insert Group button. This is necessary because you have to enter all modules for a specific user and package. The combination user smith, All Comp. Yes, package td is your group.

After you have entered a new group, you can insert multiple lines for this group. Click the Insert button. Enter **sls040** and **sls041** in the Table field and select the values modify and read from the Authorization Indicator Enum field.

You only want to give Mr. Smith read and modify access for these tables. You have to give him modify permissions because if he runs the session Maintain Deliveries, the system automatically makes changes in the actual record in the table tdsls041.

Converting to Runtime Data Dictionary

Once you have defined the user in Baan and have given him or her all the authorizations, you have to convert this data into runtime data dictionary. This session is used to acquaint the user and his profile to Baan. Figure 26.16 shows the screen use to launch this session. Complete the following steps to convert the data to runtime data dictionary.

1. Double click the Tools icon or folder.

2. Select the User Management folder.

3. Select the Convert User Data to Runtime Data Dictionary option.

Part
III

Ch

FIG. 26.16
The Convert Runtime
Data Dictionary writes
changes to the Baan
environment.

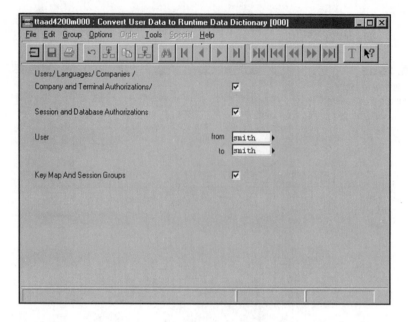

Click the Modify button, or click with the mouse pointer in the User From field. Select the range of users (in this example only from: smith to smith). The other buttons should all be marked (in ASCII switched to Yes).

Select Special from the menu bar and select Continue from the pull-down menu. The system will do the rest to acquaint the user in Baan. The user smith can now be tested.

Using Developers Data

The Developers Data subdirectory is used to set the defaults for programmers, such as the following:

- Editor
- Compiler options
- Current package VRC
- Permissions for modifying different package VRCs

To Maintain the Developers Data by User, you need to perform the following steps. This will assign the necessary permission to use the tools found in the package.

1. Double click the Tools icon or folder.
2. Select the User Management folder.
3. Select the Developers Data folder.
4. Select the Maintain Development Parameters by User option.

This session is used to define the basic tools for the programmer as shown in Figure 26.17.

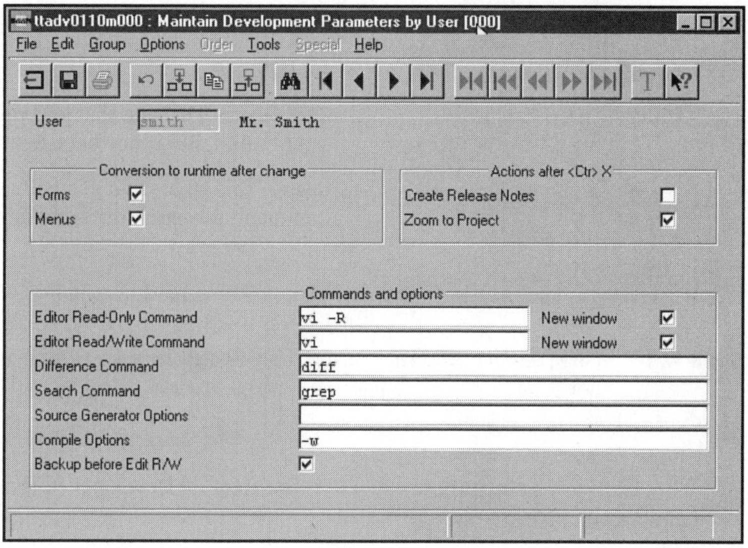

FIG. 26.17

For each developer, you need to create a profile before they can use the Baan tools.

NOTE You must to create a profile for normal users as well as for super users. ▪

Click the Insert button. Choose an existing user, smith in this case. Activate (in ASCII, switch to Yes) the Forms, Menus, and Zoom to Project fields. If you activate the fields Forms and Menus, the system automatically creates or modifies the objects for you after you leave the input mode. This is normally very helpful. Also, if the field Zoom to Project is active, the system prompts you to enter a Project and a Text every time you copy a form, session, menu, report, or program script into your own package VRC.

NOTE For every new or modified program, you should write down what changes you made, or what should be used for the new session. This documentation should be made in Baan, and therefore the Project scenario should be used. ▪

If you want to modify scripts in the tools package you will need to use an editor program. This editor program is generally the VI editor used in most programming language. Table 26.9 describes the editor options to be defined.

Table 26.9   Editor Options

Option	Description
Editor Read-Only Command	vi -R—the vi is the most used editor in UNIX, and the option -R stands for Read-Only.
Editor Read/Write Command	vi—This will state that you want to use vi as your editor program.

continues

Table 26.9 Continued

Option	Description
Difference Command	diff—This will state that you will use the Unix program diff to find difference between two files.
Search Command	grep—This states that you will use the Unix Search command to search through files.

If you want to have a new window for the editor, you have to switch the field New Window to Yes.

N O T E The values for this screen should be used as defaults. If you have other editors on your system, or if some programmers are only familiar with another editor or search command, you are allowed to change these parameters. ▨

The next session you have to execute is the General Developer Authorization. Complete the following steps to do this.

1. Double click the Tools icon or folder.
2. Select the User Management folder.
3. Select the Developers Data folder.
4. Select the Maintain General Developer Authorizations option.

This session is used to give permissions for different package VRCs to the programmer. This is shown in Figure 26.18.

FIG. 26.18
This validation program lets you change the password to access developers authorizations.

This screen is used to enter the password to modify the Developers Authorizations. If you don't know the password, contact the Baan Helpdesk, or, if somebody in your company already changed this Password contact that person. You can see how you can globally maintain parameters for all developers in Figure 26.19.

N O T E Not everybody should have the access for the Developers Authorizations session. Be very careful if you give somebody the permissions for all Package Combinations. ▨

Click the Insert button and select a user. For this example, select smith. Next, activate the Authorizations field for all package VRCs.

FIG. 26.19
Here you can globally define parameters for the developers.

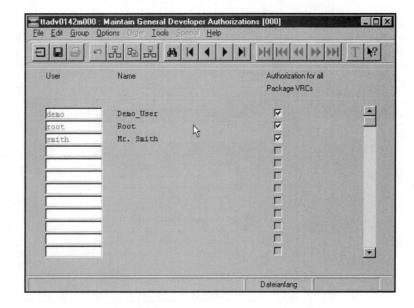

N O T E If you give a programmer these permissions, he or she is not allowed to change the standard. Only customized package VRCs can be modified by this user.

The last step is to give the user his default package VRC. The reason why you have to do is that the user currently has no package VRC defined with which to start. If he or she tries to access the Maintain Session program, Maintain Form, or Maintain Menus, the Error message Current Package VRC unknown will appear.

Using Device Management

The following sections will help you define paper types, different fonts, and printers within Baan. You will get a lot of defaults from Baan, but normally you have to define your own font or acquaint a new printer in Baan.

Maintaining Paper types and fonts

First you have to define a list of currently used paper types. These types can be assigned later to a printer device. Figure 26.20 details some examples of Paper types. Complete the following steps to maintain paper types and fonts.

1. Double click the Tools icon or folder.
2. Select the Device Management folder.
3. Select the Maintenance folder.
4. Select the Maintain Paper Types option.

Part
III

Ch
26

FIG. 26.20

Paper types can be denied using this session.

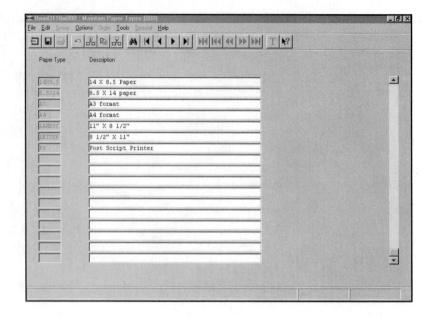

Click the Insert button. Enter **A4** in the Paper Type field and type in a commonly used word for your paper type (such as Letter or Legal) in the Description field. The next step is to define the font for your new paper type (an example is found in Figure 26.21). This is done by completing the following steps.

1. Double click the Tools icon or folder.
2. Select the Device Management folder.
3. Select the Maintenance folder.
4. Select the Maintain Fonts by Paper Type option.

Click the Insert Group button. This is necessary because you have to enter all fonts for a Paper Type. In this case, A4 is the paper type. Now, click the Insert button and select the fonts you want to have, as well as paper width and length.

Defining Printers

To set up a printer, you have to define the printer in Operating Environment. The printer file must be located in the $BSE/lib/printinf directory. In this directory, you will find different subdirectories like h (h represents the folder for all Hewlett Packard printer files). This screen is shown in Figure 26.22. Complete the following steps to set up a printer.

1. Double click the Tools icon or folder.
2. Select the Device Management folder.
3. Select the Maintenance folder.
4. Select the Maintain Device Data option.

FIG. 26.21
All the fonts to be used by Paper Types must be defined using that session.

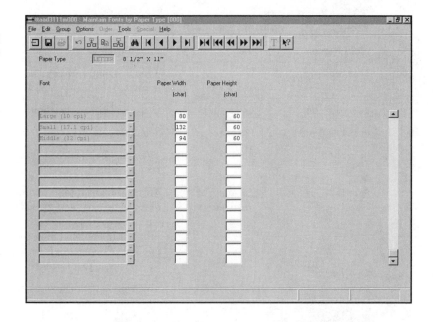

FIG. 26.22
All printers used with Baan are defined here.

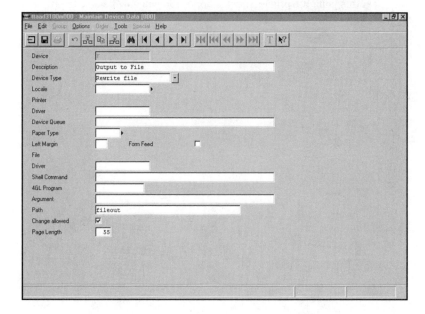

Click the Insert button. You now can define the printer. Table 26.10 gives example values and describes the field used to define a printer.

Table 26.10   Maintain Device Data

Field Name	Value	Description
Printer	LP	Type in a name that identifies the new printer in Baan.
Description	Laser Jet	Use your own explanation.
Printer Type	Printer	Select a value.
Driver	hp_lj3	This must be the driver that you would use if you want to print.
Spooler	lp -dhp_lj3 -n%d %s	This is the Operating Environment command that will be executed if you want to print anything out of Baan. -dhp_lj3 is the destination. See LPLADMIN command in UNIX. -n%d is the number of copies. %s is replaced, by Baan, with the file name that should be printed.
Paper Type	A4	This will be the default paper type for this printer.

At this point the printer setup is done. You will now be able to print out of Baan. ●

CHAPTER 27

Understanding the Integration Between the Modules

Integrating Modules

Activities occur within Baan's logistic modules, which generates financial transactions. The integrations with other modules' business object within the General Ledger module are used to map ledger accounts and dimensions in order to record these transactions. When this mapping is in place, Baan automatically chooses the appropriate ledger accounts and dimensions for all integration transactions.

The order of events described here does not represent the order in which the setup should take place, but has been represented this way for learning purposes. A diagram representing the flow of events required to set up financial integrations follows the explanation.

Assigning Ledger Accounts

Every integrated financial transaction is defined as a combination of transaction origin and financial transaction. The transaction origin identifies where the transaction originated (for example, Purchasing, Sales, or Production). The financial transaction represents the type of transaction that must be recorded within finance. For example, receipt of goods on a purchase order, goods delivered to a customer, or the revaluation of inventory.

Maintaining Accounts

The Maintain Inventory and WIP Transaction Accounts session is used to choose the appropriate ledger accounts for the various transactions. This session allows the user to identify the transaction origin as well as the financial transaction. In order to further define entries, a warehouse number, item group, item code, cost price components, or any combination thereof may be used.

A purchasing example is used to illustrate this. All raw material in a particular company is housed in a specific warehouse named RAW. Different types of items are represented financially in different ledger accounts. Raw material, which is used to produce subassemblies, is part of an item group named SUB. Goods have been received for an item within this category.

Setting Up an Account

The first required step is setting up a ledger account. The ledger account is used in the integration process. Ensure that all the accounts you want to use are created before creating the files necessary for financial integration. You find all the necessary information about general ledger accounts in Chapter 13, "Understanding the Financial Tables and the General Ledger." There is an example of a general ledger account setup in Figure 27.1.

This mapping is defined for all logistic activity, which must be represented financially. Additional setup is required if dimensions have been activated for either of these accounts.

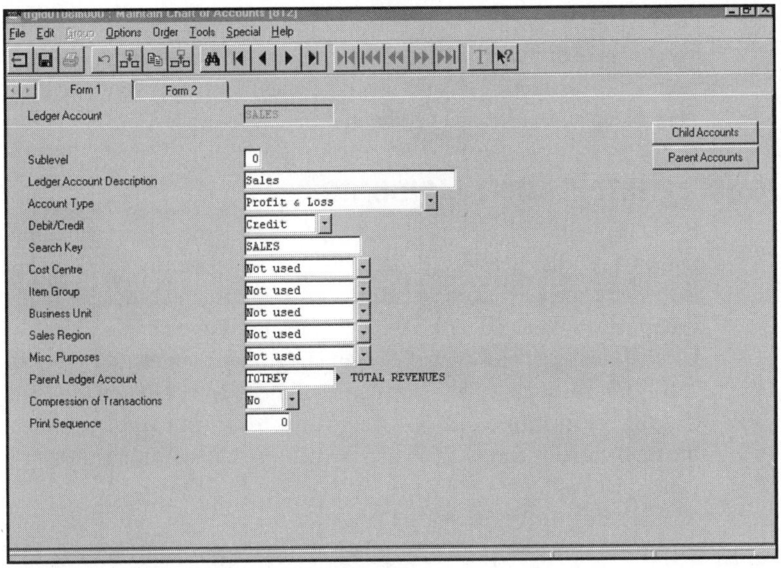

FIG. 27.1
You must set up the ledger accounts to process transactions.

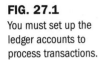

Assigning Dimensions

In order for Baan to choose the appropriate dimension code for every transaction, additional setup to the Maintain Inventory and WIP Transaction Accounts session is required. Integration elements, as well as options by integration elements, define the path in order to chose the appropriate dimension code.

Mapping Dimension Codes

Key elements are used to map the route to a specific dimension code. *Key elements* are pieces of information represented in the various transactions. For example, item, item group, warehouse, supplier, country, or area are some of the key elements available for use in the purchase/receipt transaction.

N O T E The key elements for all transactions are predefined in Baan.

Returning to the purchasing example, the ledger accounts used for the purchase/receipt transactions were subassembly inventory and goods received accrual. It was assumed that your company has defined one of its dimension types as Product Line. The Product Line dimension type consists of various codes to represent different item groups and has been activated on the subassembly inventory ledger account.

Upon reviewing the key elements available for use with the purchase/receipt transaction, several of the previously mentioned elements could be used. Item code could be used if the dimension codes represented a specific item. Item group could be used if dimensions

Part

III

Ch

27

represented a specific group of items. Supplier could be used if the supplier were used for a specific item or items of a specific group, but no other items. The key element item group is used for the example. The remaining question: How do you take the logistic information of item group and map this to a dimension?

Defining Integration Elements

First, an integration element is defined. This is a three-digit alphanumeric code used in the mapping process to assign debit and credit according to certain rules. The integration element is the template used to convert transaction information such as item, warehouse, and item group into general ledger account dimensions. For example, create a code called PUR for purchase integrations. Also create an integration element—by creating the integration element in this transaction, you indicate that no dimension is used on the credit side of the transaction. You can see in Figure 27.2 how the two necessary integration element codes were created. At the moment, this code has no logic of its own, but is used in another session as an indicator for more information.

FIG. 27.2

Integration elements to be used for purchasing transactions.

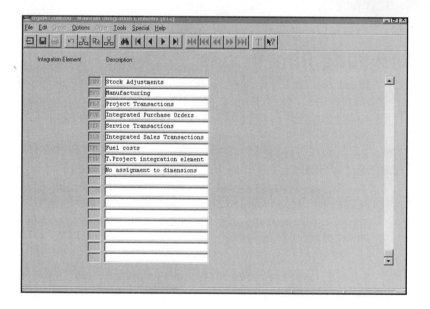

Next, use the Options by Integration Elements session to add the key elements to this code, as well as the appropriate dimension code to choose after the data has been found. To continue the example, an integration element PUR was created. The key element item group is used to map logistic information to financial information. For the item group SUB, the dimension code to choose for this transaction is 001 subassembly parts. Figure 27.3 illustrates an example of the mapping required.

Mapping may be defined by elements or by ranges. If the Element option is chosen, one item group is mapped to one dimension code. If mapping is defined by ranges, many item groups may be mapped to one dimension code.

FIG. 27.3

With this setup, any transaction with items in item group SUB is now linked to dimension 001.

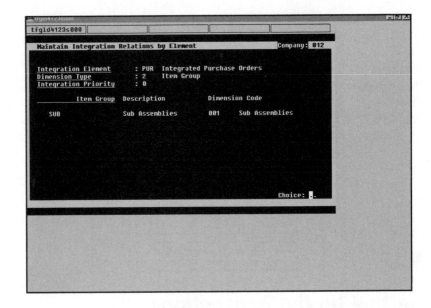

One last step is required. Use the Maintain Transaction Types by Transaction Origin session to identify the transaction origin as well as the financial transaction. In addition, define which integration element should be used for the debit and credit account as well as the transaction type to use in order to post transactions to finance. The example posts a purchase/receipt transaction and the ledger account subassembly inventory has a dimension type activated. The PUR integration element is used to map to the dimension 001 subassembly parts, as shown in Figure 27.4.

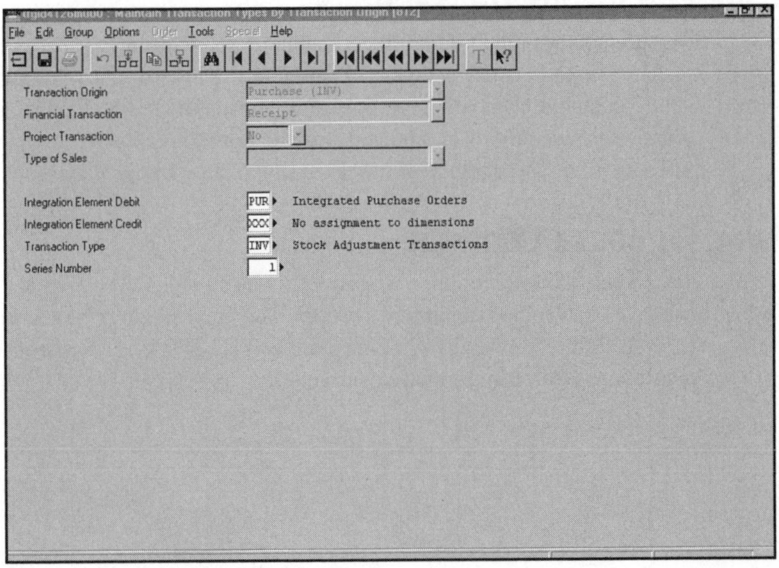

FIG. 27.4

You need to assign integration elements for every transaction type.

Figure 27.5 is a graphical representation of the setup required for purchasing, warehouse, production, and replenishment transactions.

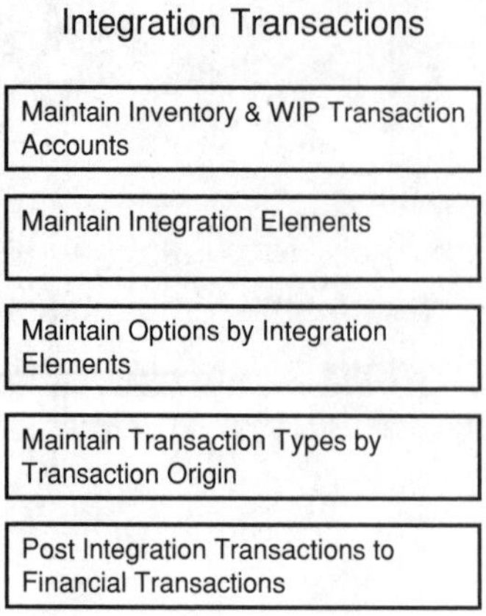

FIG. 27.5
The setup required is the same for all functions except sales.

Integration Transactions

Maintain Inventory & WIP Transaction Accounts

Maintain Integration Elements

Maintain Options by Integration Elements

Maintain Transaction Types by Transaction Origin

Post Integration Transactions to Financial Transactions

Setting Up the Transactions

The various types of transactions must be set up in the integration tables. The following sections help you set up the different sets of transactions.

 TIP Other transactions not listed must also be defined. Follow the pattern of a similar transaction.

Using Purchasing Transactions

The parameter in the INV parameters must be set in order to process transactions for purchasing. The link to Finance should read Yes. There is a session within the purchasing parameters called Maintain Financial Integration Parameters. The link to Finance should be set to Yes. If commitment accounting is required or obligations should be recognized before the receipt of goods, then the INV parameter link PUR to Finance should also be set to Yes.

Using Purchase Contract

The Purchase Contract option is used if a financial obligation must be recorded for contracts that have been copied to purchase orders. This transaction reverses when goods have been received. Table 27.1 details what the debit and credit general ledger accounts should be for all transactions related to purchase contracts.

Table 27.1 Purchase Contract Integration

Transaction Origin	Purchase Contract
Financial Transaction	Inventory on Order
Debit Account	Purchase Contracts
Credit Account	Purchase Obligations

Using Purchase Order

The purchase order option is used if a financial obligation must be recorded after a purchase order is issued. Table 27.2 details what the debit and credit general ledger accounts for all transactions related to purchase orders should be.

Table 27.2 Purchase Orders Integration

Transaction Origin	Purchase Order
Financial Transaction	Inventory on Order
Debit Account	Inventory on Order
Credit Account	Purchase Obligations

The following applies if the Purchasing module is not used, but purchases must be recorded using warehouse transactions. Table 27.3 details what the debit and credit general ledger accounts should be for all transactions related to purchase orders when only warehouse transactions are used.

Table 27.3 Purchase Orders Integration Without Purchasing Module

Transaction Origin	Purchase (INV)
Financial Transaction	Inventory on Order
Debit Account	Inventory on Order
Credit Account	Purchase Obligations

Part

III

Ch

27

Using Purchase Receipt

This option is used to record the receipt of goods or items on a purchase order. Table 27.4 details what the debit and credit general ledger accounts for all transactions related to purchase contracts should be.

Table 27.4   Purchase Receipts Integration

Transaction Origin	Purchase
Financial Transaction	Receipt
Debit Account	Inventory
Credit Account	Goods Received Accrual

The following applies if the Purchasing module is not used, but goods must be recorded using warehouse transactions. Table 27.4 details what the debit and credit general ledger accounts should be for all transactions related to purchase receipts when the Purchasing module is not used.

Table 27.5   Purchase Receipts Integration Without Purchasing Module

Transaction Origin	Purchase (INV)
Financial Transaction	Receipt
Debit Account	Inventory
Credit Account	Goods Received Accrual

Using Purchase Result

This option is used when the amount of the standard cost of an item and the purchase order amount differ. This is also used during the matching procedure, when the amount of the supplier invoice differs from the purchase order amount. This transaction is defined as a *favorable variance*. Table 27.6 details what should be the debit and credit general ledger accounts for all transactions related to purchase results.

N O T E   The transaction reverses itself automatically in the case of an unfavorable variance. ■

Table 27.6   Purchase Results Integration

Transaction Origin	Purchase
Financial Transaction	Result
Debit Account	Goods Received Accrual
Credit Account	Purchase Price Variance

Using Purchase Inventory Revaluation

This transaction is used if inventory on order is to be tracked and the standard cost of an item changes. Table 27.7 details what should be the debit and credit general ledger accounts for all transactions related to purchase inventory revaluation.

Table 27.7 Purchase Inventory Revaluation Integration

Transaction Origin	Purchase
Financial Transaction	Revaluation
Debit Account	Inventory
Credit Account	Purchase Revaluation

Using Production Material Issue

This transaction occurs when material has been issued to a production order. Table 27.8 details what should be the debit and credit general ledger accounts for all transactions related to production material issues.

Table 27.8 Production Material Issue Integration

Transaction Origin	Production
Financial Transaction	Issue
Debit Account	WIP
Credit Account	Inventory

The following applies if the Manufacturing module is not used, but inventory must be recorded as issued to production using warehouse transactions. Table 27.9 details what should be the debit and credit general ledger accounts for all transactions related to production material issue when the Manufacturing module is not used.

Table 27.9 Production Material Issue Integration Without Manufacturing Module

Transaction Origin	Production (INV)
Financial Transaction	Issue
Debit Account	WIP
Credit Account	Inventory

Using Production Operations

This transaction records the hours for man and machine recorded using the Hours Accounting module. Table 27.10 details what should be the debit and credit general ledger accounts for all transactions related to production operations.

Table 27.10   Production Operations Integration

Transaction Origin	Production
Financial Transaction	Operation Costs
Debit Account	WIP
Credit Account	Labor Absorption

Using Production Receipt

This transaction occurs when a production order is closed and goods are now ready for sale. Table 27.11 details what should be the debit and credit general ledger accounts for all transactions related to production receipt.

Table 27.11   Production Receipt Integration

Transaction Origin	Production
Financial Transaction	Receipt
Debit Account	Finished Goods
Credit Account	WIP

Using Production Result

This transaction occurs when there is a difference between the standard cost of the end item and the actual recorded production costs. Table 27.12 details what should be the debit and credit general ledger accounts for all transactions related to production results.

Table 27.12   Production Results Integration

Transaction Origin	Production
Financial Transaction	Result
Debit Account	WIP
Credit Account	Production Variance

Subcontracting

This option is used if purchase orders are issued for work processed at a subcontracting work-center. Table 27.13 details what should be the debit and credit general ledger accounts for all transactions related to subcontracting.

Table 27.13 Subcontracting Integration

Transaction Origin	Production
Financial Transaction	Subcontracting
Debit Account	WIP
Credit Account	Subcontracting

Using Production Surcharges

This transaction occurs when a surcharge has been added to the cost price structure of an item. Table 27.14 details what should be the debit and credit general ledger accounts for all transactions related to production surcharges.

Table 27.14 Production Surcharges Integration

Transaction Origin	Production
Financial Transaction	Surcharges
Debit Account	WIP
Credit Account	Material/Labor Absorption

Using Revaluation of Inventory in WIP

This transaction occurs when the standard cost of an item has been updated and the material resides in WIP. Table 27.15 details what should be the debit and credit general ledger accounts for all transactions related to revaluation of inventory in WIP.

Table 27.15 Inventory Revaluation in WIP Integration

Transaction Origin	Production
Financial Transaction	Revaluation
Debit Account	WIP
Credit Account	Inventory Revaluation

Using Inventory Transfer

This transaction occurs when inventory is moved from one warehouse to another. Table 27.16 details what should be the debit and credit general ledger accounts for all transactions related to inventory transfer.

Table 27.16 Inventory Transfer Integration	
Transaction Origin	**Warehouse**
Financial Transaction	Inventory Transfer
Debit Account	Inventory Warehouse B
Credit Account	Inventory Warehouse A

Using Inventory Adjustment

This transaction occurs if inventory is either adjusted manually or during a cycle count. Again, this transaction is set to be favorable. If this is not the case, it reverses itself. Table 27.17 details what should be the debit and credit general ledger accounts for all transactions related to inventory adjustment.

Table 27.17 Inventory Adjustment Integration	
Transaction Origin	**Warehouse**
Financial Transaction	Adjustment
Debit Account	Inventory
Credit Account	Inventory Adjustments

Using Inventory Revaluation

This transaction occurs due to the change of the standard cost price of an item. Table 27.18 details what should be the debit and credit general ledger accounts for all transactions related to inventory revaluation.

Table 27.18 Inventory Revaluation	
Transaction Origin	**Warehouse**
Financial Transaction	Inventory Revaluation
Debit Account	Inventory
Credit Account	Inventory Revaluation

Using Replenishment Order Issue

This transaction occurs when stock is to be replenished among warehouses. Stock is first sent to a transfer warehouse, and then received in the proper warehouse. Table 27.19 details what should be the debit and credit general ledger accounts for all transactions related to replenishment order issues.

Table 27.19 Replenishment Order Issue Integration

Transaction Origin	Replenishment Order
Financial Transaction	Issue
Debit Account	Transit Warehouse
Credit Account	Inventory Warehouse A

Using Replenishment Order Receipt

This transaction occurs when goods have been received at the target warehouse. Table 27.20 details what should be the debit and credit general ledger accounts for all transactions related to replenishment order receipts.

Table 27.20 Replenishment Order Receipt Integration

Transaction Origin	Replenishment Order
Financial Transaction	Receipt
Debit Account	Inventory Warehouse B
Credit Account	Transit Warehouse

Integrating Sales Transactions

The INV parameter Link INV to Finance must be set to Yes in order to record sales transactions. A session called Maintain Financial Integration Parameters (tdsls6100m000) is included in the Sales parameters. The link to Finance must be Yes and the use of invoice details should be set to Yes. The setup that must be performed for sales transactions is similar to that of those previously discussed, but some additional steps are required. Figure 27.6 details all the steps for the integration of sales transactions.

Assigning Ledger Accounts

Ledger accounts are assigned using the Maintain Inventory and WIP Transaction Accounts session, but additional accounts are assigned using several different sessions.

Dimensions are assigned to ledger accounts using the same procedure previously defined.

FIG. 27.6

The steps to building the integrations for the sales transactions are different than for other types of transactions. Here is a flow of all the sessions that need to be set up for sales integration.

Sales Integrations

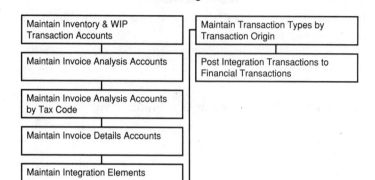

Using Sales Contract

This transaction records the obligation of issuing the sales order. The INV parameter Link SLS to Finance must read Yes to record this obligation. This transaction is set up using the Maintain Inventory and WIP Transaction Accounts session. This transaction is reversed when goods have been delivered on a sales order. Table 27.21 details what should be the debit and credit general ledger accounts for all transactions related to sales contract.

Table 27.21   Sales Contract Integration

Transaction Origin	Sales Contract
Financial Transaction	Inventory on Order
Debit Account	Sales Contracts
Credit Account	Sales Obligations

Using Sales Order

This transaction is used to record the financial obligation of a sales order being issued. The INV parameter Link SLS to Finance must read Yes to record this obligation. This transaction is set up using the Maintain Inventory and WIP Transaction Accounts session. This transaction is reversed when goods have been delivered on a sales order. Table 27.22 details what should be the debit and credit general ledger accounts for all transactions related to sales orders.

Table 27.22 Sales Orders Integration

Transaction Origin	Sales Order
Financial Transaction	Inventory on Order
Debit Account	Allocated Finished Goods
Credit Account	Sales Obligations

Using Sales Inventory Revaluation

This transaction occurs if obligations have been booked and the standard cost price of an item has been changed. This transaction is set up using the Maintain Inventory and WIP Transaction Accounts session. Table 27.23 details what should be the debit and credit general ledger accounts for all transactions related to sales inventory revaluation.

Table 27.23 Sales Inventory Revaluation

Transaction Origin	Sales
Financial Transaction	Inventory Revaluation
Debit Account	Inventory
Credit Account	Inventory Revaluation

Using Sales Issue

This transaction occurs when goods have to be delivered on a sales order. This transaction is set up using the Maintain Inventory and WIP Transaction Accounts session. Two kinds of transactions may be recorded here, but one thing to keep in mind is that revenue is recognized at the time an invoice has been issued. The following transaction setup is best used if there is a time delay between the moment goods are shipped and the time the invoice is issued. Table 27.24 details what should be the debit and credit general ledger accounts for all transactions related to sales issue.

Table 27.24 Sales Issue Integration

Transaction Origin	Sales
Financial Transaction	Issue
Debit Account	Goods Shipped Not Invoiced
Credit Account	Finished Goods Inventory

Part
III

Ch
27

This transaction may be used if no delay occurs between the time goods are delivered on a sales order and the time an invoice is issued. This may be advantageous if cost price components are necessary to record costs of goods sold. Table 27.25 details what should be the debit and credit general ledger accounts for all transactions related to sales issue when there is no delay from the time of delivery to the time of invoicing.

Table 27.25   Sales Issues Integration (No Delay)

Transaction Origin	Sales
Financial Transaction	Issue
Debit Account	Cost of Goods Sold
Credit Account	Finished Goods Inventory

Invoicing

Several transactions occur when an invoice has been issued. The first is recording the cost of goods sold, if it has not already been done using the Sales/Issue option. The accounts receivable and the sales revenue are recorded at the same time. Some T accounts represent the transactions that occur if the cost of goods sold has not been recorded. If the cost of goods sold has already been recorded, the same transaction occurs as shown in Figure 27.7, minus recording the cost of goods sold (2).

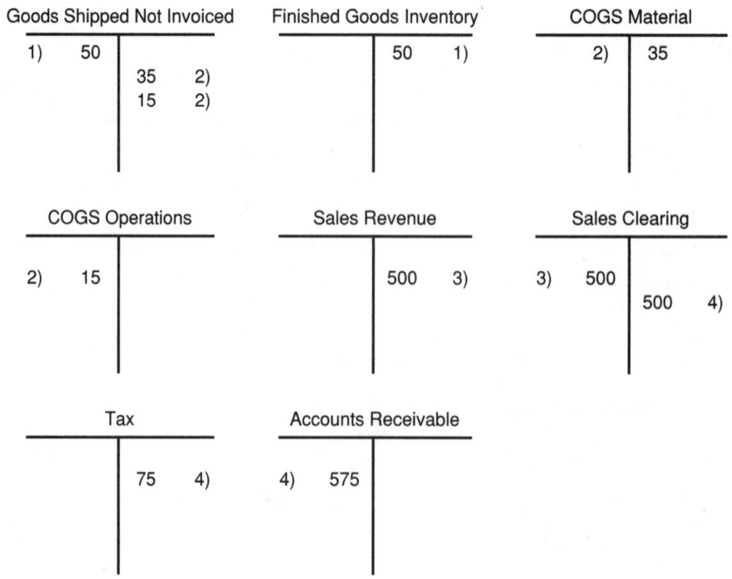

FIG. 27.7

Using T accounts here is a demonstration of the transaction results posted through the integration process.

Notes that correspond to the numbers in Figure 27.7 include:

- This transaction occurs when inventory has been delivered on a sales order and is maintained in the Inventory and WIP tables using the Sales/Issue option.
- The cost of goods sold is maintained using the Maintain Sales Invoice Details session.
- Revenue is recognized simultaneously with the cost of goods sold and is set up using the Maintain Sales Invoice Details session.
- The accounts receivable account is chosen based on the customer on the sales order. The customer belongs to a financial customer group and that is where the control account is maintained. The tax account is chosen due to the tax code, which is used on the sales order. The sales clearing account is maintained on the tax code so that the reversing entry may be made.

Using Maintain Invoice Analysis Accounts

This session is used to record the accounts for discounts on a sales invoice. This session is also used to maintain the accounts for the posting of late payment surcharges. The ledger accounts can be maintained by country or for all countries, depending on the settings.

Using Maintain Invoice Analysis Accounts by Tax Code

This session is used to record the accounts for tax as well as the sales clearing account defined on the tax code. This session is populated automatically after a tax code has been defined.

Using Maintain Invoice Detail Accounts

This session is used to record the cost of goods sold accounts as well as the revenue accounts. If different revenue of cost of goods sold accounts, they may be further defined by using the options such as customer group, warehouse, item group, or item. Table 27.26 details what should be the debit and credit general ledger accounts for all transactions related to invoice details accounts.

Table 27.26 Invoice Details Accounts Integration

Item	Debit	Credit
Material Costs	COGS Material	Goods Shipped Not Invoiced
Operation Costs	COGS Operations	Goods Shipped Not Invoiced
Turnover (Sales)	Sales Clearing	Sales

The following applies if the cost of goods sold has already been defined using the Sales/Issue option. Table 27.27 details what should be the debit and credit general ledger accounts for all transactions related to invoice details accounts when the cost of goods has already been defined using the Sales/Issue option.

Table 27.27   Invoice Details Accounts (COS already Defined)

Item	Debit	Credit
Material Costs	Clearing Account	Clearing Account
Operation Costs	Clearing Account	Clearing Account
Turnover (Sales)	Sales Clearing	Sales

Using Project (PCS) Transactions

The PCS link to Finance should read Yes (located in the PCS parameters in the Manufacturing package) to process transactions for project transactions. Projects use several different tables to map ledger accounts. The dimension mapping and structure remains the same. A list of the sessions used when mapping ledger accounts for project transactions follows. Figure 27.8 details all the steps of the integration of projects transactions.

FIG. 27.8

There is one additional session, Maintain Projects Transaction Accounts, to maintain when building integration files for projects.

Project (PCS) Integrations

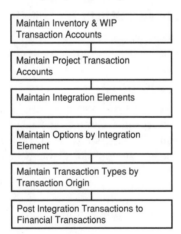

Maintain Inventory & WIP Transaction Accounts

Maintain Project Transaction Accounts

Maintain Integration Elements

Maintain Options by Integration Element

Maintain Transaction Types by Transaction Origin

Post Integration Transactions to Financial Transactions

Assigning Ledger Accounts

The Maintain Inventory and WIP Transaction Accounts session is used if standard items are included in a project. The Maintain Project Transaction Accounts session is used to assign all ledger accounts for activity that occurs for a project. The following sections assume that projects use actual costing in the proposed integration setup.

Dimensions are assigned to ledger accounts using the same procedure previously defined.

Moving Standard Inventory to a Project

If project planning replenishment has been processed, Baan automatically moves the content of the standard inventory to the Project module. You need to set up two different sessions to capture the transaction generated by this movement. You have to maintain the Inventory and WIP Transaction Accounts session and the Maintain Project Transaction Accounts session. You find all the necessary information to populate those two sessions in the following paragraphs. Table 27.28 details what should be the debit and credit general ledger accounts for all transactions related to moving standard inventory to a project.

Table 27.28   Moving Standard Inventory to a Project Integration

Transaction Origin	PRP Warehouse
Financial Transaction	Inventory Transfer
Debit Account	Project Clearing
Credit Account	Inventory

Enter the values found in Table 27.29 in the Maintain Project Transaction Accounts session.

Table 27.29   Project Transaction Accounts

Transaction Origin	PRP Warehouse
Financial Transaction	Material Cost
Debit Account	Project WIP
Credit Account	Project Clearing

If PRP is not running and inventory has been issued to a production order that has a project attached, Table 27.30 details what should be the debit and credit general ledger accounts for all transactions.

Table 27.30   Moving Standard Inventory to Project (No PRP)

Transaction Origin	Production
Financial Transaction	Inventory Transfer
Debit Account	Project Clearing
Credit Account	Inventory

Enter the values found in Table 27.31 in the Maintain Project Transaction Accounts session.

Table 27.31   Maintain Project Transaction Accounts (No PRP)

Transaction Origin	Production
Financial Transaction	Material Cost
Debit Account	Project WIP
Credit Account	Project Clearing

Issuing Hours to a Project

You must set up Integration tables to record transactions generated by the Hours Accounting module when hours are reported against projects. Table 27.32 details what should be the debit and credit general ledger accounts for all transactions related to issuing hours to a project.

Table 27.32   Issuing hours to a Project Integration

Transaction Origin	PCS
Financial Transaction	Operation Cost
Debit Account	Project WIP
Credit Account	Absorbed Labor

Surcharges

Surcharges may be added to a project or a project item to record additional costs such as overhead. Table 27.33 details what should be the debit and credit general ledger accounts for all transactions related to project surcharges.

Table 27.33   Project Surcharges Integration

Transaction Origin	PCS
Financial Transaction	Surcharges
Debit Account	Project WIP
Credit Account	Surcharge Expense

Subcontracting

This transaction is used if services are purchased to perform a task needed to produce the item. Table 27.34 details what should be the debit and credit general ledger accounts for all transactions related to project subcontracting.

Table 27.34   Project Subcontracting Integration

Transaction Origin	Production
Financial Transaction	Subcontracting
Debit Account	Project WIP
Credit Account	Goods Received Accrual

Actual Cost of Goods Sold

This transaction occurs every time a project cost is calculated. Additional transactions are recorded if there is a difference between the first and last calculations. Table 27.35 details what should be the debit and credit general ledger accounts for all transactions related to actual cost of goods sold.

Table 27.35   Actual Cost of Goods Sold Integration

Transaction Origin	PCS
Financial Transaction	Actual Cost of Goods Sold
Debit Account	Cost of Goods Sold
Credit Account	Project WIP

Sales

This transaction occurs when an invoice has been issued. An additional entry is created, because the customer belongs to a financial customer group. This dictates the accounts receivable account. The tax code used on the sales order provides the tax account as well as the reversing entry to the sales clearing account. Table 27.36 details what should be the debit and credit general ledger accounts for all transactions related to sales transactions for projects.

Table 27.36   Project Sales Integration

Transaction Origin	Sales
Financial Transaction	Revenue
Debit Account	Sales Clearing
Credit Account	Sales

Understanding the Utilities Module

Exchanging Data

Baan's Utilities module contains a set of programs called the Exchange module. This functionality allows you to import and export data from and to your Baan tables. Mastering this module allows the user to save time when preparing for implementation and provides a lot of information to be manipulated outside the Baan environment, in any spreadsheet or word processor.

N O T E   Although Baan can only import and export data in an ASCII format, programs like Microsoft Word and Excel can also import and export ASCII files. After importing an ASCII file into Word or Excel, you can add formatting and perform calculations on the data to create useful reports that might have been difficult, or even impossible, to create from within Baan. ■

The Exchange module is a user-friendly interface that allows a user with little technical knowledge to generate a file to populate any Baan table or to get a download of any field within a file.

Generating Your Exchange Scheme

You must define an exchange scheme before creating any file formats. A *scheme* acts as a folder. You may want to create more than one. This lets you create different scenarios under which you can manipulate your data. Follow these steps to create your exchange scheme:

1. Go to the main menu of the Utilities module.
2. Select the Master Data option.
3. Select the Maintain Exchange Schemes option.

The following lines direct all the interaction between Baan and your UNIX environment. Tell the system where to store the programs, where to store the log files, and where to get the sequential file. The *sequential file* is the physical file containing the information you want to import to Baan. The parameters that need to be set up for your exchange scheme are described next.

Initially, you must enter a description for your exchange scheme. You then have to define the paths where the files for the scheme are to be stored. The path for Exchange Objects and definition files can go in the /alumni/ directory. Condition errors could be recorded in a subdirectory of the Exchange Objects directory, /alumni/log for example. Sequential files could also go in a subdirectory, but not the same subdirectory as the log files. This path might be /alumni/seq. Table 28.1 summarizes the parameters necessary for setting up an exchange scheme.

Table 28.1   Parameters for Exchange Schemes

Parameter	Example
Scheme description	alumni
Path for Exchange Objects	/alumni/obj
Path for condition errors	/alumni/err
Path for sequential files	/alumni/seq
Path for definition files	/alumni/def

Importing the Data

Importing data from your legacy system saves you a lot of time. Plan your file transfer accordingly to make sure you realize all the benefits from this system feature.

There are many ways to get the data out of most computer systems. The easiest way is to print your data into a format called ASCII. This format can be used by most software. If possible, use a Report Writer program, and then create a file in the format detailed in the next section. This is by far the best way to plan your data import.

Creating the File Format

Baan requires you to create a file format, so you can have a workfile with all the necessary fields to be used in the input or output functions.

Now create your file's format. An example of a file format is found in Figure 28.1. Follow these steps to define the structure of the file to be manipulated:

1. Select the Utilities options.
2. Select Master Data.
3. Select Maintenance.
4. Select Maintain ASCII Files.
5. Click the Insert Group icon and supply the file name and the exchange scheme to be used.
6. Click the Create ASCII File button to import all the fields (if this is an existing Baan table). All fields are imported automatically.
7. Use the Insert icon to add fields or use the Delete icon to modify the file format to your specific needs.

N O T E　Changing the field type from `field value` to `fixed value` lets you experiment with your import files, which ensures acceptable data and expedites the process. This prevents the necessity of recreating your ASCII file in the event of an error message. ▮

After all the format has been created, you must generate a script for use when running the `import` function. You can find an example of this session in Figure 28.2.

1. Select the Utilities option.
2. Select the Create Script option.
3. Supply the name of the exchange scheme and the batch name to be used.
4. Click the Create Script button.

Verifying the Data

To ensure you do not corrupt your database, it is advisable to spend the appropriate time verifying the data going through the import. The system rejects any field that is not created in a reference table, but there is always the possibility that a field is improperly referenced, and that may cause problems later.

Part

III

Ch

28

FIG. 28.1

All fields from an existing Baan table can be imported automatically by using the Create ASCII File button.

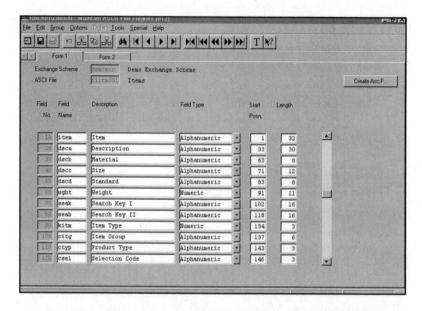

FIG. 28.2

In order to import data, you need to create a script that manipulates the data in the order you defined for each batch.

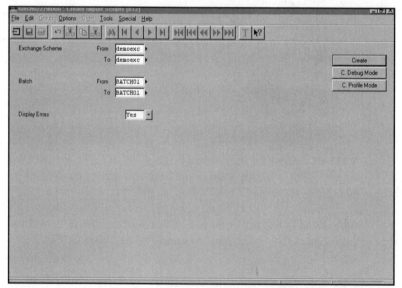

Prior to importing data, use the tool called Print ASCII File provided in the miscellaneous options. This provides you with an output of your import file broken down by all the Baan fields. This tool simplifies the task of aligning the fields.

Importing Data Options

There are two options to import data. The first is called Import Data on a Regular Basis and is used precisely as its name suggests—to import data on a permanent basis. Use this option if you have an interface running with Baan. Most customers prefer to write a program specially designed for their interface. The second option is the one to use when importing data before startup or at any point during your implementation.

Import your data to the Baan format by using the Import Data (Non-Regular Basis) option. Supply the requested information. You can use the system defaults for all the other fields. Run the program. When you have the ready message, you can activate the zoom from the choice prompt and look at the results of this upload. You see how many records were read, processed, and rejected.

Troubleshooting

You do not get the data to be loaded in your Baan file if some fields referenced to a logistic table contain data that is not created in the logistic tables. Go to the system log file to see any problems related to reference tables.

Take the following steps in UNIX to view the error log file:

1. Go to the UNIX prompt.
2. Type **cd $BSE/log** at the UNIX prompt.
3. Type **more log.bshell6.1|grep {*login*}** at the UNIX prompt.
4. Look for any error message related to the tables you just loaded.

You can see the fields that are wrong and a mention of the logistic table to which they refer.

Another problem could be preventing you from importing the data to the Baan files. Your ASCII file must be created with the exact length. Supplying records with a shorter length does not work, and you do not find any error message specifying that. Use the Print ASCII File option from the Miscellaneous menu to print your file and ensure that all the fields meet the specifications.

 T I P Comparing the size of your ASCII file to the length of the record is a good way to ensure the format is appropriate.

Creating the File Format

The next step is to create a file format that stores all the necessary information for import and export of any files. This could be all fields contained in a Baan table or just some fields. You can selectively create them.

First, assign the batch to your ASCII filename by using the Create Batch File option. Second, enter the values for the batch, the ASCII file, and the file definition. It is advisable to give a different extension than the imported file. Using .exp as a valid extension is recommended.

Third, create the file format by pressing **Ctrl+G**. Create all the fields from the file definition. You could also selectively create the field in order to create a partial file.

Part
III

Ch

28

Exporting Data

You may want to export some data out of Baan. This could be useful to pass the information to your spreadsheet program or, for the less adventurous, a word processor. Exporting data is also a good feature to use when you build a test company. You can download some fields from your production environment and import them back in the test environment.

To export your data to the ASCII format, select the Export Data option from the Export module, and enter the name of your scheme and the name of your batch while using the system defaults in all the other fields. Run the program. After you are back to the ready prompt, activate the zoom session at choice to see the results of your export. Your file is located in your home directory with the name specified in the Create File option if your export was successful.

After the file is generated, you need to use an FTP Program to move it from UNIX to your desktop environment. Contact your System Administrator if you're unfamiliar with this procedure.

Loading the Initial Values

The initial load of data is very critical in every implementation. This is an activity that can have a major impact on the project. If you follow proven paths and are very careful about how the data is imported, you begin your journey in the Baan world the proper way.

Map all the data that is available from your actual system. The critical files are shown in the following tables. Table 28.2 shows the common data. After you have the common data tables loaded, you can proceed with the manufacturing files in Table 28.3, and then with the distribution files from Table 28.4.

Table 28.2 Common Data Files

Filename	Table
Item Master	(tditm001)
Items per Container	(tiitm100)
Employee Master	(tccom000)
Customer Master	(tccom010)
Supplier Master	(tccom020)

Table 28.3 Manufacturing Files

Fileame	Table
Bills of Material	(tibom100)
Routings	(tirou100)

Table 28.4   Distribution Files

Filename	Table
Sales Order Header	(tdsls040)
Sales Order Details	(tdsls041)
Sales Deliveries	(tdsls045)
Sales History Header	(tdsls050)
Sales History Details	(tdsls051)
Inventory Data by Location	(tdinv001)
Inventory History	(tdinv700)
Locations	(tdilc101)
Inventory Data by Location	(tdilc301)

Create a load data sheet where all the Baan fields are listed, and record next to it where the equivalent information is stored in your system. Enter the value to be stored in that field in the last column. That could be the value in your system or a fixed value that you want to assign to match the Baan functionality. Your load data sheet should look like Table 28.5.

Table 28.5   *tiitm001* (Item Master)—Data Load Sheet File

Field	Description	Type	Length	Actual	Value
item	Item code	Alphanumeric	16	Item.dbf	Item.dbf-item
dsca	Description	Alphanumeric	30	Item.dbf	Item.dbf-desc
dscb	Standard	Alphanumeric	16	None	Leave blank
prdt	Product type	Alphanumeric	3	Item.dbf.001	Purchased
rept	Repetitive item	Alphanumeric	3	none.002	Always No
pric	Selling price	Numeric	20	list.dbf.pric	list.dbf-slpr

N O T E   Remember that you should always use three characters to represent the value when you work with enumerated fields; yes is 001, no is 002. Any options are represented by its position: the first one is 001, the second is 002, and so on. ■

Migration

Setting Your Parameters Properly

Using Parameters

Parameters are an integral part of any software package, and Baan software is no exception to this rule. On the contrary, Baan makes full use of parameters throughout the different modules, which are parts of the Baan package. Setting these parameters correctly when installing your Baan software allows you and your company to work in an environment configured for your particular application.

This chapter does not show you all the possible parameters' settings required to run the Baan software. The goal is to present you with a global view and basic understanding of Baan parameters in order to help you decide on the correct settings for your particular implementation.

To reach this goal, this chapter shows you where to find all the sessions used for setting parameters in every module, and you explore some of these sessions in more detail. The most important sessions in some modules are detailed.

Setting Parameters in Baan

A *parameter* is a variable—called upon by the various objects of your software package—to which it is necessary to assign a constant value in order for the system to take the appropriate action. Some parameters have settings that should be considered permanent (these parameters should not be changed after Baan's software is operational without consulting with an expert), while others have settings that are changeable as needed. Throughout this chapter, the parameters that should be considered permanent are marked with an asterisk (*).

For example, you should consider the following parameters permanent:

- Multicompany Structure* in Maintain Group Company parameters (Finance)
- Current Fiscal Year* in Maintain Company parameters (Finance)
- Production Rate Time Unit* in Maintain Routing parameters (Manufacturing)

These are changeable:

- Short Description of Currency in Maintain Group Company parameters (Finance)
- Actual Budget in Maintain Company parameters (Finance)
- BOM Unit of Measurement in Maintain BOM parameters (Manufacturing)

> **CAUTION**
> Always be careful when changing parameters' settings on your system. Many are used in multiple sessions, and the consequences of changing them could jeopardize the results expected from these sessions.

Your Baan software requires you to set a module's parameters before you can implement that module. The Common Data parameters are the first you should set, because they determine how the Common Data module will be operated.

To view or modify your system parameters' settings, select Parameters from the Common module. The menu shown in Figure 29.1 appears.

FIG. 29.1

The Parameters menu within the Common Data package allows you to select a module and modify its parameters.

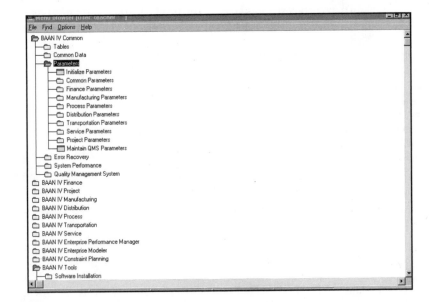

You can select the module from which you want to set or modify the parameters. The following sections describe in more detail the actual parameters that you find in these modules. It would be virtually impossible to look at all the parameters that you find in Baan software in this chapter. You are, however, shown where to find the appropriate sessions required to set the parameters; to a limited extent, this chapter discusses the main parameters in some of these sessions.

Using Initialize Parameters

This session is run only once—when you are first installing your Baan software. It should be run by your software vendor or by a Baan implementation specialist performing the installation. The use of this session is to set the default values of the parameters for the whole Baan package. You find the following in this session as well:

- Manufacturing parameters
- Process parameters
- Distribution parameters
- Service parameters
- Project parameters

Using Common Parameters

The Common parameters, as discussed earlier, are those that impact the Common Data module. Their correct settings are very important, because they affect the way your package is structured. When you select Common parameters, you see sessions shown in Figure 29.2.

FIG. 29.2

You can use the Maintain Com Parameters session to indicate whether packages like Finance and Transportation are implemented.

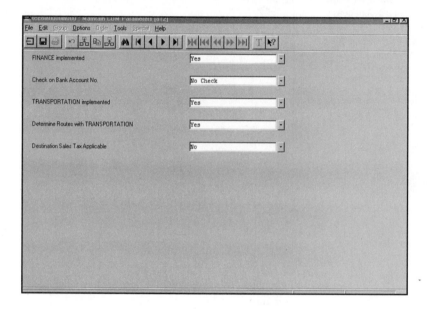

The Maintain COM Parameters session allows you to set the parameters listed in Table 29.1.

Table 29.1   COM Parameters

Parameter	Description
FINANCE implemented	This is a Yes or No parameter that indicates whether the Finance module is implemented.
Check on Bank Account No	This parameter only concerns Dutch and Belgian banks. Set this value to No everywhere else.
TRANSPORTATION implemented	This is a Yes or No parameter that indicates whether the Transportation module is implemented.
Determine Routes with TRANSPORTATION	If set to Yes, you have the option of calculating the route to a customer in the Route field of Maintain Customers session.
Destination Sales Tax Applicable	This is a Yes or No parameter that indicates whether destination sales tax is applicable.

The Maintain Intra EU Transaction Parameters session determines whether you can print, within Baan, the sales listing and statistical reports required for the European Union statistical reporting. Set this parameter to No everywhere else. In the Maintain API Parameters session, you can determine whether Baan interfaces with an external application, and if so, which type of interface providers you are going to use. Maintain Tax Provider Parameters allows you to set whether you want to use a tax provider, where the point of title passage should be (origin or destination), and whether a warning is to be issued if tax on ACR invoices.

Using Finance Parameters

All parameters in the Baan Finance module can be set in the sessions found in the Finance Parameters menu. The Group Company parameters must be maintained first, as shown in Figure 29.3.

FIG. 29.3
The Group Company parameters is a very important session to use in the configuration process. That is where you defined what general ledger dimensions will be used.

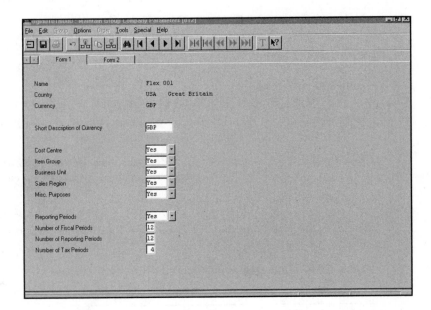

The Maintain Group Company Parameters session allows you to set the parameters in Table 29.2. Remember that an asterisk after the parameter name means that it is a permanent parameter. The asterisk is not actually part of the parameter name.

Table 29.2   Group Company Parameters

Parameter	Description
Short Description of Currency	For example, $ or US$.
Dimension 1 to 5 Used Y/N*	Dimension can be defined in your general ledger. If so, are they used in this group company? This is a Yes or No parameter.

continues

Table 29.2   Continued

Parameter	Description
Reporting Periods*	Gives you the choice of using a separate period calendar for your reporting in addition to the fiscal periods. This is a Yes or No parameter.
Number of Fiscal Periods*	The number of fiscal periods used for reporting financial transactions, usually 12 periods.
Number of Reporting Periods*	If reporting periods are used, the number of these periods.
Number of Tax Periods*	The number of periods for which the fiscal entity of this group of companies is to submit a tax return.
Multicompany Structure*	The companies' structure type within this group company; four structures are possible: single finance/single logistic, single finance/multi logistic, multi finance/single logistic, multi finance/multi logistic.
Store Data for X Years	The number of years for which detailed financial information is to be stored before it is copied in history.
Period Separator	The character to be used to separate the years and periods.
Base Company*	The company to be used to temporarily record the transactions that take place between different groups of companies.

You can set the parameters shown in Table 29.3 in the Maintain Company Parameters session.

Table 29.3   Company Parameters

Parameter	Description
Current Fiscal Year*	Enter the first unclosed fiscal year when installing the Finance module on your system. Baan automatically increments it when this fiscal year is closed.
Group Company*	The group company to which this particular company belongs.
Actual Budget	The budget code used as the default when comparing actual and budgeted figures.
Default Access by Batch	Access to a certain batch given to all users, or to the individual user who compiled the batch.

Parameter	Description
Default Finalization by Batch	Access to post a certain batch given to all users, or to the individual user who compiled the batch.
Journal Print with Finalization	Do you want a journal printout when transactions are being finalized?
History Company	The company used to store the detailed financial information after the year is closed.
Ledger Accounts Currency Differences by Currency*	Baan Finance allows you to define ledger accounts by currency. You have to decide if you want the currency differences, which result from fluctuations in exchange rates, to be entered in a ledger account by currency. This is a Yes or No field.
Currency Difference Profit Account	If you have set the Ledger Accounts Currency Differences by Currency field to Yes, you have to specify the ledger account used for currency difference profits.
Dimension 1 to 5	The dimensions to be used for the Currency Difference Profit Account.
Currency Difference Loss Account	If you have set the Ledger Accounts Currency Differences by Currency field to Yes, you have to specify the ledger account used for Currency Difference Losses.
Dimension 1 to 5	The dimensions to be used for the Currency Difference Losses Account.
Currency Difference Transaction Type Code	If you have set the Ledger Accounts Currency Differences by Currency field to Yes, enter here the transaction type from which to post the exchange rate fluctuations under.
Interim A/C Fiscal Period Change—Original	Enter here the ledger account that you want to use for the reverse entry of a transaction (in the original fiscal period), which affects two different periods, thus avoiding unallocated entries in one period.
Interim A/C Fiscal Period Change—New	Enter here the ledger account that you want to use for the reverse entry of a transaction (in the new fiscal period), which affects two different periods, thus avoiding unallocated entries in one period.

continues

Table 29.3   Continued

Parameter	Description
Interim A/C Rep. Period Change—Original	Enter here the ledger account you want to use for the reverse entry of a transaction (in the original reporting period), which affects two different periods, thus avoiding unallocated entries in one period.
Interim A/C Rep. Period Change—New	Enter here the ledger account that you want to use for the reverse entry of a transaction (in the new reporting period), which affects two different periods, thus avoiding unallocated entries in one period.

The Maintain Integration Parameters session is used to set the parameters for the integration of the financial transactions into the general ledger. You can only use this session if one or more of the Baan packages are integrated into the Finance package. Table 29.4 shows the parameters you can set using this session.

Table 29.4   Integration Parameters

Parameter	Description
Transaction Real Time to Finance	This is a Yes or No field. If Yes, the transactions go directly to the ledger and into the Non-Finalized Transactions table. You do not have to run the Post Integration Transactions to Finance Transactions session.
Immediate Start of Finalization Process	This is a Yes or No field. If the preceding field is No, you can decide to start the posting procedure immediately after the financial transactions are entered in the general ledger.
Compression	You can select one of the three following options: No Compression—All transactions are processed in the general ledger. Compression by Transaction Origin—Transactions are processed in the general ledger by origin (for example, total of sales order, purchase order, and so on). Compression—The total amount is entered in the general ledger for each processing.
Handling of Document Numbers	How you want to handle the document numbers: by date, by financial transactions/date, or by financial transactions.

Using Manufacturing Parameters

The parameters sessions for manufacturing are distributed in two folders, as shown in Figure 29.4.

FIG. 29.4
The Manufacturing parameters have been split into two folders.

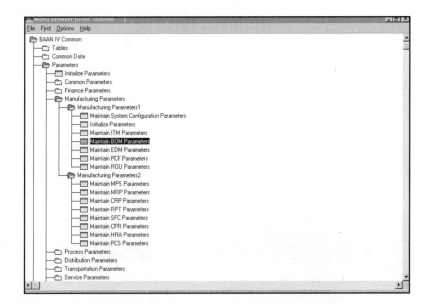

The Maintain System Configuration Parameters session is the primary session within Baan manufacturing. This is where you configure your Manufacturing module to include or exclude some packages. All the parameters in this session are of the Yes or No type. The parameters are listed in Table 29.5.

Table 29.5 System Configuration Parameters

Parameter	Description
MPS Module Implemented*	MPS (Manufacturing Production Scheduling) plays a major role in the logistical planning for most manufacturing companies. The MPS module is there to help coordinate between sales and production, determine the availability of material and capacity production, and serve as an input to Material Requirements Planning (MRP).
PCF Module Implemented*	PCF (Product Configuration) helps you generate items based on predefined generic items. The output is a completely new item with its own code, description, text, and bill of material.

continues

Table 29.5 Continued

Parameter	Description
PCS Module Implemented*	The PCS (Project Control) module is used by companies who manufacture to order. It allows you the use of project budget, project engineering, project requirements planning, and calculation.
ECOs Used*	ECOs (Engineering Change Orders) are procedures to record, approve, and execute engineering changes.
RPT Module Implemented*	The RPT (Repetitive Manufacturing) module is designed to ease the process of producing standard products in large quantities by simplifying the procedures to handle production orders within the Shop Floor Control module.

The Maintain Item Parameters session has two parameters that are used only for containerized items. Table 29.6 details both parameters.

Table 29.6 Item Parameters for Containerized Items

Parameter	Description
Prefix for Item Code Container Items	This prefix is only used by the system. The user only sees the items and the item by container. You should use special characters for this parameter (for example, ###). The prefix can have six positions. However, if you have a large item file, you should use a short prefix; the other positions are used for counting.
Signal Code Expired Container Items	When a containerized item is invalid, this code is used to alert the user by being inserted in the Signal Code field of the Maintain Item Data session. This code has to be defined in the Maintain Signal Code session.

In the Maintain BOM Parameters session, you select the BOM Unit of Measurement*—which is the length and width to be specified in production BOM—if you want the BOM to be defined by operation. This prevents components, in the case of items with a long lead time, from being stocked too early.

The Maintain HRA Parameters session allows you to set the parameters for Hours Accounting. These parameters are described in Table 29.7.

Table 29.7 Hours Accounting Parameters

Parameter	Description
Hours Accounting Type	For an employee, the hours account can be recorded by week/employee, week/order, day/employee, or day/order.
Clock Time for Hours Accounting*	If your company uses a different notation for time (for example, if your time recorder defines "quarter past 10" as being "10:25"), you select periods. If not, select minutes.
Period Length in Minutes*	If you selected periods in the previous field, you must define the period length in minutes. The period length is 0.6 minutes for the previous example.
Direct Time Recording*	This is a Yes or No field. If Yes is selected, the hours spent on an operation are recorded immediately when it is reported completed. This method requires more capacity, because the issue of orders requires the input of hours and the printing of order documents.
Actual Operation Rates*	Do you want to use estimated rates (standard costing) or man and machine rates, as entered in maintain employees and maintain machines, for the basis of the actual operation rates?
Capacity Flows*	Do you want the system to record capacity flows in your organization between main work centers only or between subwork centers?
Hourly Labor Type for Backflushing*	If hours are accounted by backflushing, what is the type of hourly labor that you use? The value has to be defined in Maintain Hourly Labor type, and it must be of the Normal Hours type.
Cover Overhead Costs in Employee Work Center*	This is a Yes or No field. It defines whether you want to post overhead costs to the financial company of the employee's work center or to the financial company where the hours are posted.

Using Process Parameters

The sessions in process parameters are, with the exception of Production Management, all found in the Manufacturing module (see Figure 29.5). Here, you only look at that particular session, which is the most relevant.

FIG. 29.5

All the parameters found in the Process Parameters menu can be found in the Manufacturing parameters—except the Maintain PMG parameters.

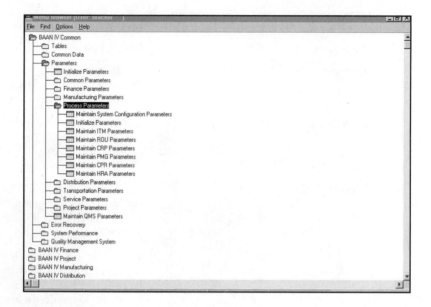

The Maintain PMG Parameters session is run to set the values for the Production Management module. The parameters are listed in Table 29.8.

Table 29.8   Production Management Parameters

Parameter	Description
Series in Production Batch Numbers	Do you want to use series in production batch number? If so, you have to decide whether one or two digits will represent the series.
Sort Materials by Associated Item	This is a Yes or No field. Do you want to group the materials by associated item before sorting them with the method selected in the next field?
Sorting Method Materials	Which method to use to sort the materials when copying from a formula to a production batch; especially important when using multilevel formulas. You can select one: Item and Operation, Operation and Item, Position Highest Formula, or Own Formula Position.
Copy Formula Text	This is a Yes or No field. If Yes, the system automatically copies the formula, material, co/bproduct, and end item texts when a production batch is created.

Parameter	Description
Engineering Revision Active	This is a Yes or No field. You need a direct link to the Engineering Data Management module if you want to be able to trace different versions of the same item.
Increment Material Positions	The factor with which to increment the position number of the estimated materials.
Increment Operation Number	The factor used to increment the operation number for the planning.
Automatic Update of Production Batch Dates	This is a Yes or No field. Do you want to modify the batch dates when the planning of the operations is adapted?
Printing Batch Documents Mandatory	This is a Yes or No field. Do you want to block the production batch until the documents (next field) have been printed?
Standard Batch Documents	You can choose one or many of the following standard documents: Batch Covering Note, Routing List, Operation Note, Material List, Material Issue Note, Checklist, Receipt Note, and Inspection Note.
Default for Comparing Actual	In the costing reports of production batch costing, do you want to see standard or estimated costs?
Use of WIP Warehouses	This is a Yes or No field. A work in process warehouse is used to temporarily store inventory for production centers. Do you want to use a WIP Warehouse?
Manual Issuing	This is a Yes or No field. If Yes, the issue of materials for production batch must be done using the Enter Material Issue for Production Batches session. If No, that session is filled automatically (direct issue). This setting has no effect on items issued via backflushing or on hold as floor inventory.
Recalculate Materials/Planning	Determines which method is used to recalculate material requirements when the size of a batch is modified. You can opt for standard, which means that the calculation is based on the actual formula, or for interactively, which prompts you to select a method.

continues

Table 29.8 Continued

Parameter	Description
Backflushing/Outbound Data	The process of automatically issuing materials in the manufacturing of an item is called backflushing. How this process is to be done can be set here.
Production Batch on Order Date Based On	The On Order Date is the date when a product is expected to be delivered in your inventory.
Calculation Method Remaining Production Time	How do you want to calculate the remaining time of a certain production? You can set this parameter to Planned Quantity (multiply the remaining by the order run time) or Time Spent, which is subtracted from the total time.
Replan Date Method	If the operation dates have to be recalculated because of changes, what method is to be used—Earliest Operation, First Operation, or operations Earliest and First?
Reporting Method for Previous Operations	When an operation is complete, how do you want the quantity reported for the previous operations to be adjusted? The choices are Automatically, Interactively, or None.
Update Allocated and Issued Quantities when Quantity Planned Changes	When modifying the quantity of a certain operation, it directly impacts the issue and allocation of materials used in this operation. This parameter determines how you want to handle these allocations and issues.
Update Method for Estimated Hours	When planning is adapted in the Maintain Estimated Batch Planning session, you can select to adjust the man hours, machine hours, and the related cost by setting this field to Automatically, Interactively, or None.

Using Distribution Parameters

The Distribution module is probably the most used module within the companies that have decided to implement Baan. Parameter settings for this module are complex. You look at four of the most important sessions in detail here.

The Maintain Base Units session determines which units of measure are to be used as base units throughout the system. You have to set the following data:

- Base weight
- Length
- Area
- Volume
- Time units

You can set the parameters shown in Table 29.9 in the Maintain CPR Parameters session, which is also used in other modules. These parameters are for the Cost Accounting module, which allows you to calculate cost prices.

Table 29.9   Cost Accounting (CPR) Parameters

Parameter	Description
Standard Cost Price Calculation Code	This predefined code determines which method of calculation you want to use for the evaluation of your items' standard cost price.
Project Cost Revaluation	This is a Yes or No field in which you have to decide if you want project costs to be reevaluated when the standard cost price is being updated for an item. This revaluation only occurs if the status of the project is Finish or Active.
Cost Price Component for Revaluation	If you have set the last field to Yes, you have to define under which cost price component to post the revaluation in the Inventory Control module.
Type of Operation Rates	Two types of rates can be used for the calculation of cost prices. You can choose between work center rate and task rate.
Number of Years to Retain Standard Cost Price History	For how long do you want the system to keep historical cost price? These could be used in the following circumstances: to determine the value of an inventory on a given past date and for transactions that take place for a certain item in your inventory, which has an old date; during cycle-count; when making an predated transaction for example.

Using the Maintain LTC Parameters session, the lot control allows you to monitor lots through-out your processes. You can trace them from their origin, as well as being able to find out where they are used. You must use lot control in conjunction with the Location Control mod-ule. In this session, you can set the parameters shown in Table 29.10.

Table 29.10 Lot Control (LTC) Parameters

Parameter	Description
Generate Lot Codes	This is a Yes or No field. If Yes, the system generates a new lot code based on the last free number every time you create a new lot. If No, enter the item-dependent lot code. Alphanumeric characters are allowed.
Series in Lot Numbering	Do you want to use series as part of the sequence number in the lot code structure? You can either select No Series, One Digit, or Two Digits, meaning that the series uses the first or first two positions of the sequence number.
Calculate Surcharges on Purchase Price of Lot Item	These surcharges, which are recorded in the CPR module, can be added to the net purchase price if the item in the item data has been defined as being valued against the lot price. If it is the case, then setting this parameter to Yes means that: The Lot Price = Net Purchase Price of Order Line + Cost Price Surcharges. On the other hand, you must set this parameter to No if you have recorded the cost price surcharges to apply only to non-lot items at the item group level.
Lot Tracking Implemented	This is a Yes or No field. Do you want the Lot Tracking submodule to be implemented?
Engineering Revisions in Control	When an item is defined as being revision-lot controlled in maintain item data, setting this parameter to Yes allows you to record the revision of that item when it is being moved inbound or outbound.
Manually Changing Potency Allowed	Setting this field to Yes allows you to manually change the actual potency of a lot item when it deviates from the standard potency.
Potency Deviation	This parameter is used if you want to set a default value for the Potency field in the Maintain Lots session.
Maintain DRP Parameters	The Distribution Requirements Planning module controls, on a time basis, the needs of your warehouses. The replenishment is based on a predefined bill of distribution for your warehouses/depot and according to a number of distribution rules. The requirements are evaluated as: Replenishment Requirements = Customer Demand/Forecast - (On-Hand + In-Transit).

You have to maintain the DRP parameters, which are described in Table 29.11, in order for the DRP Run to work efficiently.

Table 29.11   Distribution Requirement Planning (DRP) Parameters

Parameter	Description
DRP Implemented*	This is a Yes or No field. Do you want this module to be implemented?
Period Type*	Do you want the applicable period for the DRP module to be based on days, month, or weeks?
Number of Periods*	The value of this field with the period type determines the length of the period to be used.
Factor for Planning Horizon*	The planning horizon determines whether the demand/forecast is to be included in the DRP run. It is not included if it falls beyond the horizon. The Horizon is calculated as: Horizon = (Factor for Planning Horizon ¥ Order Lead Time) + Constant for Planning Horizon. The order lead time was previously entered in the Maintain Item Data session. If no values are found in one of these fields, the system considers the horizon infinite.
Constant for Planning Horizon*	Enter the constant value to be used in the previous formula.
Plan Sales Quotations in DRP*	This is a Yes or No field. Do you want the system to take sales quotations into consideration when generating planned DRP orders?
Minimum Quotation Success Percentage*	If the last field is set to Yes, enter the minimum success percentage for the quotations to take into consideration. This value is compared with the value entered in the Success Percentage field of the Maintain Quotations session.
Maximum Number of DRP Run per Day*	The number of replenishment orders allowed per item and per day.
Check Standard Routes*	This is a Yes or No field. Do you want the system to check the issue date of a replenishment order with the Standard Route and Date fields in the Maintain Dates and Times by Standard Route session?

continues

Table 29.11   Continued

Parameter	Description
Find Redundant Inventory*	This is a Yes or No field. If an inventory shortage is detected in one of the warehouses, the system might look for surpluses in other warehouses in the distribution structure.
Smoothing Factor Planned DRP Orders*	This factor lets you use part of your safety stock without automatically creating a new replenishment order. A new replenishment order is planned when the planned inventory of an item falls below the safety stock by a percentage greater than the one specified here.
Smoothing Factor Reschedule-In Messages*	Shortages in inventory are permitted up to a certain smoothing factor. A rescheduling-in message is generated when the planned inventory of an item falls below the safety stock by a percentage greater than the one specified here.
Smoothing Factor Reschedule-Out Messages*	Surpluses in inventory are permitted up to a certain smoothing factor. A rescheduling-out message is generated when the planned inventory of an item falls over the safety stock by a percentage greater than the one specified here.
Log DRP for Report*	This is a Yes or No field. If Yes, you can view the log using the Print DRP Log session.

Using Transportation Parameters

The parameters for the Transport module can be set in the sessions shown in Figure 29.6. For the purpose of this chapter, you only look at a few of these parameter sessions. Table 29.12 lists the ACS parameters.

FIG. 29.6

All the necessary parameters for the Transportation package have been split in two different folders.

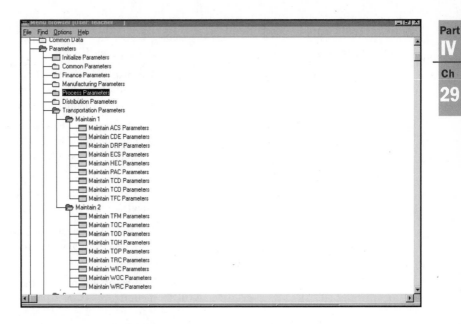

Table 29.12   Address Control (ACS) Parameters

Parameter	Description
Automatically Increment Address Codes	This is a Yes or No field. When creating a new address entry, you want the system to use the first free address number or you enter an alphanumeric code yourself.
Use of Distance Table by City	This is a Yes or No field. Do you want the distance table by city to be used in the Transport Order control and the Transport Order Planning modules?
Use of Distance Table by Zip Code	This is a Yes or No field. Do you want the distance table by zip code to be used in the Transport Order control and Transport Order Planning modules?
Search Sequence for Distances by City	The sequence to use when the system is looking for distances by city. The highest priority is given to the lowest number.
Search Sequence for Distances by Zip Code	The sequence to use when the system is looking for distances by zip code. The highest priority is given to the lowest number.

continues

Table 29.12   Continued

Parameter	Description
Based on Cities	The distances are based on the distances between the loading and unloading addresses from the Maintain Transport Order Lines session.
Based on Zip Codes	The distances are based on the zip codes of the loading and unloading addresses from the Maintain Transport Order Lines session.
Fill Distance Table by Zip Code from TOP	The distances are based on the zip codes of the start and end addresses from the Maintain Actual Stop Data by Trip session.
Date Format Address Calendar	The format to use for the address calendar. It must first be defined in the Maintain Date Formats session.
Free Address Number	This number is used if the Automatically Increment Address Codes parameter is set to Yes, or when generating addresses from other Baan packages.

In the Maintain TCD Parameters session, you set the general parameters that will be used in the Transport module, as well as in the Warehouse Inventory Control module. The data that is set for customers has priority over what is to be entered in this session. You need to define the default values for the TCD parameters shown in Table 29.13.

Table 29.13   Transportation Common Data (TCD) Parameters

Parameter	Description
Default Packing Unit	The unit used to pack the items.
Default Rate Unit	The rate entered is used as default in the Transport Rate Control (TRC) and Warehousing Rate Control (WRC) modules.
Default Weight Unit	The unit entered is used as default in the Transport Order Control (TOC) and Transport Order Planning (TOP) modules.
Default Distance Unit*	Within a company, the unit used for distances is most likely constant, meaning that you will probably only enter it once in this field.

Parameter	Description
Unit for Fuel*	This value is to be used for the fuel consumption report.
Unit for Time*	This is the time unit used in the Transport Order Planning module for the waiting time, length of stay, and the time to the first/next stop.
Unit for Hours*	This unit is needed to convert a difference in hours into a time difference in a variable unit. It is also used to determine the reminder date in the Transport Fleet Management module.
Unit for Kilogram*	Weights are always printed in kilograms on the bills of lading. It is then necessary to calculate the weight using the conversion factor of this unit.
Unit for Meter*	This unit is used to convert units from those of length to other physical quantities.
Unit for Cubic Meter*	This unit is used to convert any others into cubic meters.
Date Format for Country Calendar	The format you want to use for country calendar.
TFC/TFM Interface with Finance*	This is a Yes or No field to determine whether there is a direct link between Baan Finance and the Transport Fuel Control and Transport Fleet Management modules.
Fuel Costs Payable*	The ledger account used to post unpaid fuel bills.
Maintenance Costs Payable*	The ledger account used to post unpaid maintenance bills.
ICS Interface with Finance*	This is a Yes or No field. Do you want the invoices from the Invoice Control (ICS) module to be posted to Finance?
Revenue Interim Account*	The debit ledger account where revenues from Transportation are to be posted into Finance.
Post by Country	Do you want the late payment surcharges and line discount to be posted by country (Yes) or to your own country (No)?

The TFM parameters shown in Table 29.14 must be set before you can work with the Transport Fleet Management module.

Table 29.14   Transport Fleet Management (TFM) Parameters

Parameter	Description
Update History*	This is a Yes or No field to determine whether you want the history to be activated for the Transport Fleet Management module.
History by Warning Code*	This is a Yes or No field. Do you want to do the analysis of the history by warning code? Only accessible if the Update History field is set to Yes.
History by Cost Category*	This is a Yes or No field. Do you want to do the analysis of the history by cost category? Only accessible if the Update History field is set to Yes.
Period Table*	Which period table to use to compress the history. Only accessible if the Update History field is set to Yes.
Date Format Transport Means Calendar	The format to use in the transport means calendar.

Using Service Parameters

The parameters for the Service module can be set in the following sessions.

The Maintain Installation Control Parameters session is used to set the parameters for your Baan package's Service and Maintenance module (see Table 29.15).

Table 29.15   Installation Control Parameters

Parameter	Description
Number of Periods per Year for Periodic Maintenance*	Defines the number of periods in which you want to divide the fiscal year for periodic maintenance.
Defaults for Generating Service Orders Description	The default description when generating Service Orders. Priority—The default priority when generating service orders. Order Type—The default order type when generating service orders.
Use of Series for Generating Service Orders	Do you want to use series?
Unit of Measure*	The unit used to record the dimensions on the component and the actual cost lines if an item's unit has the physical quantity length, area, or volume. The unit must be of the type Length.

In the Maintain Parameters for Link with Finance session, you define whether you want the Service module to be linked with Finance, and if so, if you want account numbers to be defined by country. You also have to specify default values for service of the Call, Service, and Miscellaneous types.

Using Project Parameters

The parameters used throughout the Project module are defined mostly using the Maintain General Parameters session. That is where you indicate that the Project package is used, as well as what type of budgeting method is used. You find details of fields used in Figure 29.7.

FIG. 29.7
When using the Project package, you first have to maintain general parameters using this session.

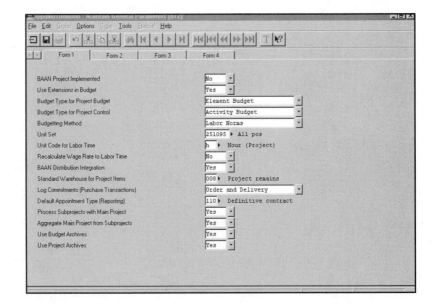

Using QMS Parameters

The Quality Management module in Baan was developed to support quality management of the companies, as well as quality control of the products. The QMS module can be linked to Baan's other modules in the Maintain QMS Parameters session. This is where you can decide for which module/function QMS is to be implemented, if you want to use order-specific inspection data instead of standard specific inspection data, what is to be done with the inspection results, and some other parameters related to the functioning of the QMS module.

Managing Your Customizations

Considering Customizing

There is no existing software in the world that would not require any customers to have some customizations done. However, adding customizations to the existing functionalities can jeopardize an installation's integrity. It is very important to manage the customizations properly. When performing a change to the software, you may enhance and ease your business process, but in the long term you are delaying any migration, as well as making support more difficult.

Customizations are an important part of any Baan implementation. Managing them makes the difference between a good and fast implementation compared to a project that seems to never start. This chapter shows you how to properly manage any changes made to the original functionality.

Important decisions must be made before you authorize someone to start coding changes to the original software. You must evaluate what the impact of this change will be on the software's functionality and evaluate whether the business needs that require this modification cannot be addressed otherwise.

Another factor to consider when planning customizations is to find out if Baan addresses those needs in future releases. Many companies have decided to wait on some modifications, knowing that the next release would do just that. It is important to spend the appropriate time, up front, saving money and a lot of headaches when it is time to migrate.

Because Baan is such a flexible software package, it is relatively easy to make customizations. The software manufacturer provides all the tools necessary to track any changes; one thing that cannot be provided, however, is the discipline and the judgment necessary to decide on customizing. Any users should consider getting the necessary expertise and speaking with actual users before drawing their customization strategy.

Customizations are beneficial if they are wisely done and well managed. This makes Baan an even more powerful tool for your company. Your implementation is harmed if the customizations are done improperly.

Customizing—Or Not

Whenever you decide to customize part of any software you should be careful and calculate what the impact of doing so will be. There are big hidden costs attached to customization. You need the actual code change, but you may also need to migrate this customization, which incurs other costs. A lot of users are currently facing this situation by having to migrate from release 2.x or 3.x to release 4. They now have to revise all changes and reapply them if they are still necessary. This is a long and costly exercise.

> **CAUTION**
>
> You must also be conscious that modifying the packaged software's functionality makes it more difficult for Baan support to help you solve any problems that may occur later, and customizations are often the first set of programs blamed for any deficiency.

On the other hand, not customizing may be a bad decision. Users do not accept a system with which they lose functionality from an actual system. Enhancements made to certain processes in Baan (to make them more appropriate to your business) are beneficial, especially in the reporting area, where everybody has different needs. You shouldn't stay away from customizing; you should simply walk this way with the appropriate caution.

Deciding

Before deciding to customize the software, make sure that the users requesting a modification understand the functionality of the program that they want modified. Sometimes workarounds are applicable and save a lot of headaches for your Information Systems staff. It is worthwhile to consult a specialist in the area. If you decide to customize, the specialist can assist you in minimizing the change to the original process. The money you invest at this early stage saves you a lot.

On a few occasions, programmers have been found writing customizations for certain processes and have been asked to stop because the users found an alternative way to use the functionality. An in-depth study of a customization's objective is necessary, and this should include study of alternatives to any problems. Over time, most of the customizations are reduced in importance and users wish they had used the standard process after they understand it fully.

Deciding Who Will Do It

Often the first level of customization does not force you to use external resources. Changes to menus, forms, displays, and reports are very easy and can be managed to a certain degree in-house. You quickly benefit from readily available expertise by investing in training for your Information System Department.

You reach a point where a required change is a little more complex, or requires the use of source code. Go to companies that specialize in writing customizations. Their staff requires less time to write any modifications, even if their rate is higher than the cost of an internal change. Some companies don't have the program's source code. The choice in that case is sometimes very obvious. Using an external firm also facilitates the migration to another release. Various Baan Global Partners offer customization services and ensure that the quality level of the changes meets the criteria established by Baan. SE Technologies, Origin in Business Technology, and Picosoft are partners accredited by Baan to perform customizations.

Employees with Baan software experience is the benefit of using an external company. You need to understand how it works in order to make good changes to the programs. It is difficult, in the early stage of your implementation, to ask that your IS staff have this knowledge. Later in the implementation, you must evaluate whether your employees' knowledge is sufficient to start making modifications.

N O T E   With Baan, the learning curve for an average IS worker is about six months. ▪

The better the specifications are written, the better the response is. When you request a quote or ask your IS department to do an estimate, make sure that you include all the details of the change, as well as include a description of any process affected by the proposed change.

Making the Request for Modification

Part of a good control system is having a good input form in which to log all the requests for modifications. A good implementation team should be disciplined in using such a form when requesting a change. You can find more information on how to create and manage your implementation team in Chapter 5, "Managing the Implementation." Figure 30.1 shows an example modification request form.

FIG. 30.1

This is an important document in your implementation process.

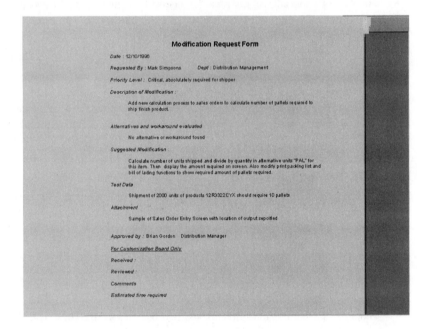

A good modification form saves everybody's time and makes your implementation run smoother. The more information you find on this form, the less often you have to go back to the users and ask them about their needs. You should find the following information on this form:

- Definition of their problem
- What has been done to find alternatives
- The potential problems of doing this change
- How the users want the change to be applied

Create a customization review board to analyze every request and prioritize them. This board should be made of representatives of business areas and include management team members.

This board has to approve requests. The board's process must be adapted to your business needs, but on average, this board should meet every two weeks. Have a one- to two-day session on customizations with this group and a consultant to educate them on the difference between a good customization, and a bad customization.

N O T E You should not have more than five members on the review board. ■

The routing for a modification form follows:

1. Have the user get approval from his or her immediate supervisor.
2. Ensure that all the fields are filled.
3. Have your customizations review team go over the proposal and approve or disapprove the request.
4. Assign a priority to the request and log it to a database. If you are dealing with a change to the item master that impacts everybody and the addition of a total for a report used by quality control, consider the item master first. Changes having impact on finances should also have high priority because of the work involved in testing the integration.
5. Periodically send a list of all open requests to all project teams to ensure that they know priorities and that they confirm the validity of those requests.

Having Customizations Done

Now that a customization has managed its way to the top of the priority list, you must manage the way this customization is performed. The customer must be involved and keep a close look on how the change asked for is added to the system.

The Information System Department is responsible for having the customizations done. Any change to the original design should be discussed with the users who requested the change and should get approval from the Customization board. This process must not be too heavy; you need enough flexibility to have the work done.

N O T E Boundaries that allow certain types of changes to customization plans without formal approval should be defined. ■

Changing the Code

The original Baan code should remain as intact as possible. It is easier to track down modifications when they are all part of a specific module or all named using some easy-to-find structure. Work with copies of original programs instead of the main object. Even if Baan provides a version release control system, you benefit from adopting a prudent strategy.

Naming your script with extensions is recommended. If you modify the item master maintenance program, you could name your modified version tiitm0101.cus, and the original script would be tiitm0101. Baan provides an alternative to this process called *program variants*. This requires you to copy the original script to a variant, modify the variant, and then compile it. The last version of a program compiled is the one to be used. This is a good process, but must be used with caution because it is very easy to recompile the first variant of a program instead of the last one—and recompile the program without the last changes.

As with in any programming language, ensure you document any change to a script with proper comments. Spending a few minutes adding comments saves hours for the person trying to do the next one. The implementation manager should ensure that proper documentation is included in the source code.

N O T E   It is a good practice to modify Help text as you modify programs. Sometimes, a customization is not noticeable to exterior people helping you on projects. ■

Documenting Your Changes

Any change to the software should be documented with a printout of the code and programming notes to explain the changes. This is a follow-up from the modification request form. A copy of this form should also be included with the previous documents.

Everything should be kept in a folder and stored where it is easy to find changes done in every Baan module. Test data used to test the changes should also be included in the folder.

Testing Your Customizations

Putting a customization into production that is not fully tested and sometimes not fully operational is a common implementation mistake. Even if you deal with professionals performing your modifications, never underestimate the task of testing changes. You end up fixing files in a few weeks if you don't express yourself clearly when asking for modifications.

Determining Your Test Criteria

Your test criteria should be defined now and modifications should be verified. Users should supply a set of data for testing as indicated in the modification request form. This is critical to ensure proper verification.

You must also specify in which environment the data should be tested. The changed program must be verified in an environment where everything is as close to reality as possible. Because of all the experiments, test companies are not always a good place for testing. Having a development area is more appropriate. Three environments make up the proper setup:

- Production for live data
- Test for training
- Development for making and testing the changes

Testing a Change

Always make sure that a change is tested in the system where it will be used. A relation to a file can be different from one system to the other. Your modification could be working at the developer's site but operate differently at your site. In addition, make sure that a person other than the developer tests the modifications. The developer knows what the system is supposed to do and sometimes it is easy to take something for granted—even if you use all the care possible.

You should prepare a set of data for use with testing when you prepare the specifications for a modification. Plan all the conditions under which you would like these enhancements to be tested. This saves a lot of headaches.

Don't put a change in your live environment before the required users have approved and signed the customization acceptance sheet. If possible, have a member of the customization board do a final check on a change before being utilized by the users. This may sound like an added burden, but it is an investment that pays off.

Keeping Track of Your Customizations

With Baan V coming, you know that you will eventually have to migrate your system. You should spend time now keeping a good log of your customizations; it saves time when it is necessary to reapply those changes during migration. Baan does not require more time for upgrading than any other software, as long as you do a good planning job. *Migrating a system* is reapplying all your customizations—always keep that in mind.

The Modification Log

Any modifications made to your system should be documented. In Chapter 22, "Understanding the Tools Module," you see how to note within a program that a change to the code occurred; adding comments in a program is insufficient. Make sure you keep a log of all the changes. That should be easy if you create all your modifications in a different module—not using any module name used by Baan.

Make sure that any modifications to the file structure are also documented. Files are often different from one release to the other, and you may have to modify the files again later. Table 30.1 is an example of a log book of customizations. This type of log becomes a valuable check list when it is time to move to a newer version.

Table 30.1   Customizations Log Book

Date	Program or File	Reason	Done By
11-10-1996	tdcus4100m000	Display for item master	D. Martin
11-15-1996	tdsls040 and tdsls050	Added field cont for continent	D. Martin
11-20-1996	tdcus5101m000	Print sales by continent	L. Pelletier
11-23-1996	tdcus5110m000	Print scales by continent and customer	L. Pelletier
11-27-1996	tdsls040 and tdsls050	Added indexes no 7, continent, and customer	R. Lacombe

Preparing for Future Changes

As specified in this chapter, preparing for the future requires you to keep yourself informed on all the future enhancements Baan is planning, as well as keeping track of all the changes you are making now. The task of migrating to release V will be easier if you do so.

The user group conferences are a good tool for keeping an eye on all future Baan enhancements. The use of the BBS and attending those events should provide you the necessary information. Reading all the White Paper Documents issued periodically by Baan is also a good way to stay in touch with Baan's future. ●

Training and Simulating

Creating the Best Environment for Training

The training and simulation of your normal day-to-day processes in Baan are an integral part of bringing the system up successfully. It is imperative that associates have uninterrupted time in order to understand not only how their processes function, but also to understand how what they do in the system integrates with other modules. When you bring the system up, the users should not only have confidence to go forward with the new system, but should have confidence that the system will fulfill their individual business processes.

Deciding where training will take place is an important decision to make before beginning any training. The users must be able to give their undivided attention while in training; a location in which there will be no interruption by their normal day-to-day work is required.

Setting Up a Training Location

A room or a specific secluded area of the office should be identified as the training area. This should be a place where the users are removed from their normal working environment. Everything needed for training should be made available in the training room.

There should be enough terminals so that all users have a terminal of their own. The same person always does the typing when a terminal is shared; the user who is watching does not get much benefit from the training. Remember that hands-on training is the only way users become confident with the package.

> **CAUTION**
>
> There are always some users who are wary of computer systems. You must make sure that these associates do not have any excuse for not being on the system.

All reference manuals should also be made available. As training progresses and you move on to the simulation stage, it is imperative that the users be able to refer to manuals for guidance.

Setting Rules for the Training Location

A schedule of all training times, along with a list of the associates who will be attending the training sessions, should be distributed to all involved parties, including management. The schedule should also be posted outside the training room. It is the responsibility of the users and their managers to ensure that they are available and on time for all training sessions.

It is imperative that everyone in the organization (other users as well as management) realize the importance of undisturbed training sessions. A constantly interrupted training room results in having to repeat parts of the training for the user(s) who left the room. It also creates animosity with the associates who have to repeatedly go over the same material.

Here is a check list for training location rules:

- Do all involved associates and management have a copy of the training schedule?
- Is there a copy of the schedule posted outside the training room?

■ Does everyone (users and management) understand the importance of being available and on time for all training sessions?

■ Is everyone in agreement that while in training the users will not be disturbed?

Training the Users

The training period during a computer system's implementation is critical. The first contact that the users have with the software must be planned to ensure that everyone feels comfortable with the process. The following sections include points that you should consider when building your training plan.

Performing the Training

Some users are nervous or apprehensive when they start training on a new system. Many people dislike change and become worried that they will not be able to navigate through the system properly, or that they will not understand how their current processes flow through the new system. Your starting point is getting the users familiar with navigating through the system. Comfort with the navigation process is critical.

Users become frustrated when they start training in their specific areas if they do not comprehend when and where they are to use specific keystrokes. It would be helpful to have some sort of a "cheat sheet" posted in the training room. That enables users to view when and where the most common keystrokes are used within the system at a glance.

N O T E Do not begin any other training until all the users are comfortable with the system navigation. ■

Important topics to cover during Baan navigation training include:

■ What are the common keystrokes used in the system?

■ What are the different form types, and how do keystrokes differ per form type?

■ How do you read the status bar?

■ What is a menu?

■ What is a session?

■ How do you know which session you are currently in?

■ How do you know which mode you are in (Find, Add, Update, Delete), and where do you see this on the status bar?

■ How do you know if there are multiple forms, and how do you navigate through them?

■ What is the difference between the Zoom and Enum commands, and how do you know when you can use these commands?

Baan provides a very complete self-study navigation manual. Ensure that all users go through that document before attending class; it saves time when teaching the software basics.

Training Key Users

The *key users* are the associates who learn the system first. They figure out how the system's different modules fit in with how the company wants to operate. They are the users responsible for setting up all pertinent tables, master data, and parameters within the system. Training the key users is intensive, because they need to understand not only how to process things through the system, but must also understand how the system functions in the background. They have to be able to test and ensure that all tables and parameters have been set up properly.

Key users typically are relieved of their day-to-day positions while training and setting up the system. They will not have the time required to devote to the system if they are not relieved of their day-to-day functions. This could result in your implementation date being pushed back.

Remember that key users are the users who are building all the background information in the system to ensure that it meets your organization's needs. It is the key user who trains the end users. They also work with the end users to produce process flows per functional area. These *process flows* enable the users to map how they are processing information today versus how it will be processed on the new system. The process flows are an important tool for ensuring that all steps of every functional area have been covered in training. They also help users know exactly how things flow through the new system.

Things to consider when deciding on key users include:

- Have you selected the proper associates as key users?
- Have you selected an appropriate cross section of key users? All operations and departments of the organization should be covered.
- Do they know how you want your organization to operate?
- Will they have the time to devote to the system, and have they been relieved of the responsibilities of their current positions?
- Does management support the choice of key users, and is there a commitment to make them available to the project?

Training the End Users

Training the end users is one of the implementation's most critical processes. These are the associates who use the system on a daily basis after you go live. It is imperative that they not only feel comfortable with the system, but that they understand exactly how they function on a daily basis when the system is up and running.

TIP For the best results, encourage all users to ask questions during the training process.

These are the associates who are familiar with the current processes. They are the ones who come up with numerous different "How do I handle this situation when it happens?" scenarios. End users are the associates who test all scenarios that commonly occur in their particular functions. They must understand how their current positions should be prepared, so that you can ensure that all current steps are being covered while training.

You create new process flows for each functional area during training. These are the process flows that are used when you go live. It is imperative during this period that users ensure that all pertinent processes relating to their jobs are processed properly in the new system. They must understand that though they may process a certain step differently in the new system, but the results must be the same.

It is during this time frame that you collect all reports currently being used to run the business—not only reports used by the users, but reports that are used by the management team. These are system-generated reports, as well as reports that are currently generated manually, outside of the system. It is imperative that all current reports considered necessary to run the business be obtained from the new system. The reports will most likely not be in different formats, but they must contain the same information.

Part

IV

Ch

31

N O T E   Some information is obtained through displays of the new system rather than by hard copy reports. It is irrelevant whether it is a hard copy or a display, as long as the users can obtain the required information satisfactorily.

The following is a checklist for use when training end users:

- Do you have current process flows?
- Do all users feel comfortable on the system?
- Have the users considered all possible different scenarios? Have they worked through all the different scenarios that occur while performing their daily functions?
- Do they understand how they carry out their day-to-day functions after the system is up and running?
- Have new process flows been created for all functional areas?
- Will all pertinent processes relating to their jobs be processed properly in the new system?
- Are they comfortable with the way the different processes flow through the new system?
- Have all reports (system-generated and manual) currently used to run the business—both management reports and reports utilized by the users—been collected?
- Will all current reports that were identified as crucial be available in the new system? If not, have you identified from where the information will come?

Training of Management Team

Management must not be forgotten in this process. They do not do any of the day-to-day functions on the system, but they must be aware of how they receive the information that's required to perform their functions. They must feel confident enough to navigate through the various sessions they require access to on the system.

Management tends to keep at arms' length during the users' training. It is important to always keep them informed of what decisions are being made. Make time to assure that they have had the proper training, so that they can move through the system comfortably.

> **CAUTION**
>
> If you wait until just before the implementation date to get management involved, you could find that they have many concerns that have not yet been addressed. This could push back your implementation date.

The management-training checklist includes:

- Have they agreed to the data integrity and the controls that will be implemented?
- Does management have any particular issues that have not come up during the training of the users?
- Have they seen and signed off on all reports that they will be receiving from the system?
- Are there any other reports that they were expecting to get that they have not yet seen? If so, is there somewhere in the system that this information can be found?

Planning the Simulation Process

The simulation process occurs throughout the project. Testing and simulations are carried out by all users. The testing and simulation process allows all users to ensure that the software is functioning the way they expect it to. It is also to ensure that all the business processes flow through the system properly.

Simulating for Key Users

Key users test and simulate processes in the system, so that they can ensure that all tables, master data, and parameters have been set up correctly. It is imperative that extensive testing be done during this stage. It is essential that the key users test to ensure that the most effective flow is used for each of the functions within the company.

N O T E There are sometimes different ways a process can be handled in the system. It is the key users' responsibility to find the shortest possible process.

All modules must be learned and tested, so that they can, in turn, train the end users. Training the end users should not begin until all areas of the system have been tested and you are sure that the system can handle all the processes properly.

After the key users have completed their testing, they simulate the processes in the system for the end users. This simulation introduces the end users to the system. It enables them to see how the system will enhance their day-to-day jobs. It is generally the first time the end users see what the system looks like and what the system can do for them.

Key users use the process flows per functional area to aid in user menu creation. It is imperative that proper security be set up within the system. Data integrity is one of the most important issues of any system and company.

Proper security is achieved through user menus. Set up a grid of all sessions and subsessions that exist in the system per module. Decide per user or user group which sessions and subsessions they have access to. Everyone can have access to display and print sessions. It is the maintain sessions that must be looked at very carefully to ensure that a particular user cannot gain access to any maintenance screens at which they should not be.

Particular attention should be paid to common data files and integration tables. These files should be accessed by only a couple of people within the organization. Logistics tables, financial tables, and all parameter files should be accessed only by key users. These tables stipulate how the system functions. End users should never have access to these files. When the menus have been created, key users test to determine that data integrity and all controls have been maintained properly.

The testing and simulating processes checklist should include:

- Have all tables, master data, and parameters been set up correctly?
- Has the most effective flow been obtained for all functions?
- Does the system handle all the processes properly?
- Will the system fit with how the company wants to operate?
- Have user menus been set up?
- Is there proper data integrity?
- Have all controls been maintained properly?

Simulating for End Users

The end users cannot go directly from training into a live environment. Practice makes perfect. They become comfortable on the system if they spend at least a couple of hours a day on the system. They must now do their own testing and simulating in the system.

Understanding the Baan Simulation Process

The methodology proposed by Baan has been proven successful over the years. The simulation process has been broken down into three major events, all of which have specific objectives in order for successful implementation. The simulation process is so important in a Baan implementation that the target methodology is based around the work needed for the three simulations proposed.

Performing Sim I

The simulation to be performed during Sim I should allow the key user team to understand the functionality of the Baan system—not to focus on the corporation's business process. This simulation can be lead by consultants and is a walkthrough of all the components to be used in the Baan software. It is preferable to use representative data for this exercise. Try to use valuable information to simulate; you may lose participants' interest if you talk about chairs and tables instead of your data elements.

The implementation team should have a clear understanding of Baan after Sim I is complete.

Performing Sim II

During Sim II, it is important to introduce all the corporation's business processes and demonstrate that the Baan software has been configured, or even customized, to meet all the business requirements. This simulation must be lead by the key users teams and must include all the external elements ready, such as customizations and interfaces. This simulation must also be done using data elements that are representative of the company database.

The implementation team should know how Baan software will be used at their site after Sim II is completed.

Performing Sim III

Sim III is a complete simulation of the use of the Baan software, including the customizations and the use of any interfaces required. This is a final check on all the implementation components. It is important that all elements are considered completed and approved by the implementation team.

Following Sim III is the time when the implementation team is in a position to confirm that the implementation is completed successfully. That is also the time to perform the final audits before going live, or to fix any last minute problems; test again, and then do the final audits.

Reviewing the Simulation

It is important to discuss the results found and address any problems immediately after each simulation is done. You can perform a specific simulation for a specific element after the business process has been modified (or the software elements have been corrected) if a software element has not been simulated to your satisfaction. Include the simulation report in the project documentation. This is a document that indicates the status of your implementation at three critical stages. ●

Going Live

Day 1 and Beyond

Preparing to Go Live

Many companies have been shocked when they see that they have done a great job planning all their implementation, but face a wall when realizing that the very first days of using the system in a live environment also needs to be planned. This chapter helps you plan the first days of operations.

Just before going live, it is important to stop and evaluate the job done during implementation. The following sections help your project team assess where you stand right now. These sections also help you verify whether you're ready to go to the next step.

Considering the Cutover Process

There are many elements that you must consider when you are ready to go live with your systems—there isn't generally enough time to ensure that everything is reviewed. This chapter offers elements for review before your going live.

Developing the Cutover Checklist

Various elements must be included in your cutover checklist. It is strongly recommended that you not go live if any element of that list is not to your satisfaction. Do not sacrifice any important step in order to meet the go-live date—the price paid later may be high.

You have to develop your own cutover checklist. Here are some elements that you must include:

- All initial values have been entered in the system.
- Dynamic files have been converted and the contents have been verified.
- Every key user has been assigned a specific role and knows what is expected of him or her.
- A contingency plan has been drafted, which means you know what to do if you need to revert to your legacy system, or if you are without a computer system for a few days.
- Every task that can be produced in advance, such as printing shop floor work orders or printing accounts payable checks, has been done in your legacy system to reduce everybody's workload during the first days of operation.
- Proper support procedures are in place, and the users know who to contact in case of a problem.
- A global cutover system check has been done.
- Transfer of ownership regarding the system has been agreed to by the different departments using Baan.
- An implementation project audit has been performed.

Remembering the Human Element

Do not underestimate the importance of the human element in the process of going live. Users have a tendency of forgetting months of training the very first day they go live with Baan software. Have your team of consultants and key user teams brainstorm about what can go wrong and add those elements to your cutover checklist. Have your project team speak with the greatest number of users possible, and ensure that everyone knows that you are there to support them and that everything has been planned.

Performing the Post-Review Process

You must also perform some more verifications when you are operating live in order to complement the cutover procedures. The post-review is completed on the business and project processes. It supports the process of continuous improvements and sets the stage for future projects through the measurement of benefits.

Obtaining User Feedback

Collect feedback from the customers when conducting the post-project review to ensure that you understand their perception of the project's success. This can be obtained from the continuous improvement process implemented with the system, surveys distributed to the customer community, and interviews with different people involved with any aspect of the final solution. Be sure to include a wide cross section of people with different responsibilities.

N O T E Allow people the opportunity to provide their feedback without any fear or discomfort. ■

Communicate all outstanding business issues to the vendor. Ensure that they are included in the next release of the vendor's product. Feedback analysis is the deliverable from this step.

Reconfirming the Business Model

Confirm that the existing business model reflects the actual process. Graphical representation of the business process is the deliverable from this step.

Highlight any differences made to the business process. Some project teams may lack the interest in completing this step. Because every business process intersects other business processes, it is beneficial to the organization to keep the model up-to-date.

Reviewing Timing

This step's purpose is to verify whether the project met the original business expectations. The set of measurements with regards to the project and the delivery of the selected solution is the deliverable from this step.

Part

V

Ch

32

The time line is an estimate of the proposed project's duration. It is a major component when determining the total project costs. The time line is also used to determine whether adequate resources are available to complete the required work. If the date can be stated, do so. Otherwise, suggest a range of dates. For example, 18 to 24 months.

 T I P Provide a rough schedule, if available. Identify the major milestones and deliverables in the schedule.

Using the Baan Methodology

Baan offers various tools to measure the progress of an implementation. Those tools can be used to plan system optimization. A project configurator program is available; this program generates your project plan, as well as analysis of the effort required to implement Baan in accordance with the target methodology.

The *target methodology* breaks down the implementation in three specific segments: mapping, piloting, and migrating. Baan-drafted reports such as activity, schedule, and responsibility charts can be used to measure the implementation's progress. The project plan is the ultimate tool for measuring the implementation's progress, as well as confirming that all tasks have been completed. The target methodology-generated project plan must be updated and distributed to all team members during the project. A review of all tasks must be done at every project milestone to ensure that no tasks have been forgotten or are incomplete, according to project team satisfaction.

Measuring Performance

This step's purpose is to confirm that business has been improved. The intention is to monitor the effect of the project completion on the business. The comparison of the business performance since the beginning of the project is the deliverable from this step.

State, in dollar values, the expected cost of conducting this project. Include all costs, both direct and indirect, such as personnel, hardware, software, outside services, overhead, and travel and living expenses. Be sure to include the elements that form part of an AR and the long- and short-term business plans and departmental expenses.

Specify the costs of ongoing support. It may not be possible to specify this in dollars. When this is the case, describe the expected resources. This helps set management expectations and commitment. Include the benefits of completing this project, both hard and soft, in dollar values where possible.

Be as precise as possible when preparing these calculations. Provide background material and assumptions to support the results.

N O T E The business case, project objective, project description, estimate of costs, and benefits are typically combined into one document. ■

Performing the Quality Assurance Check

The quality assurance check is an overall project review. A report to the steering committee and management is the deliverable from this stage. This step accomplishes the following:

- Review all steps to ensure they were completed properly.
- Confirm that scope, requirements, and assumptions from all previous phases are valid.
- Verify that all identified risks and issues are resolved.

If any of these items are not satisfactory, escalate this matter to the appropriate management level.

An appointed auditor should perform the quality assurance check. This individual should not be a member of the project team and should perform the following tasks:

- Verify that anything changed from previous steps has been documented, approved, and managed through appropriate change control procedures. Objectives, assumptions, organization, project team make-up, and impact on the business are examples.
- Suggest ways to eliminate or reduce any risk identified in the quality assurance check.
- Verify that the open issues are identified and tracked.
- Recommend whether to proceed to the next phase based on the completion of all deliverables required for passing through the next step.
- Escalate to appropriate management level if the project team does not address a critical issue.

Reporting to Steering Committee

The report summarizes the project's success or failure. A report to the steering committee or to your company's management team (if no specific steering committee has been established) is the deliverable from this step.

The report describes the strengths and weaknesses of the implemented solution. It shows the impact on the business in quantitative terms. It should also describe how the business process and the solution delivery process can be improved. Examine whether the measurements were sufficient. Describe how improvements from this point on can be measured.

Upon presentation of this report, either the steering committee or the management team should give the go-ahead or ask for a revision of a specific part of the project. If you don't get a clear decision, immediately state that is imperative to act quickly in order to keep the team's morale up; your colleagues have been investing a lot to get you at your current point. Don't hesitate to give the true picture. Don't jeopardize the start-up by not being ready if you need more time to implement.

Finding Solutions to Users Problems

Solving Problems

Users require assistance from the Information Systems Department during Baan's implementation—and even more so when going live. Baan wrote one application that helps you monitor the database. This chapter shows you an approach to solving users problems and some tools that can be used in Baan, in the tools, and in UNIX to solve problems.

Solving problems is a science that requires a lot of patience, imagination, and a lot of discipline. The following sections contain tips on how to approach any situation and discussion about certain tools available to monitor or fix problems.

Approaching Problems

Different situations occur during your implementation and when you go live. The best approach to handling problem situations is to instate a disciplined process and prioritize the problems arising. Educate your users on how to report a problem. They may be very helpful in solving problems when there is a recurring situation. It is easier to solve the problem if you receive a well-documented report on a situation.

Using a Disciplined Approach

Every situation reported by users should be well documented. A similar problem may occur at a later point and another member of your staff may have to search for a solution again if you don't document the present situation.

If possible, use a database to categorize all problems. This could be done through Baan if you create a table that can be maintained and printed in various ways. This has the advantage of being accessible to every user.

 TIP Instruct your users to always include print screens and as much documentation as possible when they report a situation to you. This saves time and eases the work of finding a solution.

Using Logical Steps

You need to have a logical approach whenever a problem is reported by a user. You save a lot of time if you have a methodical approach. Problems have often been seen before or are due to a simple mistake from the users. By considering the possible problem factors listed here, you have a proper and thorough method of identifying the problems; you also find some hints on how to get a fast resolution.

When you are facing a problem you should have those steps in mind:

1. Is this due to a mismanipulation of the data?
2. Is it a problem with a physical file? Is there any problem with the database?
3. Take a look at the data using general table maintenance.

4. Run the program in the Debugger mode if possible.

5. Re-create the situation in a test environment.

6. Report the situation to the Baan International Support Center if no solution is found.

7. Log the solution used in a database for future reference.

Performing Table Maintenance

The table maintenance program created by Baan is a very powerful tool designed to help system administrators either monitor what data is stored in a file or manipulate a portion of a table. Using this function is very dangerous. Manipulating your data improperly could seriously damage your installation.

> **CAUTION**
>
> No user—aside from those authorized by the System Administrator—should use this program.

Be very careful when using the Table Maintenance function. Data could be easily corrupted and reindexing files might be a lengthy task, depending on the size of your tables.

Using the Table Maintenance Password

The table maintenance program is protected by a password. Nobody should get this password unless they have sufficient knowledge of performing basic operations with this program. To change the password, go to Tools, Database Maintenance; then select the Change Password for General Table Maintenance function.

N O T E The System Administrator should modify the password on a periodic basis to ensure integrity of the system. ■

Part
V

Ch
33

Starting the Table Maintenance Program

There are two ways to get to the table maintenance program. The first is to call this option from the Database Maintenance menu in the Tools menu. This program can also be called directly from any menu by performing the following steps:

1. Click on File.

2. Click on Run Program.

3. Type **ttaad4100** for the program name.

4. Ensure that the External Program field is not checked.

5. Click on Run Program.

6. Supply the database maintenance program password.

The Table Maintenance screen appears. There are three fields on the header screen (see Figure 33.1). You must select the appropriate table by filling selection fields, which are listed in Table 33.1.

FIG. 33.1

The Table Maintenance screen allows you to choose which tables to maintain.

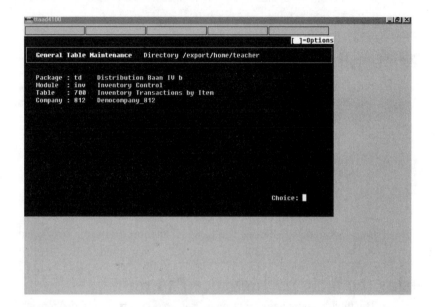

Table 33.1 Selection Fields for Table Maintenance Program

Field Name	Description
Package	Two letters representing the package. Process will be ps, distribution will be td, manufacturing will be ti, and so on. If you want a full list of the available packages, press Ctrl+Z to zoom.
Module	Modules are Business objects or portions of packages. Accounts payable is acp, common data files are under com. Press Ctrl+Z to get a full listing of the modules.
Table	You have to supply the table number for the tables with which you want to work. The item master will be 001 and the customer master is 010. The same number can be used in different modules. Press Ctrl+Z to see all the available files on the module you selected.
Company	Supply the company number, which could be the number of your test company or your production company. Files are different from one company to the other, unless they are merged using options in Tools. If you want to work with common files used by the Tools modules, or some parameters tables such as company numbers, you must specify company 000.

When you have selected the file, the cursor comes back at Choice. All the descriptions are posted next to each field if you selected a valid file. If not, you cannot get access to the file. If this is the case, revise all your selections. If you still can't access the files, contact your System Administrator to find the name of the table you want to manipulate.

If you get the error message—"File not present, Allocate Yes or No?"—answer N for No and exit. By replying Yes, you create another version of this file. You should contact your System Administrator if you get this message.

Viewing the Data

After you pass the header section, you see the first page of the detail screens. If your file has many fields, you find more than one page. Use the right and left arrows to move from one page to the other.

You can navigate using a menu in the detail screen. Simply press the Spacebar to start this menu. The various sections of this menu are shown in Table 33.2.

Table 33.2   Table Maintenance

Menu Choice	Description
Control	Allows you to print the report, to save the file, and to exit.
Browse	You find commands to find a record or to move from one record to the other. You can also change the index's order to use a different sort order.
Modify	You find all the commands to insert, copy, edit, and delete records. You can even use a global delete option.
Forms	You may choose which form to use to manipulate your data.
Miscellaneous	You find a Print Screen option and a prompt that lets you access the operating system and an option to extend fields.
?	Access to help information.
Application	There are commands whose descriptions follow.

Part
V

Ch
33

Viewing and Using Options

You can type 0 at the choice prompt to view how many records there are in the file. You see a pop-up window that indicates the number of rows in the file. Each row is equivalent to a record. This window also indicates the number of indexes on that file, if you can modify the current index, and if that index is allowing duplicates or not.

The other options available at the choice prompt include:

1. Copy Rows
2. Export Data

3. Import Data

4. Count Rows

5. Modify Rows

6. Remove Rows

Using Mass Replace

It is possible to mass replace in a field if you need to modify the value of one field in many records.

1. Press the Spacebar to activate the menu.

2. Select the Application function.

3. Select Modify Row.

4. Select the name of the field to be modified.

5. Enter the selection criteria for the mass replace. Only index fields are to be selected.

6. Enter the new value for that field.

7. Confirm by answering Yes to the OK? prompt.

All the fields within the specified range will be modified. If you want to act on part of the file that you cannot delimit using fields in the indexes, then you have to proceed through a script in the Tools menu.

Using the Debugger

Running a program in the Debugger mode can be helpful for finding out what is happening to data manipulated by users. For that, you need to compile the script of the program with the Debugger mode. You should not perform this task if you are not familiar with programming; have a tools specialist perform this task for you, and then use the debugger version of your program following the steps described in the next section.

Running the Debugger

The first time you see a program compiled with the Debugger option, you face a much different screen than usual. The debugger shows you every line of code used in the program as you run the program. You can trace the values of certain variables as you run a session. You may also set flags or break points to tell the system to stop at a certain stage in your program.

When you want to diagnosis a problem using the debugger, first identify all the variables involved in the session and trace the most valuable ones. If possible, set break points at meaningful steps during execution of the program. When you have set up your break point, type **c** at the prompt line to move to the next break point; otherwise type **s** to go the next instruction.

Using the Debugger Commands

Table 33.3 contains a list of the most useful commands in the Debugger mode. These commands are to be typed at the prompt line at the top-left corner of the screen. Figure 33.2 shows an example of a variable being traced.

Table 33.3   Debugger Commands

Debugger Command	Description
b [line number]	Create a break point at the specified line number.
c	Continue until next break point.
d [line number]	Delete break point.
t [field name]	Trace variables to trace the value of the item code: t tiitm001.item.
s	Skip to next instruction.
slow [number]	Slow down the rate of instructions displayed on screen.
stop if [expression]	Stop the program when the expression is true.
variable := [value]	Assign a specific value to a variable.
<Ctrl> D	Page-down command for source code.
<Arrow Up>	Go down the source code by one line.
<Arrow Down>	Go up the source code by one line.
q	Quit and end program. This is not recommended. The program should always perform normal termination.

Part
V

Ch
33

Getting Help Using UNIX

Because UNIX is the most popular operating software for Baan, it is important to be able to manipulate Baan in the UNIX environment. The following sections discuss some UNIX commands that you should know.

Using UNIX Commands

UNIX is a very powerful operating system with many commands. Table 33.4 lists some commands that may be useful. Perform the following steps to run UNIX from the Baan GUI menu:

1. Click on the Option Dialog task bar.
2. Click on Start Shell.
3. Type the UNIX command.

FIG. 33.2

Type **t**, followed by the variable name, to trace the item code in a program.

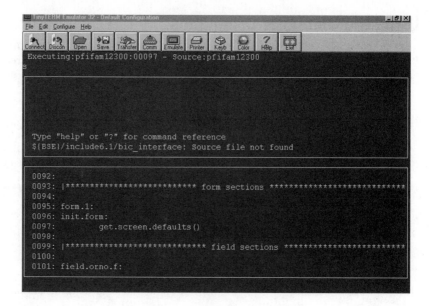

4. Type **exit** when you're done and want to return to Baan.

Table 33.4   Useful UNIX Commands in the Baan Environment

UNIX Command	Description
bdf	Check the available capacity of the different disks.
grep	Filter command to be added to other command to select a range.
lp	This command queues files for printing. You may want to print log files.
kill	Terminate running process.
ps	Find running processes status. This is used to determine who is running a job.
rm [*file*]	Remove file.
who	List all the active users on the system.

Killing a Session

Killing a session is one of the most frequent tasks performed by a system operator. Terminating a job involves:

1. Go to UNIX.

2. Type ps -ef|grep {*username*}.

3. Locate the process ID of the bshell session. bshell is the program that runs Baan.

4. Type kill {*process ID*}.

5. Type ps -ef|grep {*username*} to confirm that the job has been terminated.

Be careful when killing tasks. You can severely damage your installation or even shut down the Baan environment if you kill the wrong tasks.

Removing Files

You don't have to be told that removing files is very dangerous; this should be done with a lot of caution. There is one Baan-created file that must be removed from your system when the user doesn't log out properly. This file is named Core and eats up a lot of space on your disks.

N O T E   You should scan your disks often to find all the core files and delete them.

Do the following at the UNIX prompt to find and remove the core files:

1. Find core /*. This gives you a listing of all the core files on your system.

2. Find rm /{path}/core.

3. Find core/* to ensure that all core files have been deleted.

Reporting a Problem to Baan

There will be situations where you cannot find solutions to problems. You have to seek help from Baan when that is the case. The process is to send a form to the International Support Center nearest you; they will provide assistance.

Contacting the Support Center

Baan needs your help to speed the problem resolution process. Always have the following information available when you contact them to report a situation:

- Your customer number.
- Name of the person within your organization to contacted.
- The product where the problems occurred. The *product* is a combination of the package, the version of Baan, and the release number.

The phone number for the Support Center in North America is 1-800-925-2226.

N O T E   After you contact the Support Center, you receive a log number for your call. Always keep this number to refer to your problem when you contact Baan for follow-up on your problem.

Filling the Support Request

Filling the request form for faxing is another way to report your problem to the Support Center. When you complete the form shown in Figure 33.3, ensure that you fill all the fields of the header section. Specify what kind of problem you have. Baan also asks you about the status of your installation and if you feel that this problem is due to a customization. If this is due to a customization, you may gain time by contacting the third-party provider who did the customization; it is difficult for Baan to fix such a problem.

FIG. 33.3

The Problem Call form must be filled in a very detailed manner in order to expedite the support process.

BAAN INTERNATIONAL SERVICE CENTER
Problem Call Form

TELEPHONE 1-800-925-2226	Response Center	FACSIMILE (616) 942-8167

CUSTOMER:	Customer ABC	
ADDRESS:	10 Main Street	TELEPHONE NO: 112-555-5555
CITY:	Windsor	FACSIMILE NO: 112-555-5556
STATE/PROVINCE:	MD	MODEM NO:
ZIP CODE:	J1S 1S5	SYSTEM ADMINISTRATOR:
CUSTOMER NO:	309047	PROJECT LEADER:
LOCATION NO:	1	

DATE: 07/16/1996   CUSTOMER TRACKING NO:
TIME: 12h00
CONTACT PERSON:

KIND OF REPORT	SITUATION	INSTALLATION STATUS	TYPE of ERROR	CUSTOMIZATION
❑ system error	❑ not workable	❑ operational	❑ 10-System Standstill	❑ yes
❑ question	❑ reduced but workable	❑ testing	❑ 20-Major	❑ no
❑ special request	❑ can work around	❑ implementing	❑ 30-Minor	**REPRODUCIBLE**
❑ refer to previous call	❑ workable		❑ 40-Question	❑ yes ❑ no

Baan/Triton **VERSION** ❑ 2.0   ❑ 2.1   ❑ 2.2   ❑ 3.0   ❑ 3.1   ❑ 4.0   **RELEASE** ❑ a ❑ b ❑ c ❑ d

SESSION: tdilc0101m000 Maintain Lots

DESCRIPTION OF THE PROBLEM: As per a call entered last week, the system does not increment the lot numbers entered on the same date (the lot id structure has the dd/mm/yy as a prefix). If you try to create two lots on the same day, the system will display the message "Record already exists" for the second entry. See attached screen prints.

OPERATIONAL CONSEQUENCE: _____

Your form should contain a very detailed description of the problem; to demonstrate the problem, print screens should accompany this. The more details your provide, the faster you get a solution.

When completed, fax your form to the Baan Support Center nearest you. You receive a confirmation containing the log number for your call. The fax number for North America is 616-942-8167. ●

PART VI

Appendixes

Samples of Customization

Creating Your Own File

The next paragraphs guide you in the creation of your own customization. You learn how to create a table, how to generate a session to maintain that table, and the steps required to build a report.

> **CAUTION**
>
> The following steps should be performed by authorized users only. Ensure that you have proper access to the development tools with your Information System Department.

Creating a Table

This section details the process to creating a table. You can change the name of the fields to suit your own needs.

1. Go to the Tools menu.
2. Go to Applications Development.
3. Go to Maintain Domains and Tables.
4. Select Maintain Tables.
5. Click the Insert icon to create a new table.
6. Enter the module code (for example, **tdsls** for Sales module).
7. Select a three-digit number for your new table (you use 950 for this example).
8. Enter the file description.
9. Enter your username as the table's designer.

Creating the Fields

After this information is entered, click the Fields icon to access the field section. Follow these steps to create the fields:

1. Click the Insert icon to insert a new field on your table.
2. Enter an incremental number for field (for example, 1...2...3...4...).
3. Enter the field name. Eight alphanumeric characters are allowed.
4. If the field is a combined field, check the check box for this field.

   Combined fields are fields that consist of one or more fields already defined in the table. They are particularly useful when two or more fields combined need to be referenced to another table. For example, a table containing Year and Period might need to refer to another table also containing Year and Period.

5. Enter the domain that should be linked to this field. The domain is directly linked to the data dictionary. You can zoom and have two options:
   - The Display option lets you mark one of your choices and brings it back in the session.
   - The Maintain option lets you add a new domain.

6. Enter the description. It can be entered in different languages. The default is the user language. Runtime uses this description for:
   - Displaying above Help screens
   - Automatic form generation
   - Display on menus for text fields
   - Field descriptions in generated user documentation

7. Select whether the field should be active.

   You can make a field inactive with this attribute. By default a field is active. Non-active fields are physically not stored in the record. On form and script, you can use it for temporary or for future capabilities.

8. Enter the array depth for the field. By default, the array depth is 1. This is useful when you want 1 field for 12 periods. The array depth must be 12.

9. Enter the field's initial value. This is the default that can be stored at the moment you add a new record. Enumerated fields can also be defined by typing the set constant name.

10. Specify whether this field should contain blanks. If mandatory input is set to yes, a null value is not allowed (empty string or value zero). A message appears and the record can't be updated.

11. Enter the field name from another table you want to use as the reference. This can be used to create relations between different database tables.

12. Enter the reference mode. There are three modes for references:
    - Mandatory—The reference should be existing on the reference table.
    - Mandatory Unless Empty—Similar to Mandatory, but no check is done if the field is empty.
    - Not Mandatory—No check is done.

The belonging error message is given a reference message if a reference does not exist.

Create the fields listed in Table A.1 using the steps that you just learned. This sample table allows you to record special pricing by customer and item. Figure A.1 shows what your screen should look like while adding these fields.

Table A.1   Sample Table

Field	Description	Domain
Cuno	Customer	tccuno
Item	Item code	tcitem
Pric	Price	tcpric
Date	Date	tcdate

FIG. A.1

This screen details how to create the four fields that your table contains.

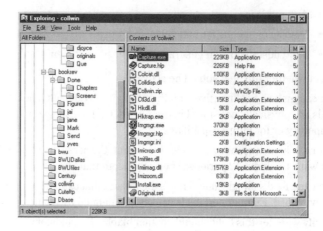

Creating the Index

You need to create an index for this table after the table and the table fields are created. The first index is the primary index. More indexes can be created based on how the user wants to access the data.

Because you store the pricing data per customer and item, the primary index is customer and item in this example. Complete the following steps:

1. Click the Index button.
2. Enter the index's description.
3. Enter the fields that are in the index.

You have just created the definitions for the table. To finally use the table, it has to be converted to runtime and the physical table needs to be created.

At the end, the user should know how to:

- Create a table.
- Create the table fields.

- Create the index for the table.
- Convert to runtime for the table created.
- Create the table physically in the database.

Generating Sessions

A *session* is the program that allows you to maintain or display the information about a table. In this example, you create a session to maintain the table created in the first section.

You need to create the table first or use an existing table in order to generate a session. This is a very effective way to start a program. You can generate the session, and then do the changes necessary to customize to your needs.

Creating the Session

Certain Baan naming conventions should be followed very strictly while creating session names. This ensures uniformity throughout Baan. You should also be careful not to overwrite an existing session. This is controlled by a *parameter*. You don't normally have authorization to change the standard program that Baan provides. Your session is generated in your current package VRC.

Enter the code for your new session. The standards used in Baan for coding/naming sessions for an example of a standard Baan session tdsls4101m000 include:

Position 1-2—td is the package

Position 3-5—sls is the module

Position 6—unique to differentiate the session

Position 7—indicates the type of session:

1 = Maintain

2 = Update

4 = Print session

5 = Display session

7 = Charts

Position 8-9—unique to differentiate the session

Position 10—m for a Main session or a s for a subsession

Position 11-13—can be used to differentiate the session, although it is used sparingly in standard Baan

If you enter an existing session, the system brings all the default. Check the value in the Replace field to make sure that you don't overwrite the session components (session/ forms/program scripts). If you want to overwrite the existing data, make sure that you either check this box or choose Yes.

Using the Session Generator

The session generator is an easy and simple way of generating a framework to develop sessions. After the basic framework is provided, further validations and complex processing can be built into the session.

No programming is needed for a simple maintain session. The generator can create the session, the forms, and the reports to add, delete, modify, and print the data.

You can generate the session based on the kind of requirement you have. If you are generating an update session without any report, you can exclude the report generation. Give the user a selection criteria and so on if you are creating a session for printing a report.

The fields listed in Table A.2 and Table A.3 need to be entered in order to generate the session for your table. The session is always generated for the user's current package VRC. Ensure that you are in the correct VRC. Figure A.2 shows what your screen should look like while adding these fields.

FIG. A.2

Using the Session Generator saves a lot of steps when creating sessions.

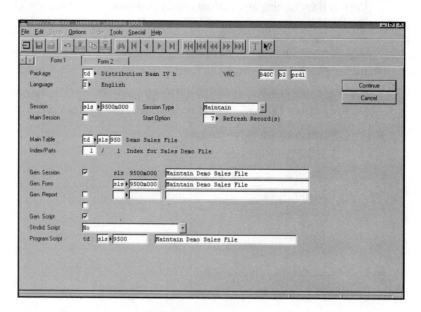

Table A.2   Form 1—Session Generator Fields

Fields	Description
Package	The user's current package
VRC	The user's current VRC
Language	The user's language
Session	The session name per the Baan standard

Fields	Description
Session Type	Whether it is maintain/display or print session
Main Session	Main or a subsession; subsessions are always used when they are not executed directly, but from within a session
Start Option	The option that needs to be executed as soon as the session is started; the start option is Modify Data as a standard for all print or update sessions Main Table; the main table for your session; data for the main table can be maintained/displayed using the session
Index	This index is used by the standard program to display/maintain the main table data; key fields in this index are used to browse the main table's data
Session, Report, and Form	If you enter Yes, the system creates forms, report, and session for you
Generate Script	If you enter Yes, the system generates a program script; user can then add extra validation/processing in the script

Table A.3   Form 2—Session Generator Fields

Fields	Description
Form Type	Type 1—Generates single occurrence on main table Type 2—Generates multi-occurrence on main table Type 3—Generates multi-occurrence with a view Type 4—Generates a form with, from, and to for each key part of the chosen index; this is used basically for print and processing (update) sessions
Maintain Session	If Yes, then add, modify, and delete choices are switched.
Transparent Box	No—Normal graphics lines Yes—Box is transparent
Column	The width of your screen
Rows	The height of the form
Report Type	Type 1—Single occurrence records in the report Type 2—Multiple occurrence records in the report Type 3—Multiple occurrence with a View field Type A—With highest sort order; these viewparts are used for large groups Type B—They have lowest sort order; these viewparts are used for small groups

Click Special, Selecting, and Ordering Fields to select the your main table's fields that you want to generate on Maintain, Display, or Report. All fields of the main table are selected if you do not specify the fields.

To generate the report, click Special, Continue; Baan generates the session for you.

Running the Program

A session can be run in different ways:

- From a menu option
- As a zoom session from within a session
- From the File-Run option

If the Run Session option is set to Yes, the system runs the session after generating the session.

Do the following to run your session externally:

1. Click File.
2. Click Run Program.
3. Enter the session number you generated.
4. Click OK.

At the end of this exercise the user should be able to do the following:

- Generate a session.
- Understand the different types of sessions.
- Run the session.

Here are some tips to keep in mind:

- Ensure that your current package VRC is correct before starting to generate the session.
- Identify the session characteristics (name, main/subsession) before starting.
- Check out the Replace field in the second form. This overwrites the existing session/forms/reports and the scripts.
- Select and order the fields from the main table using the Special option.
- Check out the column size if there are too many fields that cannot fit into the form. (For example, item code and description, when used in a multi-occurrence form, might exceed the form column size.)

Keep in mind that it is also possible to incorporate this session in an existing menu. ●

Understanding Baan BackOffice

Introducing the New Baan BackOffice

Baan is introducing a new format for its product. This is the same software used in UNIX environments, but Baan uses a different platform: Microsoft BackOffice. In addition to the original Baan functionality, you find interesting additions that use the capabilities of the BackOffice environment.

Running Baan on a PC and installing it from a CD-ROM is something that is unbelievable for the experienced user. With the newest technology on the market, Baan succeeded in developing a version of its product that can be installed easily from a CD.

Baan built its reputation by being very proactive and at the edge of technology change. It is proven here with the release of the product's BackOffice version. The next paragraphs outline the main additions you find in that release.

N O T E If you want to find more about the BackOffice environment, visit the three following Web sites:

Microsoft **www.microsoft.com/backoffice**

BackOffice Magazine **www.backoffice.com**

Microsoft BackOffice User Group **www.msboug.org**

Getting a Windows NT Version

The first release is Baan IV Release a1; it will be updated at a later point to b and c. Release a1 contains the major localizations required in various areas of the world. The first release is available in English only. Baan uses SQL Server 6.5 to speed database access and conform to the industry norms. The BackOffice version is a Baan Release 4, which operates using the new Microsoft BackOffice environment within the Windows NT operating software. Baan takes advantage of this new technology and is able to link its application to the Internet; it also uses Windows NT's powerful capabilities. That means the user can install Baan on a PC as easily any other PC software that can be bought at a computer store.

Integrating with Microsoft BackOffice

The new version takes advantage of the Microsoft GUI for presentation. Obviously, the ASCII version is not supported in this release. Users on a UNIX platform see that it finds its way easily in the BackOffice release—most of the screens are identical. One nice advantage at the user level is the use of a local Windows printer, as well as the use of the Notepad as a text editor (instead of the UNIX vi editor that is unappreciated by most users).

The Microsoft BackOffice products are a suite of products designed to take advantage of the Windows NT environment and the client/server approach. Merging the traditional database environment and the newest information networks such as the Internet and the private corporation intranets, BackOffice is designed to consolidate all information on a common Windows NT platform.

Running BackOffice

You need a PC with at least the following configuration in order to run Baan BackOffice:

- Pentium 100MHZ or Pentium 133MHZ
- Minimum storage place required is 3GB
- 64 MB of active memory

Except for the storage required, this is the configuration of the average PC used currently in the industry. You also need to operate under Windows NT version 4.0 or higher.

Because this release is new, it is inadvisable to underestimate the requirements of a system you need to run the software. Make sure you exceed the requirements from the manufacturer.

N O T E   Because of the functions available under Windows NT, Baan is able to provide better Help documentation and training tools that go with this release. A separate CD-ROM is available to demonstrate the capabilities of the BackOffice release. ▪

Opening Up to the World

Opening the Baan package to the Internet is giving users a window to the world. With all the interaction between Baan and the Internet, the possibilities are endless.

You also find the Safari Report Writer and The Enterprise Modeler tools bundled in the BackOffice version. Those two packages are similar to the version you find in the UNIX version of Baan IV.

Using Internet Access

It is possible to link with the Internet using Baan under the BackOffice umbrella. Some of the basic functions have been redesigned, making those links with the outside world possible. The specific areas in which a link has been created include:

- Customer and supplier lookup and update
- Employee lookup and display
- Item lookup and display
- Product configurator lookup and display
- MPS availability display
- Order status display
- Sales information tables and graph
- Multisite inventory by item, company, and warehouse

When using Baan BackOffice, users can extract information using their regular Internet browsers. The software can create Java applets to request information. Dynamic Link Libraries

(DLLs) are supported, as well the capability to work in conjunction with the Baan Bshell, which is the software's operating environment. Even though the software is linked to the Internet, the regular version's security rules apply.

Using Safari Report Writer

The BackOffice Baan version of the software is sold with the UDMS Safari Report Writer. This is a report writer package that runs on a PC and it extracts valuable information from the Baan database and presents it in a format easy for users to manipulate. Many installations on UNIX mainframes are using such tools with their Baan applications. When using such a product, you give your users access to all the information they need as well as the means to present it in a way that suits them best.

Safari is a user-friendly tool that is integrated with all the available drivers for the various databases used with Baan. Sold with the BackOffice version, the Safari Report Writer is shipped on a different CD and requires installation to Baan BackOffice first.

Using Enterprise Modeling

The concept of Enterprise Modeling is also found in Baan BackOffice. *Enterprise Modeling* is a concept in which the software gives the users the flexibility to configure and adapt the software to their specific needs.

The Enterprise Modeling models found in Baan BackOffice follow:

- Assemble-To-Order
- Finance
- Project industries

Those models will have been developed with the help of Baan customers and experts in their respective industries. They are, in fact, a representation of the business processes in various industries.

The users must also find different functionalities, such as:

- Enterprise Modeling Wizard tools
- Startup wizards
- Configuration or Modeling tools for Baan IV applications
- User-friendly wizards to set company-specific parameters
- Automated implementation processing based on wizard data

These tools facilitate the creation or the maintenance of all the information required to use the Enterprise Modeling tool. ●

Getting to Work in the Baan World

Getting an Education on Baan

Like many other environments, the world of Baan is a very interesting market to be in for computer specialists. Many of the key users of the original companies are now successful consultants in this area. There is a big shortage in this industry; this appendix will give you the best way to integrate into this market.

Obviously, the best place to get Baan education is to work for a company that already uses Baan. Most of the actual consultants in the industry have taken that route. If you are not already using this product in your daily functions, the other option is to get training though the Baan company.

Using the Baan Training Center

Baan has various training centers that will train you on the software. Various courses are offered. You can learn the basics of navigation or you can take a specialized course in tools programming. Many of the courses will have prerequisites, such as the self-navigation course or an introduction to a given module.

Some of those courses could be restricted to employees of companies using Baan or to employees of Alliance Partners. The amount you will invest in this education will pay back quickly.

Baan also offers training on CD-ROM; these courses were developed under a concept of Computer Base Training (CBT). These interactive courses are complete and are good alternatives to visiting Baan training centers. You can get the list of the available CBT packages at **www.baan.com/education**.

The Baan certification program recognizes that an individual has obtained a broad understanding of all packages within the Baan product. There are two levels of certification: basic and advanced. The basic certification recognizes that the student has a primary understanding of various packages of the software. Advanced certification recognizes that an individual has obtained a specific functional understanding of a particular package within the Baan software. Advanced certification tests are available in Enterprise Logistics, Enterprise Finance, Enterprise Tools, and Enterprise Modeler. Baan advanced certification is a requirement for Baan consulting and business partners.

All Baan core certification tests are administered through Sylvan Prometric's global network of Authorized Prometric Test Centers (APTC). Automated Certification Testing at Authorized Prometric Test Centers is now available in more than 1,700 locations worldwide.

You can contact the Baan Education Center at 1-800-925-2226. The schedule for the training courses can be found at **www.baan.com/education**.

Using the Baan Institute

In 1994, Baan innovated again by launching a new concept. It was a school where not only system applications were learned, but also the concept of business. Too often, individuals who wanted to integrate the implementation of business didn't master both aspects of the task. The

Baan Institute is an open, global knowledge center and expertise network for leaders who add strategic value by spanning the disciplines of business and information technology, and the art of organizational influence.

The Baan Business IT School is in Ede in the Netherlands. You can get additional information by contacting registration at +31(0) 318 696666. Obviously, once you obtain certification from this school your market value as a consultant will be increased. The Baan Institute Web site is found at **www.baan-institute.com**.

Knowing Your Options

Once you obtain the necessay knowledge and feel you can become a consultant, you have three options. You can create your own independent consulting firm, which is the route that many experienced consultants take. It would be a little bit easier to acquire more knowledge by working for an existing Baan partner. A third option is to apply for a position within the Baan company.

Profiling Consultants

Various elements will make a difference in regards to when a customer selects a consultant. This section details some of the aspects that individuals should consider before orienting his or her career path in this direction.

Because you cannot learn the entire software in a few weeks, it is better to specialize in a few areas at the beginning. The following sections detail the various areas to specialize in.

Knowing the Application

When it is time to give credentials to your potential employer, do not try to lure him or her by stating that you know all the applications. There is a handful of consultants who know this application completely. If you show that you master any part of the software, it will be more than likely that you will become very good at manipulating the other functions. Often you will be asked to answer some questions about the applications in your interview process. If you can't answer questions about every aspect of Baan after professing your complete knowledge of the software, you lose all credibility.

It is important that you show your ability to learn this application. Some customers cannot afford to hire a team of consultants to implement the package. You will be required to play with part of the software that you may never have touched before. In most cases, a consultant who masters one part of the software will be able to maneuver into other parts of the application. The problem that may arise is that the customer could be misled by his consultant if he doesn't investigate enough certain aspects of the functionality.

Knowing Business Practices

There is a philosophical debate here. Is it easier to teach good business practices to a programmer than it is to show an experienced business analyst how to implement a computer system.

The answer is that you need a person who is good at both processes. To be that person requires you to learn how the real world operates and how computers function.

Taking courses given by such organizations as APICS (American Procurement and Inventory Control Society) is a must if you are lacking business experience. Locate any association or university that could offer such courses and invest a few nights a week in building a long time career.

Being a Team Player

Joining a team that is implementing a computer solution will be demanding on your personal skills. There will be situations in which you will have to support people going through a lot of stress. You will also have to deal with individuals who are not thrilled by a change of systems and will slow this process until they realize that they don't have any other option than joining the project.

Make as many allies as you can in a project and don't turn anybody against you. You never know, in an implementation, when you will require assistance from a department or a specific employee, and you may regret not investing the proper time to introduce what you are doing and how you want that to get done. Many consultants did not have a long stay on some projects because users sensed that wouldn't be of any help to them and pressured management to look for somebody else. Usually a phone call is sufficient to boot a consultant off a project.

Becoming a Consultant

The best approach to becoming a consultant is to join an implementation team within an alliance partnership and work with senior implementers. Working with experienced individuals will help you acquire the necessary knowledge to work in this environment.

Applying for an Open Position

Prepare a résumé in which you state qualifications you think may be worth some interest. Don't hesitate to mention any knowledge of C software. This would indicate that learning the Baan tools would not require a long period of time.

Show also any business experience. If you have experience handling general ledger or handling bills of material you are an appealing candidate. Highlight the achievements you had in other projects. Successful candidates are always welcome in any organization.

Don't use the traditional format for your résumé. Use a format that is known as the résumé for a consultant. Figure C.1 is an example of this format.

Approaching Employers

You will have to convince the potential employer that you will be a good investment for him or her. If you are invited to an interview, show your enthusiasm and your willingness to join the environment. Mention that you are willing to work as a junior implementer until you gain the necessary credibility to become one of the best Baan implementers.

FIG. C.1

Example of a consultant resume.

Yves Perreault
Senior BAAN Project Manager

BAAN Implementation
Relevant Experience

- BAAN Application Manager for SE Technologies in San Jose, California,
  Yves is the Global Project Manager in the Flextronics International Implementation.
  This implementation project is for three sites— Guadalajara, Mexico;
  Karlskrona, Sweden; and San Jose, California— for a total of 500 users.

- Yves was the project Manager for the Phase I of the BAAN Implementation
  for the two Canadian Plants of the Sweetheart Cup Corporation in Toronto, Canada (Lily Cups, Inc.).
  His mandate was to implement 4 Modules— Purchasing, Location Control, Order Entry, and the
  Accounts Receivable Module. In parallel with this implementation, Yves was helping
  Sweetheart Cup in Baltimore in the installation of the BAAN Software.
  He was under contract with Quality Consultants Inc. of Atlanta.

- Also for Quality Consultants Inc., Yves was doing consulting work to help implement
  the BAAN Software at Noranda Aluminum in New Madrid, MO.

- Yves helped Americ Disc in Drummondville, QC, with their BAAN implement in the planning
  process as well as doing programming work to help them achieve their implementation plan.

- For 5 years, he was the Information Technology Manager at Wire Rope Industries, division of
  Noranda Inc. This was the first installation of the BAAN Software for this corporation; all the 35
  modules of release 2.0C were installed to replace 18 different existing software. Yves was responsible
  for user training, hardware implementation, and programming.

Positions Open at Baan

Because Baan is in constant growth, there is always a position available within the organization. The following are some of the types of positions that might be available:

- Sales
- Technical pre-sales
- Consulting services
- Product specialist
- Implementation specialist
- Account executive
- Software engineer

Table C.1 lists the main contacts for the Baan offices so you can send your résumé or inquire about open positions. You can also see all available positions on the Baan Web site at **www.baan.com** (see Figure C.2).

Table C.1 Baan Contacts

Baan Office	Address	Phone
Europe	P.O. Box 143, 3770 AC Barneveld, The Netherlands	+31 3420 28888
North America	4600 Bohannon Drive, Menlo Park, California, 94025 USA	(800) 644-4634
Latin America	1401 Ponce de Leon Blvd., 4th Floor, Coral Gables, Florida 33134	(305) 442-0034
Asia/Pacific	138 Cecil Street #13-03 Cecil Court, Singapore 0106, Singapore	+65 323 0162

FIG. C.2

Many positions are offered by Baan on their Internet site.

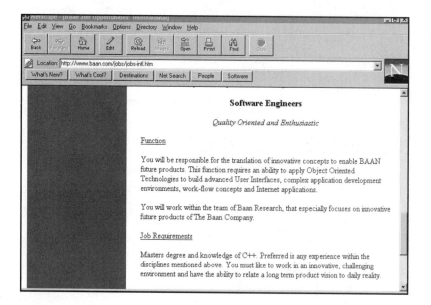

Other Companies Supporting Baan

Many companies are partners with Baan or operate in the Baan environment to support and implement the Baan solution at different customer sites. The following is a list of these partners:

Company

ADP GSI

Andersen Consulting

Arbor Software Corporation

BA Intelligence Networks

BDM Technologies

Berclain

Business Objects

Business@Web

Cap Gemini

CIMLINC

Compuware

Data General Corporation

Deloitte Touche Consulting

Digital Equipment Corporation

Disus Inc.

DP Consulting

Epic Data

Ernst & Young

FASTtech Integration

Grant Thornton

Han Dataport Benelux

Hewlett-Packard Company

HSO Business System

I2 Technologies

IBM Corporation

Information Builders

Information Services

Information System Management

Intel Corporation

Interactive Software

Intermec Corporation

JG Communication Ltd

ISM BC

KPMG

Leland Inc.

Mastech

Noblestar

NYMA Inc.

Oracle Corporation

Origin in Business Technology

Perot System

Pionner Standard Electronics

Premenos

Price Waterhouse

Process Technologies

Proloq

Quality Consultants Inc.

Resource Support Associates (RSA)

Richard Morton Co.

SE Technologies

Sequent Computer Systems

Solutions Consulting Inc.

Sterling Software

Sun Microsystems

Symbiotic Solutions

Syscom

Taxware International

Technology Solutions Inc.

Telxon Corporation

TRW

Unison Software

Vertex

Wilson Solutions

Getting a List of Companies that Use Baan

If you are not interested in the traveling that is required to be a Baan consultant, you might consider working for a company that uses the product and learn this software within your daily functions. Here are some tips on how to find a company that uses the products.

The easiest way to find which companies are using Baan is to use the Internet. Baan lists most of its largest customers on the Customer Page. You can see if one of these companies has a subsidiary in your area. The Baan Customer Page is found at **www.baan.com/customers**. The second way to find Baan users is through the Baan World User home page at **www.bwu.org**. On the welcome page you will find a button that indicates members. Click this button and you will get a list of all the companies that are members of the user group. It is easy to browse through that list and find users in your area.

Networking Through the User Group

Baan World Users

It is very important, when using any computer system, to always keep links with other users. In 1993, eight companies took it upon themselves to combine their resources in an effort to create a very active group for all Baan users. Those companies include: Northern Telecom, Noranda, Standard Data, Parr Instruments, Frisco Bay, Wire Rope Industries, Husky Injection Molding, and Flexfab. Baan and two distributors, Richard Morton Associates of Chicago and Leyland from Atlanta, supported those companies.

Attending BWU Annual Events

More than 265 companies from 21 countries have joined Baan World Users as of November 1997. This group meets twice a year, once in the spring at BaanWorld, and again in the fall at the BWU Workshop. At these events you will find companies of every size, from Boeing Commercial Airplane Group, Northern Telecom, and Noranda, to smaller enterprises. The meeting structure encourages companies of all sizes to participate. This group is totally autonomous and is funded by its members and the sponsors at its various activities.

BaanWorld is an annual event organized by Baan in which all the users are invited to see the latest development in the Baan sphere. May 1997's Anaheim meeting found more than 2500 attendees, with over 500 from the BWU. Other participants included Solution Partners and those looking to buy the software.

The BaanWorld Users Fall Workshop is exclusively designed for the members. In November 1997 in Dallas, TX, there were over 600 attendees from 11 countries. Various sessions were organized so that all its members could exchange ideas on the use of the various Baan modules. Speakers from Baan and their Solution Partners were invited to demonstrate their best techniques.

Attending these two events also gives any user or implementer the benefit of building a link with the user community.

Becoming a Member

Companies using Baan or Baan Solution Partners can join Baan World Users by submitting the form that can be found on the BWU Web page. Complete the form and send it to following address:

Baan World Users
401 Richmond Street, W., Suite 352
Toronto, Ontario
M5V 3A8

N O T E   The Baan World Users membership form can be downloaded from the Internet site **www.bwu.org**. You can also contact the Baan World Users by electronic mail at **webmaster@bwu.org**. ■

FIG. D.1

This is how the Baan World User Group welcomes you on the Internet.

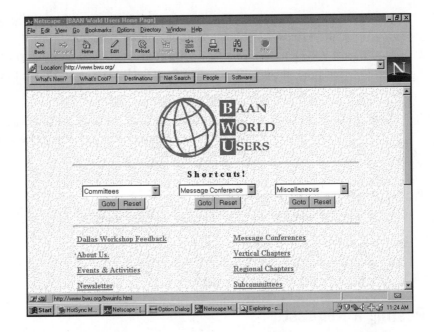

Membership fees for the BWU are charged on a per company basis. All the employees of a member company automatically become members when the company joins the group.

N O T E You can also join by calling the Management Office in Toronto, Canada at 416-593-1792. ▪

Surfing the BWU Internet Site

Baan World Users is using an Internet site to ensure communications among all its members. One of this site's best features is a BBS, which allows users to post requests or help other users who have posted earlier requests. The BBS Welcome page layout can be found in Figure D.2.

Registering Online

If you are not already a member, you can register online using the site's main menu's Registration option. Follow these steps to register:

1. Go the BWU Internet Site at **www.bwu.org**.
2. Click on Message Conferances.
3. Click on Login and Password.

4. Supply your name, the name of your company, your Baan license number, your email address, and all the configuration information requested.

5. Click Enter to send your form to the BWU Management Office. The Management Office sends you additional information about the BWU membership and an invoice for your first year of membership.

NOTE Because the User Group Web site contains a lot of secure information, you need a login and password. You can apply for one if your company is a member of the Baan World Users. ▪

Accessing the On-line Forum

To access the Baan World Users Internet On-line Forum:

1. Go to **www.bwu.org**.

2. Click Message Conferences.

3. Enter your login and password.

Posting a Request

After you are in the BBS section of the Internet site, you can post a request to be seen by all the users.

1. Click the section where you want to interact.

2. Click Post a Request.

3. Enter your name, email address, and your message.

4. Click Enter to post your message.

To reply to a request already posted:

1. Click the section where you want to interact.

2. Click the request to which you want to reply.

3. Enter your name, email address, and your reply.

4. Click Enter to post your reply.

Figure D.2 is an example of a posted request on the BWU BBS. You could reply to this request and see your answer as a follow-up.

Posting an Enhancement Request

It is possible to post a suggestion that might enhance the Baan product. The BWU has had a significant impact on Baan's products. The Product Issues Committee has a mechanism by which enhancement requests are compiled, prioritized, and presented to Baan for review.

The first step of this process can be done online through the BBS.

1. Click Enhancement Request.
2. Type in your name, company, and email address.
3. Fill in the form for an enhancement request.
4. Click Enter to send your enhancement request.

Part

VI

App

D

Index

Information Technology at Work

62 Oak Drive, Essex, Ontario, Canada N8M 3C5
Phone 519-776-9373   Fax 519-776-4911
Email tvlasic@wincom.net

Press Release

Contact: Tom Vlasic

A firm called "IT@Work" can <u>Answer</u> your Questions about Information Technology Planning and Investment.

IT@Work is focused on helping you understand the technology your company must use in order to compete in the new Digital Economy.

IT@Work is positioned to assist companies to understand and evaluate software systems

and computer technology that are necessary to compete in the new media - *the Internet.*

Electronic business is here today. E-commerce is projected to be a $200 billion market by the year 2000 - *what must your company do to be part of this electronic marketplace?* Today your company can reap huge rewards by purchasing MRO (non-production) goods on-line - *how can you realize these savings?* Shortly, Automotive Suppliers will be required by the Big 3 to conduct business over the internet or risk being left behind - *what do you need to get going with the Automotive Network eXchange (ANX)?*

Intranets (*an internet safely restricted to computers within your company*) are a highly cost effective and productive way to communicate with your staff. Consider an employee *self-serve* intranet that provides easy access to information. Eliminate multiple computer terminals and reduce the number of different computer system menus your staff must use to a single standard internet browser.

Set the stage with an Audit of your current use of information technology and produce a Report Card that will identify new opportunities. Develop a new IT plan or enhance your current IT plan to get you moving in the these areas; department structure, operating and capital budget, project alignment, service level and computer technology.

For Immediate Release

@work

MACMILLAN COMPUTER PUBLISHING USA
A VIACOM COMPANY

Technical ---- Support

If you need assistance with the information provided by Macmillan Computer Publishing, please access the information available on our web site at **http://www.mcp.com/feedback.** Our most Frequently Asked Questions are answered there. If you do not find the answers to your questions on our web site, you may contact Macmillan User Services at **(317) 581-3833** or email us at **support@mcp.com**.